CHRIST
AND THE
AMERICAS

"And all kings of the earth shall adore him: all nations shall serve him."
—Psalm 71:11

Queen of the Americas Guild

The miraculous image of Our Lady of Guadalupe as she appeared to Bl. Juan Diego in 1531, just outside of Mexico City. Our Lady of Guadalupe was pronounced Patroness of Mexico in 1754 by Pope Benedict XIV and Empress of All the Americas in 1945 by Pope Pius XII.

CHRIST
AND THE
AMERICAS

By
Anne W. Carroll

"The Lord hath spoken: and he hath called the earth. From the rising of the sun, to the going down thereof." —Psalm 49:1

TAN Books
Charlotte, North Carolina

Library of Congress Catalog Card No.: 96-61305

ISBN 978-0-89555-594-6

Cover illustration credit: *Landing of Columbus*, by John Vanderlyn, used with permission of Architect of the Capitol, Washington, D.C.

Printed and bound in India

TAN Books
Charlotte, North Carolina
www.TANBooks.com
2012

Dedication

To My Mother and Father:

Marie Harris Westhoff

Vernon Stephan Westhoff
(August 7, 1906–January 2, 1995)

"I am the Resurrection and the Life. He who believes in Me, even if he die, shall live."
—John 11:25

Contents

Acknowledgments

I am grateful to all those who have assisted in the production of *Christ and the Americas*. Bruce Clark and others at Seton Home Study made valuable suggestions which improved the text. Thomas A. Nelson of TAN Books carefully edited the text and then spent hours on the telephone going over suggested changes, most of which were adopted, producing a much better book. My students at Seton School have been the "laboratory" in which the many versions of this book have been tested over the years since the first draft was written. Finally, my husband Warren is my reliable source for an answer to almost any historical question and the reason why I am writing a history text in the first place. This book would not have existed without his support and assistance.

Foreword

As a student preparing to learn from this book, you will notice two distinctive words in the title. Each of these words tells you something about the book's focus.

The first important word is "Christ." This history book is written in the light of Catholic truth. The Catholic knows that the most important event in history was the Incarnation/Redemption/Resurrection and the most important Person in history was Jesus Christ. History is moving in a straight line from the Creation to the Last Judgment, and we judge events by whether or not they glorify God and contribute to the building up of the Kingdom of God on earth.

In this book, therefore, you will learn of the Catholic roots of our country. You will find out that Catholic missionaries were on American soil, bringing souls to Christ and dying as martyrs, long before the first settlers came to Jamestown or Plymouth Rock. You will learn how the Catholic Church has fared in our hemisphere. You will meet the great Catholic heroes and heroines of North and South America.

You will also learn to judge events from the standpoint of Catholic truth. The world judges by material and secular standards, but the Catholic looks at actions in the light of eternity.

The second important word is "Americas." This book studies all of the countries in the Western Hemisphere: in North America, Central America, South America and the Caribbean. As Catholics we need to know the history of our brothers and sisters in Christ. The histories of the United States and of the other countries in our hemisphere have often been intertwined, and many people from these other countries are moving to the United States. We need to be aware of their heritage and their history. Most importantly, Our Lady of Guadalupe is the patron of all the Americas, North and South. All of us from the Arctic Circle to Tierra del Fuego are united under her loving patronage.

Those of you who are familiar with the book *Christ the King: Lord of History* will be familiar with the Catholic way of looking at history. You will also know that the earlier book, while emphasizing the great triumphs of Catholic history, also did not hesitate to point out times when Catholics, even leaders of the Church, did not act in harmony with God's will. There have been times when Popes and bishops and Catholic rulers have been weak, have been corrupt, have been immoral. We need to be aware of these problems so that we can more fully appreciate the workings of the Holy Spirit in the Church and because truth is never served by hiding or minimizing unpleasant facts.

In *Christ and the Americas*, we have also tried to look honestly at the history of the United States. Not all of the actions of the United States government have been in harmony with the law of God; not all American historical figures have always behaved honorably. By learning the full truth about our country's history, we will be better prepared to help the United States overcome its weaknesses.

We live in a country with great natural beauty, with a system of government that was well-devised, and with many inspiring heroes, heroines and moments of history. But as with all earthly things, our country can be made better, can be brought more in harmony with the will of God. An accurate account of history can help us understand better what we need to do to help the country we love come closer to God.

In the words of Pope John Paul II on his first visit to the United States, "At a time when the struggle between good and evil, between the prince of darkness and father of lies and evangelical love is growing more acute, may the light of [the] Immaculate Conception show to all the way to grace and to salvation."

CHRIST
AND THE
AMERICAS

"Going therefore, teach ye all nations; baptizing them in the name of the Father, and of the Son, and of the Holy Ghost."
—Matthew 28:19

Chapter 1

The New World Meets The Old

WHEN HUMAN BEINGS first arrived in the New World, the Western Hemisphere, they probably came from Asia, crossing from Siberia to Alaska over what was then a land bridge across the Bering Sea. The land bridge would have been exposed because water was locked up in the huge glaciers of the Ice Age. We do not know exactly when men first set foot in the New World, but we do know that they gradually spread throughout the Hemisphere, living for hundreds of years as wandering hunters, showing little advancement or progress. Then, around 2500 B.C., the Neolithic Revolution occurred in the New World: Men began growing crops and raising animals, instead of relying for food on hunting and gathering. The New World was far behind the Old, which, according to some calculations, had achieved the Neolithic or Agricultural Revolution around 9000 B.C.

The oldest village sites in the New World date from around 2000 B.C. and appear in Central America. For some reason the vast plains of North America did not encourage human settlement and progress, but the jungles of Central America and the high plateaus of Mexico did. The staple crop was corn—unknown in the Old World—on which everything else depended. The early farmers of Mexico tattooed their bodies, turned the earth with digging sticks, and ground the corn to make a dough which was patted into cakes and baked over the fires. Their life was primitive and uncivilized, at a time when in the Old World the Egyptians were ruling a mighty empire and the Hebrews were learning and maintaining their belief in the one true God, whose name is "I Am."

Around 1000 B.C., the Olmecs, a warlike people from the eastern coastal jungle plain of Mexico, invaded the highlands to the west, establishing themselves in power. The Olmec magicians claimed special powers over nature, performing strange superstitious rituals to persuade the gods to do the will of man. If at times they appeared to be successful—after all, it takes very little magic to learn that crops sprout in the spring and die in the winter—they also knew failure, for nature is never wholly predictable. Their desire for power led the Olmecs to think of ever greater sacrifices to the gods of nature, until they began offering the greatest they could imagine: human beings. In the ancient Olmec village sites, archeologists find decapitated skeletons, smashed skulls, bodies without arms and legs, and murdered children. What they deemed the necessity of human sacrifice was fully accepted by the people of Mexico, remaining an indispensable part of their culture, even after the Olmecs were no longer dominant.

The Devil Gods

Some time after 650 B.C., the first civilization appeared in the New World. A civilization is distinguished from barbarism by the presence of cities and of writing, and the first people in the New World to achieve settled communities and written records were the Mayas of Central America and southern Mexico, whose civilization grew out of the Olmec culture. The first Mayan settlements grew up around the sacrificial altars, which gradually became marketplaces as well.

Mayan writing has not been fully deciphered to this day. It is composed of weird pictures called Maya glyphs, some of which have been given such descriptive names as the toothache glyph and the upended-frog glyph. We are able to read Mayan numbers, however, and know that their society was mathematically advanced. They developed a calendar based on an 18-month year which is slightly more accurate than our own calendar. They were excellent astronomers; a Mayan inscription gives day and month positions for astronomical objects calculated back hypothetically for more than 400 million years.

Around the time of Christ, the Mayans had their greatest cultural achievements. Though they still had stone-age tools and never did invent the wheel, they built huge temple-pyramids and also built beautiful cities. They developed irrigation, and their mathematics and astronomy reached a peak. But like the powerful ancient civilizations of the Old World, the Mayas eventually began to decline. By the 800's A.D., new tribes gained power, and in the mid-900's the Toltec people became dominant under the great leader Quetzalcoatl.

Quetzalcoatl adopted the name of the god he worshipped, a feathered serpent. He was a powerful, popular leader, who established his capital in the city of Chichén Itzá on the Yucatán peninsula. Quetzalcoatl's greatness is best illustrated by his hatred of human sacrifice. He did everything he could to stop this bloody practice, and for a brief time his civilization—freed from this brutality—flourished. But the habits of centuries could not be eliminated by one man. He was eventually overthrown, and his religious reformation died out. Human sacrifice returned. Society became collectivized: the individual person was regarded as unimportant. So little value was placed on individuals that singular pronouns—I, my, mine, me—scarcely existed. Life centered on the corn fields, the battle fields and the temple-pyramids. But there remained a prophecy which was never quite forgotten: Someday in the year "One Reed" (which occurred every 52 years), Quetzalcoatl would return, coming from the east.

Around 1450, still another tribe gained power: the Mexica—now more commonly known as the Aztecs. They came from a small island in the middle of a large lake in central Mexico and were particularly warlike and bloodthirsty. They established their capital city on their home island, which was named Tenochtitlán ("Cactus Rock"), and built there a magnificent city. The city became wealthy and powerful and remained the most important city in Mexico, which it has continued to be down to the present day, being renamed Mexico City.

The most powerful man in the Aztec Empire was not in fact the Emperor Montezuma I, but a successful warrior named Tlacaellel, who dominated Montezuma I and then picked the next three emperors. He was the effective ruler of the Aztecs for 67 years, living to be 98 (1398-1496). The one dominant policy of his rule was human sacrifice.

The two chief gods to whom the sacrifices were offered were Huitzilopochtli, the Hummingbird Wizard, also known as Lover of Hearts and Drinker of Blood, and Tezcatlipoca, the Smoking Mirror and Lord of the Dark. The universal religious symbol in the Aztec religion was the serpent.

To worship the devil gods, Tlacaellel's laws required a thousand sacrifices to Huitzilopochtli in every town with a temple, every year; there were 371 towns in the Aztec Empire, though not all had full-scale temples. There were other sacrifices as well. It is estimated that at least 50,000 were sacrificed a year, probably more. One early Mexican historian estimated that one out of every five children was sacrificed. On occasion, entire tribes, numbering in the tens of thousands, were exterminated by sacrifice.

To keep up the supply of victims, Tlacaellel invented the "Flower Wars," conflicts in which the goal was not to kill the opponent but to capture him for later sacrifice. All Mexican nobility were required to attend the great sacrifices, and all Mexican warriors were required to take prisoners for sacrifice. Then, from 1451-1454, a series of unprecedented natural disasters struck Mexico. First came a serious drought, then four consecutive years of snows and killing frosts. The corn crop, on which the whole society depended, was destroyed year after year, and the people starved. To appease the devil gods, Tlacaellel required ever increasing numbers of sacrificial victims.

In 1487 a new pyramid-temple had been dedicated to Huitzilopochtli in the center of Tenochtitlán. On the flat top of the pyramid was the principal altar, with 600 smaller altars up and down the sides. Tlacaellel organized a four-day-long dedication ceremony. With the booming of the great snakeskin drums echoing over the city and the surrounding lakes, the dedication ceremony began. Thousands of captives, in a column three miles long, were herded across the plaza. The high priest and the lesser priests, in blood-drenched robes, led the victims to the altars. Each trembling man was stretched out flat. The priest plunged an obsidian knife into the victim's chest, pulled out his heart and placed it between the gaping jaws of the stone god. His body was then thrown over the side. The whole process took 15 seconds.

The mass murder went on for four days and four nights. More than 80,000 men were killed. Most of the nobility, who had been required to be present, could not endure the seemingly never-ending spectacle and fled before its conclusion. But Tlacaellel remained to the end.

And what of the ordinary people, living in the midst of such horrors? In the Aztec society, wealth consisted of land and the men to work it, because there was no money. The emperor and his court collected a share of all the crops harvested, the pagan priests another share. Almost no one owned property of his own. The common people lived in tightly organized communities. Every man-child was dedicated to the war god at his birth and trained in the art of war from childhood. Discipline was harsh; for disobedience, a boy could be punctured with cactus spines. Any boy who failed to become a warrior was put to death or enslaved. The individual was taught that he stood for nothing: the nation was all.

He was like an ant, carrying items of tribute into the capital city, so that the aristocracy could live luxuriously and so that the priests could devote all their time to the worship of the devil gods, satisfying their ever-demanding appetites. The people lived in fear and slavery, without hope and without joy.

The Incas of Peru

Far to the south, in the high Andes mountains, in the lush valleys and barren deserts of Peru, a culture developed which was higher than that of the primitive savages of North America, but lower than that of the civilized peoples of Central America. This culture was that of the Incas, who built cities, had a highly developed governmental system, and produced amazing architecture, though they never learned to write and relied solely on oral communication.

The Inca Empire was established in 1200 A.D. In 1438, Pachacuti came to the imperial throne. He was an ambitious, talented man, probably the greatest of the Inca emperors. He built a magnificent capital city at Cuzco and elaborately decorated the Temple of the Sun. The Sacsahuaman Fort near Cuzco had walls 1800 feet long and 60 feet high. One of the stones used in the construction was 27 feet high, 14 feet long, 12 feet thick and weighed 200 tons. This construction was carried out without the aid of the wheel, which the Incas never invented. Only fleet-footed messengers and slaves carrying litters traveled the smooth roads criss-crossing the Empire.

Pachacuti and his son Topa Inca extended Inca rule from northern Ecuador to central Chile, over 350,000 square miles. They easily conquered the other tribes, often killing most of the men so that they could not rebel, or forcibly moving the inhabitants of one conquered area to another.

Incan society was tightly organized in a pyramidal structure. A government official was in charge of every 100 families and was in his turn responsible to another official, who was responsible to another, and so on up to the emperor, who had absolute authority. The Incan officials kept accurate census records, so that they knew who was born and who had died and how much in taxes was owed by every man.

All land, the llama herds and the mines were owned by the government and worked by the peasants. A peasant's day was long and laborious, and nothing he produced belonged to him. Everything went to the government officials, who then distributed food, clothing and shel-

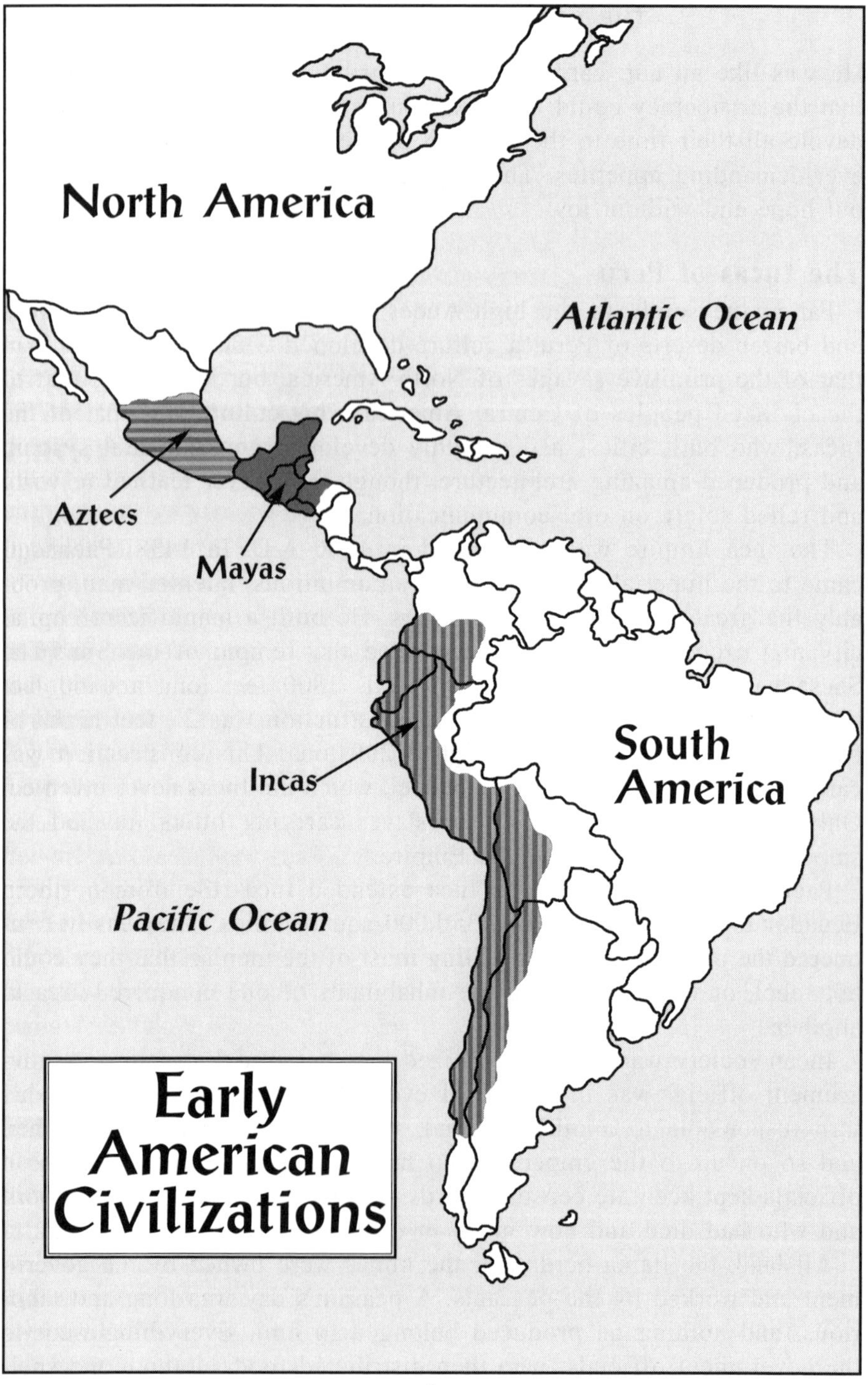
North America
Atlantic Ocean
Aztecs
Mayas
Incas
South America
Pacific Ocean
Early American Civilizations

ter to the people. As in Mexican society, the individual counted for nothing. He existed solely to serve the government. All offenses against the government were punishable by death.

The wealthy noblemen and the pagan priests lived in luxury in Cuzco, supported by the labors of the peasants. The emperor was worshipped as a god, and no one could enter his presence without removing his sandals and placing a burden on his back to indicate his humble position. When an emperor died, his body was mummified, and his favorite wives and servants usually voluntarily accompanied him in death.

Though on a much smaller scale than the Aztecs, the Incas also had human sacrifice. On solemn occasions the most physically perfect of the young boys and girls would be sacrificed to the sun god. Those chosen as victims regarded their death as an honor.

At the time of the discovery of the Americas, therefore, two advanced cultures flourished amidst the primitive Indian tribes of North and South America. In Peru, society focused on the emperor, who had the right to dispose of any man's life as he chose. In Mexico, society focused on the hungry gods and revolved around the necessity of satisfying their appetites. Thus the New World awaited the Old, and the stage was set for a clash of cultures unlike any the world had ever seen.

Visitors from the East

Many different European countries had legends of lands to the west. In our own day, scholars have claimed to find evidence that Irishmen, Phoenicians, Jews and any number of others reached the New World long before Columbus. Except in one case, these exploits remain legends. There now is compelling evidence that St. Brendan the Voyager, an Irish Saint of the sixth century, reached Newfoundland in a leather boat. The account of his voyage, *The Navigation*, long thought to be fantasy, has been confirmed in all essential respects by Brendan's fellow Irishman, Tim Severin, who duplicated the voyage in the 1970's in a leather boat made of the same materials and by the same techniques as Brendan's. Irish settlements are known to have been made on Greenland, but none are known in Newfoundland; therefore, although Brendan reached the New World, he made no lasting mark on it.

The first known New World European colonies were established by the Vikings, the fierce Norsemen who pillaged and burned throughout Europe in the ninth, tenth and eleventh centuries, destroying much of the culture that had been slowly and painstakingly created after the decline of the Roman civilization in Western Europe and the influx of original barbarians.

In the late 10th century, a hot-tempered Viking named Eric the Red was exiled from Iceland for killing two men in vengeance. He sailed on to Greenland, where he established a colony on the site of an abandoned Irish colony. In 985 he brought 14 colonists. One of them had asked his son, Bjarni Herolffson, to follow him. On his way to Greenland, Bjarni was blown off course and ended up on the east coast of Newfoundland, becoming the first Viking to reach a continental landfall, even though by accident. Later, Eric's son Leif bought Bjarni's ship and returned to Newfoundland, which he named Vinland. He wanted the timber that was there, but made no attempt to found a colony. Leif became a Christian in Norway a few years later, and soon thereafter missionaries came to Iceland and Greenland.

The next Viking New World visitor was Thorfinn Karlsefni, who organized a colonizing venture to Leif's Vinland. He could not find it, though, and ended up in a less hospitable location on the northern tip of Newfoundland. At this spot, called Vinland II, the first white child was born in the New World, the son of Thorfinn and his wife Gudrid. They named him Snorri. The colonists had trouble with the natives, much of it their own fault because they always assumed the worst of the natives. Finally, Thorfinn gave up on the colony and returned home with many of his followers.

The Viking colony lasted only a few more months, then was abandoned. The Vikings left nothing enduring; their discoveries did not change the course of history. And when the Viking power was broken, the memory of their exploits died with them, becoming only a fading and misty legend.

Christopher Columbus

In 1451, a son named Cristobal was born to the Colombo family in Genoa, Italy. He grew tall and red-haired and at the age of 22 went to sea. He took part in many expeditions, including some to the East Indies, and in his mind a strange notion began to take shape. The route to the Indies was long and difficult, involving both a sea voyage and an overland journey, along which local rulers exacted heavy taxes for the privilege of crossing their land. The Portuguese were venturing around Africa to avoid these difficulties, but Christopher had another idea. Why not sail west, coming into the Spice Islands, India and China by the back door? He was sure that it would be an easier, faster route. He calculated the distance as 2,400 miles from the Canary Islands, the last European outpost in the Atlantic, to Japan. The actual distance was 10,000 miles, and two continents stood in the way, but Columbus knew nothing about the continents and was sure his calculations were accurate.

Many people told him that his figures were in error: Among them were the advisers to the King of Portugal, whom he approached in 1484; and the advisers to the Queen of Spain, who received him in May 1486. But Columbus refused to abandon his dream. He was motivated by far more than a belief that he was right and the scientists were wrong about the size of the earth. (They did not disagree about the shape; all educated men of the time knew the earth was round.) He felt that God had called him to bring Christianity to lands where Christ was unknown. By finding an easier route to these lands, he could bring glory to God.

Just as Columbus refused to abandon his dream, so Queen Isabel of Spain could not forget him. She too had a vision of the glory of God. Columbus was ready to leave Spain, but made a last appeal to Isabel. Having just driven the Moslems from Spain, she agreed to his plan in 1492. She found financial backing for his voyage, gave him a royal commission as Admiral of the Ocean Sea, and sent with him official documents claiming the lands he discovered for Spain (along with a letter to the King of China, which she wrote in Latin though she had no idea whether this king, who she was not even sure existed, could read a word of the language).

On September 6, 1492, Columbus' three ships—the *Niña*, the *Pinta* and the *Santa María*—weighed anchor in the Old World for the last time at the little Spanish port of Palos near Seville. His course was "West, nothing to the north, nothing to the south." Columbus had great confidence in his judgment, but he knew that his men would not always be so confident, especially as they sailed farther from familiar lands. Therefore, he kept two records of the distance covered: what he called the true reckoning for his own use and a false reckoning for the eyes of the crew, so that they would not be discouraged. As it happened, Columbus overestimated his speed, so the false reckoning was more accurate.

By October, the crew was grumbling and upset. They had never been out of sight of land so long before; they were afraid they would never see land again. Finally, on October 9, Columbus promised Alonso Pinzon, his second in command, that he would turn back if they sighted no land within three days. The Admiral was not taking a grave risk with this promise. From his past experience at sea, he could recognize the signs that told him land was near. Then, at 2:00 a.m. on October 12, the lookout on the *Pinta* cried *"Tierra! Tierra!"*—"Land! Land!" "Thanks be to God!" the men prayed, as the tiny speck on the horizon grew steadily bigger. They landed on the beach around noon. Columbus went ashore, knelt in the damp sand and thanked God for the safe arrival. Thinking he was in the East Indies, not knowing he was actually in the Western Hemisphere (most probably on an island now known as Samana Cay in the Bahamas), he claimed the land for Spain and christened the island *San Salvador,* "Holy Saviour."

Throughout October, November and December, Columbus and his men sailed from island to island, searching for spices and for identifying landmarks. Instead of a flourishing and wealthy Eastern civilization, they found primitive, impoverished natives; instead of spices, they found tobacco. Still Columbus was convinced that around the next island he would finally find what he had sailed halfway around the world in search of: the East Indies.

Christmas Eve came to the men far from the *Navidad* celebrations in Spain. Yet in spite of their strange surroundings, they held a Christmas Eve feast. The officer on duty during the night had too much feasting, and thinking no one would know the difference, turned the tiller of the *Santa María* over to a young boy. The boy had no one to whom he could turn it over, so he stood sleepily at the helm until around midnight a grinding, crunching sound awakened his shipmates to the awful realization that the ship had run aground on a coral reef. The men were unable to free her and so had to abandon the *Santa María.* She was the biggest ship, and there was no room for her crew on board the smaller *Niña* and *Pinta.* Columbus had to leave the extra men on the island to establish a colony. Then, on January 4, 1493, he set sail for home.

The homeward voyage was extremely rough, in contrast to the smooth outward journey. In February Columbus ran into some of the worst storms in recorded history. Between February 13 and 14 he and Pinzon lost sight of each other as their ships were blown apart in the gale. They did not see each other again until Spain. The storm continued to rage on the 14th, and the crew had no hope left, except in God. They prayed desperately, promising to go on a pilgrimage if they were spared. Columbus himself had one of his rare moments of despair;

he wrote an account of his discoveries and dropped it overboard in a barrel, hoping that if his ship were lost the barrel might eventually find its way to shore.

But the crew's prayers were heard, and on February 15 they arrived safely in the Azores. Still, their troubles were not over because, on the final leg of the voyage home, they ran into more storms. On March 2, a storm blew away all but one of the *Niña's* sails. On the night of March 3, the ship was being blown by near hurricane-force wind toward the cliffs off the coast of Portugal. In the greatest display yet of Columbus' seamanship, the Admiral managed to turn his vessel at the last moment and save his ship, his crew and the knowledge of his discoveries.

Isabel was delighted with Columbus' news, believing with him that he had achieved his goal. He could have retired then and there a wealthy man, but he was not the retiring type. He wanted to ensure that the Faith was carried to the Indies and the area properly administered. So he set sail again in 1493 with a much larger fleet.

Columbus made new discoveries throughout the Caribbean, visiting the Lesser Antilles, Virgin Islands, Puerto Rico, the south coast of Cuba and Jamaica. He found to his sorrow that the colony left behind had been wiped out by Indians, but he established a new colony named "Isabel" on Hispaniola Island. Again he did not find what he wanted, but only a little gold, some rather poor spices and a few tropical birds. He sent these things back to Spain with one of his ships and kept looking.

When he finally returned to Spain on March 10, 1496, almost everyone but Columbus himself knew that he had not found the East Indies. But he was able to get backing for a third voyage, in 1498, during which he made the first continental landfall in the New World at what is now Venezuela.

Columbus had found a new world, thus dramatically changing the course of history, but though he is perhaps the greatest mariner of all time, he did not have the temperament or talent to administer his discoveries. His administration of the colonies was unwise; he permitted enslavement of the Indians, against Isabel's express policy. When Isabel sent a royal commissioner to investigate, Columbus was arrested and sent home in chains. The man whose vision, courage and determination had given the New World to Spain left it disgraced and humiliated.

Isabel released Columbus, and he made one last visit to the New

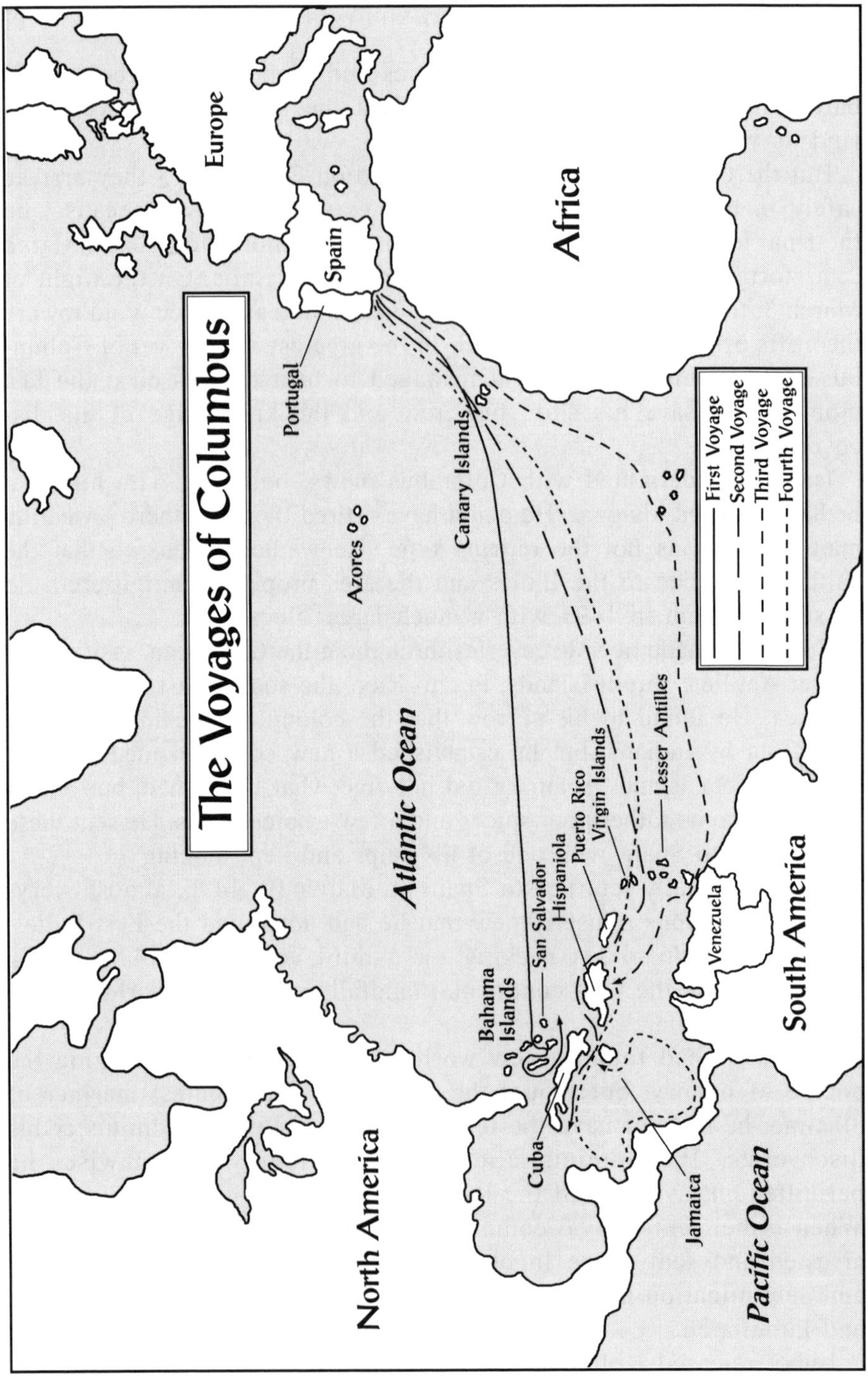
The Voyages of Columbus
Europe
Spain
Portugal
Africa
Azores
Canary Islands
Atlantic Ocean
North America
Bahama Islands
San Salvador
Hispaniola
Puerto Rico
Virgin Islands
Lesser Antilles
Cuba
Jamaica
Venezuela
South America
Pacific Ocean
First Voyage
Second Voyage
Third Voyage
Fourth Voyage

World, his fourth voyage, from 1502-1504. Now he knew that he had not found the Indies, and he spent most of the voyage looking for a way through Central America so that he could reach the East. But he did not find the way, because it did not exist. He returned to Spain, where he died two years later.

Before Columbus, men rarely sailed out of sight of land, hugging the shore, scarcely daring to sail down unfamiliar coastlines. Everyone looked east. Columbus looked west and dared to leave familiar sights and shores behind him. In so doing, he turned the continent of Europe around. The New World was drawn into the orbit of Europe and European civilization. The world—old and new—would never again be the same.

Catholic Spain Leads the Way

The knowledge that a whole new world had been discovered set fire to Spain. Before long, ships were sailing frequently from Spain to the Western Hemisphere and back again, and Spaniards were leading expeditions of discovery and colonization, slowly mapping out the shape of the New World. Some men came for gold, some for glory, some for the thrill of discovery, some for the chance to start a new life, some to spread the Gospel of Christ; most came for a combination of reasons. They were filled with enthusiasm, courage and a faith in God which let them brave any risk. Most were heroic and admirable; some were greedy and cruel. But both the good and the evil could have come only from Spain, which at this time was different from any other country in Europe.

Though all of Europe was Catholic, Spain's Catholicism was stronger and healthier. At the time of Columbus, Spain was ruled by Ferdinand and Isabel, known in Spain as *los Reyes Católicos*—"the Catholic Kings." Isabel especially lived for her Faith; her primary mission in life was to make Spain unshakeably Catholic. She succeeded in her mission. Isabel was followed on the throne by her grandson Charles I, whose primary mission in life was to defend the Catholic Church against the Protestant revolutionaries who sought to destroy it from within and the Moslem Turks who sought to destroy it from without. Some of the Spaniards who came to the New World were good Catholics, some were bad Catholics, but all were Catholics. They built a Catholic society which endures to this day throughout most of South America, Central America, and Mexico, and which has left its mark even in the United States, as we can see in so simple a thing as the Catholic names which dot the map: San Francisco, San Antonio, Trinidad, Santa Fe and hundreds more.

The Spaniards, in the very year of Columbus' discovery of America, had just won a 770-year war with the Moslems, driving them at last out of Spain with their conquest of Granada, the last Moslem stronghold in Spain, and uniting their country under one flag. They were optimistic and courageous and felt there was nothing they could not do. They were good fighters, used to winning even when the odds were against them. They could also at times be cruel and bloodthirsty, as men who have fought long and hard can be.

These were the Spaniards who left their footprints across South America, Central America, Mexico and the southern part of what is now the United States, footprints which time has not been able to erase.

Catholic Portugal Follows

Though Spain launched the discovery and exploration of the New World, another, similar nation was close behind. Though smaller than Spain, Portugal also had optimism, a deep religious faith and unshakable courage. Portuguese explorations were sparked by a prince of the royal family, known as Prince Henry the Navigator, because of his interest in voyaging.

Prince Henry's telescope looked east, toward the Indies. He, like Columbus a few years later, wanted to find a new route to the Indies to avoid the costly overland route. He also wanted to outflank the Moslem-held lands and advance the cause of Christianity. So he financed and encouraged voyages down the African coast. No one knew how far Africa extended, nor what men might find if they sailed far enough south, and most men did not care. But Henry gave his sailors and captains a share of his courage. They began sailing down the coast of Africa, going a little farther each time. Eventually, Vasco da Gama rounded the Cape of Good Hope, Africa's southern tip, and reached India in 1498, the first man to do so by an all-water route. Prince Henry had already died by this time, but the voyage would never have been made except for his vision and encouragement.

The year after Da Gama returned, King Manuel (who was married to Isabel's daughter Maria), authorized Pedro Cabral to follow up Da Gama's discoveries. Cabral outfitted 13 or 14 ships, painting the red cross of Christ on their sails. King Manuel himself came down to the harbor to

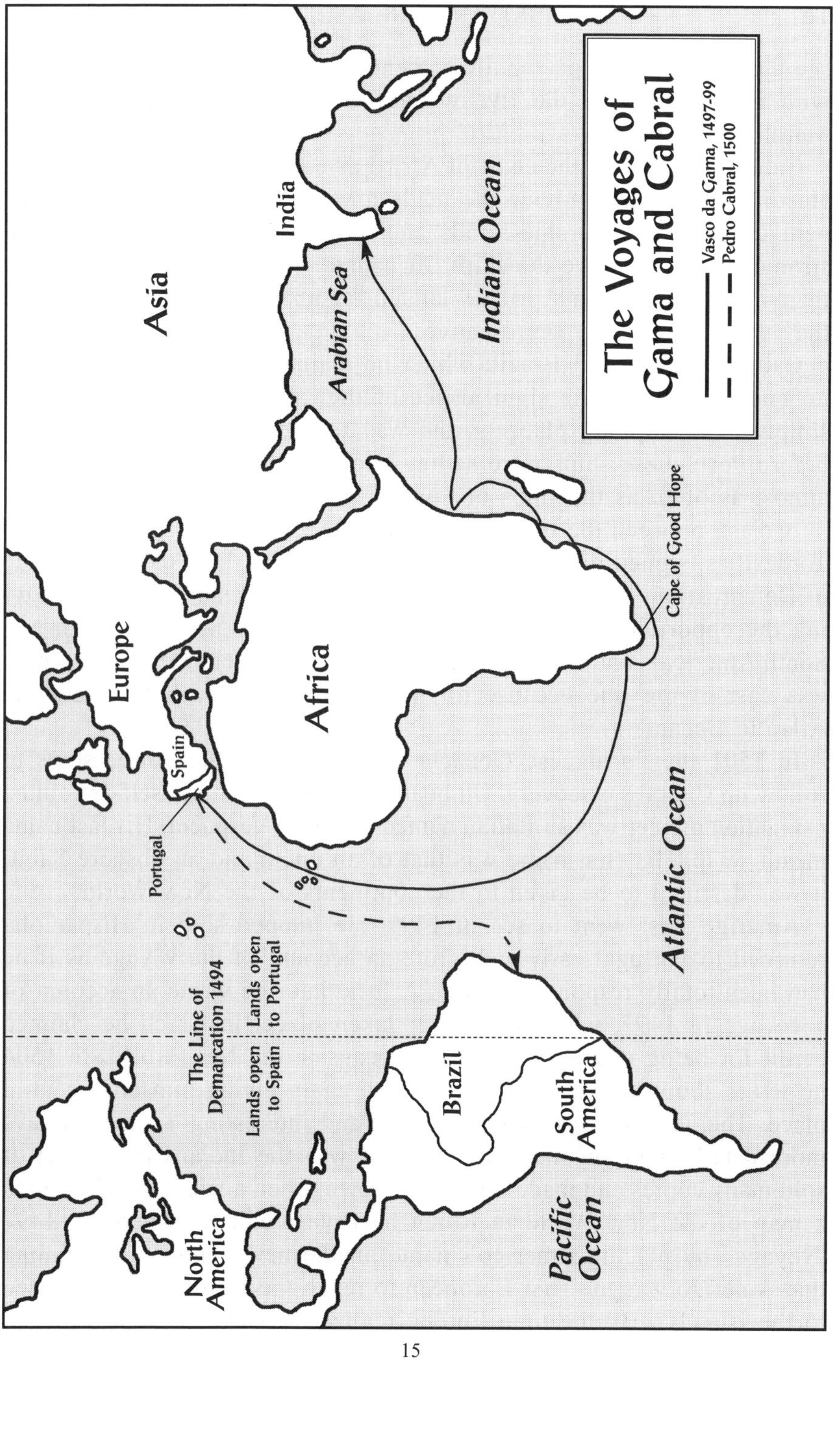
The Voyages of Gama and Cabral
Vasco da Gama, 1497-99
Pedro Cabral, 1500
Asia
India
Arabian Sea
Indian Ocean
Europe
Spain
Portugal
Africa
Cape of Good Hope
Atlantic Ocean
The Line of Demarcation 1494
Lands open to Spain
Lands open to Portugal
North America
Brazil
South America
Pacific Ocean

see the voyagers off, personally presenting to Cabral a Portuguese flag, with its depiction of the five wounds of Christ. The fleet sailed on March 8, 1500.

Cabral did not hug the coast of Africa as earlier Portuguese had done. Heeding Da Gama's advice, he made a wide sweep around the continent to pick up favorable winds and currents. But a wind shift and stronger currents drove the ships off course. They sailed more westerly than intended, and on April 21 landed on unexplored territory, where they were watched by timid natives.

Cabral had reached Brazil, which he claimed for Portugal. At first no one appreciated the significance of the discovery, regarding Brazil simply as a stopping place on the way to India, but it was not long before Portuguese ships were sailing back and forth to the New World almost as often as the ships of Spain.

A clash between the two powers was avoided by the earlier Treaty of Tordesillas, signed on June 7, 1494. An imaginary line, called the Line of Demarcation, was drawn through the Atlantic Ocean, with Spain having the opportunity to explore the western lands—most of North and South America—and Portugal the eastern—which included Brazil, which was east of the line because of the way the country bulges into the Atlantic Ocean.

In 1501 the Portuguese Gonáclo Coelho commanded three ships to follow up Cabral's discovery. On board as a passenger and self-appointed navigation officer was an Italian named Amerigo Vespucci. His last name meant wasp. His first name was that of an uncle and an obscure Saint; it was destined to be given to the continents of the New World.

Amerigo first went to sea in 1499. He jumped ship in Hispaniola, returned to Portugal early and wrote an account of the voyage as if he had been totally responsible for it. A little later he wrote an account of a voyage in 1497, which had never taken place, in which he claimed credit for being one of the first Europeans in the New World. In 1504 he wrote about his voyage with Coelho, again giving himself a central place. The account was so well-written and interesting—Amerigo gave more details than anyone else about the way the Indians lived—that it sold many copies and made him well-known. Then a friend of his printed a map of the New World in which he gave credit to Amerigo's 1497 "voyage" by placing Amerigo's name on the new continents, claiming that Amerigo was the first European to reach the mainland (as opposed to the islands). By the time Europe realized that Amerigo was not all he claimed to be, the use of the term "America" was so widespread that it could not be changed. Thus did a faker with a gift for words and a friend in the right place at the right time give his name to the two continents of the New World.

Spaniards Explore the New World

Other achievements were more genuine. Vasco Nuñez de Balboa went on a voyage to the New World, then settled in Hispaniola as a planter. Unfortunately, he soon ran out of money and was being annoyed by his creditors. So he stowed away on a ship by hiding in a provision cask that was lowered into the storage hold with the rest of the cargo. When he was discovered, the captain was first angry, but then came to appreciate Balboa's ingenuity and courage. On September 1, 1513, Balboa led an expedition across Central America. No one knew at that time just how wide it was, but everyone hoped that an easy way across could be found. Balboa and his men hacked their way through the thick growth of the tropical rain forest and waded through the swamps. Finally, on September 25, Balboa climbed a small hill and looked upon the Pacific Ocean—the first European ever to do so. He reached the shore on September 29, taking possession of this Southern Sea, as he called it, in the name of the Emperor Charles V.

Juan Ponce de Leon was red-haired, strong, aggressive and active. As a boy he had fought against the Moors for Ferdinand and Isabel. At the age of 19, he volunteered to accompany Columbus on his second voyage. He made many other voyages to the New World, becoming ever more intrigued and excited by it. In 1513, he launched a voyage under his own command, with the stated purpose of finding a "Fountain of Youth." A persistent myth had spread through the New World that somewhere there existed a spring which would restore to old men the powers of youth. Since the New World seemed strange and exotic, it is not surprising that the myth was believed. Juan found no such fountain, but he did find Florida, sailing up and down the coast of this peninsula and becoming the first white man to explore the continental United States. He also discovered the Gulf Stream, that swift current originating in the Gulf of Mexico. He was eventually wounded in a fight with Indians, dying of the wounds in Cuba.

In the meantime, the islands of the Caribbean were being colonized. Cuba, the largest, was conquered and colonized in 1511 by Diego Velazquez. From Cuba, two expeditions were sent out which reached

Mexico in 1517 and 1518. On the second expedition, Spaniards for the first time crossed into the territory ruled by Montezuma II, Emperor of the Aztecs, and also for the first time realized that this empire practiced human sacrifice. The leader of that expedition, Juan Grijalba, was not quite up to facing the magnitude of the Aztec evil, so he decided to return to Cuba.

Montezuma and his priests also had to make a decision. They knew that fair-skinned men from the "Eastern Ocean" had arrived in their domains. They also knew of an ancient legend that Quetzalcoatl would one day return from the Eastern Sea and rule again over his people. The prophecy had been very specific that he would return in the year 1-Reed in the Aztec calendar, which recurred once every 52 years. As it happened, 1519 would be a 1-Reed year.

If one of these strangers was indeed Quetzalcoatl, then Montezuma and his priests had better not antagonize them. What should be done? Montezuma, never a man of action, decided to wait and see. Wait—until the next year, 1-Reed.

Another man was waiting, rather more impatiently. He was preparing to lead Spain's third expedition to Mexico. His name was Hernán Cortés, and though he did not yet know it, he would challenge the devil gods directly and write his name forever in history.

REVIEW QUESTIONS

1. How did men first come to the Western Hemisphere? When did the Neolithic Revolution take place there?
2. Who were the Olmecs? What did they bring to American culture?
3. What was the first civilization in the New World? What was its form of writing? What were some of its accomplishments?
4. What was the significance of Quetzalcoatl?
5. How did human sacrifice come to be vastly increased? What was the significance of Tlacaellel?
6. Describe Aztec society.
7. What were the characteristics of Incan culture?
8. Why did Columbus want to find a new route to the Indies? What was his plan? Why was it rejected by most? Why did Isabel accept it?
9. When did Columbus sight land? Where did he land?

10. What happened to the *Santa María*? What were the conditions on the return voyage?
11. What happened on Columbus' second voyage? How did his third voyage end?
12. What was the main significance of Columbus?
13. Describe Spain at the time of the explorations.
14. What were the achievements of Portugal during the Age of Explorations?
15. Give the significance of Vespucci, Balboa, and Ponce de Leon.

PROJECTS

1. Do additional research on any of the explorers mentioned in this chapter and prepare a report.
2. Do additional research on Brendan the Voyager and/or Tim Severin's voyage and prepare a report.
3. Do additional research on the Viking explorations in the New World and prepare a report.

Chapter 2

Two Heroes: Cortés and Magellan

ESTREMADURA IS THE FAR western part of Spain. It is so dry and desolate that it is said that nothing grows there except soldiers and Saints. One of the greatest soldiers who ever came out of Estremadura was Hernán Cortés, who almost single-handedly brought down the mighty Aztec Empire.

Cortés departed for Mexico from Cuba in February 1519. His expedition consisted of the following: 11 ships, 508 Spanish soldiers, 100 sailors, 16 horses (unknown in the New World before the Spaniards arrived), 32 crossbows, 13 muskets, four falconets (a small cannon) and a few slightly larger cannon. With this tiny force Cortés intended to conquer an empire of millions. On his banners were these words: "Brothers and companions, let us follow the sign of the Cross with true faith and in it we shall conquer."

Cortés landed in Montezuma's territory on April 22, 1519, Good Friday to the Christians. To the Aztecs it was the year 1-Reed, the day 9-Wind. The Quetzalcoatl legend had predicted the hero's return not only in the year 1-Reed, but on his own name day: 9-Wind. Quetzalcoatl had worn black; since it was Good Friday, Cortés was dressed in black.

The Aztec records tell us that Montezuma believed that Cortés was Quetzalcoatl. He sent ambassadors with gifts. The records also tell us that Montezuma was plunged into gloom and sorrow. Perhaps two reasons combined to cause his despair: he knew that Quetzalcoatl had abhorred human sacrifice; he knew that he, Montezuma, presided as emperor over thousands of human sacrifices each year.

When his ambassadors returned and gave their report, Montezuma's despair turned into terror. They described the strangers as dressed in iron, with swords, bows, shields and spears of iron. Their report continued: "Their deer [horses] carry them on their backs wherever they wish to go. These deer, our lord, are as tall as the roof of a house. . . . Their dogs are enormous . . . their eyes flash fire and shoot off sparks. . . . They are tireless and very powerful."

In his terror, Montezuma wanted to keep the Spaniards out of Tenochtitlán at all costs. He sent them gifts, asking them to go no farther. His witch doctors worked spells to keep them in their place. Cortés, however, was unaffected by either gifts or spells. He made allies with a nearby tribe which was eager to be freed from Aztec domination. With the assent of his men, he constituted their encampment as a Spanish municipality, christened *Villa Rica de Vera Cruz*—"Rich Town of the True Cross"—and took possession of Mexico in the name of Charles I of Spain.

After building a fort and assigning about a third of his men to garrison it as the rest of the army marched inland, Cortés ordered nine of his ten ships scuttled. He wanted to leave no temptations to desertion or retreat. He then told his men that those who were afraid of the coming battle could take the tenth ship back to Cuba. No one took advantage of the offer. So Cortés scuttled the last ship as well.

Then he took 300 Spaniards and marched inland to face an empire of fifteen million. Bernal Diaz, Cortés' faithful soldier and chronicler, writes: "Let the curious reader see whether there is not much to ponder over in this which I venture to write, and whether there were ever in the universe men who had such daring."

Toward the Home of the Devil Gods

The Spaniards marched toward Tenochtitlán. Montezuma, still paralyzed by fear, did nothing to stop them. They reached Zocotlán, whose chief was allied to Montezuma. In the center of the town was a temple, where sacrifices regularly occurred. By the temple were racks for human skulls. Because they were in even rows, it was easy to count them. According to Bernal Diaz: their number "might be one hundred thousand, and I say again, *one hundred thousand.*" (Emphasis added.)

Then Cortés marched into the territory of Tlaxcala. The Tlaxcalans had maintained their independence, though many of their warriors had been captured in battle with the Aztecs and their hearts fed to the devil gods. Cortés sent Indian allies to negotiate a treaty, but the Tlaxcalans did not trust them. They attacked, and Cortés and his men faced odds of a hundred to one, odds which not even the few horses and guns the Spaniards had could overcome. Nevertheless the Spaniards won. It has been said that the Spaniards at this time were perhaps the best fighting men the world has ever known. This was only the first of many battles on this expedition which would be proof of such a claim.

But nearly every man in the army was wounded, and a few wondered if it might be better to return to the coast and send for reinforcements. But Cortés replied that the greater the obstacles, the greater would be the glory. Furthermore, he said, "we are obligated to exalt and increase our Holy Catholic Faith, which we undertook to do like good Christians, uprooting idolatry—that great blasphemy to our God—abolishing sacrifices and the eating of human flesh, which is so contrary to nature and so common here." Cortés never lost sight of the primary purpose of his expedition: the destruction of the devil gods and the winning of Mexico for the reign of Christ the King.

The Tlaxcalans now asked Cortés for a treaty of alliance, an alliance which would be crucial to his expedition. He converted one of their temples into a church, and Father Olmedo, the chaplain of the expedition, said Mass there. About this time, Cortés sent his first letter to the coast requesting supplies. The supplies he requested were hosts and altar wine. He knew that, far more than crossbows and muskets, his men must be armed with the Body and Blood of Christ.

The next stop, in the middle of October, was Cholula, where stood a temple to Quetzalcoatl. Legend had it that any army which did not believe in the Aztec gods would be drowned by a torrent of water from the pyramid. The Cholulans did not believe that Cortés was Quetzalcoatl; neither, by this time, did most of the Aztec leaders. Apparently, on advice from Aztec ambassadors, the Cholulans prepared an ambush for Cortés and his men. But the night before the planned ambush, the chief's wife came to Cortés' Indian interpreter, a young girl named Marina, and warned her about the plot so that she would not be caught in it and could marry the chief's son when it was all over. Marina pretended to go along with the woman and extracted all the information she could, then told it to Cortés. The next morning, Cortés and his men were prepared. They set upon the Cholulans and prevailed over them after a five-hour battle. Some critics of Cortés have accused him of massacring helpless Indians. But the Indians were armed and prepared for a fight, having themselves planned to massacre helpless Spaniards.

In the course of the battle, the idol in the temple was thrown down. On the top, a stone cross was erected. There was no deluge of water from the pyramid, and Cortés and his men marched on.

Montezuma ordered more human sacrifices to help him decide what to do. His council finally invited the Spaniards to enter Tenochtitlán. And so on Tuesday, November 8, they marched onto the causeway that led across the lake to Cactus Rock, the city of the devil gods.

In the Home of the Devil Gods

During the first few days of their stay in Tenochtitlán, Montezuma was a gracious host. He gave the Spaniards a palace to live in and servants to wait on them. Cortés tried to explain Christianity to Montezuma and urged him to worship the one true God, but Montezuma told him not to speak of such things.

On November 13, Montezuma took Cortés and his men on a tour of the market place and the great temple. Near the temple was a building in the form of a theater, with towers at both ends. The walls, steps, benches and towers were constructed entirely of mortar and human skulls. Then Montezuma allowed Cortés and some of the men to see the images of Huitzilopochtli and Tezcatlipoca. Bernal Diaz described them: "On each altar there were two statues, as of giants, and very fat, and the first, on the right side, they say was that of Witchywolves [the Spaniards' name for Huitzilopochtli] . . . and round his neck, the said Witchywolves was wearing some Indian faces and some hearts of Indians, some of gold, some of silver . . . and there were . . . the hearts of three Indians which they had sacrificed that day and were burning, and the walls of that chapel were so steeped black with crusts of blood, and the floor also, that it stank very badly. . . . The other big image . . . was the god of hell [Tezcatlipoca] and he was in charge of the souls of the Mexicans; and close to his body he had some figures like small devils with tails like serpents, and on the walls so much blood, and the floor soaked in it . . ."

After they climbed down from the pyramid, Cortés asked Montezuma's permission to build a chapel in the palace where they were staying. Permission was granted, the chapel was built with a cross and an image of the Blessed Virgin Mary, and Mass was said there every day.

Cortés fully realized the dangerous position he and his men were in. Soon, whatever remaining illusions Montezuma had about Cortés would dissolve, and he would finally order an attack on them. The only hope the Spaniards had was to control Montezuma himself and rule the city through him. So on November 15, in one of Cortés' characteristically bold strokes, he marched into Montezuma's palace and took the Emperor prisoner.

One of the first orders he gave to Montezuma was to end human sacrifice and remove the images of the devil gods from the temple. When the pagan priests objected, Cortés and his men marched to the temple. With his sword he slashed the curtain shielding the idols. Then, in the words of one of his soldiers, Cortés "leapt up in a supernatural way and swung forward holding the [iron] bar midway till he struck the idol high up on its eyes, and broke off its gold mask, saying: 'We must risk something for God.'"

The idols were removed, the shrines cleansed, an altar erected and Mass said in what had been the very heart of the empire of the Hummingbird Wizard and the Lord of Darkness.

The Night of Sorrows

The year 1519 came to an end and 1520 began with Montezuma still living in the Spanish quarters. At the end of April, Cortés received word that another force of Spaniards, commanded by Panfilo Narvaez, had landed in Mexico, and that Narvaez, motivated primarily by greed for the Aztec gold, had declared his intention of marching against Cortés.

Leaving behind a garrison in Tenochtitlán under command of Alvarado, Cortés marched to the coast to meet Narvaez's army. With only a small force he attacked at night and easily defeated Narvaez's men, persuading most of them afterwards to accept his authority and join his army. Narvaez, who was never accused of having too much humility, said to Cortés: "Captain Cortés, it has been a great feat, your victory and capture of me." Cortés, who had marched into the very heart of the empire of the devil gods, replied: "I regard it as one of the least important things I have ever done in New Spain."

But scarcely had he eliminated this threat than he received word that the Aztecs in Tenochtitlán had rebelled and that his men were besieged. With his reinforced army now numbering about 1400, Cortés rushed back to the capital, arriving on June 24. The city was quietly hostile, but Cortés was allowed to return to his garrison. He discovered that Alvarado had started the trouble by ordering a massacre of a number of Aztecs at a festival for the rain gods. Alvarado had feared that the festival would be the occasion for an attack on his men, but he had acted without solid evidence and now the entire Spanish force was in grave danger.

The Aztecs began day and night assaults on June 25. Cortés brought Montezuma onto the balcony to entreat the attackers to desist. But the Aztecs launched a volley of stones. One of them struck Montezuma in the head, and he died three days later.

The Aztecs had reoccupied the temple. Cortés led his men in an assault on it. They fought their way up the 114 steps of the temple. Fifty of them reached the top and faced 500 picked Aztec warriors. They battled to the chapel to find the image of Our Lady replaced by a hideous statue of Witchywolves, surrounded by the hearts of victims. The Spaniards hurled the image over the side, set fire to everything that would burn, and fought their way down again.

But their food was growing low and the constant fighting had much reduced their strength. Cortés decided that his only hope for saving his men was to escape at night, setting the night of June 30-July 1 as the date for the retreat. After Father Olmedo said Mass, they set out, carrying a portable bridge for crossing the canals.

The Spaniards crossed the first gap of the causeway safely, but at the second gap the Mexican warriors attacked. They wrecked the portable bridge, and the Spaniards had to fight for their lives. Most of the horses were killed. Half the army was killed and nearly every man remaining was wounded. But Cortés kept them moving until they finally crossed the last gap and were outside the city. They called the night *Noche Triste*—"Night of Sorrow."

Never Surrender

As the sun came up on July 1, Cortés surveyed his weary, wounded army. Almost any other commander would have ordered a retreat to the coast and an escape to Cuba. But Cortés was not any other commander. He had come to Mexico to establish the reign of Christ the King, and he would not surrender that goal. He decided to take his men to Tlaxcala to recuperate.

They started off, with the seriously wounded carried on the backs of the few remaining horses, which were themselves too exhausted to continue in the fight. But on July 7 they came to the plain of Otumba and found themselves facing an Aztec host commanded by the new emperor, Cuitlahuac, blocking the way to Tlaxacala. They had no choice but to fight. They were outnumbered perhaps twenty to one, nearly every man

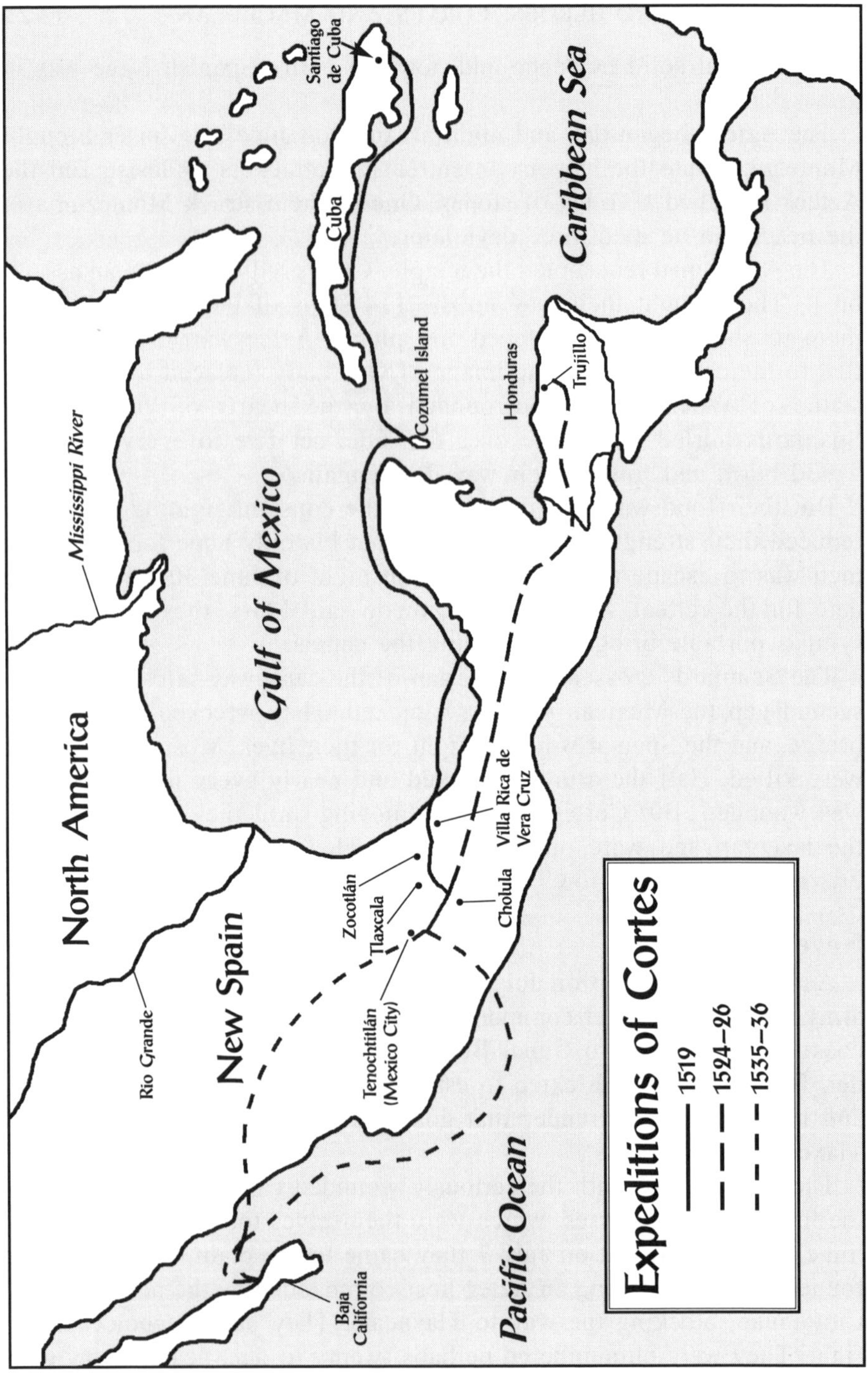
Expeditions of Cortes
1519
1524–26
1535–36
North America
Mississippi River
Rio Grande
New Spain
Gulf of Mexico
Cuba
Santiago de Cuba
Caribbean Sea
Cozumel Island
Honduras
Trujillo
Villa Rica de Vera Cruz
Zocotlán
Tlaxcala
Cholula
Tenochtitlán (Mexico City)
Baja California
Pacific Ocean

among them was wounded, and they no longer had any guns. It was Spanish courage and fighting ability against a massive Aztec host which wanted nothing so much as to capture every one of them and feed their hearts to the Hummingbird Wizard.

Cortés and his men commended themselves to God and prayed for assistance from Our Lady, St. James and St. Peter. They fought as they had never fought before. With the battle swaying now to one side, now to the other, Cortés and Juan de Salamanaca at his side spied the Aztec general. Salamanca threw his lance and the general was killed. Without their leader, the Aztec host melted away. Cortés and his men actually had the strength to pursue their retreat. The Battle of Otumba was a Spanish victory.

In Tlaxcala the men recovered from their wounds and Cortés planned the final campaign against the domain of the devil gods. He secured the surrounding territory and ordered the building of ships for the assault on Tenochtitlán. Reinforcements arrived from Spain, and Cortés trained them hard. In April of 1521, he marched on Tenochtitlán.

Victory

The siege of the city began on May 13, the beginning of 93 days of incessant warfare. Again and again throughout the siege, Cortés offered the new emperor, Cuauhtemoc, peace terms, but Cuauhtemoc, urged on by the priests of the devil gods, refused. For them, it could only be war to the death.

During the day the Spaniards would take territory from the tenacious defenders, but during the night most of the hard-won ground would have to be abandoned. But the defenders were short on food and water and suffering from disease. Nevertheless, on one assault Cortés was almost captured, to be dragged to the temple pyramid to be sacrificed, but one of his men gave his own life to save his captain, and the other men dragged Cortés to safety.

Reinforced by more Indian allies, the Spaniards secured the temple area at the beginning of August. The men fought their way to the top of the pyramid and put everything to the torch. Cuauhtemoc was captured on August 13 and the last resistance ended. The devil gods had been dethroned, and in the sign of the Cross, the Spaniards had conquered.

The Captain General

At almost exactly the same time as Cortés was leading his conquest of the empire of darkness, another great hero was accomplishing an amazing feat of seafaring.

Ferdinand Magellan was born in 1480 in Portugal. Like Columbus he was called to the sea from his youth and made his first voyage in 1505, to India. He spent eight years in the East and then joined an expedition to fight the Moslems in Morocco. Magellan then requested of King Manuel of Portugal that he might be given command of a ship. Manuel rudely rebuffed Magellan, for reasons unclear to historians, and Magellan left Portugal to take service with the King of Spain.

In March 1518 Magellan had his first audience with the young King, Charles I. Charles was impressed with Magellan, both men being deeply devout Catholics, and commissioned him to be Captain General of a voyage to find a water route through South America and then to the East Indies, though neither Charles nor Magellan, nor anyone else at that time, knew how big South America really is, nor had they any idea of the size of the Pacific Ocean on the other side.

On September 20, 1519, Magellan, with five ships, set sail from San Lucar, having dedicated his expedition to Our Lady of Victory. From the beginning, Magellan was beset by problems. The Spanish captains of his ships, under the leadership of Juan de Cartagena, had hoped to provoke the Captain General into a quarrel during their stopover at the Canary Islands, then use that as an excuse to depose him. But Magellan outwitted them by remaining calm and agreeable to everything they said until they were so confused that they did nothing. Then he deliberately sailed his fleet into the doldrums, that area of the Atlantic where winds rarely blow and ships can be becalmed in the broiling sun. He and his men sweltered and suffered for three weeks until the currents brought them into the trade winds, but he had achieved his goal: He had safely avoided capture by a Portuguese fleet that had been sent out to find him, never once suspecting that Magellan would deliberately becalm his whole fleet.

At sea, Cartagena once again attempted to goad Magellan into a quarrel during a captains' meeting. Again Magellan remained calm, and by doing so provoked Cartagena into declaring his intention to disobey the Captain General's orders. This insubordination was exactly what Magellan was waiting for. He called out his marines, who had been hiding behind the door, and Cartagena was arrested for mutiny, relieved of his command, and confined to his cabin.

On December 13, 1519, Magellan's flagship, the *Trinidad,* led the way to an anchorage in Brazil, at the present site of Rio de Janeiro. Magellan named it Santa Lucia Bay, since it was St. Lucy's feast day. A third attempted mutiny took place when a friend of Cartagena released him from custody so that he could seize control of the fleet. Magellan easily put down the attempt but felt all the more strongly his isolation and lack of friends. The fleet was repaired and reprovisioned, and on Christmas Day resumed its voyage southward.

Now the search began in earnest for the *paso,* or waterway from the Atlantic to the Pacific. Throughout the month of January they explored every inlet, only to find all of them turning to fresh water or becoming too shallow to navigate. The men were restless and the weather was turning bad.

On February 2, the Captain General faced another crisis. The Spanish captains had persuaded the entire crew to meet for a vote on whether to continue down the coast or to return to the pleasant climate of Santa Lucia Bay for the winter. But Magellan had given his oath to Charles I not to turn back until the Indies were reached. He persuaded them that they should soon find the *paso* and sail into balmier seas. They voted to continue the journey.

There were no balmier seas. The weather became worse, as wintry gales and icy seas battered the ships. The *Trinidad* was in the lead, with Magellan standing at the prow. For 60 days he had no real rest and never wore a dry garment. No fires could be lighted, so the men ate cold food. Their water-soaked clothes froze, and their beards grew icicles. Magellan suffered with his men, asking for no privileges.

By the middle of March, the Captain General realized that his men had reached the limit of their endurance, but it was two more weeks before they found a suitable anchorage. On March 31, they found a sheltered anchorage which Magellan named Port St. Julian.

Again the Spanish captains attempted mutiny, this time getting control of three ships and preparing an attack on the *Trinidad.* Magellan regained control of one of the ships by sending men with a confidential letter for the captain. Foolishly, the captain took them on board and even brought them into his cabin. He was captured and killed and the ship brought to the *Trinidad's* side. Then a loyal crewman cut the anchor cable of a second mutinous ship, which drifted toward the *Trinidad* and was personally captured by Magellan. At this, Cartagena in the third vessel was forced to surrender. A formal trial was held and of the remaining two mutinous captains, one was hanged and Cartagena was marooned at Port St. Julian.

Now Magellan discovered that the provisioners in Spain had supplied the ships with food and wine for only one year instead of two. He could not therefore afford to wait out the long Antarctic winter, so he sent out the *Santiago* under Captain Serrano to find the *paso.* After 16 miserable days of sailing, the ship was wrecked, but Serrano got all his men safely to shore. Two men volunteered to return to base for help. After 11 days of suffering they staggered into Magellan's camp. He immediately sent out a rescue crew, which brought Serrano and all his men back safely.

On August 24 the four remaining ships left Port St. Julian to sail to an anchorage that Serrano had discovered. On October 18 they departed, two ships going to explore a large bay and the other two continuing the search for the *paso.* When the two ships returned, they were flying flags and firing cannon. They had discovered the *paso,* which now bears the name of the Captain General: The Straits of Magellan.

Across the Pacific

The armada's problems were hardly over, though. The Straits of Magellan are among the stormiest waterways in the world. It took them 38 days to sail the 360 miles of the Straits. One vessel, *San Antonio,* deserted and went back to Spain. On November 28, they finally sailed out onto the Southern Sea, which Magellan christened "peaceful"—the Pacific Ocean.

Believing that the Indies could not be far away, the three remaining ships set sail across the Pacific. For two months they sailed out of sight of land—the longest time ever in the history of sailing. They crossed a third of the Pacific as food spoiled in the tropical heat and water turned bad.

On January 24, St. Paul's feast day, they reached an island which they named in honor of the Saint. Here they found water, fish and sea birds, but no fruits or vegetables. Nevertheless they were sure that they would now frequently come upon islands and weighed anchor on January 28.

They saw one small island on February 13 and then again sailed through the nightmare of endless seas. They ate all the food they had, they ate scrapings from the food barrels, they ate the rawhide wrappings from the masts. By March 5, there was nothing at all left to eat. Nineteen men had already been buried at sea; twenty-five more were dying. Those who were still on their feet were too weak to handle the sails, so Magellan left them up all the time.

Then, the next morning, a seaman named Navarro climbed the ropes to look for land—he was one of the few men left with strength to do so. Suddenly a great cry was torn from his throat: "Praise God! Land! Land! Land!"

They had reached Guam and found plenty of food to eat. But they could not linger because the natives were hostile. They sailed on, and on April 7 arrived at the Philippines. It was the second time in his life that Magellan anchored in these islands. For earlier, in 1512, sailing from Malacca through the South China Sea, he had come upon the Philippines. Since he had reached the same islands the second time, but from the opposite direction, he is thus the first man ever to complete the circumnavigation of the globe.

Death

Magellan proceeded to explore the islands. He made friends with one of the kings and opened up trade with him. The King even accepted Baptism, as did many other natives, mainly because of Magellan's influence. He seemed to be caught up in a spiritual purpose for his expedition.

But the Spanish officers in his ships still hated him, in spite of the miracle he had worked in bringing his ships thus far, and tragedy followed. On April 27, Magellan and the Christian natives were engaged in a battle with hostile pagans. Magellan and a few of his men were pinned down on the shore, until he was overwhelmed and killed.

The 108 surviving crewmen abandoned one of the ships and finally reached the Spice Islands, the expedition's original destination, on November 8, 1521. The *Trinidad* was leaking, so it was left behind to follow later. On September 8, 1522, the last remaining ship—the *Victoria*—dropped anchor in Seville, Spain, having completed the first round-the-world voyage. Thirty-one men returned in the *Victoria*; five survivors from the *Trinidad* returned later. The *Victoria* carried in its hold sufficient spices to pay for the entire voyage.

The first circumnavigation of the world is an accomplishment which can never be repeated; and it would not have taken place then without the indomitable courage, able leadership, and uncrushable spirit of Ferdinand Magellan.

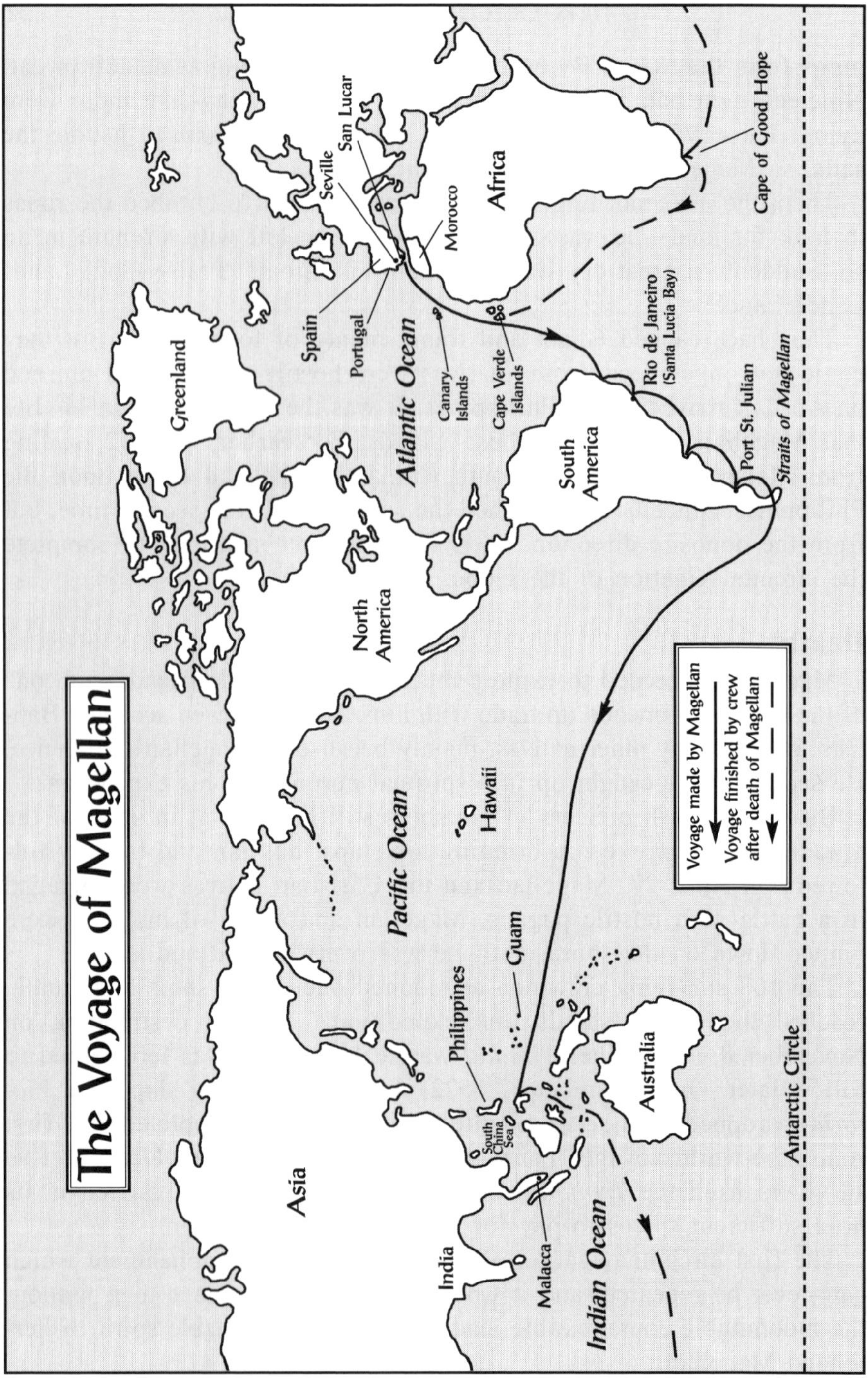
The Voyage of Magellan
Greenland
North America
South America
Africa
Asia
India
Australia
Spain
Portugal
Seville
San Lucar
Morocco
Canary Islands
Cape Verde Islands
Atlantic Ocean
Rio de Janeiro
(Santa Lucia Bay)
Port St. Julian
Straits of Magellan
Cape of Good Hope
Pacific Ocean
Hawaii
Guam
Philippines
South China Sea
Malacca
Indian Ocean
Antarctic Circle
Voyage made by Magellan
Voyage finished by crew after death of Magellan

Cortés and Magellan are two great men who combined an indomitable Catholic faith with courage and determination to open up new worlds to Christ's Church.

REVIEW QUESTIONS

1. What was the main goal of Cortes? Contrast Cortes and Montezuma.
2. Describe what happened in each of the stops on the way to Tenochtitlán.
3. What did Cortes first try to do with Montezuma? How did he make Montezuma his prisoner?
4. Give evidence from this chapter and Chapter One that the Aztecs were engaged in devil worship.
5. What caused an end to friendly relations between the Mexicans and the Spaniards? Describe the *Noche Triste.*
6. Why was Cortes finally able to defeat the Aztecs? What was the most important result of his victory?
7. What obstacles did Magellan have to overcome before he reached the Pacific?
8. Describe the voyage across the Pacific.
9. What happened in the Philippines? Why should Magellan be given credit as the first man to circumnavigate the globe?
10. How did Magellan show his strong Catholic faith?

PROJECTS

1. Dramatize one or more episodes from either the story of Cortes or the story of Magellan.
2. Prepare a time-line mural showing the steps in Cortes' conquest of the Aztecs, beginning with the landing at Vera Cruz and ending with the final surrender.
3. Imagine that you were a participant in either Cortes' or Magellan's expedition. Write a diary of at least ten entries describing your experiences and your reactions to them.

Chapter 3

Missionaries And Conquistadors

HERNÁN CORTÉS HAD BROUGHT down the empire of the devil gods, but his work was not over. He immediately set about rebuilding Mexico City and sent his men out on expeditions to explore and to consolidate Spanish rule over the tribes now freed from Aztec domination. He was concerned with land development and agriculture and made grants of land to the conquistadors and to prominent natives. These grants of lands were communal farms, which were similar to the feudal fiefs of Europe, with the owners of the land responsible for the welfare of those who worked the land. Cortés set up self-governing towns in which Spanish and natives were integrated. Except for a small number of prisoners, he allowed no slavery. There were still those who were jealous of Cortés or who opposed his rule, but on October 15, 1522, Charles I officially recognized the great conquistador as the legitimate governor of New Spain—Cortés' name for Mexico.

With the dark gods dethroned, the kingdom of Christ could now be established. The first organized expedition for missionary purposes was the Mission of the Twelve: 12 Franciscans who landed at Veracruz on May 13, 1524. When they were ready for the journey inland, they set out barefoot on the 200-mile trip through mountains and deserts. For the next 250 years, every Franciscan missionary entering Mexico for the first time imitated these 12 apostles and walked to Mexico City barefoot.

When the Twelve, under their leader Fray Martín de Valencia, arrived in Mexico City, Cortés came out personally to meet them, kneeling to kiss the hem of Fray Martín's habit. The missionaries learned the difficult languages of the people; they translated the Commandments into

Aztec verses, which they taught the people to sing; they organized processions, which appealed to the Indians' love of music and pageantry. By the fall of 1527 they had made tens of thousands of converts. Nevertheless, many Indians still held back from the New Faith, seeing it as something alien or being put off by the bad example set by many of the Spaniards.

The Bishop and the Audiencia

Cortés' rule was soon beset by problems. At the beginning of 1524, he sent Cristobal de Olid on an expedition to conquer Honduras. But Olid decided to set up his own rule over Honduras, in rebellion against Cortés. Cortés made the serious mistake of going to Honduras in person to put down the rebellion, leaving no fewer than four different men in charge during his absence. Cortés and his men hacked their way through virtually impenetrable jungle. By the time he reached Honduras, Olid had already been overthrown, and Cortés did not communicate with Mexico City again until the end of 1525.

By that time the city was in chaos, as the four men he had left behind fought each other and tried to undermine all that Cortés had done. When Charles I heard of the deplorable situation, he sent a deputy to take over the government if Cortés was dead or to conduct a thorough investigation if Cortés was alive. The deputy himself died soon after his arrival; about the same time, Cortés returned from his ill-fated expedition. Cortés' legal status was thus unclear, so the conquistador decided to go to Spain to see Charles and give a full, personal report, leaving March 17, 1528.

But Charles was still faced with the problem of government in New Spain, at least during Cortés' absence, and with the related problem of Church government, since New Spain had no bishop. Charles therefore made two appointments, one of his best and one of his worst.

For bishop he nominated Franciscan Juan de Zumárraga, who would not only be bishop of Mexico City when confirmed by the Pope, but also receive a special office: Protector of the Indians of Mexico. Charles I regarded himself as personally responsible for all the citizens of his vast realms, including the newest ones, the Indians of the New World. He wanted to be sure there would be someone to look after their interests. Then, to rule New Spain, he appointed a commission or Audiencia, under the chairmanship of Nuño de Guzman, a slave trader.

Under Guzman's leadership, the Audiencia's members began enriching themselves and their friends at the expense of the Indians and organized a flourishing trade in Indian slaves. When Bishop Zumárraga protested, the Audiencia told him to mind his own business and decreed the death penalty for any Indian appealing to the Bishop for help.

But the Indians came anyway. They told the Bishop that the Indians of Huejotzingo were being forced to pay extra taxes, which went into the pockets of the members of the Audiencia. When the Bishop confronted him, Guzman declared that he and the others were in no way accountable to the Bishop and sent soldiers to arrest the Indians who had complained. Zumárraga then appointed a Franciscan to preach a Pentecost Sunday sermon denouncing the Audiencia. In the middle of the sermon, Guzman's soldiers rushed up to the pulpit, grabbed the priest and threw him to the ground.

If Guzman thought this would silence Zumárraga, he was wrong. Though Guzman censored all mail leaving the colony, so that the Emperor could not learn of his high-handed policies, Zumárraga persuaded a sailor to carry a secret letter, hidden inside a slab of bacon which was in turn put inside a barrel of oil, to the Emperor's Council of the Indies, detailing the abuses of the Audiencia. In response to the letter, Queen Isabel, Charles I's wife and regent while he was away from Spain tending to his duties as Holy Roman Emperor, appointed a new Audiencia in March 1530. In August of that same year, a royal decree prohibited the enslavement of the Indians and confirmed Bishop Zumárraga as Protector of the Indians.

The second Audiencia took over on January 9, 1531. They came into a New Spain filled with chaos and rebellion, thanks to Guzman's misrule. Within five years they brought law and order, put down an Indian rebellion and released the captive Indians who had been taken as slaves, granted Indian communities the right of self-government under elected officers with the supervision of the missionaries, and encouraged unemployed Spaniards who had come to the New World seeking riches to marry Indian women and settle down on plots of land which the government gave them. They developed education, the arts, crafts and agriculture. Their policies were so successful that there was no further Indian trouble in the civilized parts of New Spain.

The Indian and the Queen of Heaven

But Zumárraga may have wondered if his confrontation with the Spanish leaders had come too late. The rate of conversions among the Indians was declining, at least in part because of the evils of the Spaniards. The New Faith remained alien to the Indians, and was not yet truly theirs. Zumárraga must often have gone to his knees to pray for help from Heaven to bring the pagan Indians to worship the one true God.

The answer to his prayers came on a cold December morning in 1531. Juan Diego, a 57-year-old Indian who had been among the earliest converts to Catholicism, was on his way to 6:00 a.m. Mass at the Franciscan Church outside Mexico City. Juan's wife had died; he had no living relatives except his uncle Juan Bernardino; he was poor, as most of the Indians were. As he passed by Tepeyac Hill about five miles north of Mexico City, he was startled by a burst of bird song. He could not imagine what was happening—birds never sang in December, and this song was more beautiful than any he had ever heard. He was even more startled as he looked to the top of the hill, where once an Aztec temple had stood. There stood a beautiful young girl, surrounded by light so bright that even the cactus under her feet glowed with an unearthly color. She told him that she was the Mother of God and gave Juan a message for the Bishop: "It is my desire that a church be built here for me, where, as thy most merciful Mother, and Mother of all thy people, I may show my loving clemency and the compassion I bear to the Indians."

Though his servants kept Juan waiting for hours, the Bishop received him kindly, telling Juan that he would think over what he had said. But the Lady was impatient. That very evening she appeared to Juan again and sent him back to Zumárraga. Zumárraga was half-convinced by the Indian's sincerity, but knew that the devil, as well as Heaven, could cause apparitions, so he asked Juan to bring a sign that the messenger was from God.

The next morning, Monday, December 11, Juan was in no mood for a visit from the Lady. His uncle Juan Bernardino was critically ill, and Juan cared for him all day. The next morning, December 12, Juan Bernardino thought he was going to die and sent his nephew for a priest. To avoid the Lady, Juan Diego went around the east side of the hill since she had always appeared on the west. But she was waiting nonetheless. She assured him that his uncle would recover—thereby working her first miracle for the Indians whom she loved—and gave him the sign for the Bishop: Castilian roses growing miraculously on the hillside in the middle of winter. Juan gathered the roses carefully into his cactus fiber tilma, or cloak, and rushed to the Bishop's palace.

When the cloak opened and the roses fell out at the Bishop's feet, Zumárraga saw that the Lady had indeed sent a sign. He paid no attention to the flowers, beautiful as they were, for on the cloak was an image, incredibly lifelike, of the Lady herself.

The church she requested was built, with the miraculous picture that had appeared on the inside of the cloak enthroned above the altar. The image has never faded, and the tilma has not disintegrated, though the cactus fiber cloth normally crumbles into dust within 20 years. Scientists have subjected the image to intense scrutiny and can find no natural explanation for it.

The Blessed Mother is venerated under the title "Our Lady of Guadalupe," the name she gave herself when she appeared to Juan Bernardino and cured him. Guadalupe is a famous Marian shrine in Spain, and the most likely explanation of the name is that Our Lady wanted to draw her Spanish and Mexican children closer together under this title.

At last the Indians could feel that the Christian Faith was theirs, alien no longer. There was an incredible surge of conversions, almost overwhelming the missionaries. By the time Bishop Zumárraga and Juan Diego died, within a few days of each other in 1548, *nine million Mexican Indians had been baptized,* all but about 200,000 of them *after* the apparitions of 1531, that is, in just 17 years. Catholic Indian communities were created throughout Mexico. In spite of epidemics and later oppression, in spite of the Church's own mistake in failing until recent times to ordain native priests, in spite of revolutions and bitterly anti-Catholic governments, the Catholic Faith has endured in Mexico, just as the beautiful portrait of the Mother of God still glows undimmed from Juan Diego's tilma in Mexico City.

The Great Plains

In 1535, the second Audiencia, having completed its work, was dismissed, and from then on, New Spain was ruled by Viceroys, personal representatives of the King of Spain. The first was Don Antonio de Mendoza, the beginning of a long line of able and selfless men. A sample of the actions of some of the viceroys will give an idea of their dedication and heroism: Mendoza set aside one day each week to hear Indian grievances; Don Luis Velasco, the second viceroy, was described in a letter to King Philip II as a governor "with such prudence and rectitude, doing wrong to no one, that all looked up to him as a father";

Bucarelil, a later viceroy, wrote, "I spend ten hours at my desk and still cannot complete what I would like"; Juan Vicente de Guemes would wander in disguise about the city at night to discover and correct hidden abuses—when once he found a poor girl who supported her dying mother by giving music lessons, he gave her a pension to be continued until the day of her death.

These early viceroys organized the Indians into villages, largely self-governing. These were so successful that by the end of the 16th century, no regular military establishments were needed in New Spain except along the border. The Indians were educated, taught Catholic doctrine and morality, given the opportunity to earn a living and protected from criminals and Indian leaders who wanted to enslave them. These villages still exist and were the basis of Mexican society.

And of course, through all the political changes in New Spain, hardly waiting a moment after the conquest was completed, Spanish explorers opened up the rest of the New World.

The same Panfilo Narvaez who had thought to annoy Cortés commanded a later expedition which landed in Florida at the sight of modern St. Petersburg on May 1, 1517. He sent his ships away to look for a good harbor to the west, and with 260 men on foot and 40 on horseback undertook to explore. The group met with tribe after tribe of unfriendly Indians. They ran low on food and water and had to eat their horses. They reached the Mississippi River where they built some ships, which capsized or were wrecked on the rocks. More men died until only four were left, lost in the interior of the North American continent, with nothing to aid them but their brains and their strength, determined to find other Spaniards.

The leader of the four was Alvar Nuñez Cabeza de Vaca. His improbable last name—which means "Head of a Cow"—had been adopted by his family in the 13th century, when one of his ancestors had used a cow's skull to mark a path through the mountains, which enabled a Christian army to defeat the Moslems. Cabeza de Vaca and his companions traveled inland to avoid the hostile natives along the shore. They pretended to be medicine men and made friends with the tribes along the way. Their clothes wore out as they walked barefoot through Texas, crossing the Colorado and Pecos Rivers. Often they were on the brink of starvation. But they kept going. On July 25, 1536, after an absence of seven years, they walked into Mexico City, to the amazement of the Spaniards there, who thought these shaggy, bearded men, with their skins burnt black by the sun, were creatures from a nightmare.

Cabeza de Vaca had many tales of his long walk, but his audiences kept coming back to one particular item. Some of the Indians with whom he had lived told him of cities of gold. He himself had never seen such cities, but the tales persisted. This possibility, plus the desire to explore the land, led to an expedition in 1540 captained by Francisco Vasquez de Coronado.

Coronado was from Granada, the last territory to be re-won from the Moslems, and was 30 years old when he anchored his ships at the mouth of the Rio Grande River and led his men inland. In the course of a battle with Indians (who used rattlesnake venom on their arrows), the Spaniards took a prisoner whom they nicknamed the Turk. Turk promised to lead them to the land of "Quivira," where, he told them, they could find all the gold they wanted. On April 23, 1541, Coronado and his men crossed the frozen Pecos River and began to search the eastern plains of New Mexico for Quivira.

They found no golden cities. They did find primitive Indians, buffalo, great grassy plains and a tribe of Indians who remembered Cabeza de Vaca. Finally Coronado sent most of his army back to their base to prepare for the winter, while he and 36 men, including the chaplain Father Juan de Padilla, continued on. Again they found no riches—only rabbits, wolves, deer and tribes who ate raw meat and lived in grass-roofed huts. They returned to their camp, where they suffered throughout the winter from cold, hunger, lice and disappointment, realizing at last that the Turk had lied to them. But they had added greatly to the knowledge of the inland territory and laid the foundation for Spanish colonization of New Mexico and Texas.

Finally on December 27, Coronado fell from his horse and was badly injured. He never fully recovered, and in April 1542 the expedition returned to Mexico City. Remaining behind were Father Padilla, a lay brother, and two oblates, who hoped to convert the Indians, along with Andres da Campo, a Portuguese soldier.

The lay brother was soon killed by the Indians, but nothing more was heard of the others until 1547 when three wild-looking men staggered into Mexico City. They were Campo and the two oblates. They told how the Indians had surrounded Father Padilla and pierced his brave body with arrows until he died. The three survivors had struggled through the wilderness for five years. They had carried wooden crosses to invoke

God's blessing and lived on rabbit meat caught by the dogs they had tamed. Though they had failed in their mission of conversion, their courage and dedication were to be repeated by many others who did not fail to bring Christ to the New World.

The Great River

At almost the same time that Coronado was planting the flag of Spain in the great Southwest, Hernán De Soto was also inspired by Cabeza de Vaca's tales to attempt new explorations. A superb leader of cavalry, De Soto took 223 mounted gentlemen and 400 foot-soldiers through Georgia and into the Carolinas. The Spaniards won a ferocious battle with hostile Indians at Mabilla, but lost all their supplies, even the equipment for Mass. Though by this time they had turned back toward the coast where the ships were waiting, De Soto was afraid that his men, discouraged by the battle, would want to return home immediately. Never wanting to admit failure, De Soto turned his men away from the ships and marched them through Alabama, Mississippi, and Tennessee, until at a spot a few miles below the present Memphis, they looked for the first time upon the great expanse of the Mississippi—named by the Spaniards *Santo Espiritu.* De Soto ordered the construction of barges, and his band crossed the mighty river.

By now dressed in rags, unable even to have Mass, they pressed on through Oklahoma and as far as Kansas. There a Spanish sword was found hundreds of years later, with the name of one of De Soto's officers and the motto: "Do not draw me without right; do not sheath me without honor." In 1542, exactly a year after the discovery of the Mississippi, De Soto died.

De Soto had always tried to befriend the Indians and treat them with respect, and most of them in turn respected him—calling him the Child of the Sun. His men were afraid that the Indians might turn against them if they knew De Soto was dead, so they buried him secretly at night, telling the Indians that he was only away on a visit to his father.

Now Luis de Moscoso was in command. The great river flooded their camp; they were ill with malaria. They built boats to descend the Mississippi, though their only caulking was Indian blankets unravelled into threads and their sails a patchwork of buffalo hides. The remaining men—half of the original 600—crowded into the boats and set sail. Down the Mississippi they went for 17 days, constantly attacked by savages. They reached the Gulf of Mexico, where storms nearly wrecked them. When at last they found a Christian settlement in Mexico, the first act of the survivors was to rush to church to thank God for delivering them.

Conquest of the Incas

In 1528, the Inca Emperor Huayna Capac received word that white-skinned, bearded men had been seen on the outskirts of his vast empire. This news troubled him and may have helped hasten his death. He was succeeded by one of his sons, Atahualpa, who murdered his brother and fought a bloody war to win the throne of the empire and to gain power over its millions of Indian slaves.

Atahualpa was intrigued with the news of the white men and began sending messages and gifts to Francisco Pizarro, the leader of an expedition making its way through Peru. Pizarro, who had been in the New World since 1510, had heard rumors of the vast wealth of the Incas and wanted a share. With about 200 men, including several of his brothers, he marched into Peru in 1532.

In the middle of November he reached the city of Cajamarca. As his small band of men marched into the city, they must have shivered in fear. The vast streets were practically deserted, but in the distance, on a hillside, they could see the tents and fires of a huge army. Atahualpa and 40,000 soldiers awaited the arrival of the Spaniards.

Pizarro did not have the generosity or nobility of Cortés, but he did have a generous share of courage. And he was accompanied by Spanish soldiers, the best in the world at that time, perhaps the best there have ever been. When Atahualpa was carried in a litter into the city that evening with a thousand or so attendants following, Pizarro uttered the Spanish war cry "Santiago and at them!" and his men seized the Emperor, easily fighting off the confused and uncertain natives.

Without their leader, the Inca armies were almost useless, so accustomed were they to total control from the top. They were little better than slaves, and slaves have rarely been good fighters. Atahualpa knew that his only hope for freedom was to give Pizarro what he wanted. Pizarro agreed to accept a ransom of a large room filled with gold and another with silver, and messengers went scurrying to collect the booty.

By May 3, 1533, the ransom was complete. Until June 17, the Spaniards occupied themselves with melting, refining and molding into bars the thousands of Inca ornaments and pieces of jewelry. But then, though Atahualpa had kept his part of the bargain, Pizarro refused to release him. A few of the Spaniards told Pizarro that he was being unjust, but the majority persuaded him that they were in danger from the Incas and that to release Atahualpa could result in a mass Inca attack. So in August the Spaniards held a trial of Atahualpa, convicting him of killing his own brother. On August 29, Spanish soldiers executed the Inca Emperor.

Leaving his brother Hernán in charge of Cajamarca, Pizarro marched to Cuzco, successfully defeating the vastly larger Inca force and taking the main city of the empire. He proclaimed Atahualpa's half-brother Manco as the new Emperor, but Manco was nothing more than a mouthpiece of Pizarro, doing whatever the Spaniard ordered him to do. On January 18, 1535, Pizarro founded the city of Lima, which is still Peru's capital.

But the Indians in Cuzco were becoming dissatisfied, at least partly because the Spaniards in charge were cruel and insensitive. Early in 1536, Manco told Hernán that if he were allowed to leave Cuzco he would bring back to Pizarro "El Dorado," a man made of gold. Hernán was so greedy that he fell for the trick, allowing Manco to leave. Manco promptly started a revolt. The Indians shot flaming arrows into the city to burn the straw roofs of the houses and dug deep pits into which they put sharp stakes to trap the Spanish horses.

But like their fellow countrymen in Mexico, the Spanish soldiers fought bravely, holding off the besiegers. In September, Manco had to send off a good part of his army to plant crops so that the people would not starve. The Spanish held out until a relief force, commanded by Diego de Almagro, arrived to help them defeat the Incas.

Peace had not quite come to Peru because the partisans of Pizarro and the supporters of Almagro began fighting each other. The Pizarro family won and executed Almagro on trumped-up charges. Their rule was marked by favoritism to their friends, oppression of the Indians and many abuses. At last, on June 26, 1541, Francisco Pizarro himself was assassinated by followers of Almagro's son. As he died, he traced—perhaps as a sign of repentance—the Sign of the Cross in his own blood.

The Pizarros were certainly not representative of the best in Spain. They brought many evils to the New World, and they paid for those evils with their lives. But God brought good out of the evil. The enslaved Incas were freed from their evil masters; it was now possible for them to know Christ and hope for a better future.

Argentina

On the east coast of South America, Spanish explorers had found a large river which they named the *Rio de la Plata*—"River of Silver." In 1534 Pedro Mendoza received a commission from Emperor Charles V to explore the river, establish colonies and convert the Indians. When his fleet left Spain, some 2,000 colonists, including many women, were aboard. They established the colony of *Santa Maria del Buen Aire*—"St. Mary of the Good Air"—which would eventually become Buenos Aires, the capital of Argentina.

The Argentine Indians were none too friendly. They attacked and besieged the colony. For once, the Spanish horses were not an advantage. The Indians used *bolas*—thongs of leather with lead balls on each end—to entangle the horses' feet. After a fierce attack on June 24, 1535, only 560 colonists were still alive. The Indians withdrew, leaving the exhausted colony to struggle for existence. In 1537 Mendoza left for Spain, but died at sea.

To replace him, Charles V sent Cabeza de Vaca to govern the Argentine colonies. The man famous for his walk across the southwestern part of North America, though now in his 60's, was ready to walk again. He decided to lead an expedition overland from Santa Catarina on the coast to Asunción, the new Spanish colony. He began on November 2, 1541, with 250 soldiers. As in his first journey, the men were constantly low on food, but each time they were on the edge of starvation, they would find a friendly Indian tribe to give them supplies. On the march, the Spaniards became the first white men to see the spectacular Iguassú Falls. They arrived in Asunción on March 11, 1542, having marched 2,000 miles while losing only one man.

Probably because of his past experiences with Indians—Cabeza de Vaca had more than once owed his life to them—he forbade the enslavement of the Indians and issued decrees ordering a more just treatment of the natives than they had received previously. The original settlers strongly objected to this policy, and Cabeza de Vaca was none too popular.

In 1541-1542, he led still another expedition, this one across the continent to Peru. The men encountered vampire bats and enormous ants. They established the colony of Los Reyes, but eventually were too low on food to continue, so they returned to Asunción after having pushed 600 miles into theretofore unexplored territory.

During the expedition, the hostility toward Cabeza de Vaca had increased so that, upon his return, he was overthrown by Spanish rebels. He returned to Spain, where he died in poverty and obscurity at Seville in 1556 or 1557. But his unhappy end could not obscure the achievements of this man in exploring unknown lands against great odds.

The Mighty Amazon

Francisco de Orellana was from the same part of Spain as Cortés—Estremadura. Longing for adventure and to serve the King, he had come to the New World, where he lost an eye in a skirmish with Indians. He arrived in Peru, where he earned a reputation as a courageous leader and soldier. In 1541 Gonzalo Pizarro, one of Francisco's brothers, planned an expedition into the interior of Peru to search for more gold. Orellana marched from Quito to Lima to join him.

With Pizarro in command, a large body of men marched into the Peruvian jungles. Instead of gold, they found heavy growth, a constant dampness which rusted their weapons (the crossbow and the arquebus) and rotted their clothes, unfriendly Indians and huge snakes. As they pushed farther into the jungle, they ran so low on food that their lives were in danger. Pizarro ordered Orellana to take 60 men, including all the sick and wounded, put them in their brigantine (a small boat) named the *San Pedro* and a few canoes, and sail down the Canelos River until they found food, which they were to bring back upstream, meeting Pizarro with the main force, which would be marching on the river bank. Orellana was given strict orders to be back in 12 days.

With 55 Spaniards, including two priests, two Portuguese and two Negro slaves, Orellana set off down the river, little realizing at the time that he was beginning one of the greatest explorations in history.

The weather was hot and damp, and the men were plagued by sandflies. They left on December 26 from the camp, appropriately named Christmas Camp, and as the 12-day limit neared its end, they had still found no food. The men with Orellana were becoming progressively weaker, and marching or rowing back upstream to meet Pizarro seemed beyond their strength. Orellana held a council, and they agreed to keep going until they found food. They boiled pieces of leather to make stew, fortified themselves spiritually with Mass, and continued.

As the early days of 1542 came and went, the men were eating beetles and grubs. Then, on January 3, they found an Indian village. The Indians fled at the sight of the Spaniards, who immediately began eating the food which was still warm in the cooking pots. When the Indians cautiously returned, Orellana set about making friends with them. It was always his policy to treat the Indians as brothers.

Again the men held a council and decided that it would be suicide to return upstream. Instead, they would remain in the village, building up their strength, repairing their boats and waiting for Pizarro. As the days wore on, the men became restless. Many men were sick from the unhealthful climate, and the Indians became less friendly. Finally, Orellana decided that they must leave, which they did on February 2, after celebrating a Mass in honor of the Feast of the Purification of Our Lady.

On February 12, they came to what they thought were two rivers. Upon closer inspection they found that they were branches of one river, greater than any they had ever seen before. They called it the Marañón; it would later become known as the Amazon, one of the world's mightiest rivers. Even here, where the Amazon had scarcely begun, they felt it to be more sea than river, felt themselves and the forests dwarfed by it.

Almost immediately they came to an important Indian village. Orellana made friends with the chief, who allowed them to remain there and build a second brigantine, which they named the *Victoria.* They remained for 57 days, during which time time Orellana kept perfect discipline and retained the friendship of the Indians. With the 51 men remaining in his party, he continued down the Amazon on April 24.

On across the whole of South America they sailed on the ever-widening river. The sights they saw and their adventures would remain in their memories for the rest of their lives: the Indians with the flattened, elongated heads; the Paguana Indian village, where the children led around huge spiders on strings as pets; the delicious flavor of roast parrot; floating islands of red weed which entangled the boats; the village where heads were impaled on stakes; the tall, bronzed women warriors whom they named Amazons, after the women warriors in Greek mythology, who fought ferociously using Indian men as shields; the poisoned arrows which caused a man's body to swell and turn black and which brought death within 24 hours.

The men guessed that they had traveled 5,870 miles when they began to notice a rise and fall in the level of the river, an evidence of tides. They thought they must be close to the sea, not realizing that they still had 300 miles to go. By now the Amazon was so wide that when they sailed down the middle they could not see either bank. Here the villages were populated by cannibals, so they did not dare go ashore to find food. On August 26, they at last reached the sea. They rigged the two brigantines for ocean sailing, divided the food, filled a bottle of fresh water for each man—and the 46 remaining men entered the Atlantic Ocean.

The seas were rough and many of the men were seasick. Then the *Victoria* lost sight of the *San Pedro,* and the men on board wondered if they would ever see their friends. Orellana was so concerned that he asked Father Caravajal to say Mass in the swaying bow of the boat. On September 11, at 3:00 p.m., they at last sighted Cubagua, a Spanish settlement. They had begun their voyage eight and a half months earlier. At 4:00 p.m. they docked. A Spanish woman ran up to them and asked if they were Orellana's men. Upon receiving their answer, she replied that the *San Pedro* had arrived two days earlier, and she invited them all to her house for wine and food. Bells rang throughout the island as the news spread. Maldonado, captain of the earlier-arriving *San Pedro,* borrowed the only horse on the island, galloped to the dock, and shouted: "*Viva, viva,* for the King-Emperor, Our Lord and Castile!"

Orellana had led a great expedition, exploring 6,000 miles of river. Pizarro, meantime, had become lost in the jungle. With his men dying from exhaustion and starvation, he finally brought 80 of them back to Quito, 16 months after he had left it.

Cortés

Meantime, what of Cortés, the first and greatest of the conquistadors? On December 26, 1531, Zumárraga dedicated the first church on Tepeyac Hill. He sent a special invitation to Cortés, asking the conquistador to share in the rejoicing for the great favor God had bestowed on "this land which you won." Clearly Zumárraga acknowledged that before the Blessed Mother could come to Mexico, Cortés' conquest was necessary to cleanse the land of the devil gods.

Cortés was never restored to full authority in New Spain. Unable to stand inactivity, he went on two exploratory expeditions to Baja (Lower) California. In 1540 he returned to Spain and in 1541 joined Charles I on a mission to conquer Algiers from the Moslems. A disastrous storm came up off the coast. Charles I and his war council decided to withdraw. Cortés was not invited to the council and he was not a man ever to withdraw. He asked permission to continue the expedition under his leadership, but his request was refused.

Cortés returned to court and ended up with time on his hands. He did not receive the recognition he deserved and was the victim of petty jealousies and insults. Suffering from all the injuries received in his long military career, he also became increasingly concerned with the welfare of his soul.

By 1547, the year he turned 62, he knew he had not long to live. Wanting to die in New Spain, he left Madrid for Seville. He dictated his will, endowing a hospital, a convent and a university. He stipulated his heirs to find out if any of their lands had been unfairly taken from the Indians and if so to give them back. He died on December 2 and was later buried in New Spain at his express request.

To this day, Cortés has not received the recognition he deserves. He has been accused of greed, of the destruction of native culture, of aggression against innocent Indians. The best answer to these charges is a catalog of his actual achievements: 1) the military conquest of an oppressive dictatorship at odds of ten thousand to one; 2) the total elimination of human sacrifice and cannibalism practiced by the Indians; 3) the establishment of a just government in the days immediately following the conquest; 4) the establishment of a just land policy; 5) the fostering of a blend of the two races; 6) the encouragement of culture; 7) the exploration of Central America and Baja California; 8) the encouragement and support of missionary activity.

Hernán Cortés, conquistador, had dethroned the devil gods and opened up to Christ the land and people they had ruled. Though his military achievements alone have to rank him as one of the greatest captains of all time, he really needs no other epitaph.

REVIEW QUESTIONS

1. What obstacles did the early missionaries face? How did they win the trust and confidence of the Indians?
2. Why was Juan de Zumarrága important to the history of the New World?
3. Re-tell the story of Our Lady of Guadalupe. What effect did this apparition have on the history of Mexico?
4. How was the second Audiencia different from the first?
5. In general, were the viceroys good or bad for New Spain? Give reasons for your answer.

6. Describe the first journey of Cabeza de Vaca.
7. What was the significance of Coronado?
8. Describe De Soto's expedition.
9. Who ruled the Incas when Pizarro arrived? What was Pizarro like?
10. Why was Pizarro able to defeat the Incas?
11. Describe the rule of the Pizarros over Peru.
12. Discuss the early settlement of Argentina. What role did Cabeza de Vaca play?
13. How did Orellana set out on his expedition? Summarize his adventures. Why was his journey significant?
14. What charges are made against Cortes?
15. Refute these charges by summarizing his achievements.

PROJECTS

1. Prepare a large map showing the explorations discussed in this chapter.
2. Do research and prepare a report on the Guadalupe image, to show its miraculous character and the symbolisms of the various parts of the image.
3. Do research and prepare a report on early Spanish missionaries to the New World before 1550.

Chapter 4

Bringing Christ To The New World

THE AGE OF THE CONQUISTADORS evolved into the age of the explorers, which in turn evolved into the age of the colonists. But in every phase of Spanish settlement in the New World, a key element was played by missionaries. Each of the three ages was the age of the missionaries, as the Cross of Christ was implanted in the New World.

The Apostle of Brazil

The Franciscans and Our Lady of Guadalupe were primarily responsible for the evangelization of Mexico. In Portuguese Brazil, the Jesuits brought the Good News to the Indians. The leader was José de Anchieta, the Apostle of Brazil.

Born in the Canary Islands in 1534 on the Feast of St. Joseph, José eventually entered the Jesuit order because of its missionary spirit, which was spreading the Gospel to the Far East and the New World. During his novitiate, a ladder fell on his back, permanently dislocating his spine into the shape of an S. From then on, he was never free from pain, but not once did the pain deter him from his mission.

The Jesuits sent him to Brazil in 1553 because they thought the climate would be good for his health. They must have been correct, because he stayed there for the remaining 44 years of his life. The few Jesuits who had arrived earlier had set up some villages *(aldeias)* for Christian Indians, where they constructed schools, chapels and houses, though they had inadequate equipment and almost no money. Padre Nobrega, the Jesuit superior in Brazil, had conceived plans for a Jesuit center about 30 miles inland. He envisioned a Jesuit university and seminary as well as a town for the Indians. Padre Nobrega called José and a few others to begin the settlement, which eventually became the great city of Sao Paolo.

At the time José went there, the settlement was only a few mud huts. To reach it, he had to climb over the mountains on what he called "the worst trail in the world." By the time he arrived, his feet were torn and bleeding, and he could not have imagined that this trail would one day be a modern highway known as Via Anchieta.

José was without fear as he went among the cannibals. He won their respect by his courage and his willingness to share the hardships of their life. But though the children loved José and eagerly listened to his stories of Christ, the adults were too wedded to their lives of cannibalism and superstition. A few were converted but most refused to accept Baptism.

The Jesuits knew that the constant warfare of the tribes was a hindrance to their missionary efforts as well as an occasion of sin for the Indians. In April 1563, Father Nobrega arranged a peace conference among the warring tribes, and he and José went to the hostile Tamoyo tribe to serve as hostages to persuade the Tamoyos to participate in the conference.

The two Jesuits carried on their apostolic work among the Indians with as little concern for their own safety as if they had been back in Sao Paolo, instead of virtually imprisoned by vicious cannibals. At the end of June, the first stage of the negotiations had been concluded and Nobrega returned to Sao Paulo. But José had three months more to endure among the Tamoyos. His presence there assured the continuance of the truce, while Nobrega worked frantically to reconcile the warring tribes. José submitted himself to the will of God, showing no fear when his life was threatened, as it was many times. He cared for the sick, rescued a newborn baby who had been buried alive, and wrote and committed to memory a long poem in honor of the Blessed Mother. At last a treaty was signed bringing peace, and José was able to return to friendly surroundings.

On March 1, 1565, he was present at the establishment of what was to become Brazil's leading city, Rio de Janeiro. He organized the great Jesuit college at Rio, helped bring about laws regulating slavery, traveled frequently to the *aldeias,* and wrote so extensively that he is known as the Father of Brazilian literature. In 1578, Father Anchieta was made the Jesuit superior over all Brazil. The Jesuits were so successful in

Brazil that their methods, especially the *aldeias,* were copied in Peru and Paraguay.

When Father Anchieta died on June 9, 1597, the Indians, whom he had loved and served so faithfully, grieved fully as much as his Jesuit brothers. And with good reason. The work of Father José de Anchieta and the other Jesuits had spread the Cross of Christ throughout the huge country of Brazil. Savages, who had known barbarism, murder and cannibalism, came to know justice, truth and peace.

Land of Saints

The evangelization of Peru includes the story of several Saints who lived very different lives: St. Turibius, bishop; St. Martin de Porres, a half-Negro, half-Spanish Dominican brother; St. Rose of Lima, a Dominican tertiary, or third-order member (whose maternal great-grandmother may have been an Inca and whose father had fought with the conquistadors); and St. Francis Solano, tireless missionary.

Turibius had been appointed Archbishop of Lima in 1575 by King Philip II. He lived a life of simple poverty, intense prayer and harsh penance, as he drove himself constantly in the service of all his people: Negroes, Spaniards, Indians and those of mixed blood. In 1588, a controversy between Turibius and the Peruvian Audiencia over the welfare of the Indians came to a head. The Audiencia was keeping for itself money collected for Indian churches and hospitals. Then a new tax goaded the people almost to revolt. Turibius first appealed to the King, then to the Pope. The King rebuked Turibius, but left him in his office as bishop. Pope Clement VIII was weak; he wavered and nothing was done.

But Turibius did not give up. At last, on November 24, 1601, the new King, Philip III, abolished Indian personal servitude throughout the New World, forbidding the *encomenderos* (local Spanish land owners) to exact service from the Indians as a tax and forbidding the employment of Indians on the sugar plantations. The land owners exploded. They did everything they could to delay implementation of the order. They argued that they would never get any work done if the order were carried out. Turibius supported the King completely, as did the Jesuits and Franciscans. The controversy dragged on. Then, in 1603, the King appointed a new viceroy, who simply told the landholders that they would lose their land if they did not treat the Indians fairly. Thanks largely to St. Turibius and his stubborn refusal to abandon the fight, the Indians knew a better life.

St. Martin de Porres and St. Rose of Lima worked on a personal basis to bring about reconciliation among the races and to spread the Gospel. Both of them prayed and did penance almost unceasingly, offering their own sufferings to Christ in reparation for the sins against the Indians. Beyond that, both had a gift for healing and cared for the sick of all races, no matter how loathsome the disease and unattractive the sufferer. They presented an example of brotherhood in the midst of hatred and of renunciation of material things in the midst of greed.

St. Rose had one other service to perform for her people before her early death in 1617 at the age of only 31. On July 17, 1615, a pirate, George Spillbergen, was attacking Lima. Like most pirates he wanted wealth, but he had also been hired by Dutch Calvinist Protestants to attack the Church. On the map in his cabin on board ship, the churches of Lima were marked with big black X's; Spillbergen intended to destroy the churches and desecrate the Blessed Sacrament, as the Calvinists had done throughout Europe. Rose led her fellow Limans in prayer that God would avert this disaster. All night they prayed as the guns of the ship boomed. Then suddenly Rose rushed to the tabernacle and stood in front of it, vowing that she would give her life before she would allow the sacrilege to occur. Many of the townspeople joined her and the chorus of prayer rose louder and more fervently. Suddenly, the guns ceased. The pirate ship sailed back to sea. At the moment that Rose had rushed to the tabernacle, Spillbergen had fallen to the floor of his cabin, stricken by apoplexy. Lima was saved.

St. Martin lived until 1639, continuing his tireless works of charity. As he lay dying, this humble Dominican brother, the illegitimate son of a Negro woman and a Spaniard, was visited by the Spanish viceroy of Lima, who had come to beg the blessing of a man whom he knew was a Saint.

Apostle Over the Andes

When St. Francis Solano reached Peru in 1590, his first mission was to the Tucumán Indians. To reach them, he climbed the Andes, then hacked his way through the jungle. His charity and humility greatly impressed the savage Indians. Francis made friends with Chief Tayaquin, and the two of them built a chapel halfway between the Spanish settlement and the Indian village. But large numbers of savages resisted the missionaries. On Holy Thursday evening, as Francis was praying with the Christian Indians, the pagan braves surrounded the chapel and prepared to massacre all inside. Francis rushed out, armed only with his crucifix. He began preaching so eloquently and persuasively that the Indians abandoned their attack and many of them decided on the spot to become Christians.

Eventually Francis went into the Chaco area, where a squadron of Spanish troops had been massacred to the last man in 1556. For seven years he traveled through the jungles, baptizing thousands of Indians and so endearing himself to them that they made him a hero in their folk songs. At last he returned to civilization, the first white man to leave the Chaco alive.

In 1602 he was sent to Lima, where his primary mission was to the Spanish settlers, many of whom were leading immoral lives. On one occasion he preached a sermon so moving that thousands of the townspeople flocked into the churches to pray and confess. Francis preached wherever people were found: streets, bars, arenas, theaters. His personal penances were so severe as to amaze everyone who knew of them, yet he was filled with joy: one Christmas Eve he ran through the cloister, ringing a bell and singing in praise of the newborn Babe. At his funeral in 1610, both the Viceroy and Archbishop of Lima insisted on being pallbearers.

St. Peter Claver

Indians were not the only persons needing evangelization. There were large numbers of Negro slaves in the Spanish colonies. The chief missionary to the Blacks was St. Peter Claver (1581-1654), the Spanish Jesuit who worked tirelessly in the service of the poorest of the poor.

St. Peter Claver came from Spain to Cartagena in the Caribbean Sea, the chief center for the slave trade. Slave-traders picked up slaves at four crowns per person in Africa—buying them from other Africans who had captured them in war—packed them into ships so that they scarcely had room to move, and brought them to Cartagena where those who had survived the voyage were sold for 200 crowns or more (usually a third of them died on route). Ten thousand slaves landed annually at Cartagena.

When a slave ship arrived, Father Claver would be at the dock. The stench would be nauseating and the moans pitiable. Claver would go among the Negroes, distributing biscuits, brandy, tobacco and lemons. To these people who had known only curses and lashes, Father Claver seemed Heaven-sent, as he talked to them of the love of Jesus, gave them gifts to relieve their sufferings and refused to recoil from the filth and ugliness.

Father Claver set up a hospital for sick slaves, personally dressing their wounds. He organized instruction classes in Catholic doctrine, traveling from town to town to preach the Gospel. When the wealthy women of a town objected that his confessional had an unpleasant odor, he suggested that they find another confessor, saying that his confessional was not wide enough for their fancy dresses but was suitable only for his poor Negresses.

By his heroic self-sacrifice, Claver taught the slaves that they had human dignity, bestowed on them by Christ, which not even the most brutal slavemaster could take from them.

North to New Mexico

In 1598, the first colony was established in New Mexico: 130 families, 270 single men, and 11 Franciscan friars. The story of the New Mexico colony is one of constant reversals of fortune. At first the colonists did well, planting fields and raising cattle, sheep, horses and goats. On Christmas Eve, 1599, a new train with more colonists arrived. Those who were willing to work had plenty to eat. But some had come seeking instant fortunes. When they did not find them, they took out their frustration on the Indians. At the end of September 1601, the majority of the colonists returned to Mexico and an established civilization, having lost the will to build a culture of their own. Therefore, in 1610 the new governor of the New Mexico colony moved it to a mountain plateau not far away. It was named *Santa Fe*—"Holy Faith"—and once again the colony began to flourish.

Meanwhile, the missionaries had been active. Some of the Indians said of the Franciscans: "They go about poor and barefoot as we do. They eat what we eat, sit down among us and speak to us gently." Between 1600 and 1625, 26 Franciscans built 50 churches. Most of the Indians enthusiastically adopted Christianity. Once, some of the friars found an Indian painting of a green sun and a gray moon and above each a cross. When they asked the chief for an explanation, he said: "Before, we worshipped the sun and moon because they were the strongest things we knew. But now we know that even stronger is Jesus Christ, whom we now worship."

Father Juan de Salas was in charge of the mission church south of Albuquerque. While traveling in the mountains, he met some of the

Jumanos Indians who begged him for missionaries, saying that they had been told to do so by a "lady in blue." Father Salas was amazed at this story. How had the Indians heard of Catholicism and who was this lady in blue? Unfortunately he could not follow up their request because he had no priests to spare.

But the Indians would not give up. They kept begging for missionaries. On one visit to the mission in 1629, they noticed a painting of a nun. The Indians told the priests that a woman dressed like that had been preaching to them in their own language and telling them to seek out priests. Fortunately, some new missionaries had just arrived, so Father Salas and Father Lopez went with the Jumanos. Meanwhile, back at the Indian camp, the sorcerers had been trying to persuade the chiefs to move their camp because the water hole had dried up. Finally the chiefs agreed. But that night, the lady appeared again and said that they must wait; priests were on the way.

The priests arrived and the Indians immediately requested Baptism. While the priests were with the Indians, representatives from other tribes arrived, with similar stories of a mysterious woman visitor who had told them about Christ. Clearly God had worked some kind of miracle to bring these Indians the Good News of Christianity.

Father Benevides, one of the missionaries, found out exactly what kind of miracle on a return visit to Spain. He heard of a nun named Mary of Agreda, who had reportedly traveled to the New World. He visited her in her convent, and she accurately described the New Mexico landscape, Indians, customs, churches, priests and events. Through the power of God, she had bilocated to the New World, so that the Indians could hear about Christ. Once the priests were able to minister to the Indians, her "flights" ended. But she was surely the New World's most unusual missionary.

Back in Santa Fe, old problems were reappearing. Some of the governors ignored the decrees from Madrid that the Indians should be given the same rights and privileges as white men. In 1680, the Indians, led by Chief Popé, revolted. Many settlers and priests were killed. The colonists were driven from Santa Fe. Within a few years, Santa Fe was falling into ruins. Popé was a far worse tyrant than any Spaniard, oppressing the people and amassing wealth for himself.

It was 4:00 a.m. on September 13, 1692. The sky was still dark, when the Indians living among the crumbling buildings of Santa Fe heard a loud cry in Spanish: "Glory be to the Blessed Sacrament of the Altar!"

As the sky began to lighten, they saw 200 Spaniards, led by Diego Vargas carrying a banner of the Blessed Virgin. He told the Indians that he came in peace, wanting only the opportunity to resettle the area and to reconvert the Indians. The Indians believed it was a trick; Vargas showed them his rosary and his cross as tokens of his good faith. Though his men were tremendously outnumbered, he ordered them to do nothing hostile. At first the Indians only shouted threats at Vargas and his men. But something in the Captain's courage and sincerity awed them—as other Indians had been awed by other great Spanish leaders. They accepted his offer of peace.

The next morning, a solemn procession marched into Santa Fe, singing the *Te Deum* in thanksgiving for their return to New Mexico. As word of Vargas' arrival spread, other Indian chiefs came to offer their homage and to promise peace. Vargas and his men marched into the northern provinces, accepting the surrender of 23 *pueblos* (Indian towns). He and his men showed nothing but mercy to the Indians. Two thousand Indians were baptized.

The following October the colonists returned. Peace had come to New Mexico, followed by culture and civilization, this time not to be driven out.

The Jesuits in Paraguay

In 1608, King Philip III issued a royal commission to the Jesuits, authorizing them to convert the Indians in Paraguay (which included what is now Argentina, Uruguay, Paraguay and a part of Brazil). Following the example of Father Anchieta in Brazil, they established special communities for the Indians. Called *reductions,* these communities isolated the Indians from the white men, protecting them from their bad example and from attempts at enslavement. They learned Christian doctrine and crafts. The *reductions* were self-supporting.

In 1627, Father Antonio Ruiz Montoya was made head of the Paraguayan missions. Because of attacks from raiders called Mamelucos, Montoya decided to lead his Indians to a new, safer area. Like Moses leading the Hebrews into the Promised Land, he gathered together 250 families—12,000 people. In 700 boats they sailed down the Paraná River, then carried their few possessions for eight days around rapids and cataracts, through tangled, dank forests. Even the children had to carry bundles, as leaders opened the way with machetes and all sang hymns as they marched. The Indians were exhausted, hungry and fever-ridden, but Montoya's courage and will gave them strength. They built new canoes and continued down the river until they found a new home. They had come 500 miles.

The years from 1650-1720 were the Golden Age of the *reductions.* The missions expanded and formed townships. Their fields produced abundant crops. The Indians flocked to the *reductions,* though no force was used to persuade them. The Jesuits sent missionaries into the wildest areas. Some were martyred, but others successfully converted many Indians. All looked well for the future of Spanish-Indian civilization in South America.

The Jesuits Expelled

But the Jesuits' very successes made greedy men envious of them. Europe in the 18th century was dominated by materialistic rulers who had little concern for the people and little respect for the Church.

The first assault on the Jesuit *reductions* came through the Treaty of Madrid, signed in 1750 between Portugal and Spain. In this treaty, Portugal recognized Spanish claims in the Philippines, while Spain transferred to Portugal seven Indian missions to the east of the Uruguay River and recognized Portuguese claims to territory in the Paraná and Amazon basins. In the territory newly transferred to Portugal were 30,000 Indians living in the missions. The Jesuits were ordered to turn the missions over to the Portuguese and evacuate the Indians, leaving behind everything they had built. Luis Lope Altamirano, a Jesuit representing the General of the order, told the Jesuits to obey. The Jesuit leaders knew that the rulers of both Spain and Portugal were hostile to them. By obeying this order, they hoped to avert even greater attacks in the future. The Jesuits in the missions accepted the order, but in some areas, the Indians did not. The Portuguese and Spanish had to use force to drive the Indians from the missions. Resistance was not finally put down until 1759.

But if the Jesuit leadership had hoped to pacify opposition to their society by accepting this transfer, they were tragically mistaken. In the same year as the Treaty of Madrid was signed, the Marquis de Pombal came to power in Portugal, controlling the government during the reign of Joseph I (1750-1777). Pombal was utterly hostile to the Church and to the Jesuits, and in 1759 expelled all Jesuits from Portugal and Portuguese colonies.

In Spain, the problems began in 1700, when the Hapsburg line—

which had ruled Spain and the New World since Charles I (1519-1556)—died out. The new ruling family was the Bourbons, relatives of the Bourbons ruling France. The new king was Philip V, followed by Ferdinand VI and then by Charles III. Charles III was efficient and practical, but he did not have the deep religious faith which had motivated the early Hapsburgs. He regarded the New World as a business venture, designed to bring a profit to the mother country. He reorganized the government of the New World to make it more efficient and profitable, but the end result was that society became more materialistic and government less humanitarian.

The Bourbons also believed in absolutism: that the king should have no checks on his power. They went against the system of local rights which Isabel and the Hapsburgs after her had nurtured; and they went against the Church, believing that they should dictate Church policy, rather than that the Church should judge the actions of the king.

The Bourbons believed the stories coming from the New World that the Jesuits had amassed great wealth; they did not like the influence which the Jesuits had over education; they did not like the Jesuits' loyalty to the Pope. In the Old World, they put pressure on the Holy Father to abolish the Jesuits. But even before they won out there, King Charles III, in 1767, signed an order expelling the Jesuits from Spain and all Spanish possessions.

King Charles and his ministers knew that the order must be carried out in total secrecy or the people might revolt against the government. Before dawn on June 24, 1767, officers of the Spanish Crown entered Jesuit houses, schools and missions to arrest every Jesuit, giving them practically no time to gather their belongings. The government officials were amazed to find that the Jesuits possessed little besides the clothes on their backs and the supplies they needed to convert the Indians: no gold, no silver, no riches.

When the people learned what had happened, they were furious and rebellions broke out, to be put down with fury. In Mexico, 85 were hanged, 73 flogged, 674 imprisoned and 117 banished for their part in the uprisings in support of the Jesuits.

Throughout the New World, much of the Jesuits' work was undone. In Paraguay, the missions fell first into confusion, then into ruin. The Indians either returned to the jungles or were enslaved. Within 20 years, most of the missions were deserted. All that remained was a memory of the golden days of the past, a memory so strong that a traveler in

Paraguay at the beginning of the 20th century could still hear stories of the Jesuits from the Indians, stories which remembered the *reductions* as a time of happiness, peace and prosperity.

The Evangelization of California

But though the Bourbons hated the Jesuits, they still encouraged evangelization by other religious orders. The most extensive missionary activity during the 18th century involved California, where a few Franciscan missionaries stamped what is now the Golden State with the Spanish trademark.

On March 14, 1768, a Franciscan priest left Mexico City for Lower California. Though he was already 57 years old, his greatest achievements were about to begin. His name was Fray Junípero Serra and he had just been appointed president of the missions in Lower California. Father Serra had come to Mexico in 1749. As his Franciscan predecessors had done, he walked from Vera Cruz to Mexico City. During the journey, he received a poisonous bite on the foot and an infection set in, leaving him with permanent lameness.

In command of the Lower California expedition was José de Galvez, pious, wise and farsighted. His task was to establish Spanish settlements as far up the coast as possible, in order to put a stop to Russian expansion in the area. His main troops would not be soldiers (only a few went along) but missionaries, who would have a political as well as a religious purpose.

The Russians entered the New World under Emperor Peter the Great (1689-1725), who hoped to find a passage from the Pacific to the Atlantic by driving east. The Bering expeditions of 1725-1730 and 1733-1741 discovered the Bering Strait and the coast of the American mainland. The Russians were interested primarily in the fur trade, and a rush of traders came to the Aleutians. But the Russians were also known to be interested in lands farther south. By settling these lands, the Spanish government hoped to stop Russian expansion.

Serra went first to Lower California, a land of cactus, rattlesnakes, scorpions and tarantulas, from which the Franciscans prepared to launch three missions farther north: San Diego, the nearest point in the new territory of upper California; Monterey, the best harbor the Spaniards knew of; and San Buenaventura, midway between the first two at the Santa Barbara Channel. As they planned the expeditions, Father Serra wondered that they had not chosen the name of their founder, St. Francis, for one of the missions. Said Galvez: "If St. Francis wants a mission, let him find it for himself."

Three ships left for San Diego. Father Serra marched overland with the soldiers, limping all the way on his bad leg. When they arrived in San Diego July 1, 1769, they erected a few wooden houses and a palisade fence, which was soon put to the test by an Indian attack. Many of the Spaniards were ill with scurvy because of lack of provisions on the sea voyage, but they managed to frighten away the Indians by firing their muskets.

Carmel Mission on Monterey Bay was established in December 1771 and San Antonio Mission the next summer. Father Serra would hang a bell on the bough of a tree, ring it and call out: "Come, Gentiles, come to the Holy Church. Come and receive the faith of Jesus Christ." Attracted by the prospect of a steady food supply, the Indians would come to the missions and learn of Christianity. The California Indians were not very intelligent, so Father Serra and his companions made the doctrines as simple as possible and repeated them many times. Gradually, their work bore fruit and San Gabriel and San Luis Obispo missions were founded, following the patterns which had worked well in Mexico and South America.

At first there were only about a hundred Spaniards in all of California. But in 1776 the first colonists arrived, under the leadership of Juan Bautista de Anza, who successfully brought 240 people, including women and children (three new babies were born along the way), over desolate and rugged country. Near Monterey, they established a farming community, named San José. With the expedition came a priest named Father Font, who founded a mission on San Francisco Bay on October 4, the feast day of St. Francis of Assisi—and the Franciscan founder had his mission at last.

By the end of 1783, Serra had founded nine missions, 6000 Indians had been baptized, 4500 Indians were living in the mission communities, and 200 colonists were settled at San José and Los Angeles. California was at peace, thanks to the civilizing efforts of the friars. Serra had traveled on foot in California 4,285 miles, in spite of asthma and a bad leg.

In the fall of 1783, Serra was 70 years old. He made an inspection journey to San Buenaventura from Monterey, walking as usual. When he reached home in January, he was weak and suffered from chest pains. His condition worsened, until he died peacefully in his sleep on August 28, 1784.

Serra was in every way a founding father of what is now the most populous state in the Union. It is no wonder that when it came time for the state of California to choose two men to be represented by statues in the United States Capitol, one of the men chosen was Junípero Serra.

The Black Legend

The Spaniards' great achievement in bringing civilization and Christianity to the vast area of Central and South America is rarely appreciated. Like their brothers in Europe, the Spaniards in the New World are victims of the Black Legend. The Black Legend is the common belief, fostered by propaganda from primarily English and Dutch sources, that Spaniards are unusually cruel, greedy and depraved, that in nearly every controversy Spain represents the wrong side. The Black Legend came to be accepted, especially in English-speaking countries, because the most widely read documents about Spain were written by her mortal enemies: the English and the Dutch.

In the New World, the Black Legend has three basic themes: that the Spanish killed millions of Indians, deliberately and cruelly; that the remaining Indians were wickedly oppressed and enslaved; that the Spanish government in the New World was oppressive and unjust.

The first theme came primarily from a Dominican friar named Bartolomeo de las Casas. Las Casas had been a missionary and had a genuine interest in the plight of the Indians. But to get his point of view heard, he exaggerated that plight. In his book, *A Brief Relation of the Destruction of the Indies,* he wrote that Spaniards had killed 20 million Indians. This figure has been widely and uncritically accepted. Yet it is impossible. If every Spaniard coming to the New World for a generation after its discovery had killed an Indian every day and three on Sundays, they could not have killed that many Indians. Furthermore, many of the Indian deaths were the result of tribal wars, with the Spanish arrival merely an excuse to carry on long-standing feuds. Before the Spaniards came, the Indians regularly warred against each other, with the losers often ending up on the winners' sacrificial altars or in their dinner pots. Once the Spanish conquest was completed and peace established, these deadly wars were mostly halted. Fewer Indians were killed after the Spanish came than before.

The main cause of Indian deaths was the spread of diseases for which the Indians had no immunity, particularly smallpox. But the Spaniards can hardly be blamed for these deaths, since they had no idea they were carriers of diseases which would strike down the Indians.

It is indeed true that Indians were forced to work for the Spaniards. But the Spanish government, alone in Europe, took a deep and sincere interest in the affairs of these Indians. The Spanish kings regarded the Indians as their subjects, who should be protected. England, on the other hand, regarded the North American Indian tribes as enemy nations. The Spanish kings listened carefully to every complaint brought to Spain about the treatment of the Indians, then acted on these complaints by issuing decrees to protect the Indians from forced servitude, as for example in the case of Bishop Zumárraga and President Guzman. The Spanish government ensured that the Indians would be instructed in Christianity, educated, taught trades, given land, and paid wages for their services. And the Spanish government never authorized Indians to be bought and sold, as were the Blacks of Africa. The Indians were treated as persons, not property.

We tend to think of the Spanish colonies as oppressed because they did not have elections and parliaments. But the local towns had a measure of self-government through their elected councils, the *cabildos,* as did the Indian villages. The people were left free to carry on their business and live their lives in peace. There was not a serious revolt for 300 years, during which time Spain governed the New World without professional soldiers or standing military forces, except in a few places on the frontier to protect against raids from uncivilized tribes. If the people had been oppressed, Spain would have needed thousands of troops to keep order.

Thus the Black Legend can be seen for what is: propaganda meant to blacken the reputations of the Spaniards in the New World.

The Spanish Achievement

The greatest benefit brought by the Spaniards to the New World was Christianity. The dark gods were dethroned; the Indians were converted. To this day, Latin America remains Catholic. The greatest weakness of the missionary effort was the failure to train a native clergy, so that the government of the Church in the New World remained in the hands of those of European descent.

Another strength of Spanish rule was the treatment of the natives as fellow citizens and the gradual creation of a multi-racial society in which intermarriage was common.

Spanish rule created a flourishing culture, which was truly a New World culture, a blend of Spanish and native. The University of Mexico was founded in 1553, 80 years before Harvard University in Massachusetts; by 1800 New Spain had 40 colleges and universities. The New World had poets, painters, sculptors, musicians.

A major problem was Negro slavery. The Spanish imported Negro slaves from Africa to work on the plantations and in the mines, at least partly to make life easier for the Indians. Nevertheless the Spanish slave code was far more humane than either the French or the British. Legally, the slave could persuade a less severe master to buy him; he could also buy his own freedom and that of his wife and children, or he could go to court to be freed from a cruel master. He could marry a wife of his own choice, and even at times marry into another race. As a result, there were a large number of free colored people everywhere in the Spanish colonies.

The final point to be made in evaluating Spanish rule in the New World is to distinguish between the two dynasties that ruled there: the Hapsburgs and the Bourbons. The Hapsburgs—who ruled from 1515 until 1700—believed in local self-government and local rights. The Bourbons were absolutists and greatly weakened the Hapsburg governmental system both in Spain itself and in the New World. It is quite possible that if the Hapsburg system had remained in effect, the bloody Latin American revolutions of the 1800's would never have taken place.

The Spaniards made their share of mistakes and committed their share of sins, as did all the other colonial powers in the New World. But the benefits they brought to the Western Hemisphere far outweigh the mistakes. Gone were the days of human sacrifice, cannibalism and slavery of the Aztecs and the Incas, replaced by Spanish justice and the Cross of Christ.

REVIEW QUESTIONS

1. How did the Jesuits evangelize Brazil? What problems did they face? What role did José Anchieta play in the history of Brazil?
2. How did St. Turibius of Lima work for the welfare of the Indians?
3. How did St. Rose and St. Martin contribute to the spread of Catholicism?
4. What is the significance of St. Francis Solano?

5. Summarize the work of St. Peter Claver.
6. How did the colonization of New Mexico begin? How was this colony wiped out? How was it restored?
7. What was a *reduction?* Summarize the history of the Jesuit *reductions* in Paraguay. Who were their main enemies?
8. What were the main results of the expulsion of the Jesuits?
9. Summarize the achievements of Father Serra, both religious and political.
10. What is the Black Legend? What does the Legend say about Spanish colonization of the New World? Briefly refute the Black Legend with regard to each of its three criticisms of the Spaniards.
11. What were the differences between the Hapsburgs and the Bourbons?
12. Summarize the achievements of Spain in the New World.

PROJECTS

1. Prepare a missionary map of the New World, showing the locations of missionary endeavors with the names and dates of those responsible.
2. Do research and prepare a report on the state of the Catholic Church in Latin America today. Perhaps someone from your diocese is in a Latin American mission.
3. Find out about the life of Mariana of Quito, another Saint of the New World.

Chapter 5

France In The New World

SPAIN AND PORTUGAL blazed the trail to the New World, but other nations were not far behind. Just across the Pyrenees Mountains was Spain's rival, France, a Catholic nation under a Catholic king, yet too often more concerned with advancing its own power than with advancing the Faith. More than once in the 16th and 17th centuries, French kings and prime ministers made alliances with the enemies of Christendom in order to undercut the power of Spain and the Hapsburg rulers of the Holy Roman Empire.

Nevertheless, the majority of the people of France were loyally Catholic, and most of those who led France's ventures in the New World were determined to spread the Faith as well as discover new lands and open up commercial opportunities. Ever since the barbarian King Clovis had been baptized in the fifth century—the first barbarian chieftain to become a Catholic and bring his tribe with him into the Church—France had been a Catholic nation, known as the "Eldest Daughter of the Church." The French would take this Catholicism into New France.

The first explorer who departed Europe for the New World in the name of France was a Genoese—Giovanni Verrazzano. King Francis I commissioned Verrazzano to find a passage through the North American continent—a shortcut to China. Such a passage was an object of explorations launched by many countries, but Francis hoped that France would find it first, thereby reducing the power of Spain in the New World. Verrazzano left France on January 17, 1524. Forty-nine days later he landed near the present site of Wilmington, North Carolina; he then proceeded up the coast of Virginia and Maryland and into the Bay of New York, exploring Staten Island. He continued as far north as

Newfoundland. Nothing much came of his voyage, though, because Francis I was captured in the Battle of Pavia by Charles I's army, so the discoveries were not followed up.

By 1532, Francis had been released and was making a pilgrimage at the great Romanesque monastery of Mont St. Michel. While he was there, a young man named Jacques Cartier knelt before him, asking for support for a voyage to the New World. The abbot of Mont St. Michel warmly recommended Cartier to the King, and Francis sponsored his voyage. Cartier made three voyages of discovery—sighting Labrador on May 10, 1534 and exploring the Gulf of St. Lawrence and the St. Lawrence River in 1535-1536. In May of 1535 he came upon a rocky promontory, rugged and bare, rising out of the river bank with only a few wigwams about. This place would become the queen city of New France, Quebec. Further up the St. Lawrence River he found another well-situated Indian village of log houses. When he went ashore, the Indians were sure he was some kind of medicine man and begged him to cure their sick people. Somewhat bewildered, Cartier prayed for the sick and hoped that God would cure them, since he could not. This village, known as Hochelaga to the Indians, would one day be the great city of Montreal.

Cartier and his men spent the winter of 1535-1536 in Quebec. They found the Canadian blizzards far different from the winters in France, and many of the men suffered from scurvy until an Indian recommended that they eat the leaves of an evergreen tree. Cartier returned to France the next July with many stories of the beauty of Canada and with Indian legends of great wealth "somewhere to the west."

In 1541 Cartier made his third voyage. He had asked the French officials to provide him with colonists, so they gave him convicts who had a choice of execution or Canada. After experiencing the Canadian winter, they probably wished they had chosen the gallows. Cartier took the survivors back to France in the spring. There were a few more attempted colonies, but none of them survived. The first lasting colony had to wait for Samuel Champlain, who earned the title of Father of New France.

The Father of New France

Born in 1567 in the port city of Brouage, Champlain from his earliest childhood had watched the ships and was infected with a wanderlust. He had already made voyages to Mexico and Panama when he became interested in Canada. His first voyage to New France was in 1603, when he sailed up the St. Lawrence and took possession for France of an island which he named Isle St. Jean (now known as Prince Edward Island). He spent the winter of 1604-05 at St. Croix, near the boundary between Maine and New Brunswick. The cider and wine froze in the casks and had to be served out in chunks; scurvy killed 35 out of the 79 men who were there.

But Champlain was back in 1608, when he built a colony on the site of Quebec, at the foot of the rocky promontory which had so impressed Cartier. Twenty-eight men spent the first winter there, braving the bitter cold and lack of food. Champlain set up a daily schedule to occupy the men and encouraged entertainment to keep up their spirits. The men survived and even had some food to share with a group of starving Indians who fought their way across the shifting ice in the St. Lawrence River.

As soon as the weather was warm enough, Champlain was exploring again, reaching the border between Canada and Vermont and discovering the lake which now bears his name. In 1615 he brought over the first missionaries, a branch of the Franciscans called the Recollect Fathers. Accompanied by two of them, he plunged deep into the territory of the Huron Indians, reaching Lake Ontario and Lake Huron. The Frenchmen were impressed with the deep woods, meadows, pine thickets and abundant game. One of the Franciscans remained with the Indians to preach the Gospel, while Champlain and his men continued exploring and organizing fur trading with the Huron and Montagnais Indians, with whom he was on excellent terms.

In 1625 the first three Jesuit missionaries arrived, beginning their great work of evangelization and sending letters home about their exploits. These were published in yearly volumes called the *Relations*, which were eagerly read and which served to make the New France colony better known. In addition, Champlain's letters and visits to France encouraged colonists to come to Quebec and persuaded businessmen to invest in the fur trade. Most importantly, he was able to persuade Prime Minister Richelieu to support New France. In 1627 Richelieu organized the Company of 100 Associates, which financed the journeys of 300 colonists each year and supported them in New France for another three years. Finally the Quebec colony had families instead of just single men, and artisans and skilled workers instead of just adventurers.

In 1629, however, it appeared as if Champlain's dream was to be destroyed when the greatly outnumbered French in Quebec were forced to surrender to a British fleet. But the colony was returned to France in 1632, as a reward for France's payment of the dowry of the French princess Henrietta Maria, who had married King Charles I of England.

Champlain began all over again and in the short time left in his life set the colony firmly on the road to greatness. When he died on Christmas Day, 1635, he could look back on a record of accomplishment: exploration, establishment of fur trading, a permanent colony, the beginning of missionary work, maintenance of peace with all of the Indians except the savage Iroquois, the creation of a spirit of unity and co-operation among the French colonists. Champlain's courage, faith and determination left a legacy which endures to this day in the French Canadians of the Province of Quebec.

The Blackrobes

When the first Jesuits arrived in New France in 1625, they were led by a tall, broad-shouldered man whose physique was so mighty that the Indians gave him the name "Echon"—the Bear. His French name was Jean Brébeuf, and his only desire was to bring Christ to the Indians. In October 1625, he went with a group of Montagnais to their village. Brébeuf knew that to convert the Indians he would need to understand their language, their customs, their beliefs; to achieve this understanding, he would live with them. He spent the winter with the Montagnais: eating smoked eel, wiping his hands on the nearest dog after eating, sleeping on pine needles, never complaining about the filth, dirt, grease, mice, rats, lice and fleas.

By the summer of 1627, he built a small cabin where he could say Mass and be free of the filth and smoke of the Indian huts. Every year he returned to the Indians, especially the Hurons, but made few converts. Most of the Indians preferred their superstitious world of dreams and witch doctors and demons.

In the summer of 1637, an epidemic struck the Hurons. The witch doctors blamed Brébeuf, saying that his crucifix and his prayers had brought the plague on the Indians. For months he and the other Jesuits lived in constant fear of death. In October the Jesuits were so sure that they were going to die that they imitated an Indian custom and invited all the Indians to a farewell feast. The Indians understood the food but could not understand why the priests spoke only of the joy of going to God rather than the fear of demons.

But the time of their martyrdom had not yet come, and in the meantime still more Jesuits braved the perils of New France to bring Christ to Indians who did not seem to want Him. In 1636 Isaac Jogues went to live with the Hurons, who named him "Ondessonk"—Bird of Prey. On All Saints Day, November 1, 1639, Jogues and Father Garnier shouldered packs, picked up their staffs and began moving west. Their first night out they huddled together in a small sheltered area while a fierce blizzard blew around them. Soon they ran into an even worse problem. The Indians blamed them for a smallpox epidemic and refused to allow them to stay in any of their villages. They might have starved to death if an old chieftain whom they had baptized had not taken them into his tent.

At last the Jesuits began making progress with the Hurons, but the vicious Iroquois remained hostile to Christians. In the fall of 1642, Fr. Jogues, some other Frenchmen and a few Indians were suddenly attacked by a band of Iroquois. Isaac hid in the tall grass while the battle raged, but when he saw that his friends had lost the battle and that many were already dying, he boldly stood up and asked the Iroquois to put him with the other prisoners. To the dying Indians he spoke consoling words and, wringing water out of his wet garments, baptized them.

The next few weeks were a nightmare for the Christians, both French and Indian. The Iroquois would grasp the captives' fingernails with their teeth and pull them out. They would chew their fingers until they were a jelly of blood and flesh. At every village, they were forced to run the gauntlet: dashing as well as they could between two lines of Indians armed with clubs and knives. They were given little food. They suffered from stifling heat and from insects swarming about their wounds. Isaac expected to be killed at any moment, but at last the Indians ceased their tortures, and he was allowed to live out the winter in an Iroquois village.

Came the spring of 1643. The Iroquois were constantly on the warpath, using weapons and ammunition supplied by the Dutch, who were enemies of the French. Near Montreal the settlers lived in such terror of the Indians that they scarcely dared leave their cabins.

In August a band of Iroquois came to a Dutch trading post to transact business. When the Dutch saw Father Jogues, they took pity on him and offered to help him escape. At first he was not sure whether he should take the opportunity, since it would mean that he would be free of the sufferings which he wanted to offer up for the Indians. But after long hours of prayer, Isaac at last decided that it was God's will that he try to escape. The escape was almost as harrowing as his imprisonment. He was savagely bitten by a dog belonging to one of the Dutchmen; he had to spend several days cooped up in a small attic room belonging to a Dutchman who hated Catholics and who therefore gave Father Jogues practically nothing to eat or drink; he was put on board a Dutch ship bound for England, but could not land because the Puritans had decreed the death penalty for any priest. But the Dutch ship captain slipped over to France and allowed Father Jogues to wade ashore, onto Catholic soil at last. It was Christmas Day, 1643, and Isaac was able to confess and receive Holy Communion for the first time in over a year.

He journeyed on to the Jesuit house in Rome. When he arrived there, he found that his fellow Jesuits had all believed him dead and had been venerating him as a martyr. Since he no longer had thumbs because of the tortures, the Pope gave him a special dispensation to continue to say Mass. The other Jesuits assumed he would settle down to a peaceful life in Europe, but Isaac could not remain away from his Indians. By 1644 he was back in New France.

He was first assigned to quiet duties in Montreal, but in 1646 he returned to Iroquois territory, on a mission to persuade the savages to lay down their arms and live peacefully with their neighbors. On October 14 he was captured by Mohawks (a branch of the Iroquois), and on October 18, in what is now New York state, Isaac and his companions were tomahawked to death.

As Father Jogues suffered his martyrdom, Father Brébeuf was still working among the Hurons. A few settlements for Christian Indians had been built, and the Jesuits were seeing the fruits of their long labors. But the Iroquois still hated the Blackrobes, as the Indians called the Jesuits. On March 15, 1649, Father Brébeuf and Father Gabriel Lalemant were captured while trying to help the Hurons during an Iroquois attack. Like Father Jogues, they had to run the gauntlet. They were tied to torture posts where they were burned and slashed. Boiling water was poured on them. Their eyes were gouged out. All the while Jean exhorted his companions to keep faith and think of the joys of Heaven to come. At last on March 16 the Iroquois reached the end of their cruel sport. They scalped Father Brébeuf and tore out his heart, amazed at the courage of this pale-skinned man.

Altogether eight men of New France suffered martyrdom at the hands of the Indians: Father Jogues, his two laymen companions, René Goupil and Jean de Lalande; Father Brébeuf and Father Lalemant; Father Anthony Daniel, who was killed during an attack while he was saying Mass; Father Charles Garnier, who was tomahawked not long after the death of Father Brébeuf; and Father Noel Chabanel, who was killed by an apostate Huron who confessed that he had committed the murder out of hatred for Christianity.

After the deaths of the missionaries, the Huron tribe slowly died out, through disease, starvation and the depredations of the Iroquois. The Iroquois eventually accepted the Faith, largely, perhaps, because of their admiration of the great courage of the Jesuit martyrs. The brave who murdered Father Jogues was later baptized, taking the baptismal name of Isaac Jogues. An Iroquois maiden, Kateri Tekakwitha, lived a life of chastity and consecration to God in the midst of temptation and persecution, and was the first Native American to be beatified. The Jesuits' courage was also an example and an inspiration to the settlers of New France, who remained steadfast in the Faith.

The Heroines of New France

On May 4, 1639, one of the many ships which sailed back and forth from France to New France left the Old World with three very special passengers aboard: Marie Guyard—a widow who had raised a son and was now Mother Marie of the Incarnation, an Ursuline nun—and her two companions. The three women were on their way to Quebec to set up a school for both the French and Indian children. When they arrived, Quebec was still very much a struggling colony. The women were lodged in a shack in the shelter of the great cliff. Almost immediately they found themselves nursing the victims of a smallpox epidemic. They had few supplies and very little space within their small house to care for the victims, but so well did they nurse the sick children that only four died.

Over the next 30 years, the nuns would play a great part in the growth and development of Quebec. They had to endure many hardships, especially at first. Their diet consisted of salt fish, salt pork, and sagamite (ground corn boiled into a porridge). They were constantly cold (Mother Marie gave her nuns permission to say their prayers in bed because the chapel was so cold that they could not concentrate), and they never seemed to be rid of the dirt. (Once they even found a moccasin boiling in their soup pot.) But their school was a success. The nuns educated and civilized the Indian girls so that they could be good wives to French settlers or be messengers of the Faith and of civilization back in their home tribes. The nuns provided an excellent example of Christian womanhood, since the Indian girls were used to seeing women treated as little better than slaves. Even the Iroquois sent their daughters to the Ursuline school.

The nuns suffered a great setback on December 30, 1650 when their convent burned to the ground. The sisters and the little girls escaped into the night with scarcely time to dress. But Mother Marie refused to despair. She started over again, writing to France to raise money and then budgeting it carefully so that every penny was put to good use. In the spring of 1654, a beautiful new convent school was completed. Marie proved herself both a talented executive and a mystic of deep faith and charity. Her school is the oldest convent school in North America.

What Marie did for Quebec, another woman did for Montreal. On June 20, 1653, an old sailing ship left Nantes, France with about 120 settlers bound for Ville Marie (as Montreal was then known). The leader was Paul de Maisonneuve, founder and governor of Ville Marie, who had left only seventeen colonists when he had returned to France the previous year. But now he was bringing people with all the skills necessary to start the colony on the road to prosperity. On board was Marguerite Bourgeoys, who was to be the teacher of the settlement's children.

At first Marguerite taught primarily catechism and housekeeping skills to the "King's Girls." These were girls, usually orphans or from large families whose parents could not afford the dowries they needed to be married, who were brought to New France at the expense of the French government to marry French settlers. When the girls arrived, they and the unmarried Frenchmen would look each other over; the girls would ask such questions as, "How many rooms in your house?" and, "Do you drink?" and choices would be made. Priests were on hand to marry the couples, and then they would be off to the bridegroom's house, receiving from the government wedding gifts of an ox, cow, two picks, two chickens, two barrels of salted meat and eleven crowns. Since the King wanted New France to be more thickly populated, the government also gave bonuses for large families.

Soon there were many children in the colony, and Marguerite opened her school in 1658. The first was for seven children in a small building which had once been a stable, but it grew rapidly. Marguerite recruited additional teachers, and the women formed themselves into a religious community, which eventually received the name Congregation de Notre Dame—"Congregation of Our Lady." The women opened a boarding school and a vocational school and began teaching Indian as well as French children. Her congregation grew and her nuns went throughout the territory, establishing convents and schools.

New France's Saintly Bishop

Blessed Francis Xavier de Laval, the first bishop of New France, arrived in Quebec on June 16, 1659. The saintly bishop lived simply. He rose early, opening the church doors, ringing the bell himself, and saying the first Mass of the day at 4:30 a.m., even in winter when all was cold and dark. He slept on a straw mattress, ate two frugal meals a day, and gave away most of his income to the poor. During the day he was always busy performing the corporal and spiritual works of mercy. During a fever epidemic, he worked in the hospital, doing even the most menial chores, such as making beds. When the day finally ended, he prayed the Rosary before retiring for his few hours of sleep.

Laval believed strongly that Quebec should be a Catholic society, rather than merely a society which had Catholics in it, and he encouraged the laws of the colony to reflect the laws of God. Laval set up a seminary, a high school, a technical school and an agricultural school. He was popular with the Indians and baptized the Iroquois chief, Garaktontic, in the cathedral at Quebec.

He served the people of Quebec for nearly 50 years. Even when he was old and sick, he still rose at 2:00 a.m. and dressed in the cold. He had to carry on his duties because his appointed successor had been captured by the British at sea and was being held a prisoner. On Good Friday 1708, he had to be carried to the cathedral to officiate at services. The cathedral was cold, and frostbite set in. Laval had poor circulation in his legs because of varicose veins, so he was soon afflicted by gangrene. He lived only until May. As he lay dying, one of those near asked him to give them his last words as the Saints had often done. Laval only shook his head and replied, "They were Saints. I am a sinner." At his death, all New France mourned the loss of their shepherd.

Frenchmen on the Great River

While New France gradually became civilized, brave explorers pushed into unknown territories. Count Louis de Frontenac, the wise and far-seeing governor general of New France from 1672-1682, encouraged these explorations. He appointed Louis Joliet to explore the then unknown water routes beyond Lake Michigan. With him went Father Jacques Marquette, a Jesuit priest, who undertook the journey to evangelize the Indian tribes. On May 17, 1673, with five other men in two bark canoes, they left the Mission of St. Ignatius at the point where Lakes Huron and Michigan meet, having placed their journey under the patronage of the Immaculate Conception. On June 7, they reached the limits of previously explored territory. Stopping to rest with friendly Indian tribes, they were warned of demons and serpents who would swallow them if they proceeded down the great river, which was their goal. Whether they believed in the serpents or not, Marquette and Joliet knew that many dangers awaited them, but they moved ahead anyway.

On June 10, they left the friendly Indians and portaged their canoes from the Fox to the Wisconsin Rivers. On June 17, they canoed at last into the great Mississippi, "with a joy that I cannot express," wrote Father Marquette in his journal. The priest remarked on the slow, gentle current which carried their canoes along and on the "monstrous fish" (the Mississippi River catfish).

The small expedition proceeded cautiously, not sure if the Indians along the bank were friendly. When at last they did put into a village, they were welcomed by the Indians and smoked the pipe of peace, after which Father Marquette told the Indians of God's love and mercy and they all enjoyed a great feast of sagamite, fish, dog and wild ox.

They continued down the ever-widening river, passing the Missouri River. They saw rich veins of iron and were plagued by mosquitoes. When they came to the point where a river, now named the Arkansas River, empties into the Mississippi, they debated whether to continue. It was clear that the Mississippi flowed south, and Joliet's main commission was to find a westward passage. And they might soon come into the territory controlled by the Spaniards, who could well cause more trouble than the demons and serpents their Indian friends had warned them against. So they turned back toward Canada. Afterwards, Marquette lived for awhile in a log cabin on the site of what would one day be Chicago, continuing his evangelization of the Indians. He died in 1675, looking at a crucifix.

The Mississippi beckoned another French explorer. When Joliet returned to Quebec, he found an eager listener to his tales of the Great River: Robert Cavalier de La Salle, a thirty-year-old Frenchman who had already made a reputation as a brave explorer in the wilderness, but also as a hot-tempered young man in civilized surroundings. He had made so many enemies that once his salad was poisoned, and he was ill for five weeks. La Salle could have had a well-paying job as commander of Fort Frontenac, but money did not interest him. His great dream was to explore the Mississippi to its end.

He began his journey at Niagara Falls, where he built a small ship, the *Griffin*, to carry his expedition through the Great Lakes. A total of 34 men went with La Salle, including Jesuit priest Louis Hennepin and two other priests. On August 7, 1679, they became the first white men to sail out over Lake Erie, and on August 23 they reached Lake Huron. At the entrance to Lake Michigan, La Salle sent the *Griffin* back to Quebec with furs which they had gathered to satisfy his many creditors. With the rest of his men, La Salle continued in canoes. The water was so rough that they almost capsized, but La Salle pushed forward.

Then problems mounted. They ran low on food. The *Griffin* did not reappear with supplies as promised. The men grumbled. One man aimed a gun at La Salle's back as they marched along (La Salle always insisted on marching at the head of his men), but another man knocked it out of his hand before he could pull the trigger. By the end of December they had reached the Illinois River, where they spent a bitter winter. On January 6, six men deserted, leaving poison in La Salle's porridge. For the second time, he almost died from poisoned food.

But La Salle refused to surrender his dream. He led his men in building a fort and another ship, though his two carpenters had run away. He dispatched Father Hennepin and some of the men to explore the upper Mississippi. On this journey, Father Hennepin discovered St. Anthony's Falls, which is now the site of Minneapolis, Minnesota.

When the spring thaws came in 1680, La Salle and a few men marched back through mud, up to their knees, to French settlements to get supplies. He found that the *Griffin* had sunk with all his furs aboard, that his creditors were furious, that people were calling him wasteful, crazy and dishonest. When he finally reached Montreal, he found that the only person still on his side was Frontenac, who helped him obtain money and supplies.

Having surmounted that obstacle, he returned to the wilderness, finding that more of his men had deserted, plundering the few remaining supplies. When he reached the fort, he found no sign of Tonty, the man he had left in charge. Though the whole expedition appeared lost, La Salle again refused to give up.

Eventually Tonty returned; he had been helping defend friendly Illinois Indians against the Iroquois. At long last, on February 13, 1682, they pushed their canoes onto the Mississippi itself. This was the easiest part of their exploration. The canoes floated smoothly down the wide river. They passed canebrakes and cypress forests and alligators. They passed the Arkansas, the limits of Marquette and Joliet's exploration. On April 19, 1682 they reached the mouth of the Mississippi. La Salle ordered the erection of a column and a cross. They sang the Te Deum and fired their guns. La Salle had reached the mouth of his river.

The journey back was more harrowing. They had to fight the current; they lived on wild potatoes and alligator meat. La Salle was sick for forty days. He finally reached the Illinois River and decided to stay there, sending a message to Quebec that the exploration had succeeded.

Hardly anyone believed him. Father Hennepin had been spreading stories, giving himself credit for La Salle's explorations, and Frontenac, his best friend, had been recalled to France. Not until the end of 1683 was La Salle able to return to Paris to enlist colonists for a settlement at the mouth of the Mississippi.

He returned to the New World with four ships and 400 people, but the attempted colony met one difficulty after another. The ships were buffeted by a hurricane. When they reached the Gulf of Mexico, La Salle could not find his river because of inaccurate maps and the confusing appearance of the coastal topography. He sailed past it without knowing he had done so and settled his colonists on the coast of Texas. Then began long months of searching for the river, while the colonists died from sickness and lack of food. After two years, while La Salle was leading his few remaining able-bodied colonists in search of the River, he was ambushed and shot. The colony was later wiped out by an Indian attack. Fourteen years later a French exploratory voyage found the mouth of the Mississippi. There they met an Indian who had a letter from Tonty to La Salle. Tonty had sailed down the Mississippi from the north, looking for La Salle. When he did not find the explorer, he left the letter with the Indians, who had kept it all those years.

But La Salle had opened up the Mississippi Valley, which was now the possession of the French King and was named Louisiana after King Louis XIV. In 1699 a French colony was established at Biloxi, in 1710 at Mobile and in 1718 at New Orleans, a city which retains its French character to this day.

Quebec, Montreal, Detroit, Chicago, the Mississippi Valley, New Orleans: thus did the French influence spread throughout the New World. French presence meant fur trading, attempts to convert and civilize the Indians, and gradual settlement and colonization. Though perhaps not as spectacular as the Spanish, the French contributed their share of heroes to the New World.

REVIEW QUESTIONS

1. Summarize the explorations of Verrazzano and Cartier.
2. Why is Champlain known as the Father of New France?
3. What methods did the Jesuits use to bring Christ to the Indians? Who were the leading Jesuit missionaries? How were the Jesuits received by the Indians?
4. Describe the martyrdoms of Father Brébeuf and Father Jogues.
5. How did Mother Marie of the Ursulines and Marguerite Bourgeoys contribute to the development of the French colonies and to the civilization of the Indians?
6. Summarize the contribution of Frontenac to New France.
7. Summarize the contribution of Bishop Laval to New France.
8. When and where did Marquette and Joliet explore?
9. What kind of man was La Salle? What were his successes and failures?

PROJECTS

1. Do research and prepare a report on Blessed Kateri Tekakwitha.
2. Prepare a large map showing French explorations and colonies in the New World.
3. Do research and prepare a report on French Canada today.

Chapter 6

From England To America

AS THE AGE OF DISCOVERY and exploration progressed, England was shaken by great controversy. The country was torn apart by Henry VIII's refusal to accept the Catholic teaching that marriage is indissoluble. Though Henry himself accepted Catholic doctrine, he rejected the authority of the Church. Once that authority was denied, it was not long before the doctrines were also denied, until a wholly new church was formed, the Church of England, or Anglican Church. Under Henry's daughter Elizabeth, Catholics were persecuted, only a few managing to hold to the Faith. It was then but a short step to the rapid growth of many sects, small groups professing their own particular beliefs and usually intolerant of others. These groups, too, often came into conflict with the Church of England and were persecuted. Many of these religious differences and persecutions would lead to widespread English colonization of the New World, until gradually the English dominated North America.

England's first explorer was, like Columbus and Verrazzano, a Genoese: John Cabot. He came to Bristol in 1497 and persuaded Henry VII to support a voyage in search of that elusive westward route through the American continent to the Indies. Cabot's ship eventually landed in Newfoundland, just a few miles from where Leif Ericson had dropped anchor 500 years earlier. He was amazed to see ice in the harbor, though it was already June, and he was impressed by the huge mosquitoes and abundant codfish. He arrived back in Bristol August 6. Henry gave him a pension, but Cabot later went exploring again, and he and four ships were lost without a trace.

The English did not show much interest in the New World, except for fishing expeditions off the Grand Banks of Newfoundland, until Sir Walter Raleigh came along. Brilliant, versatile, arrogant, Sir Walter was a great favorite of Queen Elizabeth. Raleigh begged her to finance a voyage; she agreed provided Raleigh remain safely in England while his ships explored the New World. In 1584 two ships sailed to the New World, where they found friendly Indians, good soil and a favorable climate for colonization. Raleigh named the area Virginia, after the Virgin Queen.

Elizabeth's main interest in the New World was to challenge the power of Spain. Therefore, she financed and encouraged Sir Francis Drake. Drake began his career as a slave-trader; then he turned pirate, attacking Spanish ships and towns. In 1577 he sailed down the coast of South America as had Magellan. He had good weather and made it through the Straits of Magellan without mishap. Then he took his ship, the *Golden Hind*, up the west coast of South America, raiding Spanish settlements along the way. He desecrated churches, stole sacred vessels and destroyed statues and crucifixes.

Drake continued up the coast of California, spending over a month at Point Reyes, about 36 miles north of the Golden Gate. He continued on to the East Indies, following Magellan's route. Having learned from Magellan's mistakes, he made sure of being well-supplied with food and water. He sailed into Plymouth Harbor on September 26, 1580, the second man to circumnavigate the globe.

The first English colony in the New World was established in 1585 at Roanoke Island. But the colonists had trouble with the Indians, so when Francis Drake stopped off at the colony, they persuaded him to take them back to England. In 1587 another Roanoke colony was established, where the first English child of the New World, Virginia Dare, was born. The next year, the colonists eagerly scanned the ocean for signs of a supply ship from England. But Elizabeth's ships were busy with the Spanish Armada, and she had none to spare for Virginia. When a ship finally arrived in 1590, it found no trace of the colony. To this day no one knows for sure what happened to the Lost Colony of Roanoke. The best guess is that they were moving to another location, but were captured by Indians, with whom they intermarried.

In 1603 James I, the son of Elizabeth's rival, Mary Queen of Scots, became King of England. With the Spanish Armada defeated, James made peace with Spain, and England had a freer hand in the New World. On May 24, 1607 the London Company founded Jamestown in Virginia with 105 people. Seven months later, the colony had a grand total of 32, primarily because the colonists were of the upper classes and did not know how to farm. Their supplies ran low and they fell victim to malnutrition and disease. In September 1608, fortunately for the remaining colonists, Captain John Smith was elected President of the Council of the colony. A soldier of fortune who had fought the Turks in Hungary, he did not have a lovable character, being ruthless and headstrong, but he made everyone go to work. No one liked him, but he kept the colony alive. In 1612 John Rolfe planted the first field of tobacco, having learned about it from the Indians. Thenceforward the colony's survival was assured. Tobacco became its main crop, and as the demand for the leaves grew rapidly in England, the colony became self-supporting.

In 1619 a General Assembly convened, consisting of 22 representatives from the towns and plantations, the first colonial legislature in the New World and the beginning of self-government in the English colonies. Government by elected representatives would be one of the most important characteristics of English settlements in the New World.

Saints and Strangers

In 1593 Parliament passed a law which was continued under James I and his son Charles I. The law declared that anyone absent from an Anglican service for more than a month could be imprisoned without bail until he pledged to conform to the established religion. If he refused, he would be exiled. This law was aimed at Catholics and at the smaller sects known generally as Separatists. The Separatists were opposed to any kind of church organization or central authority, believing that each congregation should be independent in government and doctrine.

One of the largest and most dedicated groups of Separatists was based in Scrooby, England and led by William Brewster. In 1607, when many of the Scrooby congregation were arrested, the Saints (as they called themselves) decided to leave England for Holland where the laws were more tolerant. The Saints lived peacefully in Holland for a time, but as the years went on, they became restless and dissatisfied.

After much haggling in England, the Saints made an agreement with a merchant company, receiving a royal patent to settle in a vague territory they named New England. On August 5, 1620 the *Speedwell* and the *Mayflower* put out of Southampton Harbor, headed for the New World. The *Speedwell* did not live up to its name. It leaked so badly that it had to turn back to England, and its passengers crammed into the *Mayflower*. When the *Mayflower* finally set sail for the New World, on board were 41 Saints (they would not be called Pilgrims until 1840), five hired men under contract to remain in the colony for a year, eighteen indentured servants (men who promised to work for a wealthier passenger for a certain number of years in return for having their passage paid) and 38 colonists recruited by the merchant company, whom the Saints called Strangers.

On November 10 the company sighted land. But on board ship the long voyage had brought out hostility between the Saints and the Strangers. The Strangers and the indentured servants did not get along with the straight-laced Saints. They murmured among themselves that they should break away and set up their own colony so that they would not have to take orders from anyone. The Saints' leaders decided that the solution was a written agreement between Saints and Strangers. Because their religion was based solely on the written word of the Bible, they believed that a written agreement could solve their problems.

As the *Mayflower* rolled beneath them off the coast of the wilderness, the leaders of the Saints and of the Strangers prepared an agreement which emphasized that servants and inferiors in general would not be allowed to go against the authority above them. They acknowledged that the King—"our dread, sovereign Lord"—had authority over them all, but since he was too far away to exercise that authority on any practical basis, they would govern themselves. The adult males of the Saints and Strangers—but not servants or hired men—were given the power to elect a governor. They chose John Carver, their only officer. They called this written agreement the ***Mayflower Compact***.

The Mayflower Compact and the election of Governor Carver were significant for the future history of the land the Saints were about to settle. First, they relied on the written word for law. In Europe the law was based on age-old traditions, which until the time of the Protestant Revolt, were usually interpreted and guaranteed by the Church, which was regarded as the highest authority, higher even than the King. But America had no traditions; it was indeed a New World. And the Saints had rejected the Church. So they based their government on a written document which was to be the ultimate authority.

Secondly, like their forerunners in Virginia, they set up an elected self-government. They were not ruled by a governor appointed by a king, but by an elected official. Though the right to vote was strictly limited, elections were considered the best way to choose those who would carry out the written document.

The new settlers made their permanent settlement at Plymouth, Massachusetts. They settled there December 20 and immediately faced all the perils of life in the New World: harsh climate, disease, famine. At one point during that long first winter, only six or seven of the settlers were on their feet. Over half the company died.

Fortunately most of the Indians were friendly. They taught the colonists which crops to plant and how to fertilize them. Without this help the whole colony would have starved. In April the *Mayflower* returned with additional supplies; Governor Carver died and was replaced by William Bradford, a wise, practical and efficient governor. Their first autumn brought a good corn crop; they had begun to trade in beaver skins and had built 11 houses. Though still low on food, they celebrated a thanksgiving feast in October. In November they had even more to be thankful for as another ship arrived from England with supplies and settlers.

The Plymouth colony struggled for some time before it was secure. It was never large, and in later years its influence on the course of American history was not great. But the Saints were the first permanent settlers of New England, and their attitudes toward government would influence the way the American government would develop.

The City on a Hill

The Separatist groups were never a real political power, either in the New World or in England. But one of the new Protestant sects grew until it challenged the King himself. These were the Puritans, whose doctrines came from John Calvin. The Puritans believed that man was corrupt and could do nothing to rid himself of corruption. A person's only hope was that God would choose him to be one of the Elect, overlook his sins and take him to Heaven. The Puritans believed that it was the responsibility of government to purify the nation and that government represented a covenant (a solemn and sacred agreement) with God. The Puritans were strongly anti-Catholic.

The Puritans mistrusted the Stuart kings, especially Charles I, who seemed to have sympathy with Catholicism. Many Puritans entered Parliament, hoping that it could purify the nation. But in 1629, Charles I dissolved Parliament and refused to recall it. Many of the Puritan leaders decided that the only way to avert God's wrath was to leave England altogether, setting up a new, pure commonwealth in the New World. Organizing the Massachusetts Bay Company, the Puritans arranged for the voyage. They elected John Winthrop governor, a wise choice because he was a man who could get things done. Winthrop obtained ships, provisions, passengers. He had to leave his beloved wife Margaret behind until her baby was born, but they agreed to think of each other every Monday and Friday between the hours of five and six and thereby hold communion with one another.

On April 7, 1630 the Puritan company sailed into the chilly North Atlantic, 400 passengers on four ships with 600 more soon to follow. To keep up their spirits on the stormy voyage and remind them of their goal in crossing the ocean, Winthrop preached a sermon on the deck of the flagship *Arbella*: "We shall find that the God of Israel is among us, when ten of us shall be able to resist a thousand of our enemies, when He shall make us a praise and a glory, that men shall say of succeeding plantations: 'The Lord make it like that of New England.' For we must consider that we shall be as a city on a hill; the eyes of all people are upon us."

"A city on a hill": What did Winthrop mean? He was referring to Christ's words that the Christian community must be a city on a hill, its goodness visible to all around. But Winthrop applied it specifically to the Puritan venture in the New World. He called upon the Puritans to set up an ideal commonwealth to serve as an example to all the rest of the world, sunk in the evils of false religions. The Puritans carried this vision ashore and it became an important part of American history, the phenomenon known as American Messianism. Long after the last Puritan was dead and most Americans had ceased to think of America as a specifically Christian nation, some citizens of the United States still believed that their country was better than any other and should be imitated by all. American Messianism was not true patriotism, but an exaggerated nationalism, regarding the American way of life and the American system of government as the only valid way and system for everyone.

On June 6 the Puritan company sighted land and put into shore at Salem, Massachusetts. The Puritan passengers, their minds filled with dreams of their city on a hill, stumbled ashore, already weak and hollow-eyed with malnutrition, to face the reality of the hard life ahead of them. Winthrop led them to the site of what would be Boston. Once again the dreary tale of famine and sickness was repeated. Christmas Eve, a freezing northwest gale struck the unprepared colony. They had never experienced such cold before; many died when they went outside without adequate protection.

Two hundred died that first winter. Another 200 gave up and returned to England in the spring. But Winthrop held on, encouraging the settlers, reminding them of their dream. They planted crops; new colonists arrived as more of England's Puritans became fed up with Charles I. In the autumn of 1631, Winthrop's wife Margaret came to Massachusetts, and the colonists sent gifts of venison, poultry, geese and partridge to Winthrop in gratitude for setting the colony on a sound footing.

Once the problem of simple survival was solved, the Puritan leaders turned their attention toward government. Under the charter, the directors of the Massachusetts Bay Company had unlimited authority. But Winthrop and the other leaders believed that government should be based on a covenant between the settlers and the men who were to lead them. Therefore they set up a government in which all free men (adult male church members who were not servants) would elect representatives to the legislative body, or General Court. Though later the King appointed a royal governor to administer the colony, the General Court continued to legislate for the colony through elected representatives. At the same time, the local towns were governed directly by the citizens through town meetings.

The Puritans' written document was the **Massachusetts Body of Liberties**, which set forth the fundamental laws for the colony, basing them on the Old Testament. The Puritans believed that they were God's Elect, chosen to set up an ideal government. Therefore the governors tried to ensure that the "City on a Hill" lived up to Puritan standards. Adultery, witchcraft, idolatry and giving false witness were punishable by death. Parents were required to teach their children to read so that they could study the Bible, and later free public schools were set up for the same purpose. Baptists and Quakers were imprisoned, Separatists were looked upon with disfavor, and Catholics were regarded as children of the devil. Cotton Mather, one of the leading Puritan preachers, called the Catholic Church "the Kingdom of Antichrist," and John Cotton declared that the "Holy Ghost puts no difference between Popish Paganism and Heathenish Paganism."

Intolerance was a way of life in the Massachusetts Bay Colony. A young Separatist preacher named Roger Williams came to the colony. He said that the government should have no authority in religious matters and that a Saint should not associate with anyone who was not "saved." Eventually Williams became so extreme that he said that a saved man ought not to pray with anyone not saved, even if it were his own wife and children.

Williams was charming and attracted many followers, but the Boston government could not allow him to spread his heretical views. So he took those of his followers who were willing to leave and established his own colony at Providence, Rhode Island. Gradually he became even more extreme, until he declared that he could not in good conscience pray with anyone except his wife. The narrowness of this position must have impressed itself on him because he eventually reversed himself, preaching to anyone who came to hear him.

The Boston colony was also at odds with a brilliant woman named Anne Hutchinson, who came to Massachusetts with her husband William in 1634. She soon attracted a circle of admirers who were fascinated by her teaching that all of the actions of a saved person were actually actions by the Holy Spirit, that a person's actions were no clue as to whether he was saved, and that a saved person could tell if anyone else was saved. Since she herself was saved, she went about declaring the state of salvation of everyone else.

Before long the Boston colony was divided between the pro- and anti-Hutchinson factions. Governor Winthrop could not persuade her to abandon her more extreme views, so he summoned her before the General Court. Her clever answers and thorough knowledge of the Bible marked her as the intellectual superior of the men judging her, but they had already made up their minds that she was guilty. She was banished from the colony. Like Williams, she went to Rhode Island, establishing the Newport colony. The colony became a refuge for those who could not get along with the authorities in Massachusetts.

In 1638, the New Hampshire colony was founded by John Wheelwright, another person who was banished from Massachusetts Bay. Also during the 1630's, Connecticut was founded by settlers going out from Massachusetts Bay. They patterned their government on that of the Puritan settlement.

The Dutch in the New World

Meanwhile, the small nation of Holland was gaining a foothold in the New World. In 1609 Henry Hudson, an Englishman sailing for the Dutch East India Company in search of the Northwest Passage, discovered Hudson Bay and the Hudson River and reported back that the area had great possibilities as a trading and colonization site. After several exploratory and trading voyages, the Dutch West India Company was chartered in 1624. The first permanent settlement was on Manhatten Island in 1624, when 30 families settled on the long narrow island separated from the mainland by the Hudson River. The third governor of the colony, Peter Minuit, officially purchased the island from the Indians for about $24 worth of beads and other trinkets.

Minuit was an able leader and the colony grew. Large estates were established up the Hudson River and other colonists established the town of Brooklyn on Long Island. In 1638 a group of Swedes established a colony named New Sweden, which the Dutch first assisted and then took over. This colony became Delaware.

The British, who were a more powerful nation than the Dutch, did not like the idea of a growing Dutch settlement interfering with their New World trade. In 1664, four British ships sailed into the Hudson River harbor. The Dutch had no way to defend themselves, so Governor Peter Stuyvesant surrendered the whole colony to the British. The colony was renamed New York, in honor of Charles I's brother, James, the Duke of York. Gradually New Jersey separated from New York, becoming a distinct colony.

The Maryland Experiment

An English gentleman named George Calvert had been secretary to James I but was forced to resign in 1625 when he became a Catholic. But James I liked Calvert and bestowed on him a royal title: Lord Baltimore. Baltimore had once been to Virginia and was intrigued with the New World. So he persuaded James I's son, Charles I, to grant him territory north of the Potomac River. His idea, which his son Cecil Calvert, second Lord Baltimore, carried on after his death, was to establish a colony where Catholics and Protestants could live harmoniously.

Because of his Catholic sympathies, Charles I was favorable to the idea, so he made Cecil Calvert a Proprietor with total control over the colony, and granted him a charter—**The Charter of 1632**—allowing Catholics to settle there (instead of forbidding them, as other charters did). Calvert named the colony Maryland. If anyone asked why that name, he could say that it was in honor of Queen Henrietta Maria. But Catholics would also know that the name honored the Blessed Mother. Cecil Calvert appointed his brother Leonard as governor of the colony, and an assembly of free men—even those who did not own property were eligible—legislated for the colony. Maryland prospered right from the beginning, with tobacco, timber, game and fish being its chief commercial products.

In 1633 the first colonists were twenty Catholic gentlemen and 300 indentured servants, almost all Protestant. These indentured servants received the full rights of citizenship when their contracted term of work was over four or five years after they came to the colony. Each was given a piece of land and the right to vote. Thus the colony soon had a Protestant majority. But the Protestants and Catholics lived in harmony.

Calvert was concerned about the fate of the Indians, so he established boundaries to prevent the colonists from encroaching on Indian lands. Jesuit priests had come with the colonists and set about converting the Indians. Several Indian chiefs were baptized, and many other Indians married settlers so that the two cultures blended. The Jesuits established St. Mary's Church, the oldest Catholic Church in the English colonies.

As the Maryland colony grew and came into contact with Virginia, friction arose because the Virginians disliked the Catholics, especially their missionary work with the Indians. One Virginia leader, William Claiborne, kidnapped the two Jesuit Fathers Copley and White, and sent them in chains to England to be tried under the English penal code, which at that time forbade any priest to set foot on English soil. Only by pleading that they had been forced to come to England against their will did the two priests escape execution.

Wishing to preserve his colony from religious bigotry, Lord Baltimore sent over the provisions of **The Toleration Act** in 1649. The Act granted freedom of worship to all Christians and was adopted by the Maryland assembly.

After the Puritans in England executed Charles I, two Virginia commissioners—Bennett and Claiborne—led an invasion of Maryland. They seized control of the government and summoned an assembly in 1654 from which all Catholics were excluded and which repealed the Toleration Act. Catholicism was outlawed. The priests fled, hiding for a time, as one of them wrote, "in a mean hut, sunk in the ground like a cistern or a tomb."

In 1660, the Puritan Interregnum ended, and Charles II came to the throne. The third Lord Baltimore, Charles Calvert, became proprietor, and the Toleration Act was reaffirmed. Charles II was followed by his Catholic brother James II. But in 1688 he was overthrown, and King

William and Queen Mary ascended the throne and permanently re-established Protestant rule in England. Maryland was made a royal colony; the capital was moved from Catholic St. Mary's to Protestant Annapolis; the Church of England was declared the established church of the colony with all residents required to support it; Catholics were excluded from civil rights; and priests were threatened with imprisonment. In 1692 the Act of Religion was passed with the following provisions: the Mass was illegal, the making of converts was punishable by death, a parent who educated his children in the Catholic religion would be heavily fined, a Catholic child who apostatized to Protestantism could take possession of everything his parents owned. Thus was Lord Baltimore's great experiment in religious toleration turned into a showcase of religious bigotry.

The Faith was preserved primarily through the efforts of the wealthy Catholic families who continued to have Mass secretly in their homes and to send their sons abroad to receive a Catholic education. The leading Catholic family was the Carrolls of Carrollton, who would later give a great political and a great religious leader to the United States.

The Remaining Colonies

In 1663 Charles II granted a vast territory south of Virginia to friends of his to establish a buffer against Spain. They named the territory the "Carolinas" in honor of Charles. Huge estates were set up. Since few colonists migrated to the Carolinas, they were worked primarily by slave labor. Gradually the two Carolinas became separate colonies.

In 1681 William Penn, a Quaker, received a charter from Charles II to pay off a debt owed to Penn's father. Penn was made proprietor of a colony named for him (Penn's Woods). He founded Philadelphia in 1682 and settled mostly Quakers there. The Quakers had no ministers and no church structure, believing that each Quaker was guided by an Inner Light directly from God. They were tolerant of other religions and persecuted no one. Many German Quakers came to the colony; their descendants today are the Pennsylvania Dutch (*Deutsch* being the German word for "German people").

The last of the 13 original colonies was Georgia, chartered in 1732. The charter granted liberty of conscience to all except Catholics. The founder of the colony was James Oglethorpe, who set up a series of forts to protect against the Spanish in Florida.

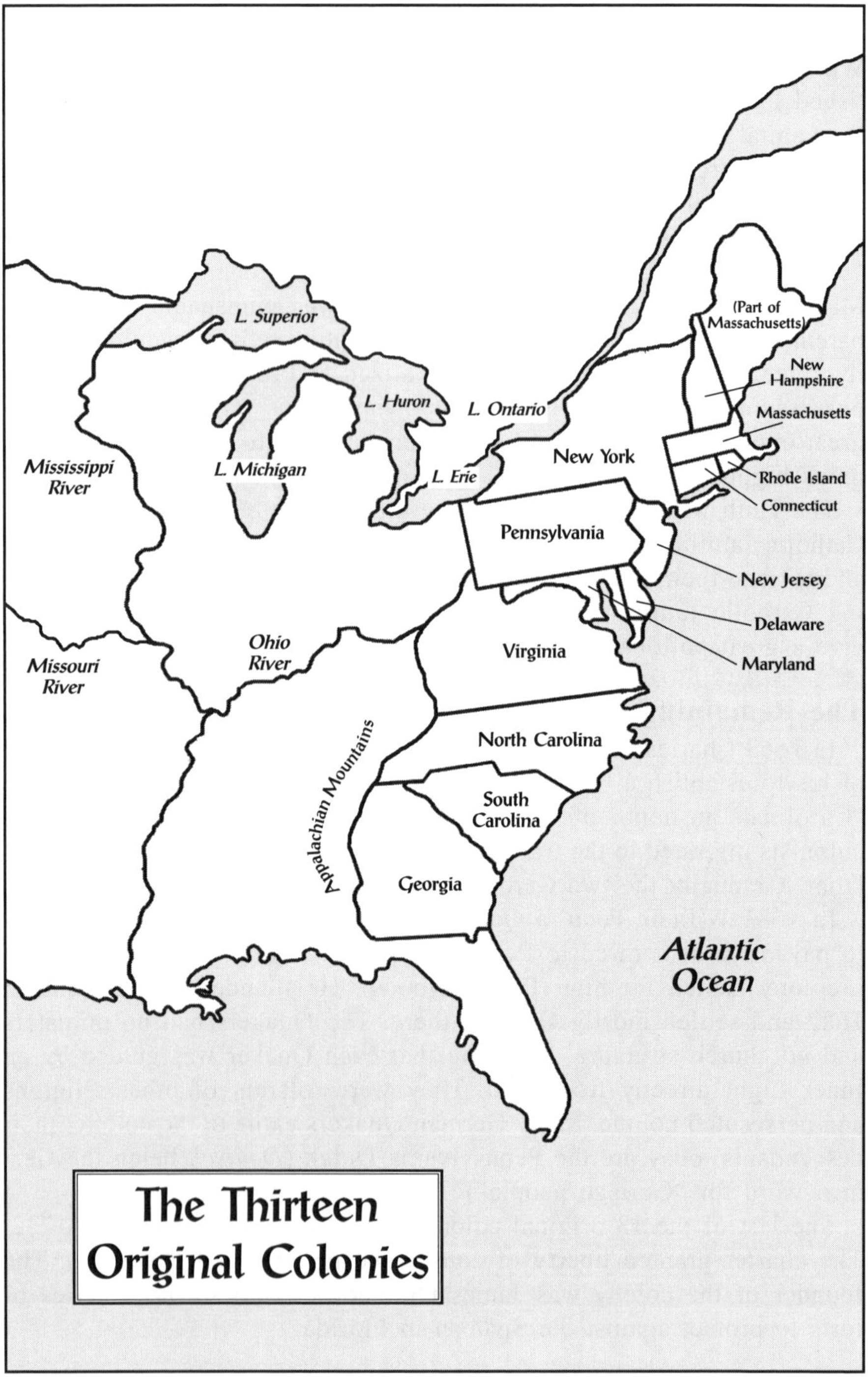
L. Superior
L. Huron
L. Ontario
L. Michigan
L. Erie
Mississippi River
(Part of Massachusetts)
New Hampshire
Massachusetts
New York
Rhode Island
Connecticut
Pennsylvania
New Jersey
Delaware
Maryland
Ohio River
Missouri River
Virginia
North Carolina
Appalachian Mountains
South Carolina
Georgia
Atlantic Ocean
The Thirteen Original Colonies

The Colonial Wars

As the English colonies expanded, they would inevitably come into conflict with the French colonies. The North American wars which ensued were part of a much larger picture, in which England and France struggled for supremacy on the continent of Europe and in overseas empires. The two nations were very different, and their colonies tended to reflect those differences: England was now ruled by a small group of wealthy men who controlled both Parliament and the King; France was ruled by an absolute monarch. England was a commercial and trading nation; France was still largely agricultural. England was Protestant; France was Catholic. The victorious nation would set the tone for the development of the whole North American continent.

At the beginning of the conflict, the French advantages were a centralized government, contrasted with the independent colonies of New England; a series of strategically placed forts; a well-trained army; Indian allies; and the French-Canadian experience with forests and trails in the area of conflict. The English advantages were the Iroquois alliance; naval supremacy; trading and financial superiority; and—probably the most crucial—overwhelming numerical advantage (over 100,000 colonists in New England alone in 1688 contrasted with 12,000 in all of New France).

The first war was known in America as King William's War (1690-1697), in Europe as the War of the League of Augsburg, where France and England fought over portions of Germany. The fighting dragged on until 1697, when a treaty was signed leaving everything about as it was before the war began.

The French colonists now decided to protect their position by establishing full control over the Mississippi Valley. They established a settlement near the present site of St. Louis in 1699 and another at Detroit in 1701. The English felt threatened by these new outposts, and war broke out anew in 1702. In America it was Queen Anne's War (1702-1713); in Europe it was the War of the Spanish Succession, a major war to determine who would be allowed to sit on the throne of Spain. The most important event of the war in America was the seizure of St. Augustine from the Spanish (who were allied with the French) by raiders from South Carolina. The South Carolinians also destroyed several Catholic missions. The war ended with the Treaty of Utrecht in 1713, which permitted a French Bourbon to reign on the Spanish throne, but which forced the French to make other concessions in return. Thus Nova

Scotia, Newfoundland and the Hudson Bay area were ceded to Great Britain.

The War of the Spanish Succession had sufficiently exhausted both sides that almost thirty years of peace followed. Both sides took advantage of the hiatus to expand their colonial empires. As a consequence, the rivalry between Britain and France became bitter once again, with Spain and Britain also hostile. The British had been sending ships to trade in Spanish waters. In 1739 the Spaniards seized one of the ships, and in the ensuing scuffle a seaman named Jenkins had an ear cut off. The English promptly declared war, appropriately named the War of Jenkins Ear (1739-1742), which accomplished little for either side. It was followed immediately by King George's War, a twin to the War of the Austrian Succession in Europe. The European War was very important, but the war in the colonies was inconclusive.

During the course of the wars, the balance of power had been gradually shifting in favor of the British. France was being weakened under King Louis XV, who was more concerned with his own wealth and power than with his people or his country. Spain, also ruled by Bourbon kings, was rapidly losing the spiritual and material strength it had accumulated in its days of greatness under Charles I and Philip II. England, now experiencing the beginnings of the Industrial Revolution, was growing materially and economically. The heavily populated British colonies spilled across the Appalachians, preceded by traders and land speculators. As they moved into the Ohio River Valley, they threatened to split New France apart. The French therefore built Fort Duquesne at the site of what would be Pittsburgh.

In 1755 the British sent General William Braddock to command the forces in America. Fourteen hundred British troops and 475 Americans under the command of George Washington marched to Fort Duquesne. The French were waiting for them. Braddock was killed and the British soundly defeated. Washington took command and conducted an orderly retreat back to Maryland.

But then the British began to win. They defeated the French in upstate New York. They expelled the French settlers from Nova Scotia, sending them to Louisiana and to some of the English colonies because they refused to take an oath of allegiance to the English king. In 1756 war officially broke out. Known as the Seven Years War in Europe, the conflict saw Britain and Prussia against France and Austria; in America it was **The French and Indian War**.

The French commander in Canada was the Marquis de Montcalm; the British commander was James Wolfe, who sailed for Quebec in 1759. Wolfe realized that a decisive attack had to come before the winter drove his fleet away. He decided upon a secret night landing. His men took the French rear guard with just a few shots. By daybreak 5000 Englishmen had formed a line of battle across the Plains of Abraham, west of the city.

Montcalm brought up his men, but Wolfe made his men lie down and not rise until the French came within 130 yards. His men had been well-trained on the battlefields of Europe, and they did not move. When the French were within forty yards, the British unleashed a volley so co-ordinated that it sounded like a single shot. They advanced four paces and fired again, then again. Within 15 minutes, the battle was over. The French were beating a hasty and disorganized retreat. Montcalm had been mortally wounded, and Wolfe himself lay dying with two bullets in his body. Quebec surrendered five days later. In 1760 all the British armies converged on Montreal and the French surrendered.

In 1763 **The Treaty of Paris** was signed, officially ending the war. England received Canada and all French territory east of the Mississippi except New Orleans.

The first effect of the transfer of power in North America was to frighten the Indian leaders. They had gotten along well with the French, who had intermarried with them and made them part of their own society. But they feared the English, who simply drove the Indians out of their lands. Pontiac, chief of the Ottawa tribe, launched Pontiac's Rebellion, the greatest Indian rebellion in history. Though he won some early victories, he was no match for the British army. Pontiac submitted, sealing the doom of the North American Indians.

The Treaty of Paris had two other important effects: The first was that North America would be English and Protestant, not French and Catholic. Except for Quebec Province itself, where the French language and religion predominated, French Catholic culture was eliminated from North America. The English colonial legacy included an intolerance of those who did not share the dominant religion, especially of Catholics; a belief that America was especially holy in the eyes of God; a trust in written documents; a trust in elected governments; and a reverence for public education.

In addition, the Treaty had an important effect on the English-American colonies. Until this time they had been fearful of the French and needed England's help to keep the French at bay. But now France was gone. The Colonies began quarreling with England as they became more aware of grievances with the Mother Country. Within less than 15 years after the signing of the Treaty of Paris, the Colonies would begin their War of Independence.

REVIEW QUESTIONS

1. Summarize the establishment of the Virginia colonies, including Sir Walter Raleigh, Roanoke, and Jamestown.
2. Who were the Separatists? Why did they come to the New World?
3. What is the significance of the Mayflower Compact?
4. Who were the Puritans? Why did they come to the New World?
5. What is the significance of Winthrop's "City on a Hill" sermon?
6. What is the significance of the government of Massachusetts?
7. Summarize the establishment of Rhode Island, New York, and Pennsylvania.
8. How did Maryland differ from other English colonies?
9. What is the significance of the Toleration Act?
10. What happened to Maryland when the Stuart kings were overthrown?
11. What were the differences between the English and the French? What were the advantages of each side?
12. What happened during Queen Anne's War? What important events happened after Queen Anne's War?
13. By the time of the French and Indian War, what new advantages did England have?
14. Who were the generals in the Battle of Quebec? Describe the battle.
15. What were the terms of the Treaty of Paris?
16. What were the three most important results of the English victory in the colonial wars?
17. Summarize the English colonial legacy.

PROJECTS

1. Prepare a chart of the thirteen original colonies showing dates, founders, and reasons for founding.
2. Do research and prepare a report on one of the colonial wars, including what happened in Europe.
3. Do research and prepare a report on one of the English colonies.

Chapter 7

The Eve of the American War for Independence

IN SEPTEMBER OF 1765, a newspaper called the *Constitutional Courant* was secretly printed and distributed in the New England colonies. On the front page was a picture of a snake cut into eight parts, with the legend, "Join or Die."

In the spring of that year, the British Parliament had given the final approval to the Stamp Act. The Act required that a stamp be purchased and affixed to every newspaper, legal document, pamphlet, marriage license, deck of cards or pair of dice in the colonies. By selling the stamps, Parliament hoped at last to get some money out of its North American colonies to pay off the debts accumulated during the long war with the French. After all, reasoned the men in Parliament, England had doubled its national debt to save the Colonies from the French. It was high time that the Colonies paid their fair share, especially since they had not paid taxes to England before.

But this last point was precisely the problem. The Colonies had long conceded that England had the right to collect tariffs (taxes) on goods shipped out of the Colonies to England and to regulate the trade of the Colonies, even to the benefit of England. But taxes on the *internal* affairs of the Colonies were a different matter. The Colonies had governed themselves and levied their own taxes for almost 150 years. The idea that Parliament at this late date could intervene to tell the Colonies what to do was unacceptable.

On June 6 the Massachusetts House of Representatives proposed a Stamp Act Congress, a meeting of delegates from all the continental

Colonies possessing representative legislatures: Massachusetts, Rhode Island, Connecticut, New Hampshire, New York, New Jersey, Pennsylvania, Delaware, Maryland, Virginia, North Carolina, South Carolina, Georgia and Nova Scotia. Massachusetts invited the delegates to plot a united strategy to meet this crisis. Nova Scotia was so dependent on Great Britain that the **Stamp Act** aroused no outcry there; the New Hampshire Assembly refused the invitation; the North Carolina, Virginia and Georgia assemblies were not in session because the governors of the Colonies (who were appointed by the king) had prorogued the assemblies (not allowed them to meet). But in early October, 27 delegates from the other nine Colonies arrived in New York City to begin deliberations.

The delegates were about equally divided between radicals (who wanted to take drastic action) and conservatives (who wanted to work out a compromise); and except for Hendrick Fisher, a German immigrant and farmer from New Jersey, were members of the upper classes and at least moderately wealthy. The majority of the delegates were lawyers, and herein lay evidence of one of the greatest stupidities of the Stamp Act. Whatever Parliament felt about the need to raise money, the members should have realized that a tax which struck particularly at lawyers and newspaper publishers would only antagonize the men who could do England the most harm—through speaking and writing against Parliament.

The delegates debated 17 days, and at the end approved petitions to King George III and to the two houses of Parliament (the House of Lords and the House of Commons). Parliament refused even to accept and debate the petitions, believing that if they did they would acknowledge that the Colonies had the *right* to come together in a congress and deal with Parliament as an equal. The Stamp Act was repealed the following year because it had proved impossible to force businesses and courts in the Colonies to use the stamps. Parliament, however, refused to deny itself the right to make other laws respecting the Colonies.

But the damage was already done. The Colonies for the first time had acted together as an effective unit, and they liked the feel of it. Wrote delegate Christopher Gadsden: "There ought to be no New England man, no New Yorker, etc., known on this Continent, but all of us Americans."

John Adams of Braintree

The Stamp Act Congress had been instigated in New England, which had been settled by Puritans. Though by 1765 much of the strictly religious motivation which had persuaded the first settlers to leave home and come to the inhospitable shores of the New World had died out, the New Englanders still kept many of the ideals of their Puritan ancestors. They still believed that America was special, superior to Europe and therefore not to be ruled by Europeans. They believed in self-government: that laws should be made and taxes levied by elected representatives, not by men thousands of miles away who had no contact with the people they pretended to rule.

With these ideas still strong in the New England Colonies, it is no surprise that a number of New England's leaders were not satisfied with the repeal of the Stamp Act. They wanted Parliament to repudiate all authority over the Colonies; some wanted to be independent not only of Parliament but of the King. When they said, **"No taxation without representation,"** they did not mean that they would be satisfied if some American representatives sat in Parliament. They wanted laws made and taxes levied for Americans only *by* Americans.

A small group of men, led by Samuel Adams, met regularly in Boston to talk of independence and how it could be brought about. They called themselves first the Loyal Nine and later the **Sons of Liberty**. One of the members of the Loyal Nine was a young lawyer, a cousin of Samuel Adams. He was John Adams of Braintree, Massachusetts, and he was one of the less radical members. When Samuel and the others talked of stirring up violence, John Adams counseled against it. But John Adams had considered carefully the relationship of England and the Colonies. He believed that the charters of the Colonies were guarantees by the King of self-government. Each colonial legislature from the beginning had possessed the power to make laws for its particular colony, just as Parliament possessed this power for Britain. Neither in theory nor in practice had New England ever accepted the legislative supremacy of Parliament beyond the shores of Great Britain.

In the summer of 1767, when John Adams' beloved wife Abigail gave birth to their first son (John Quincy), Parliament passed the **Townshend Acts**, levying taxes on glass, lead, painters' colors, tea and paper imported into the Colonies. The Colonies, Massachusetts especially, were furious. They had gotten rid of the Stamp Act, only to be confronted with other, equally hateful taxes. The Sons of Liberty stirred up riots throughout New England, and the British quickly saw that the Townshend Acts were going to be unenforceable. Therefore, on October 1, 1768, British troops landed in Boston to assert England's authority over the difficult Colony.

The situation could only get worse, and it did. The presence of the British troops angered the **Patriots**, as they called themselves, the men who believed that Parliament had no authority over the Colonies. The Patriots gave speeches and wrote pamphlets attacking Britain with ever greater emotion. They persecuted the **"loyalists,"** those who supported England, sometimes even breaking into their homes or tarring and feathering them.

Around 9:00 on the evening of March 5, 1770, John Adams was returning from a meeting when he heard firebells and cries of, "To arms!" Fearing for his family, he rushed home, finding them safe. But Boston was in an uproar. For many weeks the Sons of Liberty had been stirring up hatred against the soldiers, insulting them and provoking them to rash acts. On this particular evening a large crowd had gathered around eight soldiers doing guard duty. The mob had screamed insults and begun throwing things: bricks, rocks, snowballs. In the confusion and to protect themselves, some of the soldiers fired at the mob. Several Bostonians were killed or wounded. The Sons of Liberty immediately named the incident the **"Boston Massacre"** and demanded the execution of the soldiers and their commander, Captain Preston.

On the morning after the shooting, friends of the soldiers came to John Adams. Although they knew he was a Patriot, they also knew him as a man of honor and moral principle. They asked him to defend the soldiers, since no other lawyer would take the case. Believing that all men had the right to a fair trial, Adams agreed, though his friends in the Sons of Liberty were furious. At the trial, Adams argued that the right of self-defense is inherent and inalienable, and that the soldiers were in danger for their lives from an unlawful mob. The verdict came back: Preston was not guilty; six soldiers were acquitted; the other two were found guilty of manslaughter only.

Gradually the hostility toward John Adams died down, but not the hostility toward the British soldiers. The Townshend Acts were going the way of the Stamp Act, disregarded and disobeyed. In one last attempt to assert control over the Colonies, Parliament in 1770 repealed the taxes on every item but tea—and *that*, they intended, would remain.

The First Continental Congress

The Colonists loved their tea, but they loved their traditional rights, too. And one of those rights was under fire: the right of self-government. Letters and petitions passed from the Colony to England. Samuel Adams and his friends harangued the crowds and wrote fiery pamphlets. Then, the Boston town meeting voted to refuse to pay the tea tax when three ships laden with cargoes of the East India Company's tea arrived in Boston harbor. Thomas Hutchinson, the royal governor, ordered that the ships not be allowed to leave until the tax was paid and the tea unloaded.

On the night of December 16, 1773, a number of Patriots, disguised as Mohawk Indians, ran through the streets of Boston, rowed out to the ships, gleefully hacked open 342 chests of tea and threw them into the icy waters of Boston harbor. On March 7 of the next year more tea arrived. On March 8 John Adams wrote in his diary: "Last night 28 chests and a half of tea were drowned."

Parliament was absolutely furious and determined to punish Massachusetts. They passed the Boston Port Bill, which closed the port of Boston, thereby throwing large numbers of people out of work and virtually paralyzing the city; the Massachusetts Government Act, which deprived the Massachusetts House of Representatives of most of its powers, establishing a virtual dictatorship over the Colony; and the **Quartering Act**, which required that British troops be quartered in the private homes of the colonists. The colonists named these acts the **Intolerable Acts**. During the same year, Parliament also passed the **Quebec Act**, which allowed freedom of religion to French Canadian Catholics and extended the boundary of the province of Quebec to lands previously claimed by Massachusetts, New York, Connecticut and Virginia. Though the Quebec Act was not intended as an attack on the Colonies, the Patriots looked upon it as such, and all the old anti-Catholic prejudices came out as New England Protestants feared that the Catholic Church would take over America if Catholics were permitted freedom of worship.

The Colonists were so angry at England now that no amount of punishment could force them to accept Parliament's decrees. With a representative of the Massachusetts governor outside a locked door demanding to be let in, the Massachusetts House of Representatives approved a bill to send five delegates to a Continental Congress in Philadelphia. Then they calmly opened the door to receive notice that their legislature had been dissolved.

The steady, shimmering heat of August blanketed the land as John Adams and four other delegates rode to Philadelphia to attend the **First Continental Congress**. The Colonies had realized that the Intolerable Acts were an insult aimed not only at Massachusetts, but at all of them. They were once again acting as a unit, rather than as 13 separate Colonies. As the Massachusetts delegates rode south, they were greeted all along the way by cheering crowds, encouraging Massachusetts to stand firm.

The Congress held its first session on September 5 and soon divided between the radicals, of whom John Adams was now one, who wanted the Colonies to organize governments totally independent of England and to arm for war; and the conservatives, who still hoped for compromise. The radicals obtained the approval of the Suffolk Resolves, written by the Massachusetts delegates, declaring the Intolerable Acts and the Quebec Act illegal and advising the people to arm. But the overall tone of the Congress was compromise, and its main practical work was a non-importation, non-consumption agreement by which the Colonies agreed not to import or use any British goods until the Intolerable Acts were repealed and self-government restored to Massachusetts.

The Shot on Lexington Common

On the night of April 18, 1775, Paul Revere, Samuel Dawes and others carried word from Patriot spies in Boston to groups of Patriots in nearby communities that the British troops planned a secret march at dawn to capture John Hancock (a wealthy Patriot merchant) and Samuel Adams and to destroy the Patriots' military supplies in Concord. Groups of Patriots had been training for months, having organized into local military organizations or militia. They called themselves the Minutemen—ready to fight at a minute's notice should the British provoke them.

About 700 British troops marched toward Lexington. The **Minutemen**, with their flintlocks at the ready, lined up on Lexington Common. At first light, six companies of British infantry arrived under the command of Major John Pitcairn. Pitcairn told the Americans to lay down their arms and disperse. The Minuteman commander, Captain Parker, at first ordered his men to stand their ground. But he could see that his men were hopelessly outnumbered. He gave the order to disperse. Somehow, someone fired a shot; no one knows whether it was an American or an Englishman. The British fired a volley. Eighteen

Americans fell; the others ran, leaving the British cheering.

Pitcairn moved his men through Lexington up the Concord road. The main body of the British reached the center of Concord at seven o'clock. But no Minutemen were neatly lined up. Instead the militiamen were on the ridge overlooking the town. The British searched the town. When they set fire to the Town House, the 400 militiamen decided the moment had come to attack. A volley was exchanged as the Americans came across the North Bridge. Three British soldiers fell. Surprised at the American resistance, the British broke ranks and retreated. The fighting continued off and on until the British retreated to Lexington. There the Lexington militia, waiting all day to avenge the deaths of their townsmen, poured on an attack from all sides. The British escaped to Boston by evening, but the city now lay under siege by the Massachusetts militia.

Everyone on both sides now knew that war had arrived. **The Second Continental Congress** assembled at Philadelphia on May 10 to conduct the War. The delegates agreed on the necessity for raising an army, appointing George Washington commander-in-chief.

Meanwhile, in Boston, John Burgoyne, a playwright turned general who was commonly known as "Gentleman Johnny," arrived to take command of the War for England and, he assumed, to win it. Being a writer by trade, he issued a proclamation calling upon the rebels to give up, assuming that because it was so brilliantly written they would heed it. But it only made the Americans more angry. Then Burgoyne decided to occupy two hills overlooking Boston, Dorchester Heights and Bunker Hill. But the British were not known for keeping secrets. The plan leaked out to the Americans, who decided to get there first. On the night of June 17, they hastily built fortifications on the height. But when the sun rose, they found that they were not on Bunker Hill but Breed's Hill, a lower point where they could be easily surrounded.

The British were delighted at the Americans' mistake and proceeded to try to surround the hill from the left. They were driven back. Then they ordered a frontal assault. Because his men were so low on powder, the American Captain, Israel Putnam, issued his famous order: "Do not fire until you see the whites of their eyes!" The Americans drove off two frontal attacks. But at the third, they were so exhausted that the British succeeded. The British, though, had lost so many men that their General, Henry Clinton, said: "Another such victory would have ruined us."

Little by little, the Continental Congress realized that conciliation with England was impossible. In the fall, a force under the command of Benedict Arnold was ordered off through the Maine woods toward Canada, with instructions to take Quebec. Not a word was heard for weeks, until finally a message arrived in Philadelphia that Arnold was besieging Quebec. Then word came of the outcome. The Americans had launched a gallant assault on the city through the driving snow on the last day of the year. Arnold had been wounded and the attack had failed, the first great American military disaster of the war.

One of John Adams' greatest concerns was powder and weapons. His friend Henry Knox went off to Fort Ticonderoga in upstate New York, which had been captured back in May by Ethan Allen. He found 59 usable cannon, howitzers and mortars, but then faced the task of getting them to Boston through inhospitable country. First he floated them down Lake George to Fort George. Then he built 82 sleds, bought 80 span of oxen and hauled the cannon 300 miles through the canyons, precipices and valleys of the roadless Berkshire Mountains. Two of his cannon sank through the ice of the Hudson River, but somehow Knox fished them out. He dragged them into Boston on January 24, 1776.

Washington emplaced the cannon on Dorchester Heights in the middle of the night of March 3. When the British woke up, they were amazed to see Washington's guns pointing at them. Adams had managed to supply enough powder to blow the British out of Boston, unless they evacuated—which they did on March 17, 1776. Not another British soldier set foot in Boston throughout the entire War.

Thomas Jefferson of Monticello

Virginia and Massachusetts could hardly have been more different. Massachusetts was settled by hard-working Puritans who believed they were founding a City on a Hill to light the way for the rest of the world to earthly paradise. Virginia was founded by Anglicans (some serious about their religion and some not), many of whom hoped for an easy life in the New World and who retained affection for England. Virginia was aristocratic; a man's family and its wealth often determined how far he could advance. Massachusetts was more democratic, with few men of great wealth and every man regarded as equal to every other. Massachusetts settlers were fishermen, farmers, and shop keepers. Virginians were plantation owners.

But by the middle of the 1700's, Virginia and Massachusetts had one important characteristic in common. They were the two leading colonies in the drive for independence. Just as Massachusetts had its fiery Samuel Adams, so Virginia had its Patrick Henry, who delivered passionate speeches for independence, declaring on one famous occasion (in a phrase which was popular with the Freemasons and liberals in France who would spark the French Revolution): "Give me liberty or give me death." And just as Massachusetts had its John Adams—a scholarly lawyer who provided the intellectual arguments to go with the emotional appeal—so Virginia had its Thomas Jefferson.

Except for their views on independence, Jefferson and Adams were very different. Adams, though he was extremely hostile to the Catholic Church, was a firm believer in divine providence. Jefferson was a Deist. He did not believe in the divinity of Christ nor did he believe that God took any interest in the universe or the men he had created; in the Deist view, God simply manufactured the universe and then left it to take care of itself. Jefferson even published an edition of the four Gospels in which he removed every miracle and every reference to the divinity of Jesus Christ. Adams, as did his Puritan ancestors, felt strongly that men had a tendency toward evil and needed much assistance to live virtuous lives. Jefferson believed in the natural virtue of man: that left alone he would surely do right. Adams argued for self-government on historical and traditional grounds: The Colonies had *always* been self-governing. Jefferson argued for the same end on liberal grounds: All men are born free and each society must set up its own government, never bound by forms from the past or across the ocean. Adams said that liberty would be guaranteed if men were virtuous. Jefferson argued that virtue would be guaranteed if men were free.

In 1769 Jefferson was elected to the Virginia House of Burgesses and since that time had taken an increasingly active part in the drive toward independence. In 1774, he wrote a *Summary View of the Rights of British Americans*, denying Parliamentary authority over the Colonies. In March, 1775 he sat in Old St. John's Church in Richmond to hear Patrick Henry call for liberty or death. This meeting was actually a session of the Virginia House of Burgesses which the governor had forbidden, and it appointed Jefferson to a committee to organize a Virginia militia.

In the summer of 1775, Jefferson was sent to the Continental Congress in Philadelphia. He and Adams became instant friends and had a great respect for each other during this time. In December Jefferson had to return home because his wife Martha was ill, but he returned in

May. He brought with him instructions to the Virginia delegates to vote for complete independence from England.

Charles Carroll of Carrollton

A third key figure at the Continental Congress was one of the Maryland delegates, Charles Carroll of Carrollton. Born in 1737 into a Maryland Catholic family that had taken the lead in preserving the Faith during the years of persecution, Carroll was brought up in a society that allowed no legal rights to Catholics. He was educated at a secret Jesuit school at Bohemia Manor and then at the English Jesuit College of St. Omer in French Flanders.

He returned to America in 1765, the year of the Stamp Act, but it was not that law which caused Carroll to reject the legitimacy of the English parliamentary government. As a Catholic, educated in Catholic principles of government, he knew that the British government had been illegitimate since the so-called Glorious Revolution of 1688, when the rightful Stuart Catholic King, James II, had been overthrown by the Parliament-backed William of Orange. Parliament had taken control of the country, forbidding Catholics from ever sitting on the throne again. Carroll opposed the existing British government and worked for independence as a Catholic counter-revolutionary, who hoped and prayed that a new government, free of British Parliamentary control, would guarantee and preserve the rights of Catholics.

Since this argument against the British government could not be easily followed by Maryland's Protestant majority, Carroll also expressed his opposition to the Stamp Act and succeeding Parliamentary acts on the just grounds that they usurped the rights which Maryland's original charter had reserved for the citizens of that colony. In further violation of the rights of Marylanders in that fateful year 1765, the royal governor and the upper house proclaimed new taxes and then prorogued the lower house when it objected.

The arguments for and against these actions came to a head in 1773. Daniel Dulaney wrote a series of articles in the *Maryland Gazette* defending the new tax laws. He called himself the "second citizen" and demolished the arguments of the straw man "first citizen," which he himself had created. Carroll jumped into the fray, writing a series of "First Citizen" letters, cogently arguing the unconstitutionality of the new laws and defending the right of Maryland to govern itself.

Dulaney could not hope to match the intellectual quality of Carroll's arguments so he resorted to *ad hominem* arguments (i.e. "against the man," against the person of Carroll), declaring that Carroll as a Catholic had no right to speak on public issues. This played right into Carroll's hands. Dulaney's attacks on Carroll did not discredit the Maryland Catholic, but instead served to show the injustice of the Maryland anti-Catholic laws. Within three years, the anti-Catholic laws were wiped from the books, thanks largely to Charles Carroll's First Citizen letters.

Recognizing Carroll as a leading patriot, the Continental Congress asked him in February 1776 to join a commission to Canada to persuade the Canadians to unite with the Colonists in the south in the independence movement. Also on the commission was Carroll's cousin, John Carroll, who had been educated with him at Bohemia Manor and in Europe and who was now a priest. The Carrolls, along with Benjamin Franklin and Samuel Chase, did their best, but because the Continental Congress had shown itself to be anti-Catholic in its outrage against the Quebec Act, the commission failed to persuade the Catholic leaders of Quebec. (One interesting sidelight of the commission was that the Deist Franklin and the priest Carroll became good friends.)

The Declaration of Independence

On June 7, 1776, Richard Henry Lee, a Virginia delegate, rose on the floor of the Congress to introduce a resolution "that these United Colonies are and of right ought to be free and independent States." John Adams spoke in favor of the resolution, arguing that it would simply declare a fact already plain to those who had not blinded themselves: America had always been independent of Parliament, and the King had lost his authority by waging war against the Colonies. The Congress appointed a committee, including Adams, Jefferson and Franklin, to draft a "declaration of independence" to set forth to the world the reasons for the Colonies' actions. The other committee members quickly agreed to let Jefferson write the document, since he was the most skilled wordsmith among them.

From June 11 until June 28, Jefferson worked on his document at his homemade writing table. The opening section set forth his liberal philosophy. He stated that governments derive their just powers from the consent of the governed (not from God, not from traditions, not by inheritance, but from the people themselves); all authority comes from them. Then he listed the grievances against King and Parliament which justified the Colonies' rebellion.

The other committee members made few changes. The Congress as a whole voted to omit Jefferson's impassioned condemnation of the King for allowing the slave trade (since some colonies were involved in the slave trade), rewrote the final paragraph to replace Jefferson's words with the wording of Lee's original resolution, and added in the last sentence the clause, "with a firm reliance on the protection of divine providence."

On July 1, the Congress debated the Declaration. Jefferson took no part in the debate, leaving to John Adams the defense of the document. Adams had no easy, optimistic view that the government they were about to establish would inevitably bring happiness to all. Said Adams: "I do not expect that our new government will be so quiet as I could wish, nor [provide] that happy harmony, confidence, and affection between the Colonies, that every good American ought to study, labor, and pray for, for a long time." Nevertheless, the Colonies were free and must preserve their freedom, Adams maintained. The Declaration was approved on July 2 with no dissenting votes and was officially adopted July 4.

When it came time for Charles Carroll, the only Catholic signer of the document, to add his name, a delegate standing near remarked, "There go a few millions," meaning that Carroll was putting his considerable fortune on the line for the sake of independence. Another story goes that he added the phrase "of Carrollton" after his name when another bystander observed that there were so many Carrolls in Maryland that King George would not know which one to hang.

As well as being the only Catholic signer of the Declaration, Charles Carroll was the last surviving signer, dying in 1832 at the age of 96. Among his last words were these: "I have lived to my ninety-sixth year; I have enjoyed continued health; I have been blessed with great wealth, prosperity, and most of the good things which the world can bestow—public approbation, esteem, applause; but what I now look back on with the greatest satisfaction to myself is, that I have practiced the duties of my religion."

A Note on Liberalism

The word "liberal" has been used in this chapter to describe the views of Thomas Jefferson, especially those he enshrined in the Declaration of Independence. The word has a wide variety of meanings, but when it is used in the pages of this book, it refers to a specific political philosophy.

This philosophy was a long-term outgrowth of the Protestant Revolt, which had rejected the authority of the Church and made the individual conscience the sovereign judge of religious truth. But Liberalism was not fully developed nor widely accepted until the 18th century. Leading French philosophers—atheists, agnostics, deists—formulated the philosophy which may be summarized as follows: Liberalism rejects moral absolutes and authority, especially religious authority. It is usually opposed to hereditary monarchy. It emphasizes that men should be free to do whatever they want in moral matters and that political authority comes from the people themselves who should be free to overthrow existing governments—by violence if necessary—and to set up new governments based on the will of the majority, as interpreted and guided by intellectual leaders.

This philosophy sparked the French Revolution, where it was carried to its logical extreme, with mob violence, followed by a dictatorship of terror, all in the name of "the will of the people" and in opposition to the Church and the Monarchy.

In America, men such as Jefferson, Franklin and Patrick Henry, who were familiar with the writings of the French philosophers, adopted much of liberal philosophy and applied it to the American situation. We Americans are so used to thinking that governmental authority should come from the people that we might see nothing wrong with the political ramifications of Liberalism. We need to be reminded that all authority comes from God, and if authority is not exercised in harmony with God's law, then it is not legitimate. The standard is not, "Is it the will of the people?" but, "Is it the will of God?"

REVIEW QUESTIONS

1. What was the Stamp Act? Why was it enacted?
2. Why did the Stamp Act arouse opposition in the Colonies?
3. What was the Stamp Act Congress? What were its results?
4. Who were the Sons of Liberty?
5. What were the Townshend Acts? Why did the British land troops in Boston?
6. What were the Boston Massacre, the Boston Tea Party, and the Intolerable Acts?
7. What was the First Continental Congress? What did it accomplish?

8. How did war break out?
9. Describe the battle of Bunker Hill.
10. How were the British driven out of Boston?
11. Contrast Virginia and Massachusetts. Compare and contrast Jefferson and Adams.
12. How did Charles Carroll help to gain religious freedom for Catholics in Maryland?
13. Why did Charles Carroll support American independence?
14. Summarize the adoption of the Declaration of Independence and Jefferson's main arguments in it.
15. What is the Liberal belief about the source of a government's authority? What is the Catholic belief?

PROJECTS

1. Do research and write a report about a Colonial leader other than Jefferson, Adams, or Carroll.
2. Do research and write a report on the Loyalists during the War for Independence and what happened to them.
3. Prepare a poster illustrating the arguments in the Declaration of Independence.

Chapter 8

The United States' War For Independence

GEORGE WASHINGTON was not among the signers of the Declaration of Independence. As the men in Philadelphia affixed their names to the document, Washington was in New York, wrestling with a host of problems: the obstreperousness of the pro-British Loyalists who formed the city's majority, the difficulty of fortifying the city against the expected British attack, an outbreak of smallpox, a shortage of arms, the unruliness of his troops, and the almost daily desertions of militia. (Washington had two kinds of troops under his command: the Continental Army, recruited and paid by the Congress, and the much larger group of militiamen from the individual colonies.) Then, on June 29 British ships were seen off the New York Coast, and on July 21 troops began landing on Long Island.

Washington's strategy was to hold off the British long enough to withdraw his troops to strong fortifications in Brooklyn. But when the battle broke on July 27, the Americans soon found themselves outflanked. The British had circled around behind them and cut them off from their orderly retreat. Israel Putnam, the hero of Bunker Hill, was in command. All he could think of was to repeat the formula which had worked so well in Boston: "Don't fire until you see the whites of their eyes." Unfortunately that advice was not especially pertinent with the enemy attacking from the rear. The Americans were routed and forced into a disorderly retreat. If Sir William Howe, the British general, had pressed the attack, he might well have annihilated the American army and brought the War to a premature conclusion. But Howe may have had sympathies for the American cause and wanted to negotiate an honorable peace treaty with the Colonists. Whatever the reason, the Americans were left alone—though they hourly expected a renewed British attack—and were able to withdraw by boat to Manhattan Island on the night of the 29th.

Having suffered their first defeat, many American troops deserted in despair. Thirteen Connecticut regiments, for example, dropped from 8000 to 2000 in the week after the battle. Washington wanted to evacuate and burn the city so that the British could get nothing from it, but Congress refused to permit it. So he could only hold his discontented troops together as best he could and wait for the inevitable attack.

On September 15 British ships opened a bombardment of the American positions. Then the ships landed British and Hessians (mercenary troops from Germany, whose presence on American soil greatly angered the Colonists), and once again the Americans retreated in mad confusion, even though Washington came personally to the battle front to order them to stay. Humiliated, Washington withdrew his army to the north of Manhattan Island (Harlem Heights), leaving behind his cannon, tents and provisions. On September 30 he wrote: "Such is my situation that if I were to wish the bitterest curse to an enemy on this side of the grave, I should put him in my place."

On October 28, Washington fortified Chatterton's Hill near White Plains. The British stormed his position. His militia ran away. Confused, dispirited, hesitant, Washington decided that he must evacuate Manhattan and transfer his forces across the Hudson. Though his army daily grew smaller through desertions, he divided it into no less than four sections: a detachment under his command in New Jersey at Fort Lee, a detachment at Fort Washington (now the site of the George Washington Bridge) under General Greene, a group under General Heath at Peekskill to guard the New York Highlands, and the remaining troops under command of Charles Lee to guard the main route across the Hudson. General Lee was at this time Washington's most trusted subordinate officer, since he was the only one with previous military experience, having served in the British army.

The folly of dividing his weakened forces soon became apparent. On November 16 Fort Washington fell, and 2800 of Washington's best men were taken prisoner. Washington could not get there in time; he could only listen in despair from across the Hudson to the British bombardment. He later received word that the men had refused even to man the lines. On November 20, Washington ordered Fort Lee abandoned because the British were marching toward it. The evacuation was so hurried that pots were left boiling and tents standing.

Realizing the folly of dividing his army, Washington wrote to Lee, asking him to bring his 5000 troops to Washington's position, as he expected an almost immediate attack. On November 23 Lee replied, saying that he was sorry but had decided to stay where he was. Washington immediately wrote back, ordering Lee to bring up his troops. By December 1, 2000 militiamen were scheduled to leave because their terms of enlistment would end, and Washington desperately needed Lee's reinforcements. On the 26th came Lee's reply that he would rather fight the British where he was. Washington sent off another desperate letter, then removed his own army to Brunswick, hoping to stay a few miles ahead of the British. Then he retreated across the Raritan River and finally across the Delaware into Pennsylvania, believing now that Philadelphia itself was menaced by the British. On December 10 Lee finally made it to New Jersey, but wrote to Washington saying that he could do more good behind the enemy's lines. Faced with this insolent disobedience, Washington could only send a humiliating personal appeal to Lee, who responded by complaining that his men's shoes were worn out. Then on December 15 an express rider dashed into Washington's camp with the message that on December 13, about 10:00 in the morning, at White's Tavern three miles from the American lines, General Lee was captured by a British patrol just as he was finishing breakfast. Washington wasted no time mourning Lee's interrupted breakfast but instead welcomed General Sullivan to his camp with Lee's troops.

When in Doubt, Attack

Washington's situation was truly desperate. He had less than 8000 troops, and by the first of January would have only 1500 because of the end of enlistments. Since leaving Boston, he had lost every major battle, and in most of them the Americans had been humiliated. The only reason the war was still going on was that the British had not moved to wipe out the American army. The American commander-in-chief had made a number of serious mistakes. But Washington was neither a coward nor a quitter. As December neared its end, he made a courageous decision which changed the whole complexion of the war: he would attack.

On Christmas night he moved his troops and artillery to the Trenton River, where blocks of ice floated past as the wind rose. Across the river the Hessian patrols assigned to guard the encampment had been excused because of the bad weather. Boat after boat went across. Wash-

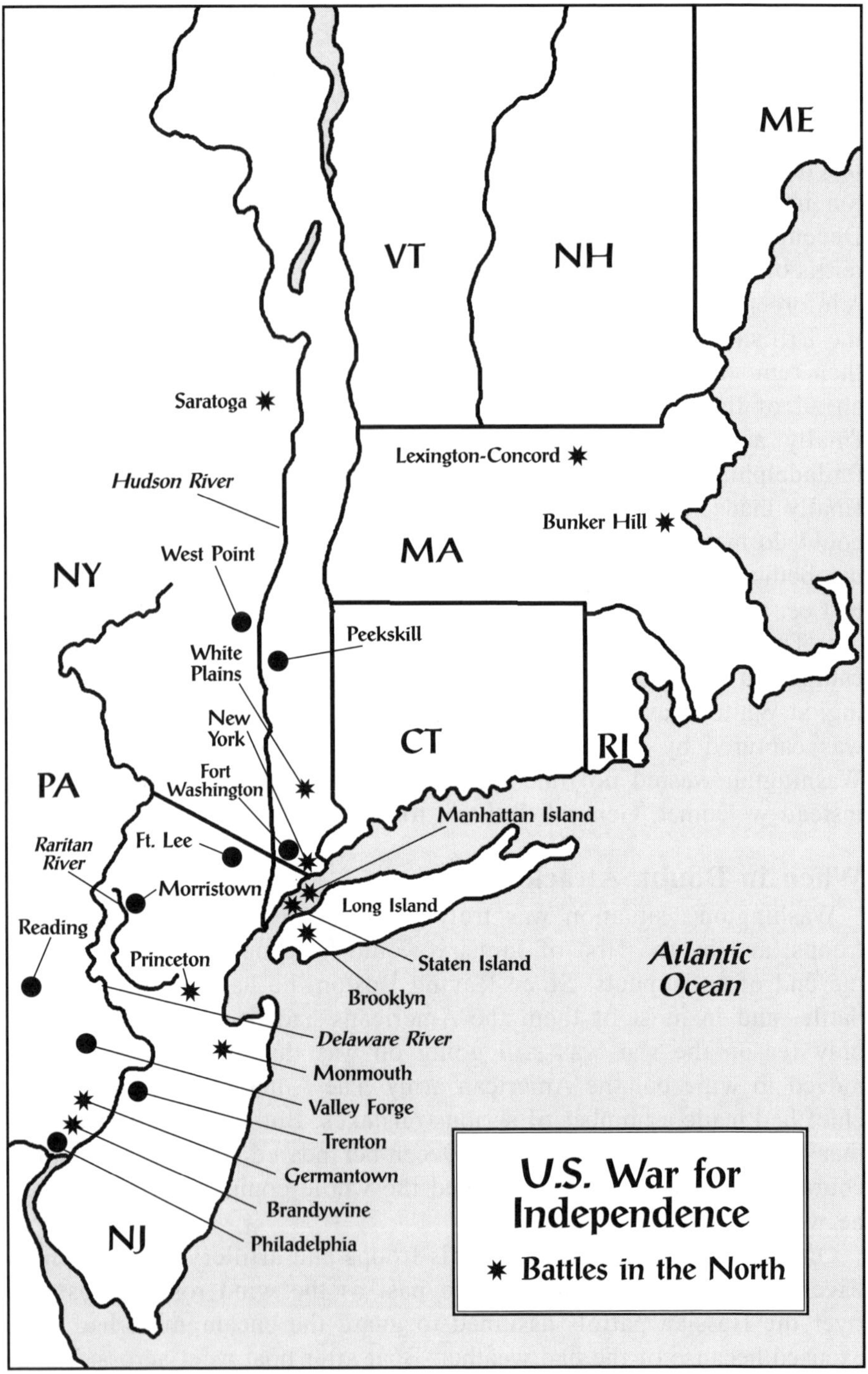
ME
VT
NH
Saratoga
Lexington-Concord
Hudson River
Bunker Hill
MA
West Point
NY
Peekskill
White Plains
New York
CT
Fort Washington
RI
PA
Manhattan Island
Raritan River
Ft. Lee
Morristown
Long Island
Reading
Princeton
Staten Island
Atlantic Ocean
Brooklyn
Delaware River
Monmouth
Valley Forge
Trenton
Germantown
Brandywine
NJ
Philadelphia
U.S. War for Independence
Battles in the North

ington had hoped to have his army across the river by midnight, but because of delays they did not all arrive on the opposite shore until 4:00 a.m. and then had nine miles to cover before daylight revealed their position. Through the snow and sleet the Americans marched. The surprise was total. They attacked at 8:00 a.m. By 10:00 a.m. the Hessians had surrendered. Only two American lives had been lost and only five other Americans were wounded; 918 prisoners were taken.

With this victory—and the promise of a bonus—many troops agreed to stay on past the expiration date of their enlistments. Washington decided to attack again. Marching his troops through the muddy roads resulting from an unseasonable thaw, he outflanked Lord Cornwallis' troops, winning the Battle of Princeton on January 3, 1777, then put his troops into winter quarters at Morristown, New Jersey.

As spring came, the Americans were still weak, but the British were disinclined to attack. Howe proceeded to evacuate New Jersey, and then did not march up the Hudson to meet General Burgoyne's force coming down from Canada, a maneuver which would have divided the colonies and been a severe blow to the Americans. At the Battle of Brandywine on September 11, the Americans guarded Chad's Ford, where they expected the British to cross the Brandywine River. The British outflanked the Americans, crossing at an entirely different ford. The Americans were soundly defeated and lost hundreds of men and many guns.

On September 21 the British marched toward Reading, Pennsylvania, where the Americans had cached their supplies. Washington immediately marched in the same direction to protect his stores, but overnight the British shifted their march, turned back and entered Philadelphia—America's largest city—without opposition.

Once again, the American army had been humiliated, and once again Washington turned to the strategy which had worked the preceding winter: a surprise attack. He started a secret night march on October 3 toward the British camp at Germantown. In the fog and confusion, the British broke through to the rear of the American lines. The Americans panicked and by morning the battle was lost. The only consolation was that the American army had fought well, giving Washington some hope for the future.

On October 14 good news came to Washington's camp. General Burgoyne had attacked at Saratoga in upstate New York, but General Benedict Arnold led a charge that broke Burgoyne's flank. Though Arnold's horse was shot and the General received a bullet in the leg, the charge carried the day. Burgoyne surrendered his entire army to the American commander, Horatio Gates—who received all the credit for the great victory, thereby earning Arnold's lasting hatred.

Knowing that his army was too weak to attack, Washington put them into winter quarters 18 miles northwest of Philadelphia at Valley Forge and devoted all his energies to keeping his barefooted men from starving or freezing. One officer wrote of Valley Forge that the site must have been selected on the advice of a traitor or by a council of ignoramuses. There were no buildings. It was windy and hilly. Food was hard to come by. Washington wrote the Continental Congress that if they did not receive provisions soon, the army had only three choices: "starve, dissolve, disperse." They had to build their own cabins, and not until the middle of January, 1778 were the last of the troops under a roof. Some of the men could not leave the cabins because they had no clothes. Many had to sleep on the floor with no blankets. Washington and his officers lived in constant fear of mutiny, but through the strength of his personality Washington kept the men under control and held the remnant of an army together, while Baron von Steuben of Prussia trained the troops and gave them much-needed discipline.

The Shifting Fortunes of War

At last the snow melted and the flowers bloomed on the Pennsylvania hills. With the spring came General Charles Lee, who had been exchanged for a British officer whom the Americans had captured in bed. Lee had not been changed by his experience; he still believed that he was America's best general and need take orders from no one. But at the end of April, far better news arrived. Washington received a letter stating that France, because of the American victory at Saratoga, had recognized the independence of the United States on December 17, 1777 and signed a formal treaty of alliance. Washington wrote: "I believe no event was ever received with more heartfelt joy." He lined up his ragged troops to fire a salute and shout, "Long live the King of France!" Individual Europeans—such as Baron von Steuben, the Frenchman Marquis de Lafayette and Thaddeus Kosciusko of Poland—had already come to America to help the fledgling nation, but Louis XVI's France was the first government to offer badly needed assistance.

As Washington was debating whether to attack the British or stay put, he received word that General Henry Clinton, who had replaced

Howe, was preparing to evacuate Philadelphia for New York, because he had heard that the French fleet was on its way to America. Washington decided on an attack, the Battle of Monmouth Courthouse, with Lee and Lafayette in command.

About noon on June 28, Washington sent Lee to attack the British rearguard. Soon rumors reached Washington: Lee's men were retreating. Washington could not believe it until he saw for himself the men running frantically down the road. He galloped ahead to find Lee, who told the commander-in-chief that he did not feel like attacking. Disgusted, Washington took command and rallied the troops. The Americans counterattacked and drove off the British.

On June 30, Lee sent a letter saying that Washington had insulted him and demanding an apology. Washington's return letter demanded an explanation as to why Lee had ordered "an unnecessary, disorderly and shameful retreat." Lee smugly replied that if Washington did not like his actions, the commander could court-martial him, upon which Washington ordered Lee's arrest on charges of disobedience, misbehavior before the enemy and disrespect to the commander-in-chief. To the surprise of no one except Lee, he was found guilty, and that was the end of his career in the American army. Though Lee was the worst example, Washington was plagued throughout the war by the lack of reliable subordinate commanders.

The remainder of 1778 saw little significant action. The French fleet arrived, to the great joy of the Americans, but accomplished almost nothing at first. In 1779, the war shifted south. On December 29, 1778 the British took Savannah and on January 29, 1779 Augusta, both in Georgia. A joint French and American attack to regain Savannah failed in October, whereupon Admiral D'Estaing took the French fleet off to the West Indies. Washington decided to send his Virginia regiments south to help out there, and put the rest of his troops into winter quarters reminiscent of Valley Forge in the hardships the men had to undergo.

The new year of 1780 began with a six-foot snowstorm. Washington tried a raid on the British position at Staten Island, but it was driven back, as many soldiers suffered frostbite. In May Washington sent reinforcements south under the German General De Kalb to try to save Charleston, South Carolina, but the city fell on May 12 before he could get there.

When summer came, Washington decided to give top priority to fortifying West Point because of its key position. If the British captured

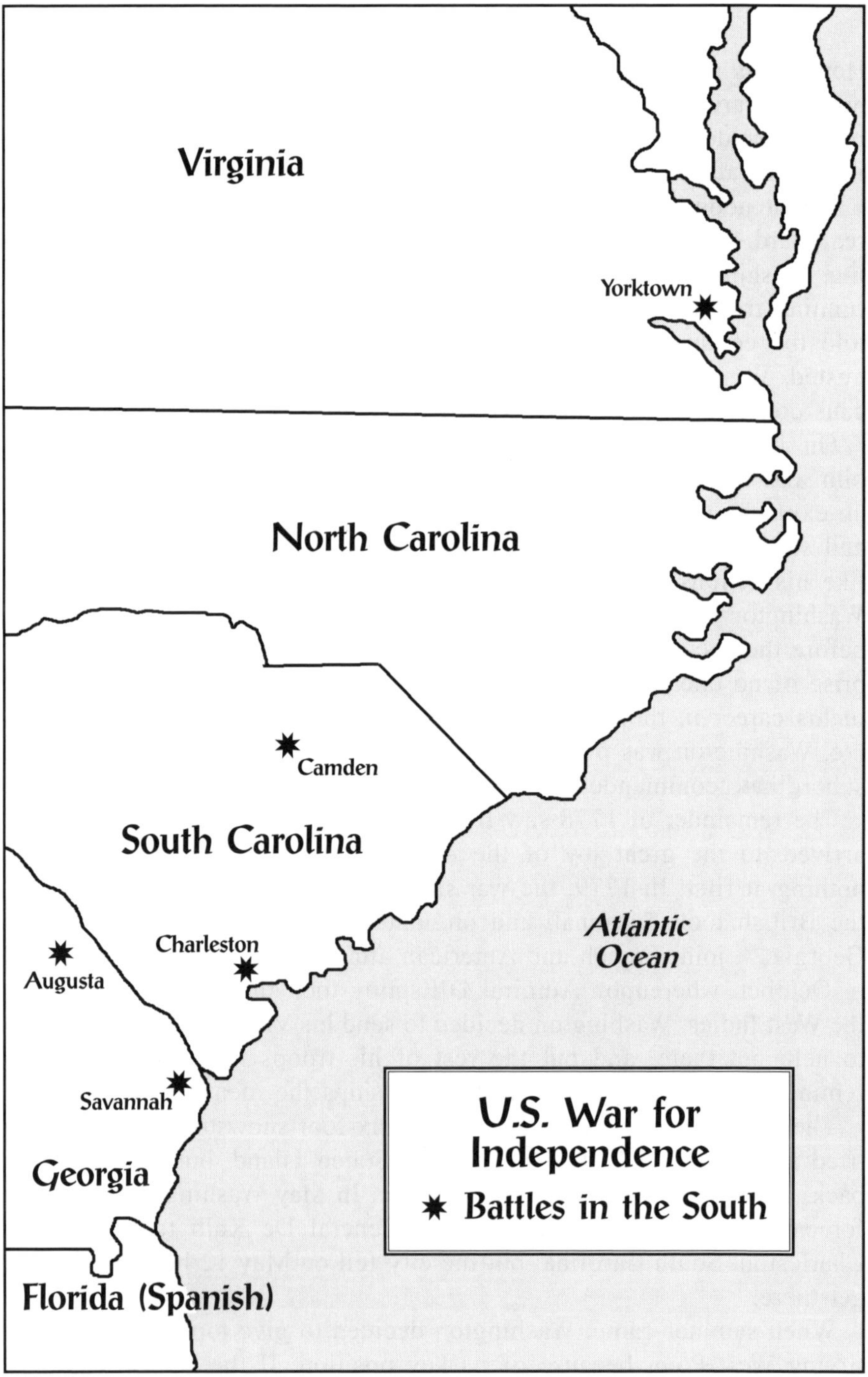
Virginia
Yorktown
North Carolina
Camden
South Carolina
Atlantic
Ocean
Charleston
Augusta
Savannah
Georgia
Florida (Spanish)
U.S. War for
Independence
Battles in the South

it, they could cut off New England from the rest of the Colonies. Benedict Arnold asked Washington for the West Point command, saying that his wounded leg was still not strong enough for battle. Washington sent Arnold to New York with orders to strengthen the fort. In July the French Count Rochambeau landed with 6000 troops, but in September Washington learned of the American defeat at the Battle of Camden, South Carolina on August 16 and of the shameful behavior of American General Gates, who was found after the battle 40 miles from the scene of action, mounted on the army's fastest horse.

With his mind preoccupied by the dual front of the north and the south, Washington decided to inspect Arnold's progress in fortifying West Point. When he arrived on the morning of September 25, he was surprised to find that Arnold was not on hand to meet him and that no one could seem to find the general. He made his tour of inspection nonetheless, finding the fortifications in disrepair. In the afternoon Alexander Hamilton arrived with the shocking news that a man who called himself John Anderson had been caught on the road to New York with a packet of confidential papers regarding the military situation at West Point, including a pass in Arnold's handwriting. "Anderson" admitted that he was British Major General John Andre and that he had carried messages from Arnold to British General Clinton. Washington was dumbfounded. He soon learned that Arnold had deliberately allowed the situation in the fort to deteriorate, having planned to allow the British to capture West Point in a "surprise" attack, to get revenge on the American government for not adequately recognizing his victories of the past. With Washington's inspection imminent, Arnold had escaped to a British ship. Washington ordered the damage repaired as quickly as possible and with a heavy heart returned to New Jersey to face another bad winter, which this time included a mutiny of 200 Pennsylvania volunteers.

Victory with the Help of France

During January and February 1781, Washington had nothing but bad news. The French fleet was idle. General Nathanael Greene was being pursued by Lord Cornwallis and had evacuated almost all of North Carolina. Desperate, Washington sent Lafayette and a detachment of troops south to intercept Cornwallis. On July 6, Cornwallis defeated Lafayette.

Washington faced a crucial decision: Should he attack New York or march his troops 450 miles to the south? On August 14, he heard that the French Admiral De Grasse was coming to Chesapeake Bay with 28 ships and 3000 troops, but could stay only until October 15. Washington took 2500 Americans and all the French troops to Virginia.

As he rode south, Washington began to be optimistic for almost the first time since he had ridden victoriously out of Boston, over five long years before. With the French blockading the coast, the British forces under Cornwallis would be unable to escape by sea.

Cornwallis and his men were in an encampment called Yorktown. On September 28, Washington ordered his army to begin a general advance. On September 29, the British evacuated their forward positions. Washington brought up his siege artillery and his men dug trenches. On the night of October 6, the Americans moved to a line of trenches nearer the British position. On October 9, the bombardment began. On October 11, they moved up again. On October 14, Washington ordered Lafayette to try an assault with 400 infantry.

Lafayette attempted a surprise attack, but when Washington heard the British guns firing, he knew that the surprise had failed. But word came back that Lafayette had captured two British redoubts (small fortifications). On October 16, the British tried their only attack of the entire battle, surprising a small group of Americans who had been permitted to go to sleep. The Americans suffered 16 casualties and the British spiked six guns.

Suddenly, on the 17th, a British officer appeared with a white flag and a letter from Cornwallis: "Sir, I propose a cessation of hostilities for 24 hours, and that two officers may be appointed by each side, to meet at Mr. Moore's house, to settle terms for the surrender of the positions at York and Gloucester. I have the honour to be, &c. Cornwallis." Cornwallis had expected the British navy to rescue him. But the British Admiral Graves was one of the few poor admirals Britain had produced. De Grasse had defeated him, and Cornwallis had no place to go. Rather than fight it out, he decided to surrender.

Washington was elated with this, his greatest victory, though he knew full well that he could never have won without the French fleet. But he was also concerned that the victory be followed up. He tried to persuade De Grasse to join in an attack on Charleston or Wilmington, North Carolina, but the French admiral refused and sailed off to the West Indies, where his fleet was annihilated by the British.

Washington rode to his home at Mount Vernon, where he picked up his wife Martha and headed north. He went personally before Congress, trying to persuade them to keep up the struggle and not become overconfident because of the victory at Yorktown. But the enemy was quiet, and Washington spent most of his time in Philadelphia at a round of parties.

On August 4, 1782, Washington received a letter from the British General Sir Guy Carleton: "We are acquainted, Sir, by authority, that negotiations for a general peace have already commenced at Paris." The letter asked Washington to negotiate with him for surrender terms. Washington sent the letter on to Congress, suspecting some kind of trick. But it was not a trick. The British began evacuating New York in December. On November 30, 1782, a treaty of peace was signed by the American Colonies and Great Britain, recognizing the independence of the Colonies.

Why America Won

The War for Independence was not a war of brilliant strategy or titanic battles. The winning side had no militarily great generals, and throughout the entire war its army was constantly plagued by a shortage of supplies and a turnover in troops as the state militias' short-term enlistments came to an end. The British had an army which had won victory after victory in Europe during earlier wars, and a navy which would soon deal a mighty defeat to Napoleon.

But the Americans won for three reasons. One was the steadfastness of Washington. Though he was not a brilliant strategist and made a number of crucial mistakes, he was a man of great integrity who refused to give up. Wrote one German officer who visited Washington: "In short, he impresses you as a good man, who can be trusted." Washington kept the army together against all obstacles, inspired the trust and loyalty of his men, and would never admit the possibility of surrender. When all seemed darkest, he ordered the attack at Trenton, the turning point of the war. Without Washington, the British could have won in six months.

The second factor in the American victory was the British failure to press their advantages. Throughout the war, the British generals, especially Howe, showed little inclination to wipe out the feeble American army, as they could have done on a number of occasions. The British generals did not seem to be taking the war seriously. If the British had been commanded by even one talented general with a determination to win, probably not even Washington could have saved the day.

Finally, the Americans could not have won without the French, especially the French fleet. Though the French admirals spent most of their time chasing about the West Indies, at the crucial point, where their help was absolutely necessary, the French ships stood off the coast of Virginia and prevented Cornwallis' escape.

Revolution or War for Independence?

The war between the American Colonies and the British is often called the American Revolution or the Revolutionary War. But this is not an accurate term. A revolution is properly defined as a total upheaval in government, values and way of life. But the Americans were fighting to keep their traditional way of government, and their independence made little or no difference in values and way of life. A revolution is destructive of moral standards and civilized order. But no such destruction took place in America.

A more accurate designation is the American War for Independence. The Americans fought for their independence against a British government which had become increasingly tyrannical. The Americans had a right to defend their traditions against British aggression.

So a new nation was born—from the early enthusiasms of Concord Bridge and Bunker Hill, through the humiliation of New York, through the daring of Trenton through the disobedience of Charles Lee and the treachery of Benedict Arnold, to the trenches of Yorktown and the French fleet off Chesapeake Bay. Washington rode back to Mount Vernon, longing for a well-earned retirement, while the new nation tried to decide what to make of itself, now that it had burst forth upon the world.

REVIEW QUESTIONS

1. Summarize the battles around New York. What mistakes did Washington make?
2. Summarize the role of Charles Lee in the War.
3. Why did Washington attack at Trenton? Why was this a turning point of the War?
4. Summarize the battles around Philadelphia.
5. Describe the conditions at Valley Forge. What good results came out of the winter at Valley Forge?
6. What happened at the Battle of Saratoga? How did it affect Benedict Arnold?

7. Why did France enter the war on the side of the Colonies? How did France help the Colonies?
8. What happened when Benedict Arnold was given command at West Point?
9. Summarize the battles in the South.
10. What happened at Yorktown? Why did the British surrender?
11. List and briefly explain the reasons the Americans won.
12. Why is the American Revolutionary War an incorrect term?

PROJECTS

1. Imagine that you were a soldier in George Washington's Continental Army. Write a diary of at least ten entries describing your experiences and your reactions to them.
2. Do research and prepare a report on some phase of the War.
3. Do research and prepare a report on an important figure of the War other than George Washington.

Chapter 9

The Birth Of The American Government

THE UNITED STATES had won independence. A new nation had appeared on the world scene. But no one yet knew what kind of nation it was going to be. In 1777, the Continental Congress had approved the **Articles of Confederation**, providing for a confederation of the thirteen States to be known as the United States of America. The Confederation would be governed by a Congress in which each state would have one vote and which would have both legislative (lawmaking) and executive (law enforcement) power. Little power was vested in the Congress; it was made subservient to the States. Congressional delegates were appointed and recalled by state legislatures. Money to carry on the government came from the States, but there was no way to force them to provide it. There were no federal courts. The main purpose of the Congress had first been to carry on the War—which it had done—and then to handle foreign affairs and those domestic affairs which individual states could not handle or which the States disputed (for example, the disposition of the lands to the west of their boundaries).

The new nation's government was beset by a host of problems, primarily economic. The Congress had had only two ways of paying the expenses of the War: borrowing money or printing paper money. These expedients, necessary at the time, now came back to haunt it. The huge debt—both of the national government and the state governments—had somehow to be paid. The paper money had rapidly depreciated. Virginia, for example, called in its paper money at a ratio of a thousand old bills to one new bill. Those holding paper currency wanted to use it to pay their debts, but creditors demanded payment in gold or silver (also called **hard money** or **specie**). When state governments levied heavy taxes—payable only in specie—to pay their own war debts, many a farmer who saw little hard money from one year to the next was subject to court action, loss of property and even debtor's prison. These people demanded the privilege of paying taxes in paper. But the state governments did not want the paper money because *their* creditors would not take it. And the national government was not able to pay any debts because the states were not sending it any money. Robert Morris, a leader of the Confederation, said that talking to the States about money was like preaching to the dead.

In 1783 the prestige of the Confederation was so low that some States no longer sent representatives. When John Hancock was elected presiding officer of the Congress in 1785, he did not even come to New York for sessions. The Articles had required seven affirmative votes to approve any action. Often there were not seven delegates present, so that no action could be taken. Wrote Alexander Hamilton: "The republic is sick and wants powerful remedies."

The years from 1783-1787 are called the **Critical Period in American History**. While far from the only crisis the United States has faced, these years brought the first fundamental choice that the leaders of America had to make: a choice between two radically different forms of government. The first choice was a form of the Confederation, with revisions of the Articles to meet the needs that had manifested themselves at the close of the War, making the United States a union of independent states with the national government serving as the representative of the States for those matters transcending state boundaries. The authority of the national government would be delegated by the States.

The second would be a national government, in which power would rest in the central government. The States would be subservient to the central government, its authority delegated from all of the people, taken as a whole, regardless of which state they lived in.

In 1786, a veteran of the War for Independence, Daniel Shays, took command of a band of Massachusetts farmers who were angry with the Massachusetts legislature for refusing to authorize paper money to pay debts. Shays' "army" prevented courts from sitting and released debtors from prison. They marched to the Springfield arsenal to seize guns, planning to continue to Boston to force the legislature to rescind tax-debt laws. The governor called out the state militia, which easily put an end to **"Shays' Rebellion"** by a few cannon shots.

But the episode had showed the extent of the discontent within the States. Shays and the men like him were primarily interested in their own economic problems. They were not calling for a new national government. But those who did want a stronger government pointed to the rebellion as evidence of the need to change the Confederation. These men, known as **Federalists**, seized the initiative in the confusion afflicting the young nation and persuaded the Congress to authorize a **Constitutional Convention** to draw up a new plan of government. Many of those who supported the Convention believed that amendment of the Articles of Confederation would suffice to meet the demands of the situation, but the leaders of the convention fully intended to start all over again with a new form of government, which would give primary power and authority to the national government, not to the states.

Madison and the Convention

The Convention was scheduled to begin on May 14, 1787. James Madison of Virginia arrived eleven days early, but his patience soon became taxed as the Convention could not muster a quorum of seven states until May 25. Madison—brilliant, enthusiastic and strong-willed—was a committed Federalist who believed that those who arrived first would be able to dominate the Convention.

When the other Virginians arrived, Madison convened a series of meetings which produced the **Virginia Plan**, proposing a three-part system of government: a national executive, legislature and judiciary. The legislature would consist of two houses, one elected, the other appointed by the elected body from a list of nominees submitted by state legislatures; it would have the power "to legislate in all cases to which the separate states are incompetent, or in which the harmony of the United States may be interrupted by the exercise of individual legislatures." The Plan called for a strong national government with authority over the States.

The Convention opened with the unanimous election of George Washington as chairman. Washington had received a tumultuous welcome in Philadelphia, complete with fire bells and cheering crowds. This admiration for Washington helped the Federalist cause since Washington himself wanted a strong national government, no doubt because of his experience during the war with independent state militias disappearing just when he needed them most.

The Virginia Plan was introduced on May 29, to be countered on

June 15 by the New Jersey Plan, which would have retained the Confederacy but given power to Congress to tax, to regulate foreign and interstate commerce, and to appoint a Supreme Court. After three days of debate, the Convention voted seven to three to work toward a wholly new government with the Virginia Plan as a basis, rather than modifying the Confederation.

Now the Federalists began to quarrel among themselves. The most acrimonious controversy in the Convention concerned representation in the national legislature. The small states wanted a system like that in the Confederation with each state having the same number of votes. Without this provision, Delaware, Connecticut and Georgia argued, they would be constantly outvoted by the large states and their own particular needs would not be met. Their claims to the western lands would not be honored; they would lose the power to issue paper money to pay their debts. They feared that they would be swallowed up and lost in the national sea.

The large states—New York, Massachusetts, Virginia—wanted representation to be proportional to population, so that they could dominate. Madison, a Virginian, argued strongly for proportional representation. The debate became so heated that on June 28, Benjamin Franklin proposed having each session begin with a prayer in order to calm frayed nerves and relieve tension. But the delegates could not even agree on that; the proposal was defeated, and such was almost the only reference to God in the entire convention. Finally, just before the Fourth of July recess, the Convention appointed a committee to work out a compromise so that they could get on to other matters. The stubborn Madison was deliberately left off the committee in order to ensure that a compromise could in fact be reached.

On July 5, the committee reported the **Connecticut Compromise** to the delegates. One house of the legislature would have proportional representation; the second would have equal votes for each state. The small states were happy; the large barely agreeable; Madison was furious. But the vote on July 16 was 5-4 in favor, and the compromise was adopted.

The second major controversy concerned the wording of the grant of power to the federal government. The Federalists, led by Madison, wanted a general wording in order not to put unnecessary restrictions on the government. The anti-Federalists preferred a specific enumeration of powers, beyond which the government could not go. Again the debate was hot and heavy; again compromise was essential. But this time the compromise was more to Madison's liking. A list of specific powers was included, but then the national government was given the authority to make all laws "necessary and proper" to the carrying out of the enumerated powers. To Madison, this wording implicitly gave the national government all the power it needed. In addition, federal laws were made supreme over state laws. The preamble reflected this emphasis: the draft had read, "We the people of the states of Massachusetts, New Hampshire, etc."; the final version read, "We the people of the United States . . ."

The issue of slavery split North from South. The debate was finally resolved by permitting slavery in the U.S., but prohibiting the importation of slaves after 1808. Then the Southerners, who had been arguing that slaves should be regarded as their property, reversed themselves by wanting to count slaves as persons when determining the number of representatives to which each state would be entitled. The compromise here was to count each slave as three-fifths of a person for purposes of representation. These compromises enshrined a fundamental contradiction in the Constitution: America was supposed to guarantee human rights, but the nation's basic document denied the humanity of slaves. This contradiction, together with the sharp division between North and South, would eventually erupt in war.

At last, on September 17, at 6:00 p.m.—two hours past the time scheduled for adjournment—Washington rose and put the final question to the delegates. The roll was called. In every delegation, the majority voted yes. The Constitution was sent to the States.

Ratification

The ratification procedure required the people of each state to elect a convention, which would vote upon the Constitution. As soon as a majority—seven states—had voted yes, the Constitution would be ratified and the new government formed.

Bitter controversies erupted in the States. Those in favor were commercial and manufacturing interests, who regarded a united country under a strong national government as necessary to economic prosperity; creditors, who wanted a strong national government to collect taxes and pay the government debts; veterans of the War for Independence, who wanted their back pay; and the Federalists, like Madison, Hamilton and Jefferson, who wanted the United States to be an important power in the world. Perhaps the biggest asset of the Federalists was George Washington. If he was for the new Constitution, large numbers of people thought, it must be good.

Against ratification were those who believed in the local rights of the States; debtors and others who favored paper money and therefore did not want to see the States lose the right to print their own currency; farmers, who mistrusted the manufacturers and traders of the cities and the coasts, seeing them as the cause of high prices and other economic woes and as likely to dominate any national government because they had money and power; some of the original Patriots such as Samuel Adams, who had not fought for independence from England's authority only to turn it over to a new central authority; men such as Patrick Henry, who regarded a strong central government as a threat to individual liberty.

On December 6, Delaware became the first state to ratify, doing so unanimously. It was followed rapidly by Pennsylvania, New Jersey, Connecticut and Georgia. But the three states essential to the union—New York, Massachusetts and Virginia—delayed. In Virginia, Patrick Henry fought violently for the Constitution's defeat. In New York, Federalist John Jay threatened that New York City might secede from the state and ratify on its own if the state as a whole did not act. Jay, Madison and Hamilton wrote a series of articles known as the ***Federalist Papers***, to argue the case for the Constitution. In the last, Hamilton wrote, "a Nation without a National Government is in my view an awful spectacle." Finally, on February 6, 1788, Massachusetts ratified. Maryland became the seventh state, followed quickly by South Carolina and New Hampshire. In Virginia, the Constitution was finally approved by only ten votes, and then only because Madison and the Federalists promised to introduce a series of amendments—later known as **The Bill of Rights**—to protect individual rights. New York, seeing ten other states already in the union, finally voted yes on July 26, but by only three votes. North Carolina did not get around to ratification until November, 1789; and Rhode Island, whose economy was in chaos, was the last, May 1790.

The people responded to the news of ratification with great enthusiasm, parades and celebrations. Though men like Patrick Henry and Samuel Adams were still unhappy, Dr. Benjamin Rush of Philadelphia summed up the majority view in a letter to John Adams: The Constitution "has a thousand . . . things to recommend it. It makes us a nation. It rescues us from anarchy and slavery. It revives agriculture and commerce. It checks moral and political iniquity. In a word, it makes a man both willing to *live* and to *die.* To *live,* because it opens to him fair prospects of great public and private happiness. To *die,* because it ensures peace, order, safety and prosperity to his children."

The Constitution

The checks and balances system of the Constitution was its greatest contribution to political thought. Power in the national government was divided among legislature, executive and judiciary, with each having a measure of authority over the other. Power was further divided between States and national government, with neither supreme. Much of this system developed because of the conflicting interests at the Convention—farmers, merchants, plantation owners—each wanting advantage for themselves. But the system also represented a genuine attempt to establish a government which could not become tyrannical. If power were shared, no one could monopolize all of it.

This is sound political theory. The Christian governments of the Middle Ages, Isabel's Spain, and the Holy Roman Empire, for example, all had working systems of checks and balances which preserved the freedoms of the people and prevented concentrations of power. In the United States, the system worked well—until the 20th century. Then it began to break down, first with the national government taking power from the States and then with various branches of the government dominating the others. For example, in the mid-20th century, the Judiciary Branch gained dominance. The framers of the Constitution never dreamed of such an event. But step by step the Supreme Court of the United States became virtually absolute with no real check on its power.

Why did this theoretically excellent system break down? The Constitution itself had one serious flaw. Madison, rightly regarded as the **Father of the Constitution**, stated that *sovereignty* (the source of authority) should rest in the people. In other words, the government received all its authority from the consent of the people. Thomas Jefferson had made the same point in the Declaration of Independence: "Governments derive their just powers from the consent of the governed." This idea came from 18th century Liberalism and was hostile to previous political theory. Since the rebirth of civilization after the Dark Ages, men had regarded sovereignty as coming from God. If power were not exercised in harmony with God's laws, it was not legitimate, no matter how many people consented to it. But God is not mentioned in the Constitution. By placing sovereignty in the people, rather than in God and Divine law, the framers of the Constitution left the door open for any evil, so long as it was justified by majority rule. In Christian societies, the Church was the ultimate check on any would-be tyrant. But this check did not exist in the United States.

Ultimately, therefore, the reason the Constitutional system could be perverted is not the fault of the governmental system set forth in the Constitution. Rather the reason is that the Constitution allows matters of truth and morality to become open questions, not anchored to Divine law. In a governmental system where rulers are chosen by elections, the rulers will reflect the moral values of the people, or of those among them who can exert the most pressure on the electoral process. If the moral values of the people decline, then so will the values of their rulers. They will find ways to subvert—or they will simply ignore—the checks and balances of their constitution in order to impose the kind of government they want.

We Americans should admire the governmental system of the Constitution, but we should not pretend that there is anything within the Constitution itself that will guarantee wisdom and morality in government. Unfortunately the "City on a Hill" mentality has too often led Americans to believe that their governmental system was virtually flawless and should be adopted by everyone else. Many people have put far too much faith in the Constitution, so that almost anything could be justified if declared "constitutional." Because the U.S. Supreme Court was the interpreter of the Constitution, that body would inevitably grow in power.

No governmental system is flawless. Any system is only as good as the people who live under it. If our Constitution has failed in any way, it is not the fault of the governmental system laid down in the Constitution. It is the fault of those who ask, "Is it constitutional?" instead of asking, "Is it in harmony with natural law and with the law of God?"

First in Peace

With the Constitution safely ratified, everyone began talking of Washington as President. There was even a new song: "Great Washington shall rule the land / While Franklin's counsel aids his hand." The writers of the Constitution, believing that the majority of the people were not wise enough to be entrusted with so serious a matter as electing the President, had set up a system called the Electoral College. The voters of each state would choose electors, the number equal to their number of representatives in Congress, who in turn would each cast two votes of equal value. The man with the highest total would be President, the second highest Vice President. In the first election, Washington was the unanimous choice of the Electoral College. But there was a struggle for the office of Vice President, as Federalists and Anti-Federalists fought for power. John Adams, the choice of the Federalists and of Washington, won by a narrow margin.

Washington's government was brand new, and he found himself constantly making decisions which would set precedents for years to come. But only one significant controversy arose in his first term, and it signified the direction the new government would travel.

In 1790, the brilliant New York Federalist, Alexander Hamilton, Washington's Secretary of the Treasury, proposed his plan to bring order out of the chaos of the American economy. First, Congress would repay all war debts contracted by the States. Madison objected on grounds that some states—especially his own state of Virginia—had already paid most of their debts. But enough states had not paid to pass the plan by three votes.

Then Hamilton proposed the establishment of a national bank. Congress was sharply divided; did the Constitution give Congress the authority to set up a bank? The southern representatives and Thomas Jefferson said no, since the Constitution nowhere had any specific provision authorizing a national bank. The New England states—with their commercial and trading interests—said yes. Again the bill narrowly passed, and it was up to Washington to sign or veto. Hamilton argued that the Constitution stated ends only; whereas the government had to choose the means to the ends, even if those means were not explicit in the Constitution. The President believed that a strong central government was essential to avoid the chaos of the Confederation, and therefore the national government could not be limited to what was specifically in the Constitution. On February 25, 1791, Washington signed the legislation.

By these two actions, precedents were set to give the national government authority over the states and to interpret the Constitution broadly—a continuation of the trends in the Constitutional Convention, trends which would continue, with occasional setbacks, throughout America's history. The controversy also led to a lifelong animosity between Jefferson and Hamilton, who became the leaders of two factions which gradually developed into the first U.S. political parties.

Washington never made a formal announcement that he wanted a second term, but the electors chose him anyway. The contest for Vice President was an ugly fight between Federalists, led by Hamilton and Adams, and Anti-Federalists—known as Republicans—and led by Jefferson; but once again Hamilton's faction won and Adams was re-elected.

REVIEW QUESTIONS

1. Summarize the Articles of Confederation. What were their weaknesses?
2. What was the fundamental choice during the "Critical Period in American History"?
3. What were Madison's main political views?
4. How were the three major controversies of the Convention resolved?
5. What groups were on each side in the ratification controversy?
6. What was the most significant political event of Washington's first term?
7. How did political parties begin in the United States?
8. List the strengths and weaknesses of the Constitution.
9. Why should we neither worship the Constitution nor blame it for America's problems?

PROJECTS

1. Make a poster illustrating the Bill of Rights.
2. Study the Constitution and make a list of the powers specifically given to each branch of the government.
3. Do research and write a report on the events of Washington's administration not covered in the text.

Chapter 10

Catholics In The New Nation

THE CONSTITUTION CONTAINED only one reference to religion, stating that no one could be forbidden from holding office in the national government because of his religion. The Bill of Rights, in the First Amendment, added that "Congress shall make no law respecting an establishment of religion [i.e., use tax money to support a specific church], or prohibiting the free exercise thereof . . ." These clauses referred only to the national government; the states could do whatever they liked. Some of the states continued their legal persecution of Catholics, forbidding them to practice their religion or to hold public office; only five states granted Catholics equal rights.

Though these legal discriminations gradually died away, popular feeling against Catholics remained. When Bishop Briand of Quebec proposed visiting Maryland and Pennsylvania to administer Confirmation, Catholics there asked that he not come. They preferred to forego the Sacrament rather than risk stirring up trouble in bishop-hating America.

But it is not the nature of Catholicism to hide its light under a bushel. On September 14, 1789, Pope Pius VI appointed John Carroll as Bishop of Baltimore, a diocese which at that time included all of the United States.

The First Bishop's Background

John Carroll was a member of one of the wealthy Catholic families in Maryland which kept the faith alive during the persecution following the Glorious Revolution. At the age of 14, he was sent to Flanders to be educated by the English Jesuits at St. Omer's. He entered the

Society of Jesus (the official name of the Jesuits) and was ordained in 1769. But in 1773 the Jesuits were suppressed and so Father Carroll came home. As we have seen (Chapter 7), he was a member of a deputation which included his cousin Charles Carroll and Benjamin Franklin sent to Quebec to try to persuade the Quebec government to support the American War for Independence. He had no illusions about this mission, and it failed because the Quebec Catholics knew of the anti-Catholic prejudice in the Colonies. All Carroll gained from this mission was the friendship of Benjamin Franklin because he took care of Franklin when the Philadelphian came down with an attack of boils on the way home.

At this time, most of the priests in America were Jesuits, but with the suppression of their Society they were at loose ends. Carroll took the problem in hand, developing in 1782 a plan to protect Jesuit property. He then began organizing an ecclesiastical structure for the Church in the United States. He wrote to the Pope on April 10, 1784, stressing loyalty to Holy See but saying that the U.S. must not be under European bishops and that "the only connection they [the Catholic clergy and laity here] ought to have with Rome is to acknowledge the Pope as the spiritual head of the Church." He said, "I have observed that when the ministers of religion leave the duties of their profession to take a busy part in political matters, they generally fall into contempt; and sometimes even bring discredit to the cause in whose service they are engaged." Rome contacted U.S. representatives in Paris, one of whom was Benjamin Franklin, regarding the appointment of a Vicar Apostolic. Franklin said there would be no objection so long as his authority was spiritual, not temporal. He supported Carroll as the best qualified man for the job. Carroll believed that "Congress should have the privilege of deciding whether Rome's choice was acceptable or not," though Congress was not in fact consulted. That same year, Carroll was officially made "head of the missions in the provinces of the new Republic of the United States of North America."

Here we see two potential problems. One is the idea that bishops should not involve themselves in political matters. The other is that Congress should have some control over Church appointments. But having been brought up in an environment hostile to Catholicism, Carroll was trying to protect the Church from future persecutions. He could not have dreamed of a later situation where moral values were precluded from the public conversation on the grounds of "separation of Church and state."

Carroll's first task was to give a thorough report of the condition of the Church. His territory covered the Atlantic to the Mississippi, Canada to Florida. There were about 16,000 Catholics in Maryland, 7,000 in Pennsylvania, 1,500 in New York, and 200 in Virginia. There were 19 priests in Maryland and 5 in Pennsylvania. There were only two priests in New York City, and they could not get along with each other. Carroll tried to reconcile them, but one of them left the country. In his report, he asked the Vatican that Catholics be allowed to marry first cousins, as a means of preserving the Faith in an overwhelmingly Protestant land. He wrote: "The abuses that have grown among Catholics are chiefly those which result with unavoidable intercourse with non-Catholics . . . namely, more free intercourse between young people of opposite sexes than is compatible with chastity in mind and body; too great fondness for dances and similar amusements; and an incredible eagerness, especially in girls, for reading love stories which are brought over in great quantities from Europe." He also sought permission to celebrate Sunday Mass in the afternoon since many had to travel long distances to attend.

In 1789 there were newspaper attacks on Catholics being allowed to vote and hold office, on the argument that the U.S. was built and won by Protestants. New York and New Jersey prohibited Catholics from exercising these rights. Under the pen name Pacificus, Carroll refuted these ideas. He said that the U.S. based its liberties and government "on the attachment of mankind to their political happiness, to the security of their persons and their property, which is independent of any religious doctrine and not restrained by any." Therefore persons of all religions should possess equal political rights. He was thus defending religious liberty, but as an alternative to persecution of Catholics, not as a means of denying that the Catholic Church is the one, true Church. John Carroll no doubt discussed this matter with his brother Daniel, who had helped shape the First Amendment to the Constitution.

An ex-priest and an ex-Jesuit wrote vicious anti-Catholic pamphlets John Carroll had to refute. With all of these problems facing the Church, Carroll believed strongly that a bishop, not just a Vicar Apostolic, was needed. He met with the Italian Catholic Filicci, who offered to intercede in Rome. William Seton, a non-Catholic friend of Filicci, offered the use of his commercial firm for correspondence between Carroll and the Vatican.

In 1789 news came from Rome that the U.S. clergy was to select the see city and nominate a bishop. The vote was 24-2 for Carroll. On September 14, Pope Pius VI confirmed the appointment after Thomas Jefferson told him that Carroll's appointment would not give offense to "our institutions or opinions." Shortly after the appointment of the first bishop, the first U.S. President was elected. Carroll congratulated George Washington on his election: "We pray for the preservation of them [full rights for Catholics] where they have been granted and expect the full extension from the justice of those states which still restrict them."

The First Bishop in Office

John Carroll was consecrated in London on the Feast of the Assumption 1790. He arranged with the Sulpicians to build a seminary and to supply four teachers, money, and even five French seminarians. St. Mary's Seminary in Baltimore opened in 1791. No Americans persevered at first, only the Frenchmen who had been driven from their homeland by the French Revolution.

In the fall of 1791 (though it was actually founded in 1789), Carroll opened what would become Georgetown University, to provide general education and preliminary training for future priests. The XYZ Affair (see Chapter 11) led to a wave of hatred for anything French, which almost drove out the Sulpicians (who had earlier been driven out of France by the Revolution). Also in 1791, Carroll held the first national synod. A main topic was marriage. The clergy set up rules for mixed marriages, a major issue in the U.S. because of the small number of Catholics. Carroll emphasized the importance of valid marriages according to the laws of the Church. In his own family, Charles Carroll's son was going to marry an Episcopalian. Her family intended to have a morning ceremony by Carroll and an evening one by an Episcopalian bishop. Bishop Carroll said that there must be only a Catholic ceremony and carried the day.

In 1793, Carroll performed the first ordination on U.S. soil: Father Stephen Badin, a refugee from the French Revolution. That same year Leonard Neale, a native of Maryland, was appointed Coadjutor Bishop, though the document did not arrive until 1800. His main responsibility was running Georgetown University.

In 1795, the second priest was ordained, Prince Demetrius Gallitzin, one of the more colorful characters from early American Catholic history. His father was from a noble Lithuanian family; his mother was the daughter of a German field marshal. He was born in the Hague while his father was Russian Ambassador there. His father, who was a follower of Voltaire, had prepared his son for a military career and brought him up to scoff at religion. His mother had been led away from the practice of her faith by her husband, but when she became seriously ill in 1786, she returned to the Church and prayed for her son's conversion. Because of his mother's conversion, he said, "I soon felt convinced of the necessity of investigating the different religious systems, in order to find the true one. . . My choice fell upon the Catholic Church, and at the age of seventeen [in 1787], I became a member of that Church." He still pursued a military career and fought with Austria against the French Revolutionary army. Then the Austrian army dismissed all foreigners, and he came to the U.S. to try his luck in the infant army of the U.S., arriving in 1792. He immediately noticed the need for priests and decided to study for the priesthood. He studied in Baltimore and was ordained in 1795, the first American trained priest. He worked in Virginia and Maryland for four years, then was assigned to western Pennsylvania, where he labored for 41 years, traveling by horseback through the forest wilds, being caught in the rains and suffering the heat. He used his own money to build a mission center at Loretto, Pennsylvania. His work covered an area that now includes the dioceses of Pittsburgh, Harrisburg, Greensburg and Erie. He also wrote books defending the Catholic religion. He concealed the fact that he was a prince, introducing himself as Father Smith. When he was naturalized as an American citizen, it was under the name of Augustine Smith. He was a great civilizing as well as Christianizing influence in the frontier Church.

Also in 1795 Carroll began missions to the Indians of Ohio with two priests who received government subsidies (urged by George Washington). In 1799 both Pope Pius VI and George Washington died, leaving Carroll bereft of two men to whom he had been quite close.

In 1803 the Louisiana Purchase doubled Carroll's diocese. In 1805, five American women established the Visitation Convent and Girls School on property adjacent to Georgetown. They chose this particular rule because they found a book of rules and constitutions of the Order of the Visitation. This left their canonical status in doubt, but the Vatican finally confirmed their foundation in 1814, and their school is still in business today. Kentucky, which was mission territory, saw two foundations. The Dominicans opened a motherhouse there, and Belgian born

Father Charles Nerinckx, assisted by a young Kentucky woman named Mary Rhodes, founded the Sisters of Loretto at the Foot of the Cross in 1812. In 1814 the Society of Jesus (the Jesuits) was restored and took over Georgetown.

A major controversy facing Carroll was "trusteeism." Parish trustees, who were something like today's parish councils, would try to set up a Protestant system in which laymen would control the parish property and hire and fire priests. Carroll strongly opposed this system because he knew it undermined hierarchical authority. In Philadelphia he had to excommunicate two priests who went along with trusteeism, whereupon they went into schism. When Carroll went to Philadelphia in 1798 to resolve the controversy, the trustees had him arrested, denied in court his authority and jurisdiction, and criticized canon law, Catholic doctrine, the Church government, the Holy Father and the Council of Trent. Carroll bore it calmly, continuing negotiations, until they finally saw the error of their ways, repented and were reconciled. Trustees also attempted a takeover in Baltimore and several other places as well.

The American Church suffered from a shortage of priests. Though there was a trickle of European priests coming into the U.S., most were either unsavory characters or too independent (one supported himself working in a traveling circus).

As the U.S. population grew, Carroll saw the need to divide his diocese. Rome responded by suggesting that there be four or five new dioceses. The Vatican asked Carroll to recommend the see cities and the prospective bishops. On April 8, 1808, Pope Pius VII created the new dioceses of Boston (Bishop Cheverus), Philadelphia (Bishop Egan), Bardstown, Kentucky (Bishop Flaget), and New York. Carroll had not recommended any candidate for bishop of New York because he did not think there was anyone truly worthy there. The Vatican appointed Irish-born Dom Concanen, who never arrived because he was stranded in Italy because of the Napoleonic Wars. Then the Holy Father appointed a Dominican, John Connelly, who arrived two days after Bishop Carroll's death. The Vatican also appointed an Apostolic Administrator for Louisiana—Father Nerinckx. With bishops under his authority, Carroll was now an archbishop. In one of their first actions as a group, the American bishops denounced Napoleon's treatment of Pope Pius VII.

When Egan died in 1814, trusteeism controversies resulted in no bishop being appointed for Philadelphia for six years. Carroll died December 3, 1815 with the Diocese of Philadelphia still vacant. There were now 70,000 Catholics, 70 priests and 80 churches in the United States. John Carroll, the initial builder of the Catholic Church in the United States, had made sure that the Church in the infant nation got off to a good start.

Was John Carroll a Liberal?

John Carroll's views on separation of Church and State are controversial. As we have seen, he always supported that practice in this country. Does that mean he was a Liberal? He was not a Liberal in his views on papal supremacy and papal authority. He was not a Liberal in his views on the importance of a bishop's exercising his full authority. He was not a Liberal in his views on mixed marriages. He opposed Napoleon and he opposed the Freemasons.

Did Carroll see separation of Church and State as the only policy that would have worked in early 19th century America? He was so used to seeing persecution that he thought the American system was great by comparison. "In these United States, our religious system has undergone a revolution, if possible, more extraordinary than our political one. The United States have banished intolerance from their system of government, and many of them have done the justice to every denomination of Christians, which ought to be done to them in all, of placing them on the same footing of citizenship, and conferring an equal right of participation in national privileges." Because of his delight that Catholics were not persecuted by the U.S. government, he perhaps did not see the danger that this policy had of leading to religious indifferentism (the belief that one religion is as good as another, or even to the belief that a person is free to choose to practice no religion at all) and to the belief that the Church should not interfere in politics.

As we shall see, many American Catholics came to believe precisely this second point (that the Church should not interfere in politics), as well as rejecting the spiritual loyalty to the Holy Father that John Carroll held to so firmly.

Elizabeth Ann Seton

As wars raged and governments fell, a beautiful young American woman set about laying the foundations for the growth of American Catholicism. Her constructive efforts are a bright light in the midst of the problems of the early 19th century.

Elizabeth Ann Bayley was born in New York City on August 28, 1774, the same year that John Carroll returned to Maryland and the First Continental Congress met. Her father Richard was a distinguished New York doctor and her mother Catherine the daughter of an Episcopalian minister. Elizabeth was a descendant of Calvinists; both of her grandmothers were Huguenots. Mrs. Bayley died in 1777 and Elizabeth's father remarried Charlotte Barclay. Dr. Bayley was hard-working and had a special concern for helping the needy, a concern which he taught to his daughter. During the American War for Independence, Dr. Bayley was staff physician to Lord Howe.

From her earliest days, Elizabeth had a habit of prayer and always tried to see things as God would want her to see them. As a teenager, in spite of the social whirl common to her prominent family, she persevered in a daily examination of conscience and drew up a plan for spiritual perfection.

The talented Elizabeth Ann became the wife of the young merchant, William Seton, in January 1794. An Episcopalian, Elizabeth and her sister-in-law Rebecca were sometimes referred to as the "Protestant Sisters of Charity" for their many charitable activities, including an organization they founded to help poor widows. The two women were very close, and both strove for spiritual perfection.

Elizabeth and William had five children: Anna Maria born in 1794, William in 1796, Richard in 1798, Catherine in 1800 and Rebecca in 1802. William's father died in 1798 and William junior had to take over the business in shaky economic times. Elizabeth managed the large Seton home and became her husband's business secretary. In 1801, Dr. Bayley died of yellow fever, caught while caring for the sick during an epidemic. In 1803, the family fell on hard times. William's business suffered severe reverses, and he contracted tuberculosis. Though he had not been a churchgoer, his trials led him to draw closer to God.

To try to regain his health, he set sail for Italy with Elizabeth and their oldest daughter, Anna Maria. When they docked at Leghorn, the family was quarantined in the Lazaretto for fear of yellow fever, and there William's condition deteriorated. They were released from quarantine on December 19, and William died at the home of his business associate, Antonio Filicci, on December 27, leaving Elizabeth a widowed mother of five at the age of 29.

Elizabeth stayed with the Filicci family. At the urging of the Filiccis, she began to read about Catholicism, and was convinced of its truth, especially the doctrine of the Real Presence. She returned to New York in May of 1804. Her sister-in-law Rebecca died soon after her return, leaving her without the one person who would have understood her desire to convert to Catholicism. Her family and friends tried to dissuade her from entering the Church. Her dear friend, Episcopalian minister Rev. Henry Hobart, asked her to undertake a study of the Episcopalian faith. She did, and underwent a trial of spiritual desolation. She did not yet have the spiritual and intellectual formation needed to answer the arguments against Catholicism and in favor of Episcopalianism. Antonio put her in touch with Father John Cheverus of Boston (later bishop of that city). He encouraged her to enter the Church as soon as possible in order to receive the graces available to her there. She was received into the Catholic Church on March 14, 1805, despite the bitter opposition of her relatives, at the only Catholic Church in New York City, St. Peter's. She made her first Holy Communion on the Feast of the Annunciation. She was rejected by family and friends, who could not understand why she wanted to join a religion which in New York City was mainly that of the poor and lower classes.

Elizabeth had no money, and though the Filiccis and some others helped her, she wanted to be self-supporting. An English gentleman and his wife opened a small school and hired Elizabeth to teach. The school soon failed for lack of pupils. In November 1804, a man whose dying wife Elizabeth had nursed helped her open a boarding house for young students. Just a few years earlier, no one could have imagined the fashionable Mrs. Seton as proprietor of a boarding house.

In the spring of 1806, her sister-in-law Cecilia entered the Catholic Church. The family had tried locking her in her room to change her mind, to no avail. At this point, those who had been helping her broke off all connections. There seemed to be more anger at this conversion than at her own, as her family and friends believed she was dragging people away from Protestantism.

Father DuBourg, President of St. Mary's College in Baltimore, met Elizabeth and encouraged her to found a society for pious women which could set up a school for girls to supplement the three for boys in the Baltimore-Washington area (Georgetown, St. Mary's, and Mt. St. Mary's). In June 1808, she set out for Baltimore. The school began with seven pupils, including Elizabeth's three daughters. But Elizabeth was not concerned with the trappings of earthly success. She was advancing in the spiritual life, and without omitting any of her duties she lived, as she said, "in the secret of the tabernacle."

Soon Archbishop John Carroll persuaded her to establish the first native American religious order, the Sisters of Charity, and she pronounced her vows to Archbishop Carroll on March 25, 1809, the 175th anniversary of the landing of the first Catholic colonists in Maryland and the offering of the first Mass in the Colonies. Elizabeth and her four companions pledged to work with the poor, the sick, the sorrowful and children. Receiving a donation of land in Emmitsburg, Maryland, she established her motherhouse there, along with another school. She and the young women who joined her suffered many privations in the early days. Harriet Seton, who was received into the Church in Emmitsburg, died in November 1809 and Cecilia Seton died in April 1810.

They moved into the White house in February 1810, where Elizabeth opened a boarding school for girls and, in February 1810, a free school for neighborhood children, including Blacks, the first parochial school in the United States. Her constitutions were based on those of St. Vincent De Paul's Daughters of Charity.

The first superior of the order was Father J. B. David, a stern disciplinarian who suggested removing Elizabeth as Mother Superior. He favored Sister Rose White, a widow who had joined Elizabeth in June 1809. Elizabeth found out about this plan just after the death of her beloved sister-in-law, Cecilia. She received a letter from Father David that he was going to install Sister Rose as superior and telling her to inform the other sisters. She chose to wait until Sister Rose returned to Emmitsburg. But before the plan could be fulfilled, Archbishop Carroll vetoed it and sent Father David to Bardstown, Kentucky. The new Father Superior was Father John DuBois.

In September 1811, Anna Maria became ill and endured excruciating pain until her death on March 12, 1812. Later that year Rebecca fell and injured her leg. A tumor formed on her thigh. After long months of suffering, she died in her mother's arms in 1816. The deaths of her daughters were Elizabeth's greatest trials. Yet she kept her spirit of poverty, mortification and recollection. She remained a loving mother to her own children, her pupils and her nuns.

In 1812 her permanent rule and constitutions were approved, though her Sisters of Charity were not formally united with the French Daughters of Charity because of Elizabeth's unusual status as the mother of young children. But in the 1830 Miraculous Medal apparitions, the Blessed Mother told St. Catherine Laboure that the union would take place, and in 1850 it did so.

In 1814 three sisters were sent to Philadelphia to take over an orphanage, to which a free school was later added. In 1817 a foundation was made in New York.

Elizabeth had been suffering from tuberculosis since 1810. In August of 1820 she was thought to be dying, but recovered temporarily. Confined to bed, she stayed in a room next to the chapel so that with the door open she could always contemplate the tabernacle. One of her greatest trials in the last months of her life was the knowledge that her two sons were leading wild lives. It would not be until after her death that they would settle down. (Will's son Robert would become an archbishop.)

Finally, in January 1821, the hour of her death had arrived. As she was dying, she recited her daily ejaculation: "May the most holy and high will of God be accomplished forever." Her last words of advice to her sisters were, "Be children of the Church." Her last words of all were, "Jesus, Mary, Joseph . . . Jesus."

By the time of her death, she and her sisters had laid the foundations for today's vast network of American Catholic institutions—schools, orphanages, hospitals and the rest. Almost single-handedly she left a monumental legacy of charity and devotion to the welfare of others which has benefitted America to this day. Canonized in 1975, Elizabeth Ann Seton was America's first native-born Saint.

Other Early Catholic Leaders

In 1818 the Religious of the Sacred Heart came to St. Louis under the leadership of Mother Rose Duchesne. She had thought she would be able to work among the Indians, but the bishop said no. So she and her nuns established the first free school west of the Mississippi, the beginning of the great work of education that the Sacred Heart nuns would accomplish. She also started a boarding school, a novitiate and an orphanage, despite incredible hardships.

Finally, in 1841, Rose Duchesne (at age 72) received permission to begin mission work among the Indians of Kansas. It was impossible at that age for her to learn the Indian language, so she spoke the international language of kindness and love. Daily she spent four hours in the morning and four hours in the evening in the chapel, praying for the success of the missionary work. The Indians named her "Woman Who Always Prays," and she remained among the Indians until her death in 1852.

In 1820 John England was appointed the first bishop of Charleston, a diocese which included South Carolina, North Carolina and Georgia. He had worked for Catholic Emancipation in Ireland before coming to the United States. He eliminated entirely the trustee system in his diocese. He set up the area's first seminary and taught in it himself.

He believed very strongly in a well-educated laity, so he traveled and preached incessantly, set up a book society and library, published *U.S. Catholic Miscellany* (the first Catholic newspaper in the United States), and compiled a catechism and English missal.

Bishop England did not neglect the many Blacks in his diocese. He established the Sisters of Our Lady of Mercy to educate girls, including free Blacks and slaves; he said Mass for Negroes every Sunday and had a regular Sunday service for them with a sermon. Sometimes he was too busy to preach his sermon to the white people, but he was never too busy to preach to the Blacks. He set up a school for black children and was one of their teachers.

With large numbers of Irish immigrants coming to the U.S., there would be many great Irish bishops, of whom John England was the first.

REVIEW QUESTIONS

1. What do the Constitution and the Bill of Rights say about religion?
2. Summarize the background of John Carroll before he became Vicar Apostolic.
3. What were his accomplishments as bishop?
4. Summarize the career of Prince Gallitzin.
5. Summarize the trusteeism controversy.
6. What were John Carroll's views on separation of Church and state? Why did he hold these views?
7. Summarize the background of Elizabeth Ann Seton before her conversion.
8. Summarize the circumstances of her conversion and the reaction of her family and friends.

9. Summarize the crosses she endured.
10. Summarize her accomplishments.
11. What were the accomplishments of Rose Duchesne?
12. What were the accomplishments of John England?

PROJECTS

1. Do research and write a report on one of the religious orders mentioned in this chapter.
2. Do research and write a report on one of the persons mentioned briefly in this chapter.
3. Prepare a mural illustrating the life and accomplishments of Mother Seton.

Chapter 11

The French Revolution And The New World

EXACTLY TWO MONTHS after George Washington took his oath of office, the Estates General convened in Paris for the first time in 175 years. May 4, 1789 marked the beginning of a chain of events which rocked France to its foundations, bringing 10 years of chaos, bloodshed and terror to the French people. The shock waves of the French Revolution also traveled across the Atlantic to the New World, unleashing war and revolt from Canada to Argentina. The liberal ideas which sparked the French Revolution found a home in Hispanic America among the wealthy Creoles (American-born Spaniards). And the United States was drawn into the wars into which France plunged Europe. The effects on the Western Hemisphere were as long-lasting as the effects on the Eastern; the French Revolution scoured out a chasm which sharply separates history before from history after, throughout the entire world.

Revolution in Haiti

The island of Saint Domingue (Santo Domingo) lies between Cuba and Puerto Rico. It was a strange sort of island: half French colony, half Spanish. The society of the French colony on Saint Domingue was rigidly divided. The *Grand Blancs* ("Great Whites") were the oldest, wealthiest, most powerful Creole families. The *Petit Blancs* ("Little Whites") were the island's middle class—not as wealthy, not as powerful, not as respected. They were susceptible to liberalism, as a way of bringing the *Grand Blancs* down to their level. The *Petit Blancs* tended to be racist, despising the Blacks. There were also two classes of Blacks: the free people of color and the 450,000 slaves who worked the plantations. The free coloreds hated the slaves and were servile to the Whites in hopes of advancing in society. The colony was governed by officials from France and was generally peaceful and prosperous.

When the French Revolution exploded, the National Assembly passed decrees ordering liberty, fraternity and equality for all in Saint Domingue by providing elections and giving the free coloreds rights of citizenship. The result was civil war, as each faction grabbed for power, with England and Spain jumping into the fray from time to time.

Then, in the dark nights of early 1791, the slaves decided their turn had come. When they met in the forests for their voodoo rituals, relying on their witch doctors to drive away the evil spirits, they had a new purpose: organizing for revolt. By late summer, plans were complete, and on August 22, the slaves revolted all over the island. They were untrained in military matters, but anyone can kill if he is angry enough, and the slaves were angry. They slaughtered white people on the island and burned plantations to the ground.

In the early days of the rebellion, a young slave named Toussaint worked among the Negroes as a doctor. He had been the overseer on a plantation, and his master had educated him well. He was a devout Catholic, very intelligent and respectful toward the Whites. Though he recognized the Negroes' problems, he knew that his people deserved better than they had received. He also knew that their mindless rebellion would only lead to brutal repression. Because he was well-educated and talented, he soon rose to a position of authority and set about training a proper army. As an avid reader of Julius Caesar's *Gallic Wars,* he knew something about military strategy. He gave himself a new last name: *L'Ouverture*—"the opening"—an opening to freedom for his people.

Toussaint also knew something about politics and how to play off one force against another. First he joined the Spaniards against the French. Then he supported the Royalists (defenders of the French monarchy) against the *Petit Blancs.* When the National Assembly emancipated all slaves in 1794, he cast his lot with the French Republic against Spain and Britain. Whatever side he was on, his men won nearly every battle. The National Assembly was so much in the little man's debt that they named him Lieutenant Governor on April 1, 1796.

Toussaint was by far the most talented man—black or white—in any position of leadership on Saint Domingue and soon had most of the power on the island in his hands. Toussaint administered the island with great energy, trying to improve the lives of all the people of whatever color. In June 1801, he proclaimed a new constitution, which abolished slavery, gave Blacks political rights and made him Governor General for life. Everyone had to work, but workers would receive one-fourth of the profits of the plantations and were guaranteed reasonable hours and humane treatment. The colony reached new heights of prosperity as trade flourished. Ironically, among the discontented were former slaves, because they had hoped that emancipation from slavery would also mean emancipation from work. But Toussaint regarded the island as one large plantation, in which everyone would contribute his share under the Governor General's benevolent and watchful eye.

Given time, Toussaint might have made his system work, but Napoleon, who had seized control of the French government in 1799, wanted to use Saint Domingue as a base for the building of an overseas empire and began to be nervous about the black man's power. He gave his brother-in-law Charles Leclerc command over 60 ships, the greatest maritime force ever gathered for an overseas expedition, and told him to take over the island.

Toussaint's former slaves took on the finest soldiers in the world and fought them to a draw. Entire divisions of French soldiers would be trapped in narrow mountain passes and shot without seeing a black man. The French would no sooner gain a mile than Toussaint's men would close in behind. French night sentinels in the mountains had such heavy casualties that some preferred to be court-martialed rather than stand that hazardous duty.

But the various races under Toussaint's command were still jealous of him and of each other. They fought among themselves, each group wanting all the power. Toussaint saw no point in continuing the war. He arranged honorable terms and surrendered his army in April 1802, the French promising that he could return to his estate for a peaceful retirement. But Napoleon was not known for keeping promises. Toussaint was arrested, sent to France and imprisoned in the mountains, a far different climate from the tropical heat of his island home. He died alone and friendless in April, 1803.

But once Toussaint was gone, his people realized what they had lost. They rebelled again. After a year of bitter fighting, Napoleon reluctantly withdrew the rest of his army, and the independent republic of Haiti was born. Napoleon was so disgusted with his attempt to maintain an empire in the New World that he decided to get rid of it all and concentrate on Europe. Hence the American commissioners in Paris found a willing seller when they came to inquire about perhaps purchasing some of the Louisiana Territory.

President Adams

Meanwhile, back in the United States, news of the French Revolution was mostly welcomed. Jefferson wrote that "99 in 100 Americans" were in sympathy with the Revolution. Though that was surely an exaggeration, many Americans saw the French Revolution as similar to their own War for Independence, a justified rebellion against a tyrannical king. This misconception of the French Revolution has been widely believed in America ever since.

Jefferson added that the "liberty of the whole earth was depending on the issue of that contest," but President Washington was not quite so enthusiastic as his Secretary of State. He had to consider the Revolution's effect on world politics and especially the role of the brand new nation in those politics. He could foresee a general war, with great pressure on the U.S. to get in on one side or the other. Yet he knew that the last thing America needed was a war, just as it was recovering from its War of Independence.

When war did break out between France and the other European powers, the U.S. was divided between supporters of the French Revolution, who wanted to get into the war on the side of France (these tended to be members of Jefferson's Republican Party) and those who wanted neutrality or perhaps a show of favoritism toward Britain (these tended to be members of the Federalist Party). Washington took matters into his own hands, issuing a Neutrality Proclamation on April 22, 1793, in which the U.S. declared that it had no intention of going to war with anyone. Jefferson did not like it and eventually resigned as Secretary of State. U.S. ambassador to France James Monroe did not like it and eventually had to be recalled because he was too pro-French. But Washington kept the U.S. out of war.

Washington refused to run for a third term. The Federalist candidate in the election of 1796—as Napoleon Bonaparte led troops against Austria—was John Adams, who deeply distrusted the French Revolution because it denied all authority; Charles Pinckney ran for Vice President. The Republican candidates were Jefferson and Aaron Burr, who attacked Adams as a monarchist, because the Federalist candidate did not think it wise of France to cut off the head of its king. Boston's French sympathizers wore ornamental guillotines pinned to their coats to show where their loyalties lay, but in an election marked by insults, threats and fraud, Adams won by three electoral votes over Jefferson. Because the Constitution designated the second-place candidate as Vice President, Adams found himself saddled with a Vice President who, though once his good friend, was now his bitter enemy.

Adams, recognizing the military danger threatening his country, tried to persuade Congress to build up the U.S. Navy, but the Republican-controlled Congress only approved the building of three merchant ships. Then Talleyrand, France's foreign minister and a former bishop who had managed to escape the guillotine by being more devious than everyone else, decided that the U.S. was so eager for peace that he could make a profit out of it. In October 1797, he dispatched three agents to speak to the three U.S. commissioners to France, informing them that if they paid the reasonable sum of $250,000 and gave France a loan of $1.3 million, France would not go to war against the U.S. The U.S. commissioners sent details of the offer to President Adams, designating the three French agents as X, Y and Z. Adams was furious and released the correspondence. Americans were so outraged over what came to be called the **XYZ Affair** that the majority rallied behind Adams and turned against the French. Congress pushed through legislation to build 12 armed vessels and raise an army of 10,000 men. Talleyrand—who had really wanted money, not war, especially now that the French fleet had been wiped out at the Battle of the Nile—issued a public apology. A few naval battles were fought, with the Americans winning most, as each side tried to seize some of the other's ships, but Adams had successfully called Talleyrand's bluff and kept America out of war.

In 1798, Congress—still concerned about the possibility of war with France—passed a series of laws known as the **Alien and Sedition Acts**. The Alien Act and the Alien Enemies Act were aimed at the large number of French citizens in the United States, many of whom were actively agitating against the U.S. government. The Sedition Act was aimed at the Republican newspapers which were supporting the French and attacking the U.S. government. Adams favored the acts on the ground that if war should come, the President would have some way to curb enemies of the U.S. who were active within its borders. But the Republicans, a large number of whom were still sympathetic to the French, attacked the acts as violations of the right of free speech. None of them explained why free speech included the right to try to overthrow one's government, but the Republicans used the Alien and Sedition Acts as a potent weapon against Adams in the election of 1800.

During the electioneering, the Adamses moved into the still uncompleted White House in the new capital city, Washington, D.C. Abigail got lost on the back roads on her way to the District of Columbia; when she arrived, she had to hang her laundry in the East Room, and the unpaved streets were a sea of mud, but at least the President had a home of his own.

The Election of 1800

The election of 1800 was one of the strangest in the history of the U.S. The authors of the Constitution had tried to create a foolproof system for guaranteeing the choice of the country's best man as President and the second best man as Vice President. But the framers of the Constitution had not imagined the emergence of the party system, and their blueprint did not take into account human greed for power. By 1800 the electors running in each state were men pledged to support one or another party. The electors of each party would agree among themselves that one of them would "drop off" his vote for the man designated Vice President by their party so that he would finish second, one vote behind the Presidential candidate.

But when the Electoral College met in 1800, the electors got their signals crossed. The Republican Party won, but *all* of their electors had voted for both Thomas Jefferson *and* Aaron Burr, so that they were tied. According to the Constitution, the election had to be decided by the House of Representatives. Burr decided that he wanted to be President after all and refused to withdraw in Jefferson's favor.

The House of Representatives was dominated by Federalists who liked neither Jefferson nor Burr. Thirty-five ballots went by with neither getting a majority, as partisans of both worked frantically behind the scenes, trying to influence Hamilton and the other Federalist leaders. For six days the Representatives slept on the floor of the House and had food brought in to them. Then on February 17 the Federalist leader of Delaware, Mr. Bayard, announced that Jefferson had promised not to abolish the navy John Adams had worked so hard to build nor to eliminate the public credit system, both of which Jefferson had earlier said he would eliminate if he became President. Jefferson later declared that he had made no such promises, but the announcement swung Vermont and Maryland to Jefferson, giving him victory. Congress, not wanting to go through such sleepless nights again, recognized the reality of the party system and passed the twelfth amendment to the Constitution to provide for separate balloting for President and Vice President.

Marbury v. Madison

On March 1, three days before his term ended, John Adams appointed Federalists to various judicial positions. The Republicans were not happy at Adams' last minute appointments, and James Madison discarded 17 commissions for justice of the peace rather than deliver them to the men appointed. Most of the men involved did not care because the position was unsalaried. But Mr. William Marbury filed suit in the U.S. Supreme Court for the delivery to Madison of a writ of mandamus (a court order requiring a specific thing to be done) ordering delivery of the commission, basing his suit on a clause in the Judiciary Act of 1789 authorizing such legal action.

Chief Justice John Marshall, a Federalist appointed by Adams, ordered Madison to show cause why the writ should not be issued. Madison ignored the order and refused to appear in court, arguing with Jefferson that the Supreme Court did not have the right to oversee the functions of the executive branch.

Marshall knew that Jefferson would go on ignoring him. So he had to find a course of action which would avoid the Court's being humiliated by the executive branch and preserve the powers of the judiciary. He did not issue his ruling in the case of ***Marbury v. Madison*** until February 24, 1803.

In the ruling, Marshall declared that Marbury had a right to the commission and that Jefferson was violating that right. But according to Marshall's reading of Article III of the Constitution, the Supreme Court can issue writs of mandamus only in cases of appellate jurisdiction (cases appealed from a lower court), not in cases of original jurisdiction (cases originating in the Supreme Court). Marshall wrote: "Thus, the particular phraseology of the Constitution of the United States confirms and strengthens the principle, supposed to be essential to all written constitutions, that a law repugnant to the Constitution is void; and that courts as well as other departments are bound by that instrument." The law in question was the Judiciary Act of 1789, which Marshall was saying could not be used because it authorized an action which the Constitution did not allow.

This case might have been a minor footnote in American judicial history except for the way it was used in the 20th century. Marshall, it was said, had declared an act of Congress to be unconstitutional. The Supreme Court therefore becomes the final arbiter of what Congress, the Executive Branch, and what the States as well, may or may not do. This view of the Court is called "**judicial supremacy**." Instead of three equal branches of government, judicial supremacists in the 20th century elevated the judiciary to be the paramount branch, with supremacy over the other branches and the States, through its power to declare laws and actions by the other branches and the States to be unconstitutional and therefore forbidden and to replace those laws with "laws" the Court itself writes through its decisions.

Judicial supremacy, however, is a false conclusion drawn from *Marbury v. Madison.* Marshall was in fact admitting that the judiciary cannot force the executive branch to do something it does not want to do. He does not say that he is striking down a law. He simply says that the court cannot be forced to do something that the Constitution does not authorize it to do. The equality of the three branches is maintained. Nowhere does Marshall say that the Court can determine which laws Congress may pass. Nor does the Constitution give the Court the power to decree laws.

Marbury v. Madison has been used as a justification for the amassing of power by the Supreme Court. As we shall see in later chapters, this power has had serious consequences in the United States, as the Court went beyond judging constitutionality to, in effect, dictating legislation.

President Jefferson

Thomas Jefferson was the nation's first non-Federalist President. His Secretary of State was fellow Virginian James Madison, the Father of the Constitution. The first crisis they faced came from the far-off Mediterranean Sea. Under Washington and Adams, the U.S. government had paid tribute to the Moslem pirates of the Barbary States (Algiers, Morocco, Tripoli and Tunis in North Africa), who found piracy and protection money far more lucrative than trade and manufacturing. Jefferson refused to pay, and when the Pasha of Tripoli declared war on May 14, 1801, Jefferson dispatched ships to the Mediterranean.

The pirates were amazed to find themselves facing opposition from this upstart nation. The Americans captured a few pirate ships; and Morocco, Tunis and Algiers decided friendship might not be such a bad policy. But the ship *Philadelphia* was captured by Tripoli, leaving Commodore Preble with one frigate and a handful of brigs. To even the score, the Americans captured a Tripolitan ketch, renamed her the *Intrepid,* and loaded her with combustibles and 84 sailors under the command of Lieutenant Stephen Decatur. On the night of February 16, 1804, the *Intrepid* sailed into the Tripolitan harbor, bumped into the *Philadelphia* and unloaded its sailors. They set the *Philadelphia* afire and escaped back to sea without losing a man. On June 4, 1805, the Tripolitan pirates capitulated and signed a treaty of peace favorable to the U.S. The most important result of the war, however, was the experience the fledgling U.S. navy had received. The experience would stand America in good stead before too many more years had passed.

Elsewhere, Napoleon's clash with Toussaint made him want to get out of the Western Hemisphere. But he was left with a rather large chunk of the North American continent known as the **Louisiana Territory**, the huge area on either side of the Mississippi River explored by La Salle. So when U.S. commissioners Robert Livingston and James Monroe came to Talleyrand to buy the port of New Orleans for $2 million, Talleyrand offered them all of Louisiana for a bargain price of $20 million. The U.S. offered $4 million and the haggling went on. The final price agreed upon was $15 million. Though neither the Constitution nor Congress had authorized the President to purchase territory, Jefferson approved the deal and found the U.S. doubled in size.

When Monroe asked Talleyrand, "What are the boundaries of Louisiana on the west?" the Frenchman replied, "I do not know. You will have to take the province as it stands." To find out how the province stood, Jefferson commissioned Captains Meriwether Lewis and William Clark to find out. On Monday, May 14, 1804, they set out from St. Louis with 28 men. They returned two and a half years later. They did not find the mountain of salt which legend said was there, but they did go all the way to the Pacific and saw Mount Rainier, a suitable substitute.

The War of 1812

After Jefferson's re-election, the French Revolution moved closer to home. The British were not pleased with French trade being carried in American ships, so they began seizing the ships and impressing some of the sailors—usually British citizens but sometimes Americans, too—into the British navy.

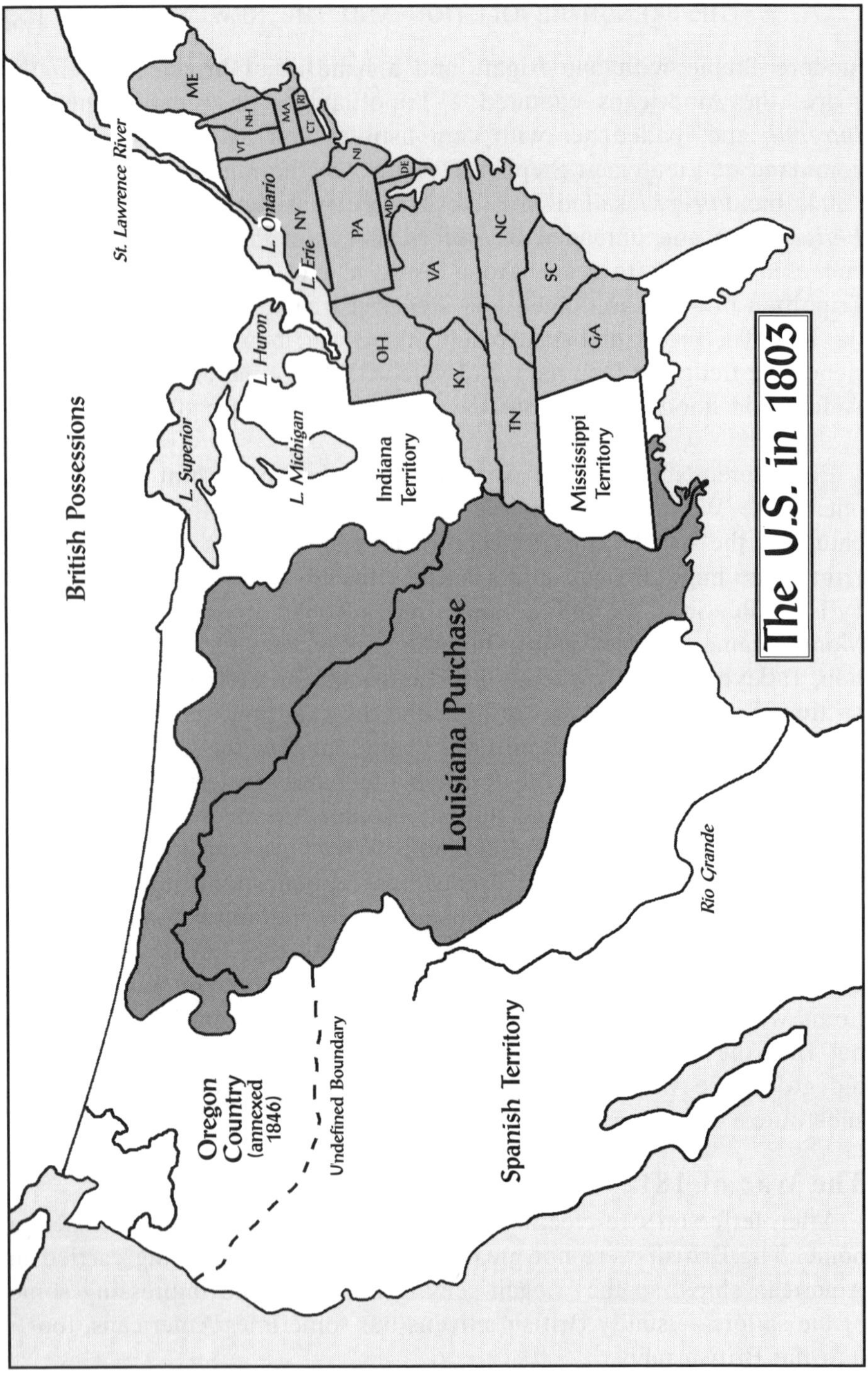
The U.S. in 1803
British Possessions
St. Lawrence River
L. Superior
L. Michigan
L. Huron
L. Erie
L. Ontario
ME
NH
VT
MA
RI
CT
NY
NJ
PA
DE
MD
VA
NC
SC
GA
OH
KY
TN
Indiana Territory
Mississippi Territory
Louisiana Purchase
Oregon Country (annexed 1846)
Undefined Boundary
Spanish Territory
Rio Grande

Jefferson passionately desired to avoid war. When the U.S. ship *Chesapeake*—which had no cartridges to fit its guns and no matches to fire the guns even if it had cartridges—was attacked by the British ship *Leopard,* Jefferson's only response was a proclamation ordering British warships to leave U.S. waters. Later Congress passed an Embargo Act, forbidding all U.S. trade with foreign nations. This hurt the U.S. more than it did the British, and Americans consistently evaded the law. Jefferson's popularity sank.

The Presidential election of 1808 was won by James Madison, Jefferson's hand-picked successor. But in the Congressional elections of 1810, the people turned out those who wanted compromise with the British and elected men who called for armed resistance. Said Henry Clay, one of the new Congressmen: "Are we never to manage our affairs without the permission of His Britannic Majesty?" A feeling also arose at this time that the U.S. had a right to increase its territory, and war with Britain would provide a golden opportunity to seize Canada.

The final push toward war came from the revelation of a British plot to stir up a revolution in New England. After a day-long secret session of Congress on June 18, 1812, horsemen galloped through the streets of the District of Columbia, shouting, "The Nation is at war!"

As in the War for Independence, the odds were with the British. The U.S. Army had only 5000 men, scattered all over the country. The state militias which had given Washington so much trouble were little help; Connecticut, Rhode Island and Massachusetts all refused even to raise a militia. The Navy's 165 gunboats were always capsizing or running aground. But the War was fought in and near the U.S.; the British were preoccupied with Napoleon; and the experience during the Barbary war was invaluable.

The War on land began inauspiciously. The U.S. wanted to take Canada, but the attempt was under the command of too-old generals left over from the War for Independence. Before the end of 1812, General William Hull had surrendered Detroit to the British without firing a shot, an American attack at Fort George on the Niagara River had failed because the New York militiamen had refused to provide reinforcements on the grounds that they were could not be ordered to leave their home state, and a projected attack on Montreal failed because the militiamen would not cross the Canadian border.

The War on sea almost did not begin at all. Madison decided that the Navy must wage a defensive war and ordered his captains to stay in port. Isaac Hull, commander of the *Constitution,* knew the orders were coming and sailed out of port to avoid them. He encountered the British ship *Guerriere.* The Americans fired every gun, and 25 minutes later the British surrendered for the first time since 1798. The U.S. had made great advances in naval gunnery, especially in long range firing. In the next four months, the U.S. Navy fought two more battles and won them both, more victories than all the navies of the world had won over Britain in the preceding nine years. These successes persuaded Madison to order his ships out to fight the British. In the next five naval battles, the U.S. won four.

To revitalize the Army, the young and vigorous William Henry Harrison was commissioned a major general on February 27, 1813 and sent off to retake Detroit. But he could not achieve this so long as the British held Lake Erie. Therefore Madison ordered Commodore Oliver Perry to Lake Erie to do battle with the British. Perry hoisted a blue flag embroidered with the motto, "Don't give up the ship," and on September 10 sailed out to meet the British. The U.S. fleet was mauled, men were falling on all sides and Perry's ship was about to lose its mast. So Perry gathered the few able-bodied men left, grabbed his flag, piled into a boat and rowed furiously to the ship *Niagara* as British shot fell on all sides. The captain of the *Niagara* had held back from fighting because he was angry with Perry, so the ship was relatively undamaged. Perry took it into action against the weakened British fleet and won the day. His message to headquarters proudly declared, "We have met the enemy and they are ours."

Perry's victory forced the British to evacuate Detroit, and the War shifted east to the Buffalo area. Fort Niagara fell to the British just before Christmas, when the gate was left open so the commander could return after helping his family decorate their Christmas tree. The British burned Buffalo, and Ft. Niagara remained in British hands until the end of the War.

In early 1814, Napoleon abdicated and was sent off to the island of Elba. The British now had more troops to spare for the American war and dispatched 14,000 of the Duke of Wellington's veterans to the New World, planning a three-pronged attack—on Lake Champlain, Chesapeake Bay and New Orleans. They tightened their already effective blockade on the American coast.

On August 18, 4500 men landed at Benedict, Maryland on the Chesapeake Bay. The militia were sent out to stop them at Bladensburg. President Madison and his cabinet rode out to watch the battle. They did not like what they saw. The experienced British soldiers attacked from both flanks, and the militia ran. The British then had to encounter U.S. sailors and marines, who proved tougher opponents, but after a four-hour battle the British broke through. They camped outside the Capitol and burned it the next day. Then they piled furniture in the living room of the White House and burned that too.

But Washington was not the strategic key; Baltimore was, because it was the port of the privateers which were preying on British shipping. On September 13, the British launched an all-night bombardment on Fort McHenry, which guarded the harbor. But the fort would not surrender, and the British left the next morning, leaving behind an American prisoner who had watched the battle from one of the ships and spent his time writing a poem to the tune of an old song. The prisoner's name was Francis Scott Key, and his poem is known as "The Star Spangled Banner." The British gave up this prong of the attack and went back to Nova Scotia.

In the northern prong, the Americans won the fierce Battle of Lundy's Lane near Niagara Falls on July 23. At the September 11 Battle of Lake Champlain, outnumbered U.S. ships were backed up against the shore with no room for maneuver. Eventually all the batteries on the engaged side except one were out of action. Their masts were gone so they could not use sail to change position. Suddenly a burst of cheering came from the American ships. The U.S. *Saratoga* was being turned with cables which Captain Macdonough had placed under her bow before the battle. Her fresh batteries were brought into action. The British were wiped out and that was the end of the northern prong.

As well as the U.S. Navy performed, the War could not have been won without the privateers: privately owned vessels armed with guns and a government license to commit piracy on enemy merchant ships. The U.S. privateers drove British shippers to distraction. The ships were fast and light and could be built in only 35 days. Within just two weeks, the ship *Argus* sent eight British ships up in flames. The *Scourge* and the *Rattlesnake* spent a summer in the North Sea, taking 22 ships and breaking up the Baltic trade. The *Yankee* alone captured $3 million worth of British shipping. One British captain was captured three times in a single voyage. The resulting shortage of goods in England angered the people, who brought pressure on the government and forced England to get out of the War.

Peace terms were already being negotiated when Andrew Jackson took 2500 volunteers, feeding them on roots and berries and bark, to New Orleans, where he arrived in December 1814, to face the British southern prong. On January 8, 1815, his mixed crew of sailors, Louisiana Creoles, Saint Domingue Blacks, and Dominic You's pirates stopped the well-ordered British troops, who marched right into his rifle fire. Said one British lieutenant, "I never saw men shoot so fast."

The peace treaty, known as the Peace of Ghent, was ratified by the Senate on February 15, 1815, and henceforth no one doubted that America would never be reconquered by Britain.

Though the War as a whole had been ineptly fought, the U.S. victory boosted optimism and nationalism throughout the country. Andrew Jackson became a major national hero. The Federalist Party, which had opposed the War, disappeared. In the 1816 Presidential elections, Madison's Secretary of State, James Monroe, won an overwhelming victory, garnering 183 electoral votes to his Federalist opponent's 34.

REVIEW QUESTIONS

1. What caused the outbreak of rebellion in St. Domingue? How did Toussaint become head of the rebellion? Summarize his character and abilities.
2. How did Toussaint become head of the government? What did he try to do for St. Domingue?
3. What were the results of Toussaint's leadership?
4. What were the two attitudes in the U.S. toward the French Revolution? What was Washington's goal?
5. What was the significance of the XYZ Affair?
6. Summarize the election of 1800.
7. What did Marshall rule in *Marbury v. Madison* and why did he make this decision?
8. How has the case been used to promote judicial supremacy? Why is this an incorrect reading of the decision?
9. Summarize the causes and results of the War with the Barbary pirates.
10. Why was Jefferson able to buy Louisiana?
11. Why did the War of 1812 break out with Great Britain?
12. Summarize the main land battles of the War.

13. Summarize the main naval battles of the War.
14. What were the results of the War.

PROJECTS

1. Prepare a map showing the main engagements of the War of 1812.
2. Another interesting Supreme Court case around this time was *McCulloch v. Maryland.* Do research and prepare a report on this case.
3. Do research and prepare a report on the life and career of John Marshall.

Chapter 12

Spain Is Driven From Latin America

SPANISH AMERICA ALSO felt the shock of the French Revolution. During the 17th century, the Spanish colonies were gradually becoming more independent. More of their wealth was remaining in the Colonies; the Creoles were achieving a greater measure of self-government. Given time and peace, they might have achieved full self-government within the Colonies while being united with the Mother Country in foreign policy.

But then the Bourbons came to power in Spain. As we have seen, Charles III believed that the Colonies existed to benefit the Mother Country. He eliminated local self-government, raised taxes, and tightly controlled trade. The Creoles were resentful and thought seriously for the first time of rebellion. They were encouraged by the circulation in the Colonies of liberal writings—Voltaire, Rousseau, Jefferson. The Creoles found their excuse to rebel when Napoleon deposed King Ferdinand VII and placed his brother Joseph on the throne of Spain in 1808. Throughout the New World colonies, the Creoles took over the governments in the name of King Ferdinand.

But the new governments had serious problems. Factions fought among themselves. The Indians did not support the revolts (except in Mexico) because they suspected that they might be even more oppressed without the royal officials to appeal to for help against the Creoles. Thus royal authority was restored in every country except Argentina by 1815 (the year of Napoleon's final defeat and the restoration of the Spanish monarchy). But powerful forces had been unleashed which could not easily be stifled, especially by a Bourbon leadership which did not command the moral strength to oppose revolutionary ideas. The Revolution was far from over.

Uruguay and Paraguay

The earliest hint that Latin America had not regained peace and stability came in the one area which had clung to independence, Argentina, where the revolutionary government had stayed in shaky control because of British support. The government in Buenos Aires passed back and forth among rival factions, each seeking to gain control over the masses of the ordinary people, whose lives had not changed for the better with the coming of the liberal republic. Scarcely able to keep order within Argentina itself, the government could not control the outlying provinces. Uruguay broke away from Buenos Aires and, after a number of bloody battles, declared its independence. Upper Peru (modern Bolivia) broke away, and when an army from Buenos Aires massacred innocent people, the Upper Peruvians pledged their allegiance to the Spanish viceroy in Peru.

Then there was Paraguay. Paraguay repudiated the authority of Buenos Aires and in 1811 declared its independence. The Creole aristocracy tried to organize a Congress, hold elections and write a constitution; but as they played with ideas they did not understand, José Gaspar Rodriguez de Francia, a Creole official and lawyer, quietly gained the support of the owners of the small estates, the farmers and the peasants. In the election of 1814, over 80 percent of the country voted for him, and an exhausted Congress made him "Supreme Dictator of the Republic" for five years. Francia soon persuaded Congress to appoint him "Perpetual Dictator" for life and then to adjourn. He adopted the title "El Supremo" and ruled Paraguay absolutely until his death in 1840 at the age of 74.

To establish himself in power, he had to eliminate his enemies. First was the Creole aristocracy; when he uncovered an attempt by some Creoles to overthrow him, he imprisoned and tortured the leaders, harassed their families and confiscated their property. The Church was next. Francia seized the lands of the religious orders, took away the Church's income, closed the schools and prohibited all contact with Rome. The army he turned into a personal private guard. He set up an espionage network so that it seemed that half of Paraguay was spying on the other half.

To prevent Paraguayans from realizing that life was better elsewhere, he outlawed newspapers and books, prohibited all mail and trade, and allowed no one to enter or leave the country without his rarely given personal permission. Foreigners caught in Paraguay when the trap closed suffocated in the country for years. Francia had absolute control over the economy, told the farmers what to plant and how much, terrorized Spaniards and continued slavery and the slave trade.

The vast jail that was Paraguay for 25 years is an extreme example of what can happen when traditional values and rightful authority are overthrown.

The Rebellion in Chile

Across the Andes from Argentina, the Spaniards had re-established their authority in Chile. But by the end of 1816, a 4000-man Army of the Andes was on the move under the leadership of Creole aristocrat and liberal, José de San Martín and a liberal aristocrat Bernardo O'Higgins, son of an Irishman in the Spanish colonial service and a Chilean mother. On the plains of Chacabuco, the Army of the Andes handed a stinging defeat to the royalist forces, though San Martín was so ill that only heavy doses of opium would keep him in the saddle. O'Higgins was made supreme dictator of Chile and established himself even more absolutely than the Bourbons because he believed it necessary to avoid anarchy. Said aristocrat O'Higgins of the lower classes, "If they will not become happy by their own efforts, they shall be made happy by force." He confiscated royalist property, set up an extensive educational system and established some control over the Church to eliminate the royalist clergy and to control public actions of the priests.

But many of the Creoles had not fought the revolution in order to establish a liberal absolutism worse than the Bourbons'. O'Higgins' increasing power led to a Creole revolt. He was forced to abdicate in January 1823, and Chile plunged into anarchy. Finally, after seven years of confusion, a traditionalist movement took power and restored order. The new government acknowledged the authority of the Church, protected property rights, balanced the budget, and restored stability. The Chileans were thus fortunate enough to end up with a government no worse and perhaps even better than that which they had back at the beginning of the century.

New Granada

San Martín turned his attention to Peru, where he was briefly successful. Peru declared its independence on July 28, 1821, and San Martín was named protector with supreme civil and military power. He proceeded to anger the colony's Spaniards by confiscating their property and to alienate the Liberals by establishing an authoritarian regime. With no support left, he was forced to resign on September 20, 1822. He went to Europe, where he remained until his death in 1850, disillusioned with the notion that order and stability could be maintained in an independent Latin America. Peru was reconquered by the Spaniards in 1823.

But liberal revolutionaries did not forget Peru. Waiting in the wings was the most determined of all: Simón Bolívar. Bolívar was a Creole aristocrat born in 1783 to one of the richest and most powerful families in Latin America. He was an atheist, an admirer of Voltaire and Rousseau; he proclaimed that liberty is the "only object worth the sacrifice of a man's life." But for whom exactly he wanted the liberty was another question, since he also declared that a "terrible power" was needed to achieve independence and that a centralized government was necessary because Latin America was not ready for democracy.

Before he turned to Peru, Bolívar's strategy called for the "liberation" of the province of New Granada, the northern viceroyalty of South America. On December 31, 1816, he landed an expedition at Barcelona in Venezuela and established a base in the great plains of the Orinoco River. He won a number of victories with the help of the *llaneros*, the cowboys of the Venezuelan plain. Then he took his men through rain-soaked plains, marching in water up to their waists, then over the cordillera at 13,000 feet to Colombia. Bolívar's forces won battle after battle. On August 10 they entered Bogotá; Colombia was independent. Bolívar returned to Venezuela and won the decisive battle there on June 24, 1821.

Then Bolívar turned toward the last province of New Granada, Ecuador. At the end of 1821, he marched south from Bogotá to Quito. Across his path lay the mountain province of Pasto—Catholic, traditionalist and royalist. Bolívar's men were badly defeated by the determined men of Pasto, but he had drawn most of the royalist attention to himself so that rebel General Sucre was able to surprise Quito in an attack from the north. On May 24, 1822, Bolívar won the decisive battle on the slopes of the snow-capped extinct volcano, Mt. Pichincha. He established Sucre as president, and the whole area of New Granada was now in Creole control.

As elsewhere in Latin America, the wars of independence brought much devastation to Ecuador, Colombia and Venezuela. The economy was destroyed, crime increased, the different factions of the victors quarrelled among themselves. Bolívar had hoped to see the three states united under one government, but the regime in Colombia was so corrupt that Venezuela and Ecuador both broke away.

The Creole aristocracy was in power in all three countries. The Indians had stayed out of the war on either side though they tended to favor the royalists because they regarded the King as their protector. Now the Liberals in power said that the Indians must have the same rights as everyone else—a theory which sounded fine but did not work. Under Spanish rule, the Indians had lived on communal farms where they worked under the supervision of the Spanish authorities. The Liberals broke up the farms and gave each Indian his own parcel of land. But the Indians did not like the idea of working by themselves on a lonely piece of land. The Liberals' good intentions produced only disruption, and the Indians ended up with less security than before.

Bolívar and Peru

Bolívar now turned his attention to Peru. On September 1, 1823, he entered Lima and was invested with supreme military and political authority. Authority was a cheap commodity—at that moment Peru had a congress, two presidents, and a dictator. When Bolívar fell ill in January 1824 and was forced to rest in a small village, he commented that he saw "discord, misery, discontent and egoism . . . Peru no longer existed." But Bolívar would not draw the conclusion that because rebellion had made Peru the "chamber of horrors" which he said it was, the rebellion should cease. He began rebuilding his army. Bolívar brought 9000 troops to the plateau of Junín on August 6, 1824, where he defeated the royalist force in a battle of swords and lances and horses, not a single shot being fired. The last Royalist stronghold capitulated on January 23, 1826.

The usual pattern of independence was followed. The economy fell into chaos; the Creole aristocracy established control, while the life of the masses of the people remained unchanged; the Indians suffered because they were plundered by both sides. Again Bolívar wanted to give the Indians their own land. But to give the Indians land without money, equipment and protection was to invite them first to become indebted to more powerful landowners, then to surrender their land in payment, and finally to end up in serfdom.

Meanwhile Upper Peru held out under Casimiro Olañeta, a traditionalist general, who was determined to fight to the bitter end for King and Religion against Liberalism. But when Bolívar's General Sucre invaded Upper Peru, the Creoles deserted Olañeta because they wanted to be on the winning side. Cornered and isolated, Olañeta—one of the few men in the whole story of Latin American independence who fought for the genuine good of the people and high moral values—was mortally wounded at the Battle of Tumusla on April 1, 1814 and his forces defeated.

The government, dominated as usual by Creoles, named their country Bolivia, after Bolívar. Sucre was established as first president but was unable to bring order out of the post-rebellion chaos. In April 1818 he was wounded by mutinous elements and had to resign.

In Peru, Bolívar had himself named president for life, but resentment built against his growing power. With everyone turning against him, he returned to Bogotá, but did not find peace even there. He barely escaped assassination; Colombia was disintegrating; Venezuela villified Bolívar as a traitor and declared him an outlaw.

As he lay dying of tuberculosis in 1830, Bolívar summed up the revolts he had done so much to carry through: "I am ashamed to admit it, but independence is the *only* benefit we have gained, at the cost of everything else. . . . America is ungovernable. Those who serve the revolution plough the sea. The only thing to do in America is to emigrate."

Mexico's Agony

In Mexico the early rebellions had come from the lower classes, the only place in Latin America where this was true. Miguel Hidalgo, a liberal Creole priest working among the rural poor, had led a peasant army of 60,000 in 1810. But the atrocities committed by his army alienated potential supporters, and his undisciplined followers were of little use against trained troops. Hidalgo's army was routed in January 1811, and he was captured and executed. The leadership of the revolution passed to José Morelos, a mestizo (mixed Spanish and Indian) priest who had trained a small, disciplined army. But he could gain no support among the Creoles; the royalists defeated him, and he was captured in 1815, found guilty of treason and shot.

The royalists re-established control but with a liberal government. It suppressed monastic and hospital religious orders, ordered the arrest and confiscation of the property of known anti-liberals, including the Bishop of Puebla and other bishops, abolished the military courts, and abolished the *repartimientos* (the large estates on which the Indians worked for Creole owners). The Creoles believed that the royalist government no longer safeguarded their interests and began to support independence. Their leader was the Creole Agustín de Iturbide, a Catholic, landowner and army officer. On February 24, 1821, Iturbide published the *Plan de Iguala*, in which he offered something for everyone: a constitutional monarchy, protection for the Church, and citizenship and equality for all citizens. His flag was a tricolor—white for religion, green for independence and red for the union of Europeans and Indians. The only supporters the viceroy had were the liberal Freemasons and a handful of Spanish soldiers. On his 38th birthday, September 27, 1821, Iturbide led his army into Mexico City. Thus ended three centuries, one month and two weeks of Spanish rule of Mexico. The tricolor was hoisted from Louisiana to San Francisco, from the mountains of Guatemala through the Great Plains and high sierras of North America. In his proclamation, Iturbide announced: "Mexicans, now you have liberty and independence. It is for you to find happiness."

They did not find very much. Iturbide set up a military dictatorship; he spent his days designing chivalric orders and inventing titles for his court. As the treasury lay bare and anarchy threatened, he planned his royal coronation as Emperor Agustín I.

His main prop was the army. But he could not pay the army. So under the leadership of the Mexican commander in Veracruz, Antonio Lopez de Santa Anna, and the royalist general José Antonio Echavarri, a force marched on Mexico City. Emperor Agustín I was forced to abdicate on March 19, 1823, having held power only a little over a year. He went to Italy, but returned a year later. Within two days of setting foot on Mexican soil, he was captured and shot.

The new government, a liberal republic, repeated the dreary story of the republics to the south. The leaders fought among themselves; the Creoles held control; the economy suffered; the communal lands of the Indians fell into the hands of the wealthy. (When one Indian was asked whom he wanted to represent him in the new Congress, he replied "the Holy Spirit.") Control of the missions which Father Serra and others had labored so hard to build was taken from the Franciscans; the missions fell into disuse and much of the good that had been done for the Indians by the brown-robed priests was lost.

John Quincy Adams and American Foreign Policy

While Hispanic America tore itself apart, its neighbor to the north closely followed events. President Monroe and his Secretary of State, John Quincy Adams, spent much of their time dealing with things Spanish.

The first controversy was over Florida. Everyone agreed that Spain owned east Florida, the peninsula, but the two countries fought over west Florida, the panhandle. Andrew Jackson had an easy solution. He invaded Florida on the excuse that the Seminole Indians were stirring up trouble and put the U.S. in possession of the entire territory. Faced with this seizure, Spain panicked that the next target of the Americans would be the Texas territory. So the Spanish ambassador entered into negotiations, lasting about six months. Adams was a hard bargainer. Probably his greatest dream was to see the U.S. in total possession of North America. He forced concession after concession out of the Spanish, giving in only over Texas. Finally the Transcontinental Treaty was ratified on February 22, 1819. The U.S. now owned all of Florida, and the previously disputed boundaries of the Louisiana territory followed the Sabine River, the Red River, the Arkansas River and the 42nd north latitude west to the Pacific Ocean. The treaty was the biggest step taken since the Louisiana Purchase itself to make the U.S. master of the continent.

Having secured the ratification of the treaty by Spain, Monroe and Adams could then turn their full attention to South America without fear that they would imperil the treaty negotiations. Both Monroe and Adams were pro-revolt and anti-Spain, a position understandable in Monroe, who was a protege of Jefferson, but more difficult to understand in the son of John Adams, who had stood virtually alone among U.S. leaders in opposing the French Revolution. Perhaps Adams saw the Latin American countries as reflections of the U.S. in asserting a tradition of self-government against a tyrannical monarch, a false view which has been commonly held by Americans ever since.

Guided by Adams, the Monroe government extended diplomatic recognition to the new republics—the first government outside Latin America itself to do so—thus boosting the ambitions of the rebels. Adams and Monroe feared intervention by traditionalist European powers on behalf of Spain. So they worked together to formulate the policy statement known as the **Monroe Doctrine**, though it is in fact as much Adams' as Monroe's.

Delivered to Congress on December 2, 1823, the Monroe Doctrine included three important statements: 1) "The American continents . . .

are henceforth not to be considered as subjects for future colonization by any European power." 2) The U.S. for its part would not become involved in European wars. 3) Any attempt by any European power to re-establish Spain in control in Latin America would be regarded "as the manifestation of an unfriendly disposition towards the United States." This last principle was known as the **Hands-Off Policy**.

What the U.S. would have done if a European nation had challenged the Monroe Doctrine is unknown. But no one did challenge it. Though the traditionalist powers of Europe were no doubt more afraid of Great Britain (which supported the rebels in order to gain commercial advantages) than of the U.S., the U.S. role in supporting the Latin American revolutions played a real part in the success of those revolutions by encouraging their leaders and supporting them in their belief that a liberal republic was the best possible government, in spite of their immediate practical experience to the contrary.

The Experience of Brazil

When a French army approached Lisbon, Portugal near the end of November 1807, the royal family fled to their colony, Brazil. The Prince Regent, Dom Joao, arrived in Rio de Janeiro in March 1808 and set up his government there. Brazil prospered by having the royal court in residence; Dom Joao liked Rio so much that even after Napoleon's defeat, he did not want to return to Portugal. So he proclaimed the United Kingdom of Portugal and Brazil with Brazil equal in status to the Mother Country.

But after a liberal revolt in Portugal in 1820, Dom Joao was forced to return, leaving his son Dom Pedro, 24 years old, as regent. The new liberal government in Portugal, resentful of Brazil's status, passed restrictive laws against the South American country and ordered Dom Pedro to return to Portugal. Dom Pedro absolutely refused. Finally on September 7, 1822, while on a journey to Sao Paolo to get support, Dom Pedro was overtaken near a stream called the Ipiranga by a messenger from Rio with the latest Portuguese demands. Dom Pedro threw the dispatches to the ground and cried, "The hour has come! Independence or death! We have separated from Portugal!" This is known to Brazilians as the "Cry of Ipiranga." September 7 is their independence day. Crowned Dom Pedro I, Emperor of Brazil, the new ruler managed, with very little bloodshed, to defeat the Portuguese forces and establish his authority.

Unfortunately, power went to his head, and Pedro I became more high-handed as time went on. Finally, a revolt forced him to abdicate in favor of his five-year-old son Dom Pedro II. For ten years a regent ruled in the name of the little boy, while Brazil suffered violence and disorder. When Pedro II officially took control at the age of 15, the nation heaved a collective sigh of relief; it was in desperate need of authority.

Pedro was highly intelligent, possessing a prodigious memory and a logical mind. He ruled for 49 years in a spirit of compromise and conciliation. He was no believer in democracy as a cure-all, but neither did he want all power for himself, sharing it with the landed and professional classes. Brazil had an interlude of peace and progress remarkable on the South American continent, and the credit goes to the common sense of the Brazilians in keeping a member of the royal family in authority and in the wisdom of Pedro II in restraining the natural human desire for power.

The Legacy of Independence

By 1830, all of Latin America—save the islands of Cuba and Puerto Rico—was independent. What had this independence brought? It had first brought suffering and bloodshed, as wars and revolutions always do. Throughout Spain's proud history, the tendency toward violence as a solution to problems had usually been kept in check by religion and tradition, to be called upon only in just causes. But in Latin America the liberal attacks on authority and the Church meant that this tendency would too often be indulged simply as a means of obtaining wealth and power for one or another faction. The armies left over from the wars of independence would contribute to the violence and instability of the country.

The Indians would be increasingly isolated because of impractical schemes to give them economic independence. The Negro slaves were usually better off; steps would be taken toward freeing them, though total emancipation would not come until the 1850's.

The basic governmental structure was unchanged. Whereas before, Spaniards held the reins of power, now the Creole aristocracy held power, and they usually exercised it less wisely and with less restraint than had the Spaniards. Governmental bureaucracies would grow rapidly, as whatever faction held power proceeded to distribute offices to friends and relatives. Government thus became extremely costly, leading to inflation and economic decline, as well as to increasing the temptation to factions out of power to try to gain control.

Thus, Latin America can hardly be said to have gained by independence, as Bolívar finally realized when it was too late.

REVIEW QUESTIONS

1. Summarize the rule of Francia in Paraguay.
2. Who was San Martín? How did he bring independence to Chile? What kind of government did O'Higgins establish? What was the ultimate result for Chile of independence?
3. What finally happened to San Martín?
4. Summarize the philosophy of Simón Bolívar.
5. How did Venezuela, Colombia and Ecuador become independent? What were the results of independence?
6. How did Peru become independent? What were the results of independence?
7. Who was Olañeta? How did he resist revolution? Why did he fail?
8. What did Bolívar conclude about independence?
9. How did Iturbide bring independence to Mexico? What kind of government did he establish? Why was he overthrown? What kind of government took over?
10. What were the terms and significance of the Transcontinental Treaty?
11. List the three main provisions of the Monroe Doctrine.
12. Summarize the role the U.S. played in Latin American independence.
13. Summarize the legacy of independence.

PROJECTS

1. Prepare a map of Latin America, locating events from this chapter.
2. Choose a South American country, and prepare a report on its history since independence.
3. Choose a South American country, and prepare a presentation using audio-visual aids on that country's culture.

Chapter 13

Manifest Destiny

THE 25 YEARS FROM 1825-1850 are a watershed in American history. Before this time the new nation was establishing itself on the world scene, showing by the War of 1812 that it meant to be taken seriously. From 1825-1850, the United States was expanding throughout the North American continent with a spirit of optimism, courage and individualism.

"Old Hickory" in the White House

By the time of the 1824 election, it had become almost traditional in America for the Secretary of State to succeed to the presidency. Hence John Quincy Adams announced his candidacy for the office he believed rightfully his. But America had a surplus of talented, ambitious men, and Adams found himself opposed by Kentucky Senator Henry Clay, by the War of 1812 hero Andrew Jackson and by Congressman William Crawford. When the electoral votes were counted, Jackson had 99, Adams 84, Crawford 41, and Clay 37. With no candidate having a majority, the House of Representatives had to choose from among the three leading candidates. Since he was eliminated from the race, Clay advised his friends to vote for Adams. As a result, Adams—though he had received a minority of both popular and electoral votes—became President. When Adams then appointed Clay Secretary of State, Jackson partisans charged collusion. Though there was never conclusive evidence that Adams had made a deal with Clay, Adams was not a popular President. The Republican Party split into two groups: the Whigs, led by Adams and Clay, and the Democrats, led by Jackson.

Adams' presidency was relatively uneventful, but the 1828 election campaign was one of the liveliest in American history. Jackson's friends screamed "corrupt bargain" at the Adams forces. Adams supporters attacked the personal morality of Jackson and his wife Rachel, on the grounds that Mrs. Jackson had been married before and divorced (at a time when divorce was far from common in America) and that she and Jackson had apparently been invalidly married for two years, having had to undergo a second marriage ceremony. Jackson was furious at the aspersions on Rachel's virtue and blamed the Adams partisans for driving his wife to her death in early 1829.

Rachel's death devastated Jackson, but he had won the presidency. Though from an aristocratic background and a large landowner, Jackson was fundamentally a frontiersman who would just as soon fight as not. He had a bullet in his arm and another resting next to his heart, the souvenirs of two brawls. His followers poured into Washington for the inauguration, sleeping on floors and pool tables. They begged Jackson to put them on the government payroll. Jackson did the best he could, firing a number of government employees for no other reason than that they had supported Adams and replacing them with his friends. Putting one's supporters into government jobs is called the Spoils System, and Jackson introduced it on a large scale into the federal government.

As a frontiersman, Jackson believed that white settlers had the right to seize Indian lands. After the military campaigns of 1813 and 1814 against the Cherokees and Creeks, they had been pushed into Georgia, and the Choctaws and Chickasaws into Mississippi and Alabama. Solemn treaties had been signed guaranteeing the Indians these lands if the Indians in turn would adopt white men's ways. The Indians had kept their promises. The Cherokees adapted especially well to civilization; they built houses and roads, manufactured cloth, kept herds, and had just laws and few crimes. But by settling down peacefully, they frightened the whites, who saw good lands forever denied to them. So the state governments of Georgia, Mississippi and Alabama annexed Indian lands and ordered the Indians to go to the Oklahoma territory. Some of them did leave, but the Cherokees refused. They hired a lawyer to take the case to the Supreme Court, asking for an injunction against Georgia on the grounds that the States had no right to break a federal treaty. The Supreme Court denied the injunction, and Jackson supported the States. The controversy dragged on until 1835, when the Cherokees surrendered all their lands east of the Mississippi to the U.S. and went wearily off to Oklahoma.

The next controversy of Jackson's administration was known as the **Nullification Controversy** and involved tariffs. South Carolina opposed high tariffs, while Jackson supported them to make imported goods more expensive than goods made in America. Tariffs were a lively controversy throughout much of American history, but they had little lasting historical importance. But on this particular issue, the tariff was the occasion for the airing of a matter of much larger significance.

Led by Vice President John C. Calhoun, South Carolina announced its intention to disobey the federal laws mandating protective tariffs and threatened to secede. Jackson asked Congress for authority to use military force to collect the tariffs and announced that if Congress did not act, he would give himself the authority. Faced with Jackson's intransigence and without the support of any other state, South Carolina gave in, obeyed the tariff laws and stayed in the Union. But for the first time, the word secession had come into the American vocabulary and it could not quite be forgotten.

Jackson also took on the U.S. Bank. By Jackson's time the Bank virtually ruled the commerce, industry and agriculture of the nation through its power to control the amount of money in circulation. Its president was Nicholas Biddle, probably the single most powerful man in the country. By telling the various Bank branches how much they could lend, he could help or hinder business in almost any locality in the country.

Jackson called upon Congress to abolish the Bank. Biddle responded by adopting a generous loan policy toward key Congressmen. Daniel Webster of Massachusetts received a $22,000 loan, gave a speech in support of the Bank and received another $10,000. Jackson then issued instructions to cease depositing U.S. funds in the Bank, announcing: "Sooner than live in a country where such a power prevails, I would seek asylum in the wilds of Arabia." Biddle replied that Jackson might "as well send at once and engage [his] lodgings," and manipulated credit and called in loans to cause financial distress throughout the country, blaming it all on Jackson. When people came to Jackson asking him to do something about the financial crisis, Jackson replied, "Go to Nicholas Biddle." Soon that became a theme song of the Anti-Bank faction. Eventually the people caught on to what Biddle was doing. On April 4, 1833, Congress voted not to recharter the Bank, and Nicholas Biddle was out of a job.

Through all of these controversies, Jackson had shown what a strong President could do.

The Birth of the Texas Republic

Jackson had a good friend from his fighting days named Sam Houston, who was governor of Jackson's home state, Tennessee. Like his friend, Houston had lived a stormy life, but in 1829, at the age of 35, he decided to settle down. He married 18-year-old Eliza Allen, and the newlyweds seemed blissfully happy. But just 48 hours after the wedding, Eliza told her friend that she wished Houston were dead; and twelve weeks later, Houston resigned as governor, sent his blonde bride home to grow up, and under an assumed name went off to live with the Cherokees in Oklahoma. Neither Sam nor Eliza would talk, but eventually it was discovered that Houston, subject to towering rages, accused his wife of infidelity. Houston later apologized and begged her to come back. But her honor and the honor of her family would not permit it. She remained at home, and Houston left for Oklahoma. If Mrs. Houston had been a trifle more forgiving, the history of the expansion of the United States might have been different.

For Houston did not remain in Oklahoma. He went to Washington to visit his friend the President and received from him a secret commission to check out Texas. On December 2, 1832, Houston crossed into the Texas territory, held by Mexico.

Americans had been settling in Mexican territory for years. Though many were peaceful farmers, others considered the possibility that they could seize Texas and either become independent or join the U.S. When Houston returned from his mission, he enthusiastically wrote Jackson that "nineteen/twentieths of the population of the province" desired "the acquisition of Texas by the United States." Though this was a typical Houston exaggeration, rebellious sentiment was strong enough to persuade Houston to purchase a uniform with general's stars on it and to begin recruiting volunteers.

General Santa Anna, who had seized control of the Mexican government in 1830, was becoming increasingly dictatorial. When he ordered the Mexican constitution abolished, a convention of Americans in Texas at the end of 1835 declared provisional independence, with Houston as commander-in-chief of the scattered bands rather optimistically known as the Armies of the Texas Republic. By early 1836, Santa Anna was north of the Rio Grande River with 7000 troops. Houston ordered his men to retreat, believing that they were not ready to take on such an imposing force. The leaders of some of the bands, overconfident, disobeyed. One group withdrew into a small fortress called the Alamo, outside San Antonio, which the Mexicans then besieged. Just before dawn on Sunday, March 6, 1836, the 188 defenders heard the bugles of the besieging Mexican army. Three Mexican columns advanced on the former mission, which had withstood two weeks of bombardment. Troops poured through the breach in the northwest wall; the defenders fell back to the two-storied convent building. By dusk all the Texan soldiers were dead. The only survivors were Mrs. Dickinson, whose husband had been killed, her 15-month-old baby Angelina and commander Travis' Negro servant Joe.

It was a victory for the Mexicans, but it turned into a defeat. The Americans were incensed by the wanton slaughter of the men and screamed for revenge. Six weeks later, Santa Anna's army faced Houston's 800 men on the plain of San Jacinto. Just before the battle, Houston told his men: "Victory is certain. Remember the Alamo!" Santa Anna had not believed that Houston would attack, so when the battle broke, he was in his carpeted tent enjoying a siesta. The Mexicans were routed. Houston's men went wild, clubbing, knifing, shooting every Mexican they could find. The next day, a party rounded up Mexican stragglers. One dejected man was found sitting on a stump near a ruined bridge. When he was brought back to camp, the Mexican prisoners shouted "El Presidente!" It was none other than Santa Anna himself. He bowed to Houston and said, "That man may consider himself born to no common destiny who has conquered the Napoleon of the West; and it now remains for him to be generous to the vanquished." Houston replied: "You should have remembered that at the Alamo." But much to the dismay of his troops, Houston did not order the execution of the "Napoleon of the West." After negotiating a withdrawal of all Mexican troops from Texas territory, he released Santa Anna.

On October 22, 1836, in a big barn at a table covered with a blanket, Houston took the oath of office as the first president of the Republic of Texas, and the Lone Star flag replaced the Mexican tricolor. The Republic then petitioned the U.S. government to be admitted to the Union. But because Texas had legalized slavery, the annexation question became entangled with the slavery issue, which was heating up at this time. Annexation was not finally approved until 1845. In the meantime, Houston proved to be an excellent president, bringing order out of chaos and guaranteeing that Texas would never slip back under Mexican rule.

The U.S. Looks West

The next ten years were marked by a growing feeling that the United

States should include California and New Mexico, the names given to all the territory held by Mexico north of the Rio Grande, and the Oregon Territory, held jointly by the U.S. and Great Britain under the terms of a treaty negotiated by John Quincy Adams as Secretary of State. The editor of *The United States Magazine and Democratic Review* coined the term **"Manifest Destiny,"** calling for the "fulfillment of our manifest destiny to overspread the continent allotted by Providence for the free development of our yearly multiplying millions." Americans picked up the term, firmly believing that it was God's will that the U.S. control the North American continent from Atlantic to Pacific. In gradually increasing numbers, people began moving into the California and Oregon Territories.

The Presidents during this time encouraged westward movement: Martin Van Buren (1837-1841), the aristocratic New Yorker who incongruously was Jackson's hand-picked successor; William Henry Harrison (1841), whose reputation mainly rested on his victories in the Indian wars (most notably that at Tippecanoe, which, combined with his vice-presidential candidate's name, led to the slogan, "Tippecanoe and Tyler too"); John Tyler (1841-1845), who became President upon Harrison's death of pneumonia, after only a month in office, probably brought on by the miserable weather in which he gave his hour-long inaugural address. Tyler's most important act was to sign the annexation bill making Texas part of the United States.

In 1844, the Democrats nominated James K. Polk. He ran on an expansionist platform and the slogan **"54-40 or Fight."** That strange combination of numbers referred to a latitude line in Canada. Polk and the expansionists declared that America should own the Oregon territory up to the latitude line of 54°40', without sharing it with anyone.

Expansionist fever was at its height, for a number of reasons: 1) the desire of the slave states to legalize slavery in the empty lands and to regain some of the power they were losing in Congress because of the more rapid population growth in the North; 2) the desire of land speculators to get rich selling the uninhabited lands; 3) the desire of industrialists for new markets; 4) the desire for adventure and excitement; 5) the desire by quite ordinary people for cheap land and the chance to make a new start in life; 6) the desire for security by eliminating foreign powers from U.S. borders; 7) and of course Manifest Destiny; the U.S. must spread its system of government across the Continent because that was its God-given destiny.

Polk easily defeated his anti-expansionist opponent Henry Clay, but having won the election, Polk was not eager for war with Britain, especially since he also faced the threat of war with Mexico over the annexation of Texas. So in his own mind he was willing to compromise at the boundary line of 49 degrees, the latitude line marking the rest of the U.S.-Canada border. But he could not simply go to the British ambassador and present the compromise—which the British were willing to accept because there were already six or seven thousand Americans in the Oregon territory who had come there along the Oregon Trail. Polk had aroused the people over 54°40'; if he initiated the compromise, their anger would turn away from the British and toward James K. Polk. Therefore he had to persuade Congress to make the suggestion. Polk decided that the way to achieve this goal was to convince Congress that war with Mexico was imminent. Congress, not wanting to fight two wars at once, would then suggest the compromise.

Polk did not really want war with Mexico either, but he wanted the California and New Mexico territories—what would become the states of California, Nevada, Utah, Arizona, New Mexico, Wyoming and Colorado. Remembering Andrew Jackson's successful scheme of marching into Florida to persuade Mexico to surrender territory elsewhere, Polk sent General Zachary Taylor and his troops marching into a 120-mile wide strip between the Rio Grande and Nueces Rivers, then in dispute between the U.S. and Mexico. Taylor was known as "Old Rough and Ready," but his army was far more rough than ready.

Half of Polk's plan succeeded and half failed. Congress was sufficiently frightened of war with Mexico to propose a compromise on the Canadian boundary. Polk pretended to think this cowardly, but on June 15, 1846, the treaty with England was signed, giving Oregon to the U.S. But in the meantime, Mexico had actually gone to war with the United States.

California and New Mexico

Polk had committed the first aggressive act by sending armed troops into Mexican territory, but the first shots were fired by Mexican cavalry at 60 American dragoons on April 25. The war was fought on three fronts: California, New Mexico and Mexico itself.

While still hoping to seize California without war, Polk had planned to encourage a native rebellion and then move in the U.S. Army on the grounds that Mexico could not keep order. While the idea was being secretly discussed, a young American army officer in California, Captain John Fremont, had ideas of his own. He had been in California at Sutter's Fort—built by an independent Swiss on the present site of Sacramento—since December 9, 1845, after crossing the Great Salt Desert. This crossing had won him fame, but he wanted power too; and when he heard that the U.S. was on the verge of war with Mexico, he decided that his moment had come.

His plan was to provoke the Mexican commandante in northern California, Señor Castro, to attack some Americans. Then Fremont could ride to the rescue. So Fremont sent a dozen marauders to raid Castro's horse herd. Castro, who also knew about hostilities between the U.S. and Mexico, thought this raid the prelude to full-scale attack. He therefore sent out an order mobilizing troops. Immediately (June 14, 1846), Fremont's men seized the tiny hamlet of Sonoma and announced the formation of the California Republic. Fremont also seized Sutter's Fort from the peaceful Swiss. With the help of mountain man, Kit Carson, he captured a few Mexicans, whom he ordered shot.

Fremont was a bit frightened that his unauthorized revolt might cause him trouble, but to his relief Commodore Robert Stockton, now in command of the U.S. Fleet in California, commissioned him a major and mustered his men into the Navy. On July 29, Stockton and Fremont issued a proclamation accusing Castro of lawless violence and the Mexican army of pillage and murder (neither charge was true), and on August 14, they occupied Los Angeles.

America was not prepared to fight a full-scale war. General Winfield Scott, the most talented general in the Army, urged Polk to allow him to train and equip an army. But Polk wanted quick victories so he left Taylor in command—even though Old Rough and Ready's army was undisciplined and untrained—and ordered Stephen Kearney to occupy New Mexico.

From Bent's Fort in Colorado, Kearney marched his hastily recruited volunteers through the intense heat of the Southwest. (One day their thermometer registered 120°.) Water was in short supply and the dry winds made the men even thirstier, but they slogged through the sand, enthusiastic to conquer the "Greasers," as they contemptuously called the Mexicans.

On August 18, they reached Santa Fe, a small, poor town, but nonetheless the capital of New Mexico and older than any U.S. settlement. Kearney marched into the central plaza. With a few Indians and Mexicans looking on, the tricolor was lowered and the U.S. flag raised. For the first time in history, U.S. troops had conquered a foreign capital, and they did it without firing a shot.

Kearney and his battalion continued on to California, where he was authorized to take command of all troops there and set up a government. Stockton and Fremont had enjoyed their game of running a government and refused to cooperate with Kearney. Not until February 1847 did Kearney have things under his control. But Kearney kept order, and Polk had California.

To the Halls of Montezuma

But none of this territory could be retained if Mexico could not be defeated. American newspapers stirred up hatred against the Mexicans, criticizing them as dirty, uncivilized (though their territory had been civilized longer than the United States) and ignorant. The public called for a high "butcher's bill" of dead Mexicans. Volunteers responded by pouring into the recruiting centers, where they were treated to lectures attacking the Mexicans, primarily their Catholic religion. (A number of Irish, French and Polish American Catholics joined the Mexican Army as the St. Patrick's Battalion. They fought well, but when their unit was defeated, the U.S. Army proceeded to execute them all.) But in spite of the troops' enthusiasm, they remained untrained, for Taylor's army was in confusion. Polk tried espionage. He negotiated an agreement with Santa Anna, then in exile in Cuba, to return to Mexico with U.S. help, seize the government and negotiate a treaty. All worked well except for the last step. Instead of negotiating, Santa Anna turned his army against the U.S.

At last Polk was forced to approve Scott's plans for taking the port of Veracruz and then moving on to Mexico City. Polk did not especially enjoy giving Scott command since he knew a Scott victory would make him a powerful political rival, but he also knew that a long drawn-out war could finish his political career. Scott took half of Taylor's troops and marched toward Veracruz. Taylor also had political ambitions, so he deliberately disobeyed orders, planning to take his abbreviated army to Mexico City himself. He got as far as the mountains near Buena Vista when Santa Anna attacked. The Americans, in a good defensive position, managed to hold off the Mexican army for two days at the cost of many lives. On the third day Santa Anna finally retreated, and Taylor got the credit—which should have gone to the individual sol-

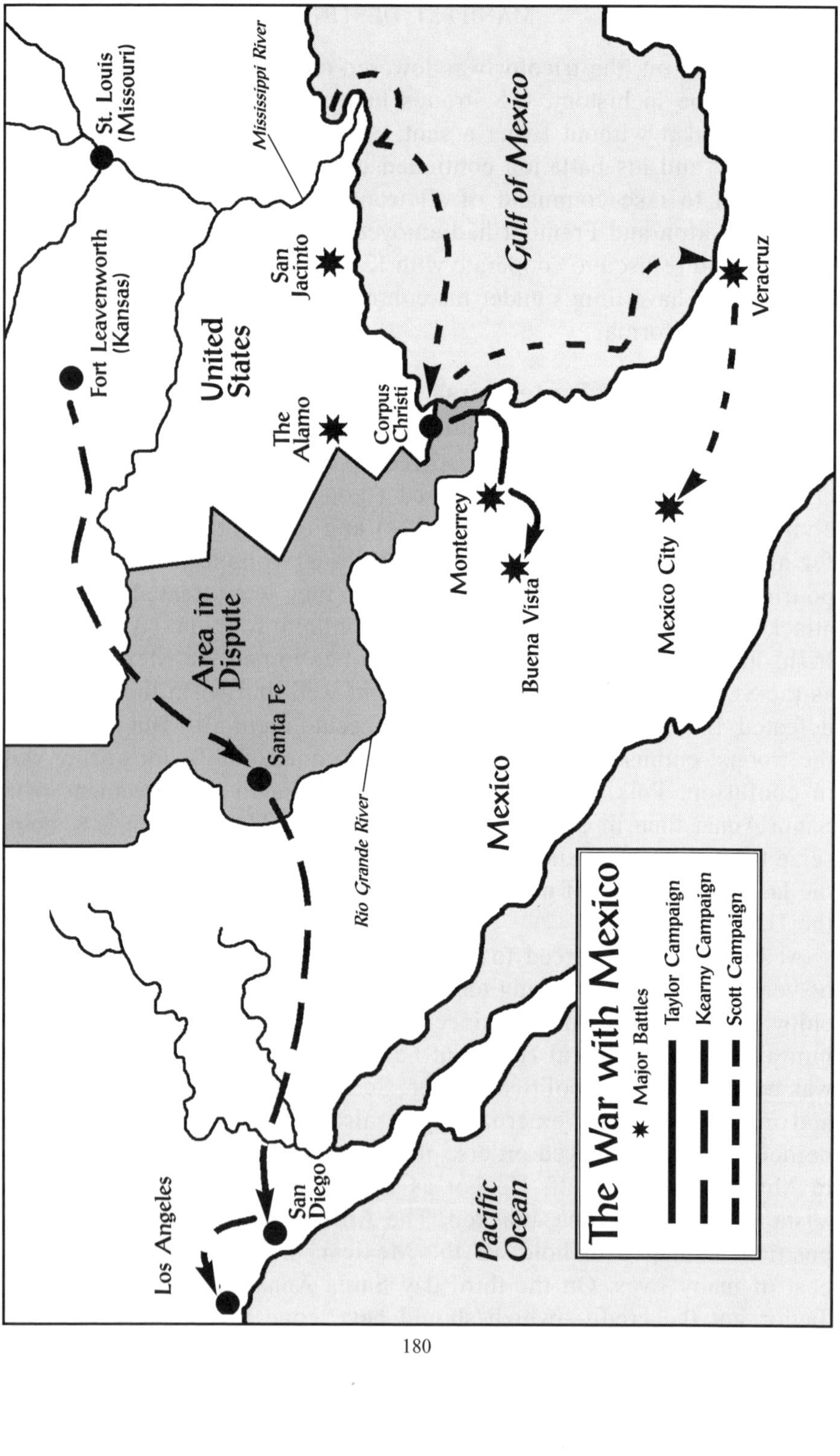
The War with Mexico
Major Battles
Taylor Campaign
Kearny Campaign
Scott Campaign
St. Louis (Missouri)
Mississippi River
Fort Leavenworth (Kansas)
United States
San Jacinto
Gulf of Mexico
Veracruz
The Alamo
Corpus Christi
Area in Dispute
Santa Fe
Monterrey
Buena Vista
Mexico City
Mexico
Rio Grande River
Los Angeles
San Diego
Pacific Ocean

diers—for a great victory. But his army had been shot to pieces, and he had to give up the chance for any more heroics.

Scott never had half the troops or supplies he needed, but he kept the Army moving, and incidentally, gave his subordinate officers—Ulysses Grant and Robert E. Lee, among others—invaluable training. On March 29, 1847, Veracruz surrendered after the fortress was battered by guns sited by Lee. On August 7, Scott took his army over the mountains to Mexico's great central plateau, following Cortes' route of conquest. On August 19 and 20, he won two bloody battles, which led him to the gates of Mexico City. The Mexican men were courageous and immovable fighters—a far cry from the lazy Greasers the Americans had expected—but the Mexican generals were more cowardly than not and constantly betrayed the courage of their men.

On September 13, at the Battle of Chapultapec, two divisions stormed the hill on which Mexico City's key fortress was located. The men clawed their way up an almost vertical slope, climbed the palace walls and fought a savage bayonet action. Young cadets from the military academy tenaciously defended their city, but were at last driven off. On the 14th, the American flag was raised in the Plaza de Armas, and the War was over.

Zion in the Desert

While the war was going on, hundreds of Americans were journeying westward to Oregon and California. The first significant migration of settlers to Oregon took place in 1843, followed by a bigger movement in 1845; but the migration of 1846 was decisive, making it clear that Americans intended to fill up the West. Despite the hazards of the journey, individuals headed for what they were sure would be a better life in the West, as Americans had done from the earliest days of the nation. They underwent many hardships and sufferings, but kept their optimism and their hope.

One especially hopeful group was the Church of Jesus Christ of Latter Day Saints, more popularly known as **Latter Day Saints** or **Mormons**. Their church had been founded by Joseph Smith (1805-1844), who claimed to have seen visions of angels who gave him revelations on golden plates, which afterwards disappeared. He wrote of the revelations in the *Book of Mormon*, published in 1830, and gained many followers. Leading his settlers to a point of land north of Quincy, Illinois, which they named Nauvoo (Beautiful Place), the Saints, as they

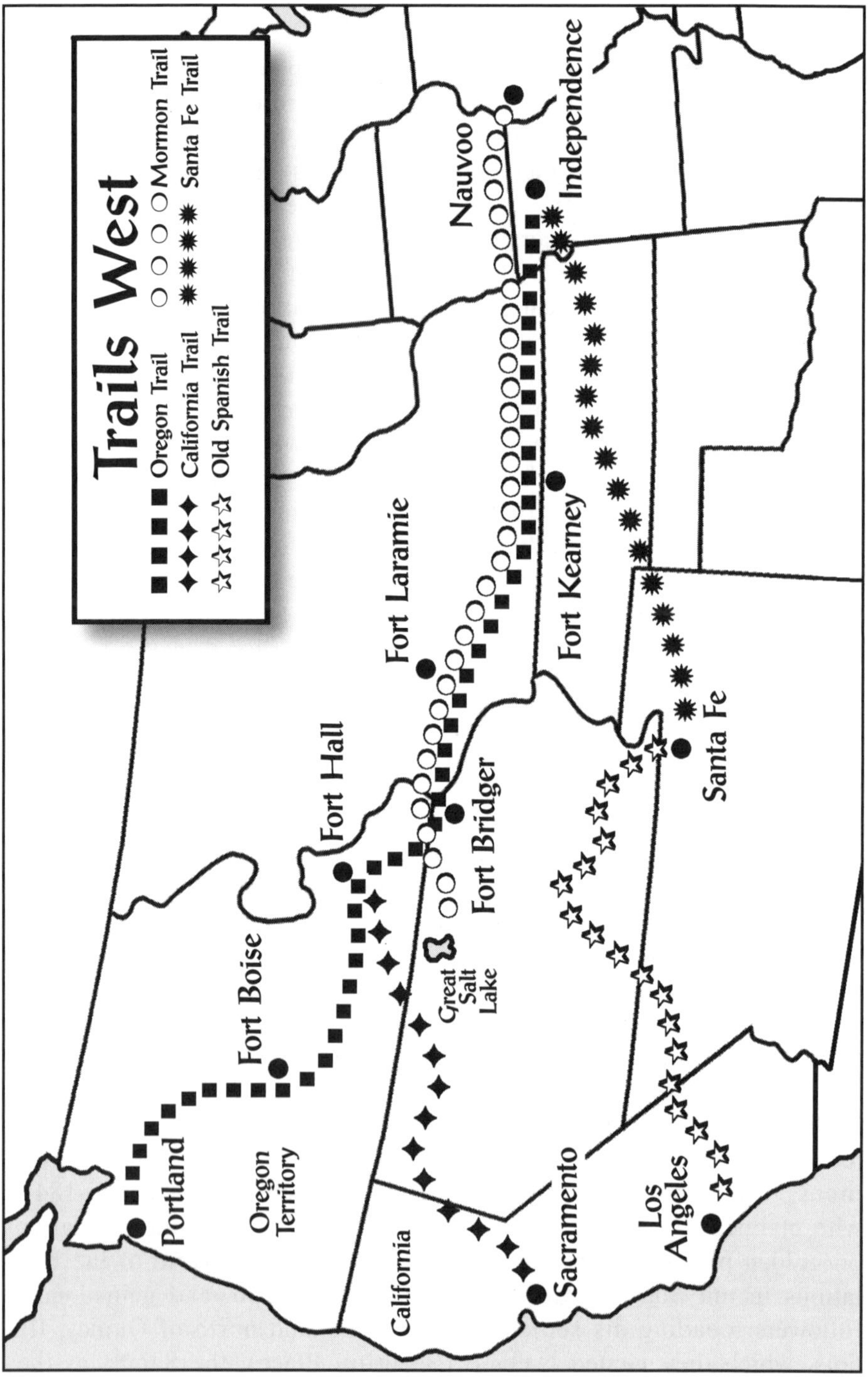
Trails West
Oregon Trail
California Trail
Old Spanish Trail
Mormon Trail
Santa Fe Trail
Portland
Oregon Territory
Fort Boise
Fort Hall
Fort Laramie
Fort Bridger
Great Salt Lake
Nauvoo
Independence
Fort Kearney
Santa Fe
California
Sacramento
Los Angeles

called themselves, came into conflict with the local residents. Smith organized a military group called the Nauvoo Legion and asked President Polk for permission to conquer the West. When an opposing newspaper criticized the Mormons, Smith had its press pounded to pieces in the street. But the final blow was Smith's sudden pronouncement that he had received a divine revelation ordering the practice of polygamy. Smith and his brother were eventually arrested and murdered in jail by an enraged mob, while authorities looked the other way.

But the Mormons had two great assets: a strong sense of community, working together and helping each other; and their new leader, Brigham Young. After Smith's death, the Latter Day Saints nearly split into a hundred pieces, which would have eliminated it from history. (One faction, which has survived, was led by Smith's original wife Emma and his son, and it rejected polygamy.) But Brigham Young was a powerful leader and of strong character. He held the Mormons together, prepared them for the westward migration and gave them courage to face the unknown.

The first year, the Mormon migration stopped at the Missouri River, the last stragglers from Nauvoo arriving November 27, 1846. They named their winter quarters "Misery Bottoms," for sickness was rife. But Young kept up their spirits and set up a tight organization to guarantee that responsibilities were fulfilled. When spring came, the Mormons were off again. On the morning of July 24, 1847, Young, though weak from a severe fever, came to a high plateau overlooking the Great Salt Lake Valley in Utah. Brigham said: "It is enough. This is the right place."

The rest of the emigrants arrived and immediately set to work transforming the desert into Zion—paradise. They used irrigation to turn the desert into fruitful farming land. They built a prosperous city. Eventually Utah would be admitted to the Union, on condition that polygamy be outlawed. Many of the Mormons regarded this as a betrayal and went to desolate areas in Mexico or practiced polygamy in secret. But in general the Mormons have become loyal Americans, even regarding the Constitution as divinely inspired. And the state of Utah bears their imprint to this day.

The Donner Tragedy

Another group of pioneers set off in 1846, much better equipped than the Mormons. The party was led by James Frazier Reed, whose luxurious covered wagon was nicknamed the Prairie Palace Car. The other leaders of the group were George and Jacob Donner, and the group was known as the Donner Party. Their journey began on April 16, and all went well at first.

All the emigrant parties followed a standard trail to Fort Laramie, Wyoming. There the trail made a wide V to avoid the Watsatch Mountains and the Great Salt Lake Desert. But an ambitious man named Lansford Hastings had been trying to persuade groups of emigrants that he knew a short-cut through the mountains and the desert which would save time and energy. Experienced mountain men said that Hastings was crazy, and the majority of wagon trains rejected his advice. But the Donner Party listened; it seemed obvious that it would save time to make a straight line rather than a V. They made a bargain: Hastings would meet them at the Wasatch River to show them his Hastings Cut-off. The Donner Party, a total of 87 people, left Fort Bridger on July 31, confident that they were on the last leg of their journey and would soon be in California.

But when they reached the Wasatch, they found no Hastings, only a letter from him pointing the direction and apologizing for not showing them through personally. They were worried, but it was too late to turn back. So they plunged into the Wasatch Mountains. In modern days, there is a highway through the mountains—but it was built with the aid of dynamite. The Donner Party had to make its own road through the narrow, twisting canyons, through the aspen and cottonwoods and choking underbrush and the sunken boulders. They felled trees and leveled off hills and bridged brooks. Up inclines, over ridges, around spurs of rock they went. Several times they had to go back over part of the road they had built because they had come to a dead end. It took them fifteen days. By the time they finally came out, they were exhausted, panicked and inclined to blame Reed for everything.

Then they came to the Great Salt Desert. Hastings had told them it was 40 miles across. It was 80. It took them six days and nights to cross its blinding glare under a burning blue sky as twisting whirlwinds of salt blew past them. Oxen, maddened by thirst, stampeded into the wasteland. The Reeds abandoned the Palace Car. Others threw out anything they could spare to lighten the load. They staggered out of the desert on September 8. No one had died, but they were much weaker, they had lost many animals, and—most importantly—they had lost their sense of community. Now it was every man for himself, and hatred simmered. They almost killed Reed before he agreed to go on alone, leaving his wife and four children behind, hoping that the other emigrants would not turn on them. Theft became common as morality was jettisoned with the excess baggage.

With only twelve wagons left, they reached Truckee Meadows, the last resting spot before the final push over the Sierra Mountains. They decided to rest one day because the oxen were exhausted. But in the night came a snow storm. The mountains were impassable. They could neither go nor return. They faced a winter of starvation.

Though they cooked every part of the animals, even the hides, the remaining oxen did not provide food for very long. There seemed virtually no hope of surviving until spring. Finally on December 16, fifteen of the healthiest members of the party, including five women, made snowshoes, nicknamed themselves the "Forlorn Hope," and with rations of one ounce of food per day for six days set out to cross the mountains and to bring back a rescue party. Thirty-three days later, the seven survivors staggered into a settlement at the edge of Sacramento. They had survived only by eating the bodies of those who died.

Reed, who was alive and safe, immediately gathered together a relief party and set out over the mountains. They had to turn back because of the snow, and it was not until February 18 that the first relief party arrived at the Truckee Meadows Camp. Those still alive were emaciated skeletons, who had lived on hides, twigs and human flesh. Most of them were scarcely rational, having lived through such horrors. All four of the Donner parents died. A total of 47 Donner Party members finally reached California. But the Reed family was reunited. They all lived and never once had they eaten human flesh. Mrs. Reed's courage and religious faith had kept her children from despair, and the entire family entered California.

There were other tragedies on the westward migration, but nothing could stop it. The rich, fertile land of California and Oregon beckoned, and the covered wagons flowed westward in a steady stream, as Americans sought a new and better life.

1848

1848 was the year General Zachary Taylor, **"Old Rough and Ready,"** won the Presidential election. His Vice President was Millard Fillmore, who succeeded to the presidency when Taylor died. He in turn was succeeded by Franklin Pierce, who managed to persuade the American people that a wound received in the Battle of Veracruz when he fell off his horse qualified him to be President.

1848 was the year John Fremont became a hero in the newspapers, though he had been found guilty at a court-martial of disobeying orders. Fortunately he had a father-in-law who was a U.S. Senator.

1848 was the year of the **Treaty of Guadalupe Hidalgo**, formally ending the Mexican War and handing over the New Mexico and California territories to the U.S., thus completing Manifest Destiny (except for the small strip of the Gadsden Purchase of 1853).

It was the year that James Marshall, working on a sawmill site at Sutter's Fort, saw something shiny and stooped to pick it up. It was the first nugget of the California gold rush.

And 1848 was the year that America, having achieved its Manifest Destiny, could begin thinking about other nagging problems, the most nagging: would slavery be allowed in the new territories? Could America continue to declare that all men were equal while treating men with black skins as property, not persons? The slavery controversy exploded and did not die down until long after half a million Americans had died fighting over it.

REVIEW QUESTIONS

1. Summarize Jackson's personality. What were the three main controversies of his administration? How did he handle them?
2. What kind of person was Sam Houston? Why is Eliza Allen Houston important to history?
3. What was the significance of the Alamo?
4. What was Manifest Destiny?
5. How did the U.S. gain possession of the Oregon Territory?
6. Why did war break out with Mexico?
7. How did the U.S. gain California and New Mexico?
8. Contrast Taylor and Scott.
9. What was the significance of the westward migration?
10. Summarize the Mormon migration.
11. Summarize the Donner tragedy.
12. What important events happened in 1848?

PROJECTS

1. Prepare a poster or mural illustrating the events of 1846 or of 1848 or of the Mexican War.
2. Research and prepare a report on Joseph Smith.
3. Prepare an illustrated talk on the westward migration.

Chapter 14

No Irish Need Apply

"NO IRISH NEED APPLY" was written on signs that went up on businesses all over the East Coast during much of the 19th century. In the first quarter of the century, Irish immigration to the U.S. increased. Many Irish, scraping together what little money they had, took passage on ships to America, where—they had been told—jobs and land were plentiful, everyone had an equal chance to succeed and there were no English landlords.

But when the Irish came to America, they found hatred, prejudice and persecution. Many Americans were afraid they would lose their jobs to the Irish, who were willing to work for low wages. Others saw the Irish as poor and dirty, a blot on the landscape of the City on a Hill. "This country has become the great receptacle for the miserable outcasts from European society," reported the commissioners of the New York almshouses. Also, many Americans were still infected with anti-Catholic prejudice, and the Irish were—almost all of them—strong Catholics.

Maria Monk and Friends

The first phase of anti-Catholicism in the 19th century was unorganized but fueled by a variety of anti-Catholic publications. The overall movement was called "Nativism," on the grounds that its participants were defending native American values against Irish Catholicism.

In 1829, *The Protestant*, a magazine, was founded in New York. Its purpose was to "inculcate Gospel doctrines against Romish corruptions—to maintain the purity and sufficiency of the Holy Scriptures against Monkish traditions." *The Protestant* and other anti-Catholic publications warned Americans that Catholics owed their political loyalties to a foreign prince (the Pope) and therefore could never be true Americans. Dire predictions were made that the Pope and a papal army would soon land on American shores to set up a new Vatican in, of all places, Cincinnati, and establish the Inquisition with Bishop John England as the Grand Inquisitor. Public speeches of the time had such titles as "Is Popery Compatible with Civil Liberty?" and "Is the Roman Hierarchy that man of Sin and Son of Perdition who was predicted by Paul in his second Epistle to the Thessalonians?" Samuel Morse, inventor of the telegraph, published in 1834 a book entitled *Foreign Conspiracy against the Liberties of the United States*, which contained the following dire warning: "They have already sent their chains, and oh! to our shame be it spoken, are fastening upon a *sleeping* victim. Americans, you are marked for their prey, not by foreign bayonets, *but by weapons surer of effecting the conquest of liberty* than all the munitions of physical combat in the military or naval storehouses of Europe . . . Will you be longer deceived by the pensioned Jesuits, who having surrounded your press, are now using it all over the country to stifle the cries of danger, and lull your fears by attributing your alarm to a false cause? . . . Awake: To your posts! Let the tocsin sound from Maine to Louisiana. Fly to protect the vulnerable places of your Constitution and Laws."

Fears for their jobs, distrust of Catholics because they were different and even somewhat mysterious, and rabble rousing by Nativists led some Americans to violence. The Ursuline Convent of Charlestown, Massachusetts was one of the best schools of Boston and was attended by the daughters of many prominent non-Catholic families. On Sunday, August 10, 1834, a Nativist leader preached a sermon accusing the Pope of a plot to seize the Mississippi Valley. The next night the convent burned to the ground. Firemen watched unmoved as nuns and children fled in the middle of the night. Only one man was brought to trial for the crime, and he was acquitted to wild cheers in court and showered with gifts.

Because many Catholic immigrants came to New York City, violence broke out there as well. In June of 1835, there were three days of anti-Catholic violence, to which the Irish responded in kind. There was much bloodshed, including the death of Dr. William McCaffrey, the Irish father of a large family, who was knocked to the ground while hurrying to a patient and trampled to death.

In 1836, anti-Catholic books, which fed upon the ignorance of many

Americans regarding Catholic customs, especially convent life, reached heights of popularity. There was *Nun*, which purported to tell of the escape of a Turin heiress from a convent dungeon, as well as *Six Months in a Convent*, which described sadistic penances imposed on Ursuline nuns by a flute-playing bishop.

But the best-seller of the year was *The Awful Disclosures of Maria Monk, as Exhibited in a Narrative of Her Sufferings During a Residence of Five Years as a Black Nun in the Hotel Dieu Nunnery in Montreal.* In it Maria Monk (that was her real name) told of the horrors of the Hotel Dieu Convent, in which nuns and priests engaged in shocking immoralities, with any nun who refused to participate being smothered between feather beds. Maria had escaped the convent, she said, because she was about to have a child by a Father Phelan and wanted to save it from death. It was even possible to obtain pictures of Maria, baby in arms and a priest behind her, with the caption "Maria Monk and Old and Young Father Phelan."

Maria's mother promptly appeared on the scene and said that her daughter had a deplorable habit of telling wild stories and that she had never been near the convent. She said that Rev. William K. Hoyt, a Canadian Protestant minister, had offered Mrs. Monk a hundred pounds if she would swear that Maria had been a nun, but that she had refused. Maria had, in fact, been a resident of a home for wayward girls and her child was fathered by a local Montreal boy. With the permission of Montreal's bishop, two Protestant clergymen were allowed to tour the Hotel Dieu, even the cloistered areas, and reported that the book had no basis in fact.

Nevertheless, *Maria Monk* was a runaway best seller, with 300,000 copies sold prior to the Civil War.

Dagger John

In 1838 John Hughes became Bishop of New York. Irish-born himself, he fought for the rights of Irish Catholics, and he encouraged the immigrants to hold fast to their faith against the temptations to give it up for worldly advancement.

His biggest battle as bishop was with the Common School Society, the governing authority of the public schools of New York. If a Catholic child went to a public school, he would be subjected to ridicule because of his faith and to anti-Catholic textbooks which contained such passages as, "If any person denied the Pope's authority he was burned alive"; and "Abbeys and monasteries became seats of voluptuousness"; and "To this day they consider St. Patrick as in Heaven, watching over the interests of Ireland. They pray to him, and to do him honor, set apart one day in the year for going to Church, drinking whiskey and breaking each other's heads with clubs."

Some parishes set up free parochial schools in Church basements, but parishes were so debt-ridden that they could not afford to accommodate many. So in October 1840, Hughes and his people petitioned the Common School Society for a share of education funds. The Society turned down the petition by a vote of 15-1. Hughes thereupon turned to the state legislature, asking them to take control of education away from the Common School Society. Politicians being politicians, the legislators postponed any consideration of the issue until after the 1842 election.

Hughes, willing to use any weapon at hand, ran his own slate of candidates in the election. They did not win, but they pulled enough votes away from the Democrats, for whom the Irish normally voted, to give victory to four Whig candidates. Hughes was therefore charged by the New York *Herald* with attempting "to organize the Irish-Catholics as a distinct party that could be given to the Whigs or Democrats at the wave of his crozier." The legislators got at least part of the message. They abolished the Common School Society, but they prohibited public funds to any school that taught or practiced "any religious sectarian doctrine or tenet."

In the long run, the government's refusal to help the Catholics turned out for the best. Hughes then told his people that no matter what the sacrifice, they would have to build their own schools. And build them they did. Workers making a dollar a day and Irish servant girls making six dollars a month sacrificed their pennies to build churches and a fine parochial school system.

But Hughes had still more battles to fight. After Nativists won the April 1844 New York City elections, they went on parade through Irish districts, carrying weapons and shouting insults. They hoped to provoke the Irish into violence, but the Irish remained peaceful. When the mob came to the cathedral, they found it protected by several thousand men brought there by Hughes. That was the end of the parade.

Then the Nativists planned a mass meeting for May 9. Hughes told his people to be peaceful, but prepared to act in self-defense. He organized forces to protect each church in the city and threatened that "if any Catholic church is burned here, New York will be a Moscow." He urged the mayor to cancel the meeting. The mayor agreed and New York was saved. It was such actions as these that earned Hughes his nickname: "Dagger John."

But Hughes was not satisfied merely with defensive actions. He told his people of their responsibility to evangelize their new country. In an 1850 sermon he declared: We Catholics "have for our mission to convert the world—including the inhabitants of the U.S.—the people of the cities, and the people of the country, the officers of the Navy and the Marines, commanders of the Army, the Legislatures, the Senate, the Cabinet, the President, and all."

Nativist Political Action

In the early 1840's, Nativism moved from unorganized actions fueled by the likes of *Maria Monk*, to middle class, "respectable," organized political activity. In June 1843, the American Republican Party was formed on a specifically nativist platform. Among its platform planks was a requirement of 21 years of residency before an immigrant could become an American citizen. In the next few years, they elected a number of candidates, including the mayor of New York in 1844.

But even though the Nativists were now engaged in political activity, violence did not therefore cease. In May 1844 there were riots in Philadelphia which resulted in the destruction of two churches, two rectories, two convents and a library, and left 40 dead. Another riot in July left 14 dead. When the grand jury investigated, they blamed the Catholics and indicted for murder several Irishmen who had tried to protect their homes. Riots also broke out in St. Louis after rumors spread that the cadavers used in the Jesuit medical school there were the bodies of Protestants tortured to death by the Inquisition.

In 1845 the potato crop in Ireland sickened and died. Other crops were grown on Irish soil, but since the soil belonged to English landlords, these crops were shipped off to England to earn a tidy profit for the owners. The people who worked the land starved. The population in Ireland fell by one-half because of the famine. Men, women and children died by the thousands.

The U.S. responded generously to the needs of the Irish. Protestant churches took up special collections. Quakers and various U.S. leaders such as the President of Harvard organized famine relief. But sadly, the U.S. was not so ready to welcome the Irish famine survivors who now emigrated in large numbers to the "Land of the Free." Nativists organized parades protesting immigration and urged laws to keep out immigrants.

"I Know Nothing"

The new wave of immigration led to the next phase of the Nativist movement: the era of the **"Know-Nothings."** Their official name was the Order of United Americans. They received their nickname because of the secrecy surrounding their organization. Whenever a member was asked about the group, he replied: "I know nothing."

The Know-Nothings accepted as members only native-born Protestants unrelated to Catholics by blood or marriage. Their motto was "Americans must rule Americans." They had secret hand shakes, passwords, oaths and recognition signals.

The Know-Nothings engaged in a variety of anti-Catholic actions. In 1855 they seized control of the Williamsburg section of Brooklyn and would have burned down the Church of St. Peter and Paul had not four Irishmen held them off until the militia arrived. Also in 1855 Know-Nothings took control of the polls in Louisville and prevented Irish and German Catholics from voting; they later went into the Irish section of town and destroyed 12 houses. Know-Nothings gained control of the school committee in Philadelphia and fired all Catholic teachers.

The Know-Nothings also stepped up Nativist political activity. In November 1854, Massachusetts Know-Nothings elected the governor, every seat in the Senate, and 376 out of 379 seats in the House. In 1855 the Know-Nothings carried every state in New England except Maine, won in Maryland and Kentucky and showed significant strength in New York, Pennsylvania, California and the South. In 1856 they even nominated a Presidential candidate, Millard Fillmore, who won 22 per cent of the popular vote and carried the state of Maryland.

But then, like every other group in the U.S. at this time, the Know-Nothings had to face the slavery issue. Some of their members supported slavery, some opposed it. The party split on the issue and was never again a major force. It lingered in Maryland until about 1860, existing mainly to keep Catholics from voting. One gang, called the Blood Tubs, collected animal blood from butcher shops in tubs and then spent election day squeezing sponges filled with the blood over the heads of German and Irish Catholics who dared to come to the polls.

In the midst of all these provocations, the Irish behaved with remarkable restraint and a sense of humor. One Catholic newspaper, for example, said that the Declaration of Independence should be amended to read "Life, liberty and the pursuit of Irishmen." Many of them responded by becoming better Catholics. They expanded their parochial school system, which in many areas soon rivaled the public schools in quality. They trained more priests, welcomed more young women into convents. Some translated their strong Irish nationalism into a strong American nationalism.

And some, unfortunately, went to an extreme to prove that Catholics were not foreign agents but loyal to the Constitution. They convinced themselves that America really was morally better than any other nation, that Catholic Europe was corrupt, that America was the City on a Hill, that the Catholic Church in America should be allowed to go its own way without undue interference from the Vatican. These beliefs eventually led to the "**Americanist Heresy**," condemned by Pope Leo XIII in his Apostolic Letter *Testem Benevolentiae* ("On True and False Americanism in Religion"), January 22, 1899. Among the propositions condemned in the letter were the following: that the Holy Spirit can guide men in their spiritual lives so that they do not need the Sacraments or organized church structure; that the natural virtues are higher than the supernatural; that the active life is better than the contemplative life; that religious vows are a restriction on freedom; that the Church needs to accommodate its doctrines and practices to attract more Americans into it.

At the time of the letter, American Catholic leaders affirmed their adherence to Catholic doctrine and their rejection of Americanism. But Americanism never fully died out and would reappear in full bloom in the next century after the Second Vatican Council.

St. John Neumann

But in the midst of persecution, there are always saints, and out of the Nativist era came a great American saint.

On May 21, 1836, John Neumann disembarked from the *Europa* in Brooklyn harbor. He knew no one in New York; in his pocket were a rosary, about a dollar in change and the address of the bishop of Brooklyn. Within a month he was ordained and on his way to Buffalo to minister to the many German Catholics who had practically no priests. He was given responsibility for 400 Catholic families; no two lived within a mile of each other. At his first Mass in his new parish, Catholic-haters threw pebbles, cow dung and corncobs through the space where the door would be when they could afford one.

Neumann built a school and did all the teaching himself. He walked through the snow and rain to minister to his parishioners. He brewed herbal medicines and doctored their illnesses. His people loved him and their faith grew stronger. But Father Neumann felt deeply the need of an ordered spiritual life. Convinced that his own lack of holiness was the cause of every problem in the parish, he left New York and became a Redemptorist novice in Pittsburgh. He pronounced his vows on January 16, 1842 and was assigned to St. James parish in Baltimore, where he spent two years teaching catechism, instructing converts, baptizing and counseling immigrants. These he would later see as the happiest years of his life.

But in March 1844 he was sent to Pittsburgh as superior of the Redemptorist community there, although the last thing he wanted was a position of authority. In Pittsburgh, Nativism scourged the Catholic community: churches were burned; pamphlets attacked the American Church as "that foothold of the Austrian Kaiser in our midst"; priests were beaten when making sick calls. To protect his people from the materialism and Protestantism dominating American culture, he made Catholic education his top priority.

In 1847 Neumann was made superior over the 10 Redemptorist foundations in America. The order was saddled with a debt of a quarter of a million dollars at a time when most of its parishioners earned 50 cents a day. The Redemptorist superiors in Europe appointed Neumann because they knew he was best fitted to curtail material expansion in favor of spiritual growth. Father Neumann taught humility and abnegation by example: his cell was the size of a broom closet; he wore a patched habit. Many of the priests in the order were not responsive to the call for spiritual renewal; they complained that Neumann promoted "disharmony." John blamed his own spiritual inadequacies for all of the Congregation's problems and asked to be relieved.

He returned to Baltimore. But soon rumors began to circulate that he would be appointed bishop of Philadelphia. Panicked, John asked the nuns he directed to make novenas "to avert impending harm to the Church in America." But the novenas were not answered—or rather were answered in the way John did not want. In 1852 he was consecrated bishop.

In Philadelphia, he lived as humbly as a parish priest, spending as much time with his people as he could. He doubled and redoubled his prayers and penances, in spite of his deteriorating health. He made pastoral visitations, often falling into bed at night covered by a film of coal dust. He established Catholic schools all over the diocese, to the dismay of the Know-Nothings. Asa Symington, one of their leaders, called on his followers to "unmask this Neumann for the enemy of American institutions: free elections, free speech, public schools, the whole democratic process."

But in spite of the often violent anti-Catholicism, Neumann's work bore rich fruit. He inaugurated the Forty Hours devotion, started an order of nuns, saw the solemn placement of the cross on the roof of the new cathedral, and founded a preparatory college for aspirants to the priesthood. By 1854 the diocese had 34 parochial schools enrolling 9,000 children.

The Christmas season of 1859 came, and Bishop Neumann attended school Christmas pageants, made his monthly day of recollection at the Redemptorist House, heard confessions and celebrated Midnight Mass. It was during that Mass that he experienced a sharp pain in his chest, so great that he could scarcely move for several minutes. But he continued working without rest. On January 5, 1860, returning from the freight depot where he had gone to mail a chalice to an impoverished upstate parish, he collapsed on the street, dying in a nearby home. His funeral procession was the largest Philadelphia had ever seen.

John Neumann guided the Church in America through perilous times. He is an example and an inspiration for all American Catholics, past, present and future.

REVIEW QUESTIONS

1. List the reasons some Americans were hostile to Irish immigrants.
2. What were the views of Samuel Morse on Catholics?
3. Summarize the claims of Maria Monk. What effect did they have?
4. Summarize the conflict between Bishop Hughes and the School Society.
5. How did Bishop Hughes protect Catholic lives and property?
6. How did Bishop Hughes encourage evangelization?
7. What were the aims of the American Republican Party?

8. Give three examples of anti-Catholic violence in the 1840's.
9. How did the Know-Nothings attack the Church?
10. How did American Catholics respond to persecution (two main ways)?
11. Why did Leo XIII write *Testem Benevolentiae*? What did it say?
12. Summarize the accomplishments of St. John Neumann before he became bishop.
13. Summarize the accomplishments of St. John Neumann after he became bishop.

PROJECTS

1. Do research and write a report on the Irish Potato Famine, with particular emphasis on how it led to emigration to America.
2. Do research and write a report or prepare an exhibit on Catholic history in your own area during the time covered in this chapter (1830-1860).
3. The Knights of Columbus were founded around this time. Find out more about this organization.

Chapter 15

The Coming of the Civil War

THE PERFECT GOVERNMENT does not exist. No matter how a government is structured, every government must exercise power, and the temptation to those both within and without the government to seize power will be ever present. The best resolution of these problems was the Christian system of government as it evolved during the Middle Ages. There was a strong central authority with power to act in certain areas. But there were also strong local authorities, with power to act in other areas. The power of both the national government and local authorities was limited by institutions independent of both, particularly the Catholic Church through its moral teachings.

The men at the Constitutional Convention knew that power should be limited. That is why they set up a three-part system of government and why power was divided between the States and the federal government.

But in spite of the checks and balances of the Constitution, there was always a tension between those who wanted the federal government to have more power than the States and those who wanted the States to have more than the federal government. Though the distinction was not always clear, usually the Southern States upheld the authority of State over federal government and weak central government over strong; whereas, the Northern States held the opposite view. These two tendencies exemplified wider differences between the two areas. The North was a center of the Industrial Revolution; the South kept to a farm-centered way of life. The North was more democratic—everyone was thought to be the equal of everyone else and elections the best way of solving any controversy. The South was hierarchical—in the family, the father held authority; on the plantation, the owner's decisions were final; within the community, the oldest, wealthiest families were the leaders. Northerners still tended to hold to the "City on a Hill" idea; they were more Messianic, regarding the Union as divinely decreed. The South would honor home and family and land ahead of the Union.

Though the South honored many sound values, its leaders tragically chose to regard its whole way of life as dependent on slavery—the buying, selling and owning of innocent men, women and children against their will. Therefore all that was good in the South was infected by the belief that men of one color had the right to dispose of men of another color as they would any other property. This belief, which the South came to hold ever more fanatically as the North challenged it, would lead to the United States' bloodiest war.

The Compromises

The slavery controversy surfaced at the Constitutional Convention and was finally resolved by compromise. To satisfy the North, the importation of slaves would be illegal after 1808, with the unspoken hope that without being able to import new slaves into the United States, the South would soon realize that slavery was really an expensive, inefficient form of labor and this "peculiar institution," as it was called, would gradually die out. To satisfy the South, the Constitution permitted slave owning and allowed the South to count slaves in determining its number of representatives in Congress, each slave being worth three-fifths of a white man. Of course, this compromise represented a contradiction. Slaves were property, said the Southerner in justifying his buying and selling of them. But slaves were persons—or at least three-fifths persons—when it came to representation. As a result of the compromise, the South dominated Congress during its first fifty years, and most of the Presidents during that time were Southerners or at least sympathetic to slavery.

But the compromises of the Constitutional Convention had not taken into account the possibility of new territory being added to the United States, neither slave nor free at the time of the annexation. Until 1820 the balance was maintained by alternately admitting slave and free states to the Union, so that at the end of 1819, there were eleven free and eleven slave states. But Missouri's application for statehood raised the question of the legal status of slavery in Missouri and in the rest of the territory west of the Mississippi which had been added to the Union through the Louisiana Purchase. After a ferocious debate—the forerunner of many such debates—the **Missouri Compromise** was adopted in 1820: Missouri was admitted as a slave state, balanced by Maine's admission as a free state, and slavery was excluded from the Louisiana Territory north of the latitude line 36°30' and permitted south of it. Southerners breathed a sigh of relief. They had been afraid that their influence in Congress would wane with the more rapid growth of the North's population, but enough Northern representatives (nicknamed "doughfaces") joined the Southern delegates to pass the compromise.

But the situation had changed more than the Southerners perhaps realized. In the North, slavery was coming to be regarded as much more than a political issue—that is, simply determining which section would have the most representatives—or even as a mild moral issue motivating men to work to prevent its spread. It was becoming *the* moral issue of the day, with the growing belief that slavery should be abolished altogether. The earliest leaders of the **Abolitionist Movement** were the Quakers of Philadelphia, whose belief that all men's religious beliefs were of equal value led them to conclude that *all men were of equal value*, whatever the color of their skin. The idea of abolition really took hold in the North and spread like wildfire after the Great Revival in the 1830s—an evangelical Protestant revival movement, which saw thousands flocking to tent meetings to hear preachers call upon them to reform their lives and to reform their country. In part, the Great Revival was a reaction against the harshness of Calvinism; the revivalist preachers rejected the idea that man was totally evil. Instead they taught that he could and should do good and that the best good he could do was to improve society. Thus a spate of social reform movements appeared, working for more humane prisons, better schools, aid to the poor, and—as an issue rising above all others—the abolition of slavery. A third factor resulting in the growth of abolitionism was Liberalism, because one of the few beneficial doctrines it preached was that slavery was evil.

The abolitionists were first led by Theodore Weld, who founded antislavery societies throughout New England. Their first leader in Congress was John Quincy Adams, who had been elected representative from his ancestral home of Braintree, Massachusetts upon his involuntary retirement from the Presidency. Writing in his diary that slavery is "a great and foul stain upon the North American Union," Adams introduced petitions in Congress calling for the abolition of slavery in the District of Columbia and the Territories.

Adams and Weld were moderate abolitionists. They did not call for the immediate and total end of slavery because they could foresee the great disruption that would result. But others were not so temperate. The leader of the radicals was William Lloyd Garrison, who termed the Constitution "a Covenant with death and an agreement with Hell" because it permitted slavery. Garrison soon commanded a widespread movement which violently condemned the South and encouraged slaves to escape and come north. Abolitionists throughout the North secretly aided these fugitive slaves by hiding them in their homes in what came to be called the **"Underground Railway**." Northern newspapers took up the abolitionist cry, fanning the flames of discord higher, as the press reached its greatest power in the United States up to that time.

The South responded to the radical abolitionists by hardening its own position. Instead of simply maintaining that slavery was necessary for the cultivation of their plantations, a false though defensible position, the most radical pro-slavery advocates—such as South Carolina Senator John C. Calhoun—called it a positive good, the foundation stone of all that was valuable in Southern society, and a benefit to the slave, who had security and care throughout his entire life. With the help of Northern Democrats, who wanted Southern votes for their party, Southerners in Congress pushed through **"Fugitive Slave Laws**," requiring the return of run-away slaves, and the **"Gag Rule**," prohibiting Congress from acting on anti-slavery petitions. These actions in turn brought more Northerners to the abolitionist side. They accused the South of trying to extend its power to the North through fugitive slave laws and of denying free speech through the gag rule.

Each side hardened its own position and hurled ever greater vituperation at the other. New England and the Deep South faced off against each other, while the border states leaned South and the middle states leaned North, as their leaders looked frantically for some way of compromising the two intransigent foes.

The Compromises Collapse

The expansion of the United States made the already sizzling slavery issue even hotter. Abolitionists fought the annexation of Texas because they knew it would come in as a slave state, delaying it until 1845. But the controversy over Texas was nothing compared to the battle royal over the territory annexed after the Mexican War. In January 1849, Calhoun, as spokesman for 69 Southerners in Congress, delivered the "Address of the Southern Delegates," accusing the North of aggression against the South by prohibiting slave-owners from taking their "property" into the territories. But the Southerners were even more upset when California applied for admission to the Union—its population, swollen by the gold rushers, desperately needing a state government—because its entry would destroy the balance of fifteen slave, fifteen free states. Seeking compromise, Kentucky's Henry Clay proposed the admission of California as a free state, but the organization without restriction on slavery of the balance of the territory acquired from Mexico.

The Senate's consideration of Clay's proposals was known as the **"Great Debate."** Calhoun—too weak from the illness that would soon kill him to speak on the Senate floor—listened as his speech opposing the compromise was read by a Virginia Senator. William H. Seward, a strong abolitionist, opposed the compromise as well, arguing that slavery should be totally abolished because God's law was higher than the Constitution—a premise which is of course true, but which fell on deaf ears at the time. Each side in the debate was absolutely convinced that it was right and everyone else was wrong. Though the actual sundering of the Union would not take place for eleven more years, the chasm between the two positions was already wide and deep.

At last an exhausted Congress approved a series of laws known as the **Compromise of 1850**. California was admitted as a free state. The New Mexico territory was organized without restriction on slavery, with the provision that when applying for statehood, the territory "shall be received into the Union, with or without slavery, as their constitution may prescribe at the time of their admission." The fugitive slave laws were tightened to please the South; and the slave trade was abolished in the District of Columbia to please the North.

The Compromise of 1850 was like a band-aid holding together two parts of a broken bone. The enmity between the two sections grew stronger with each passing day. In March 1852, Harriet Beecher Stowe wrote her famous novel ***Uncle Tom's Cabin***, inflaming Northern sentiment against the South still more; Northern States continued to circumvent the fugitive slave laws; Southern leaders met in conventions to discuss the possibility of secession, convinced that secession was their right because several states, both North and South, had affirmed the right of secession at the time the Constitution was ratified.

Then in the spring of 1854, Illinois Senator Stephen Douglas,

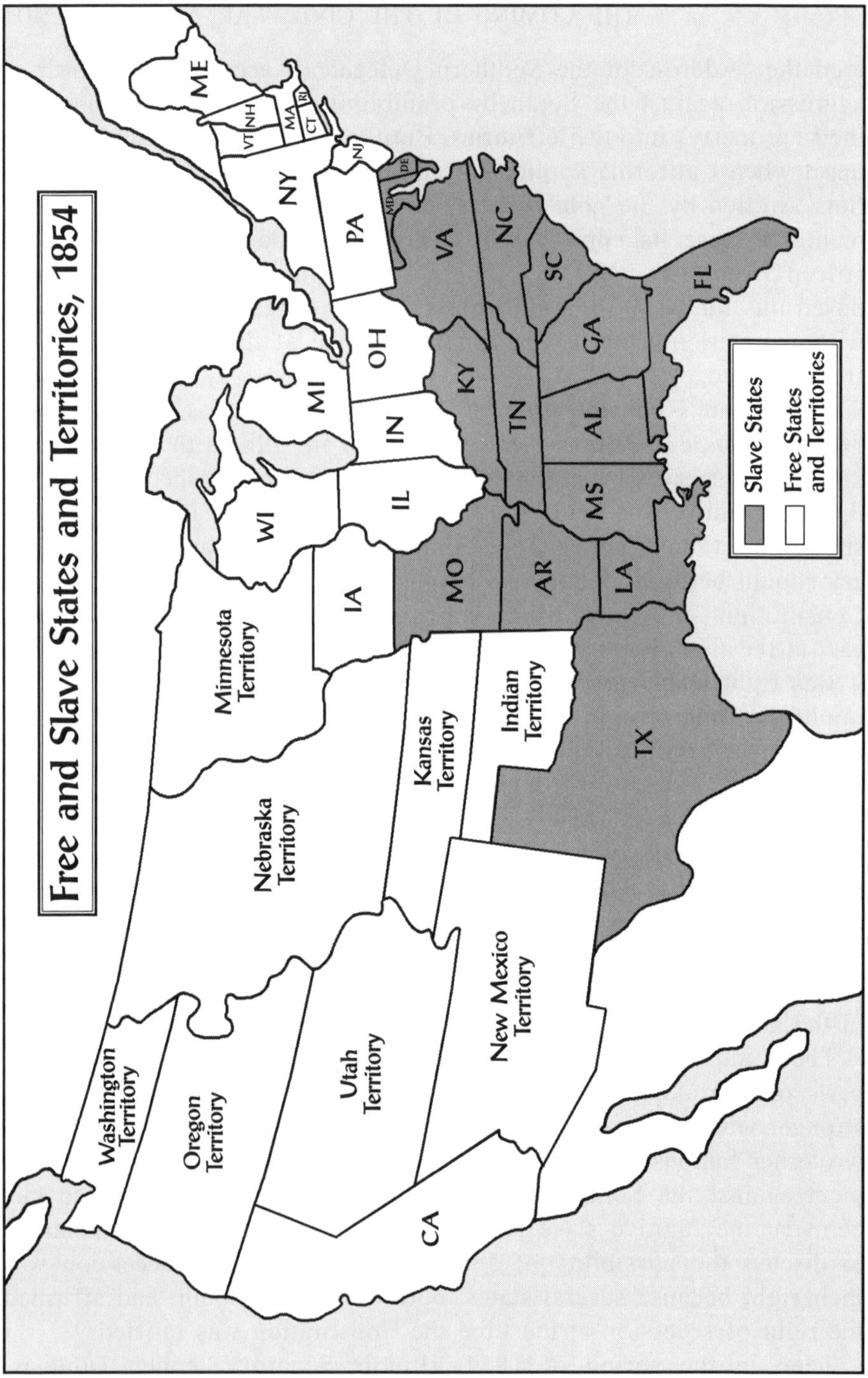
Free and Slave States and Territories, 1854
ME
VT
NH
MA
RI
CT
NY
NJ
PA
MD
DE
VA
NC
SC
GA
FL
OH
MI
IN
KY
TN
AL
IL
WI
MS
MO
AR
LA
IA
TX
Minnesota Territory
Nebraska Territory
Kansas Territory
Indian Territory
New Mexico Territory
Utah Territory
Washington Territory
Oregon Territory
CA
Slave States
Free States and Territories

nicknamed the "Little Giant," introduced a bill for organizing the territories of Kansas and Nebraska. His proposal rejected the Missouri Compromise, which had left these territories north of the slavery line. Instead he proposed that **popular sovereignty** govern the question of slavery, declaring that the territories could be admitted to the Union with or without slavery, depending on the Constitution voted for by the people at the time. Douglas thereby tried to change the slavery question from a profound moral issue to one that could be settled by a show of hands. Douglas himself had no objection to slavery, believing that Whites were the superior race, and probably conceived of his plan as the surest way to get support for himself from every area of the nation in a future presidential race. After a vicious debate on the proposal, Douglas rammed the **Kansas-Nebraska Act** through Congress.

Congress could probably not have made a worse mistake. The immediate reaction of both sides in the controversy was to flood the territories with settlers to tip the elections to their side. And neither side was opposed to using violence to frighten the opponents away.

Though slave-supporters thought they had won a victory in the repeal of the Missouri Compromise, all the different anti-slavery groups finally stopped bickering with each other and joined together as a result of the Kansas-Nebraska Act. Whigs, anti-slavery Democrats and members of the recently formed Free-Soil Party organized the Republican Party, calling for repeal of the Kansas-Nebraska Act and the fugitive slave laws and for the abolition of slavery in the District of Columbia.

Bleeding Kansas

On October 16, 1854, at Springfield, Illinois, a 45-year-old lawyer delivered a speech condemning the Kansas-Nebraska Act and calling for the gradual emancipation of slaves. His own conviction that slavery was immoral was gradually growing stronger, but he nevertheless believed that Congress had no Constitutional right to abolish slavery where it already existed and that any abolitionist movement must proceed carefully, in order not to inflame unnecessary hatreds. He refused to condemn the South as irredeemably immoral, arguing that slavery was a *national* evil and that the North was not totally free from sin in this regard. A former Illinois legislator, Abraham Lincoln came to national attention by his reasoned and intelligent speech.

Reason and intelligence were in short supply, and the year 1856 was to see both of them all but disappear. On May 19, Senator Charles

Sumner of Massachusetts rose to deliver a speech on Kansas, where slavery and anti-slavery factions seemed to be competing for a prize in lawlessness. He marshalled all the power of his considerable oratorical ability against proposed legislation to make Kansas a slave state. In a speech entitled "The Crime against Kansas," Sumner called the bill a "crime against nature, from which the soul recoils and which language refuses to describe." But Sumner's language managed to describe it throughout that day and again the next before he finally finished. Though Sumner must be credited for recognizing the evil of slavery, his speech itself was one long litany of hatred for the South, and especially for Senator Andrew Butler of South Carolina, whose desk was in front of Sumner's.

On May 21, a pro-slavery mob—designated a posse by the pro-slavery sheriff and joined by "Border Ruffians," rioters from across the state line—ran wild in Lawrence, Kansas. They burned the hotel, robbed homes and destroyed the offices of two anti-slavery newspapers. Two men were killed. Anti-slavery men called for retaliation, heeding the words of Henry Ward Beecher, a Protestant abolitionist minister, who had said that where Kansas was concerned, a rifle was a greater moral force than the Bible. Gunsmiths promptly nicknamed rifles "Beecher's Bibles."

On May 22, Sumner was working at his desk. Preston Brooks, a South Carolina Congressman and Senator Butler's nephew, strode into the chamber. "I have read your speech twice over," he said. "It is a libel on South Carolina and Senator Butler." He raised his heavy cane and brought it down on Sumner's head. Brooks struck him again and again as Sumner was unable to get out from behind his desk, which was fixed to the floor. At last he wrenched the desk loose from its fastenings and staggered to his feet. Brooks knocked him to the floor, but by this time his cane was broken and he turned and left. Southerners sent Brooks more canes in the mail, while Northerners pointed to the attack as evidence that the South would never listen to reason.

On May 24, a bearded man with piercing eyes led seven men armed with swords through the twilight shadows in the ravines bordering Pottawatomie Creek, Kansas. John Brown was unbalanced, unsuccessful at everything he had ever tried, and a fanatical abolitionist. Somehow he had come to believe that five men had been killed in Lawrence. He was determined to kill five pro-slavery men in retaliation. First, the small band came to the cabin of the Doyle family, poor Whites from

Tennessee who had no love for slavery. But Brown ordered the father and two sons outside, where they were hacked to death. They killed Wilkinson, a pro-slavery leader, in his dooryard. Finally, they captured William Sherman, who had been in the Lawrence riot. They split his head, stabbed his chest and cut off his hand. They washed the blood off their swords in the creek and went home satisfied.

By June, guerrilla warfare was raging throughout **"Bleeding Kansas"**; crops were burned, horses stolen, men shot from ambush. On June 2, the Democratic National Convention nominated James Buchanan for President. Buchanan had been ambassador to England and was not associated with the slavery controversy, the Democrats hoping that a noncontroversial candidate would bring victory. Their platform affirmed the Compromise of 1850 and supported the Kansas-Nebraska Act. The Republicans held their first national convention and nominated John C. Fremont, who hoped to ride his California escapades into the White House. The Know-Nothings nominated Millard Fillmore and joined the Democrats in attacking the "Black Republicans." In November the Democrats won the key states of Pennsylvania, Indiana, Illinois and New Jersey, along with the entire South. Fremont carried only New England and New York, while Fillmore and his anti-Catholic party ironically won Maryland, once the only colony tolerating Catholics.

By inauguration day, Kansas governor John W. Geary, with the help of U.S. troops, had brought an uneasy peace to the Bleeding Territory. In his inaugural address, Buchanan condemned the slavery agitation, supporting noninterference with slavery in the States and popular sovereignty in the territories. Buchanan hoped only that the controversy would quiet down and leave him in peace.

But peace was far away. Now the Supreme Court stepped into the fray. Just two days after the inauguration, Chief Justice Roger Taney, a Southerner appointed by Jackson, delivered the decision in the case of ***Dred Scott v. Sanford***. Scott was a slave who had been taken by his master from Missouri to the Wisconsin Territory, where slavery was prohibited by the Missouri Compromise. Upon returning to Missouri, Scott went to court to be freed, holding that he had become free because of his stay in a free territory. The case involved three issues: whether Scott was a citizen of Missouri and thus entitled to sue in the courts; whether his temporary stay on free soil had given him a title to freedom; and the constitutionality of the Missouri Compromise.

The Court ruled against Scott on all three counts: Negro slaves were not citizens; his temporary residence in free territory had not made him free upon his return to slave territory; the Missouri Compromise was unconstitutional because it deprived persons of their property without due process of law and hence violated their rights under the Fifth Amendment. This decision was the first time since *Marbury v. Madison* that the Court had declared unconstitutional an act of Congress. The South cheered; they had been vindicated on every point. Horace Greeley, a leading Republican newspaperman, said that the decision deserved no more respect than if it had been handed down in a barroom. At that moment, the U.S. Constitution was officially determined as decreeing that Negroes were property, not persons, with no rights. It would not be the last time that the Court would deny humanity to a whole class of persons.

Lincoln v. Douglas

In 1858, Abraham Lincoln challenged Douglas for his Illinois Senate seat. In accepting the Republican nomination, he made his famous "house divided" speech, declaring: "A house divided against itself cannot stand. I believe this government cannot endure permanently half slave and half free. I do not expect the Union to be dissolved; I do not expect the house to fall; but I do expect it will cease to be divided. It will become all one thing, or all the other." Lincoln challenged Douglas to a series of debates, seven of which were held in the course of the summer. The two candidates made a striking contrast. Douglas was short, compact, intense; Lincoln tall, gangly, soft-spoken. Douglas pounded home his theme of popular sovereignty as the only solution to the question, carefully avoiding the moral issue. Lincoln, while denying that he thought it practical to abolish slavery in the South, condemned slavery as immoral and called for an end to its extension. At this time, senators were still chosen by the state legislatures; though Lincoln had more support among the people, the legislature was controlled by the Democrats. Douglas returned to Washington.

Lincoln made up his mind to win in 1864. But his supporters had bigger things than the U.S. Senate in mind. Lincoln had emerged as the most thoughtful of all the anti-slavery leaders. His friends arranged speaking engagements in the East to spread Lincoln's reputation, and Lincoln quietly urged them to line up delegate support for the 1860 Republican presidential convention.

In the meantime, John Brown had been raising money from abolitionists.

He planned to seize the federal arsenal at Harper's Ferry, Virginia, arm Negroes, lead a rebellion, and set up a free state in the southern Appalachians to serve as a focal point for spreading Negro revolt throughout the South. On October 16, 1858, eighteen men, including five Negroes, seized the federal arsenal and armory and held some local people as hostages. After two days of battle, a force of U.S. Marines, commanded by Colonel Robert E. Lee, recaptured the arsenal and took Brown and his followers prisoners. Brown was convicted of treason and hanged in December. His raid frightened the Southerners, who were terrified of Negro rebellion; and his death inflamed the Northerners, who proclaimed Brown a martyr and made "John Brown's Body" their theme song.

During the 1860 presidential campaign, the Democrats split, just as the nation had. The more moderate Democrats nominated Douglas, and the southern radicals nominated John Breckinridge of Kentucky. A few left-over Know-Nothings and Whigs, who could not find a home in either Democrat or Republican parties, formed the Constitutional Union Party and nominated John Bell of Tennessee on a platform upholding "the Constitution of the country, the union of the States and the enforcement of the laws."

The Republicans met in Chicago, where Lincoln supporters worked among the delegates, promising cabinet posts to get support. On the third ballot, Lincoln was only one and a half votes short of nomination. One of his supporters rushed to the Ohio delegation, which had been supporting Ohio's Salmon P. Chase, telling them, "If you can throw the Ohio delegation to Lincoln, Chase can have anything he wants." Four votes immediately switched to Lincoln, and he was the Republican presidential candidate. The division among his opponents made Lincoln's election almost a certainty. Though his three opponents garnered a total of a million more votes than he did and though he won not a single vote in the entire South—making him both a minority and a sectional President—Abraham Lincoln had a majority of the electoral votes and was President of the United States.

Secession

From the time of Lincoln's nomination, radical forces in South Carolina had declared that their state would secede if the Black Republican won. On December 20 a state convention voted unanimously that "the union now subsisting between South Carolina and the other States, under the name of the United States of America, is hereby dissolved."

South Carolina was followed in rapid succession by the other six states of the Deep South: Mississippi, Florida, Alabama, Georgia, Louisiana and Texas (though Sam Houston had made every effort to prevent Texan secession). In February, delegates organized the Confederate States of America, with a Constitution similar to that of the U.S., though it protected slavery and stressed "the sovereign and independent character" of each state. Jefferson Davis, a Mississippi Congressman who had been a leading pro-slavery spokesman, was elected president; Alexander Stephens, who as late as November 1860 had spoken out against secession, was chosen vice president. Four slave states—Virginia, Arkansas, Tennessee, and North Carolina—did not secede, though they warned that they would oppose any attempt by the federal government to use force against the Confederacy. The border slave states—Maryland, Delaware, Kentucky and Missouri—wavered, as pro and anti-secession factions fought for control.

In Washington, D.C., meanwhile, panic reigned. The nation's capital was surrounded by slave territory, and had scarcely a soldier to defend it. Buchanan was paralyzed by the contradictory beliefs that states could not legally secede and that the federal government could not legally stop them from seceding, and so did nothing. The air was so full of wild threats to assassinate Lincoln that the President-elect was brought into Washington in disguise.

The other focus of everyone's attention was Fort Sumter off Charleston, South Carolina, the only federal fort on rebel soil. Major Robert Anderson and his 70 troops looked out at the rebel cannon, calculated that it would take a government army of 20,000 to rescue them, and watched their food supplies dwindle.

As he took office, Lincoln hoped desperately to avoid violence, but he knew that he must take a strong stand. He sent a message to the governor of South Carolina, announcing that he was sending a cargo of food to resupply Fort Sumter, but that he did not intend this as an aggressive act. Immediately the Confederate forces, commanded by General P. T. Beauregard, demanded the Fort's surrender. Anderson, a brave man in a difficult situation, said that he could not do that, but if the Southerners were patient, he would soon be out of food and they could march in and take over. But Beauregard and his troops wanted a total and dramatic victory. At 4:30 a.m., April 12, 1861, the first shot of the Civil War was fired. Thirty hours later, Anderson's small band surrendered.

Believing that the Constitution denied the right of secession, Lincoln refused to recognize that the South had in fact seceded or that a state of war existed between two separate nations. He issued a call for 75,000 militia to volunteer for three months to "restore order" and enforce federal laws. But throughout the North, the issue was clear: this was a war to whip the South, to end slavery, and to reunite the Union. Volunteers poured into recruiting offices. In Iowa, twenty times as many as could be taken came forward and refused to go back. Detroit raised $81,000 in a few days to equip the militia. A New York woman wrote, "It seems as if we never were alive till now." Everyone looked upon the conflict as promising action and glory and excitement. Blood and pain and suffering and death were far from the minds of both North and South, each of which was sure that it could win this little war in no time.

With the coming of secession and war, each side, while still keeping the slavery issue paramount, saw other goals to be achieved. The South came increasingly to feel that it was fighting for independence and the preservation of its land and culture from Northern capitalism and greed; the North came to feel that it was fighting to preserve the Union and to demonstrate the superiority of American government. In his July 4 address to Congress, Lincoln declared that upon the fate of the Union hung the fate of democracy everywhere in the world.

On April 25, the Seventh New York Regiment entered Washington and garrisoned the city, preventing its being seized by the South. Virginia, Arkansas, Tennessee and North Carolina seceded after Ft. Sumter. Maryland stayed in the Union because Lincoln sent troops to turn back pro-secessionist legislators on their way to a special session of the Maryland assembly to vote on secession; those who would not turn back willingly were arrested. Delaware, surrounded by Maryland, had no choice but to stay with the Union. The Governor of Missouri wanted to secede, but Lincoln had put Captain Nathanial Lyons in charge of armed forces there. Lyons marched on Jefferson City, scattered the state militia, and forced Governor Jackson to flee, leaving Missouri in the Union. In Kentucky, Lincoln did not quibble at assuring a delegation of Kentucky congressmen that he had neither the right, power nor disposition to violate Kentucky's neutrality, while a few hours later suggesting the kidnapping of secessionist Governor Magoffin and ordering a shipment of guns, in boxes labeled "circular saws," to the U.S. arsenal at Watervliet. In response, Confederate General Leonidas Polk occupied Columbus, Kentucky. This violation of their neutrality angered the Kentucky lawmakers, and they voted to stay with the Union.

Robert E. Lee

Across the Potomac from Washington, D.C. stood the mansion of the Custis family, descendants of Martha Custis Washington. Inhabiting the house now was the family of Robert E. Lee of the United States Army, who had married Mary Custis. Lee's father was Lighthorse Harry Lee, a cavalry hero of the Revolutionary War, from whom he had inherited his love for the military. His mother was Ann Lee, who had instilled in her children a high standard of morality and of honor.

Lee looked upon secession as a tragedy of the highest order. On January 23, 1861, he had written his son Custis: "I can anticipate no greater calamity for the country than a dissolution of the Union. . . . Still, a Union that can only be maintained by swords and bayonets, and in which strife and civil war are to take the place of brotherly love and kindness, has no charm for me. . . . If the Union is dissolved, and the Government disrupted, I shall return to my native State and share the miseries of my people, and, save in defense, will draw my sword on none." Lee was no defender of slavery, having once said that if he owned all the slaves in the South, he would cheerfully give them up to preserve the Union. But he was a true Southerner in his loyalties to his home, his land and his native Virginia.

On April 18, Lee rode across the bridge from Arlington to Washington to speak to Winfield Scott, commander-in-chief of the Union armies. Scott was eighty years old and so overweight that he could not mount a horse, but there was nothing wrong with his brain. He had warned Lincoln that it would take three years and 300,000 men under good generals to defeat the South. He also knew that the best general of all was the Virginian who had been his chief of artillery in the Mexican campaign, and he had summoned Lee to his office to offer him the field command of the Union armies. But Lee could not raise his sword against the South. When he refused Scott's offer, the general replied: "Lee, you have made the greatest mistake of your life; but I feared it would be so." Having turned down the highest honor that the country could bestow on a military man, Lee returned to Arlington to learn to his dismay that Virginia had seceded. He resigned from the U.S. Army and left Arlington for Richmond, never to return, having been appointed commander of the military forces of the state of Virginia. Echoing Scott, Lee told the Virginia secession convention that they were "just on the threshold of a long and bloody war," and he wrote to his son that nothing could be done to avert the calamity which was befalling the United States, North and South alike, but that "in God alone must be our trust."

War

Having lost Robert E. Lee, the best Lincoln and Scott could do was appoint General Irvin McDowell to take command of the Army of the Potomac. The troops were raw and untrained—a not uncommon sight was a captain on the training ground consulting an army textbook to decide what to do next as he drilled his army—but newspapers and politicians alike clamored for a quick attack on the Southern army and then a drive on Richmond to seize the capital of the Confederacy and end the war. Scott warned against it. Far better and less bloody, he said, to blockade the Southern coastline and slowly starve the South, dependent as it was on European trade (a plan nicknamed the "Anaconda Strategy"). But the politicians and the newspapers were noisier than Scott. Lincoln ordered McDowell to prepare an attack on the important Confederate railroad junction at Manassas, Virginia. The battle is known as **First Manassas** or the **First Battle of Bull Run**.

McDowell's men marched out of Washington on July 16, 1861, with bands playing and crowds cheering. On the morning of Sunday, July 21, his troops began a wide flanking movement to surprise the Confederates. But General Beauregard knew what was coming (helped, no doubt, by the battle maps the Washington newspapers had printed). Probably those most surprised were the sightseers from Washington who hurried out to see a real live battle before the war was over. They had not realized that a real live battle involved real dead men.

Union General Patterson was supposed to occupy Confederate General Johnston in the Shenandoah Valley to prevent his joining Beauregard. But a few Confederate outposts made lots of noise to occupy Patterson, while Johnston's men marched to Manassas. Their arrival, together with the brave stand of the Virginians under Thomas Jackson (earning him the nickname "**Stonewall Jackson**") turned the tide of battle. McDowell ordered a retreat. But an orderly retreat is a difficult maneuver for untrained troops. The situation was not helped by the carriages of the sightseers and a wagon which broke down and blocked the main bridge over Cub Run. Before long, the retreat had turned into a rout. Fortunately for the North, the South's equally untrained and exhausted troops were in no condition to follow up the victory.

McDowell was replaced by McClellan, who began the arduous task of building a real army. The call now went out for three-year, rather than three-month, volunteers. And the North increased its resolve to fight to the finish. This determination was best brought home in Lincoln's inaugural address: "I hold that in contemplation of the universal law and of the Constitution, the union of the states is perpetual. . . . I therefore consider that the Union is unbroken and shall take care that the laws of the Union are faithfully executed in all the states . . . You [the South] have no oath registered in heaven to destroy this government, while I have the most solemn one to preserve, protect and defend it." Lincoln had pledged before God to keep that union perpetual; he would never abandon his pledge.

REVIEW QUESTIONS

1. What were the good points of the North and of the South before the Civil War? Why were the South's good points morally compromised?
2. How had the slavery controversy been handled at the Constitutional Convention?
3. Summarize the terms of the Missouri Compromise.
4. Summarize the terms of the Compromise of 1850.
5. Who were the moderate abolitionist leaders? Who were the radical abolitionist leaders? How did their views differ?
6. What were the Fugitive Slave Laws? What was the "underground railway"?
7. What was the Kansas-Nebraska Act? What was its fundamental error?
8. What were Lincoln's views on slavery?
9. Summarize the violence of 1856?
10. What was the Dred Scott decision?
11. How did John Brown become an abolitionist hero?
12. How did Lincoln win the Presidency?
13. How did war break out?
14. Why did each of the border states remain in the Union?
15. What were Lee's views on the war? How did he become commander of the Virginia army?
16. Why did McDowell attack at Bull Run? Why did the Union lose? How did this loss affect the North?

PROJECTS

1. Read *Uncle Tom's Cabin* and prepare an oral or written book report.
2. Do research and prepare a report on the Underground Railway.
3. Find out how the invention of the cotton gin affected the slavery question.

Chapter 16

The Civil War

THE CANNON SMOKE settled into the plains of Manassas, and the rain washed the blood from the ground. Lincoln fired McDowell as commander of the Army of the Potomac—the first of many changes he would make in the field command—and on July 24 appointed George McClellan, who had been successful in early skirmishing in the West, so successful in fact that the Northern newspapers, hungry for heroics, bestowed on McClellan the title, the "Young Napoleon." Winfield Scott, who had never been compared to Napoleon but who had more strategic sense than most of those who had been so compared, still pressed his "anaconda strategy" and warned against trying to win the war overnight. This advice was not what anyone wanted to hear. Though the blockade was instituted, Lincoln and most Northern Congressman still wanted heroics, so Scott was eased out and McClellan was named General-in-Chief in his place.

While the officers drilled their troops and taught them which end of a rifle to point at the enemy, the North's naval blockade went into effect. Soon cotton mildewed on the wharves because ships could not escape to carry cargo to Europe. The English government, which had built up a lively trade with the South, protested to the U.S. ambassador, Charles Francis Adams (son of John Quincy Adams), and declared neutrality. Adams then had to carry the heavy burden of persuading the British government neither to go beyond neutrality into active aid nor to extend official diplomatic recognition to the South as an independent nation. But Adams had the intelligence and diplomatic skill of earlier Adamses and succeeded in his mission.

On January 15, 1862, Lincoln appointed Edwin M. Stanton as Secretary of War. Lincoln's friends exploded. Stanton had been one of Lincoln's bitterest enemies, calling him "the original gorilla" and the "Illinois Ape." But Lincoln had a war to win, and he wanted the best man for the job. Stanton was that best man. He was an outstanding war minister, equipping a huge army for a full-scale war. The South never had anyone of even half Stanton's ability. As a consequence, the Southern army was constantly low on supplies, to the great detriment of its war effort.

Besides the worries of generals, war secretaries, blockades and military strategy, Lincoln carried the weight of personal tragedy. His beloved son Willie died, and his wife nearly went insane. Deep lines of strain and worry etched Lincoln's face, and he found himself turning toward God for consolation much more than he had in his youth.

But the War had to go on. The strategy worked out by Lincoln and his generals was to dispatch an army to seize Richmond, the capital of the Confederacy, while sending another force west to capture the Mississippi and Tennessee Rivers and divide the Confederacy. The two armies would then join and crush the South. The Confederates proposed to wage a primarily defensive war, in support of their right to exist as a nation, with any offensive actions in the North intended strictly to persuade the North to sue for peace.

The War During 1862

Lincoln finally had good news with reports of the Battle of Shiloh, in Tennessee on April 6-7, 1862, in which both sides lost over 10,000 men. Union General Ulysses S. Grant had failed to scout the enemy and been caught by a surprise attack, suffering heavy losses on April 6. But Confederate general Albert Sidney Johnston was wounded in battle on the first day and bled to death. His successor, P. T. Beauregard, did not press the attack, thinking the Union was in retreat. Instead Grant counterattacked on the second day. By sheer determination and the help of reinforcements from Ohio, his army forced a Confederate retreat. Though many Northern newspapers and Congressmen complained at the heavy casualties the Union had suffered, Lincoln supported Grant because he was not afraid to be aggressive and take chances.

Grant was the opposite of McClellan, who was refusing to attack. Lincoln removed him from overall command, naming General Henry Halleck as General-in-Chief, but leaving McClellan with the Army of the Potomac, the main Union force. More good news came from the

West with the Union's capture of New Orleans by Admiral David Farragut, thus giving the North the largest, wealthiest, strongest Confederate city and the South's main port and the key to the Mississippi River. In the East, the news was not so good. On June 1, Robert E. Lee had been given supreme command of the Army of Northern Virginia, and he promptly worked out a brilliant plan to stop McClellan's projected invasion of Richmond. Stonewall Jackson's maneuvers in the Shenandoah Valley frightened Lincoln into keeping 50,000 troops around Washington instead of sending them to McClellan. McClellan was almost within sight of Richmond but would not attack. Jeb Stuart and the Confederate cavalry destroyed $7,000,000 worth of supplies. By June 27, the Federal Army was virtually encircled. But in the June 30 Battle of Frayser's Farm, Stonewall Jackson unaccountably did not move his men in their part of Lee's pincer's movement until too late. Lee revised his plan and tried to cut the Union column in half, but again Jackson moved too late. On the seventh day of what came to be called the Seven Days' Battle (June 26-July 2), Lee launched a general assault, but the Union had its cannon in place and the Confederate attack failed. But the Union's strike toward Richmond had been halted, and the Army settled down in a fortified camp on the James River, while McClellan wrote frantic letters to Washington to "prove" that Lincoln had deliberately refused to give him enough men to defeat Lee's "huge" army. (Lee's armies always seemed to double from the time they fought McClellan to the time he wrote his reports.) Lincoln was not impressed, putting General John Pope in command of the Armies of Virginia and ordering a strike south.

Lee heard of Lincoln's plans and sent Jackson with 25,000 men on a circuit behind Bull Run Mountain and through the only real pass, Thoroughfare Gap. Pope, thinking the mountain protected him, had forgotten about Thoroughfare Gap. The few men who were there, mostly by accident, were amazed to find Jackson's whole division falling upon them. The next thing Pope knew, Jackson and his troops were in Manassas. When the Union army finally reached Manassas, Jackson's men had moved upstream, and Lee's army was rushing through Thoroughfare Gap. Pope, obsessed with Jackson, forgot about Lee and ordered an attack. His men ran into Lee's artillery, Lee sent Longstreet to attack the weakened line, Jackson's men advanced, and Lee took 7,000 prisoners.

Encouraged by this victory at Second Manassas, Lee ordered an invasion of Maryland in September, hoping that Maryland would join the

Confederacy. Lincoln fired Pope and put McClellan in charge of Washington's defenses. McClellan interpreted his authority broadly and went in pursuit of Lee, though he worried that Lee had too many troops and held back from a decisive engagement. But then one of McClellan's men found a copy of Lee's battle plans in a campsite that the Confederates had just vacated. The plans showed that Lee was dividing his forces and that McClellan faced just part of the Confederate Army. Even "Cautious George," as he was sometimes known, could not resist an attack in those circumstances, though instead of attacking immediately, he waited until the next day to be sure his army was ready.

That gave Lee the time he needed. A Confederate sympathizer had been among the crowd of local citizens in McClellan's tent when the captured orders were brought in. He rushed the news to Lee, who sent out messengers to recall his scattered forces. At Sharpsburg on September 17 the two armies fought a bloody battle. Lee outsmarted McClellan, who neglected to order his reserves into battle in time. Lee held his lines and the battle was a draw, though the total of 26,000 casualties was harder on Lee than on McClellan. Because the Confederates had their usual shortage of men and supplies, Lee was unable to press another attack and withdrew to Virginia. McClellan claimed credit for a victory and complained that Lee had outnumbered him with 100,000 men. Said Lincoln upon hearing McClellan's report: "Sending that man reinforcements is like shoveling flies across the room."

But the Battle of Antietam had consequences far beyond the strictly military. Because the Confederates had retreated, the battle appeared a Union victory. The British and French governments, on the verge of recognizing the Confederacy after the early string of Confederate victories, now held back. British and French aid to the South could have changed the entire course of the war.

And because of Antietam Lincoln decided to issue the ***Emancipation Proclamation***. The radical abolitionists had been after Lincoln for some time to free all slaves. Though Lincoln was opposed to slavery, he had held back; he did not want to antagonize the border slave states, and the Constitution gave him no power to free slaves. But as he became convinced that the Proclamation would aid the war effort by disrupting the South and that morality required it, he wanted a Union victory as an occasion to announce emancipation. Antietam was the best he could do, so on September 21, Lincoln proclaimed the freedom of all slaves in rebel areas as of January 1, 1863, carefully exempting slaves in border states. The Proclamation had no immediate effect. The South ignored it, and the radical abolitionists condemned Lincoln as not going far enough. The Democrats swept the November elections, and Lincoln was in serious political trouble. The day after the election disaster, Lincoln removed McClellan, a Democrat, and appointed Ambrose E. Burnside (after whom sideburns were named).

Burnside decided that he would succeed where everyone else had failed: he would outwit Lee. He sent a decoy toward Warrenton, then pushed to Fredericksburg on the way to Richmond. But when he arrived at Fredericksburg, Burnside was shocked to find Lee waiting for him. Though the Confederate Army was outnumbered 113,000 to 75,000, Lee's army was entrenched behind fortifications on the top of nearly vertical hills. Yet Burnside nevertheless ordered a frontal assault of 100,000 men on December 13. The Union fighting men courageously charged across the stream and up the hills in the face of withering fire from above. The Union lost 1,284 killed and 9,600 wounded; the Confederates half that many. The remaining troops spent a miserable Christmas in the rain. On January 21 Burnside ordered another frontal assault. His men nearly mutinied. General Joseph Hooker sent a frantic message to Lincoln, reporting Burnside's suicidal order. Burnside responded by trying to get Hooker fired. Lincoln responded by firing Burnside and appointing Hooker.

The Absolute Masterpiece

Spring came early in 1863, and General Hooker was delighted to see the blossoms covering the trees along the Potomac. For with the coming of good weather, he could put into action his plan for the final, crushing defeat of Robert E. Lee and the Army of Northern Virginia. It was a perfect plan, an "absolute masterpiece," everyone called it; and though Lincoln was more cautious than most, he too had hopes that at last he had found a general equal to the Virginian, Robert E. Lee. The plan appeared foolproof. To begin with, Hooker led more than 120,000 men, battle-tested, well-drilled and well-equipped. Lee's ragged, hungry army contained no more than half the Union total. Hooker planned to march his army up the river, crossing the Rappahannock and Rapidan Rivers 20 or 25 miles northwest of Fredericksburg, Virginia, then swing down and come in on Lee's flank. In the meantime, two smaller forces would act as decoys, crossing lower down the river to distract Lee while the main force outflanked him.

On April 27, Hooker's troops began to march and all of the pieces of the "absolute masterpiece" fell into place. Lee rose to the bait, concentrating his main force against the decoy led by Sedgwick. Hooker's force came around Lee's left. By the afternoon of April 30, he had more troops than were in Lee's entire army outflanking Lee, with Sedgwick and 40,000 men squarely in front of the Virginians. Lee was outnumbered, outmaneuvered and outflanked, his men caught like a nut in a vise between the wings of the Union.

Hooker sat in his headquarters near a crossroads known as Chancellorsville. He announced to his troops: "The enemy must either ingloriously fly, or come out from behind his defenses and give us battle on our own ground, where certain destruction awaits him." Lee had never ingloriously flown in his life, but he obliged Hooker by moving his army out from behind the Fredericksburg entrenchments. At the same time he did what seemed utterly rash; he divided his already greatly outnumbered force. He left ten thousand men to hold the line against Sedgwick's 40,000, and with the rest of his Confederates set out for Chancellorsville. Around noon on May 1, the first skirmish lines collided. The Union commander sent a message to Hooker, asking instructions. Hooker had talked confidently the night before, but now that his army was actually face to face with Lee's, he was worried. He ordered his advance troops back to the trenches and told them that tomorrow was soon enough to complete the "certain destruction" of the Virginians. He told one of the other officers, "I've got Lee just where I want him," adding that Lee's army was now "the legitimate property of the Army of the Potomac."

Meanwhile Lee held a conference with Stonewall Jackson. While Hooker was boasting how he would soon destroy Lee, Lee and Jackson planned how they would destroy Hooker. In his daring plan, Lee would divide his force still another time, sending Jackson and 25,000 men on a long circuit around Hooker, until the Confederates were due west of the Union troops, to attack the Union's exposed right flank. This long march would take until early evening. Meanwhile, Lee, with fewer than 20,000 men, would hold off Hooker's 80,000 so convincingly that Hooker would not guess Jackson had gone.

The next day, May 2, Lee hurled his small force against Hooker with such vehemence that Hooker kept all his attention on Lee. He heard about Jackson, but misinterpreted the movement, thinking it a retreat and sending out a few divisions to hurry Jackson along. Just before sundown, Jackson struck Hooker's right, totally surprising and utterly devastating the line. The fighting died out with the darkness, but Hooker's army had been shaken and had lost its confidence.

However, Lee and the South lost more than that. Late in the night Jackson rode out to reconnoiter the line, probing for a weak spot to strike the final blow come morning. There was confused fighting all around (one federal division had collided with other federal troops and fought a savage battle). When the men of the 33rd North Carolina Regiment heard a noise behind them, they were sure it was a federal move. They fired their guns and mortally wounded General Stonewall Jackson, Lee's right arm and probably the best general, save perhaps Lee himself, in the entire War.

Lee had loved Jackson like a brother, and hearing the news was one of the greatest shocks of his life. But he could not afford the luxury of mourning. When dawn came, he sent cavalry commander Stuart to take command of Jackson's offensive. The two wings of Lee's army came together, almost surrounding the Union force, which had lost the will to fight, and shoving them across the river. Then Sedgwick re-attacked, and Lee calmly re-divided his forces, leaving a few brigades to hold Hooker and sending the rest to trap Sedgwick in a bend of the river. After a day of hard fighting, the Union forces retreated, glad they were still alive. Lee regrouped his army and prepared to attack again.

Hooker did not give him the chance. His men still outnumbered Lee's, but Hooker simply crumbled. In the dark and rain he retreated, abandoning his invasion of Virginia, his perfect plan in ruins.

But the Battle of Chancellorsville *was* an absolute masterpiece after all, and none knew it better than the Confederate troops who rose to their feet and let out a mighty cheer as Lee rode among them. Chancellorsville was Lee's greatest triumph, probably the most masterful battle ever fought by an American general. Lee loved his men and acknowledged their cheers with gratitude, but in his heart lay a dull, throbbing pain. Jackson was dying, 12,000 Confederates had been put out of action, and the long weary road of war still stretched into the future, with no end in sight.

Gettysburg

In the North, they were getting sick of war. Not everyone to be sure, but much of the enthusiasm of the early days had been eroded by the string of Confederate victories. Besides the growing casualty lists, there was much dissatisfaction stemming from other causes. The Emancipation Proclamation was criticized, both by those who thought it too harsh and those who thought it too lenient; in the Midwest, secret societies (nicknamed Copperheads) sprang up, speaking openly in favor of the South and encouraging defiance of the law. In response, Lincoln had ordered the arrest of many of the Copperhead leaders and revoked the right of *habeas corpus* for all those imprisoned by military order (meaning that they could be kept in prison without being charged with a specific crime). Still a third cause of discontent was the new draft law. Before this time, soldiers had been strictly volunteers, but as the flow of volunteers lessened, Lincoln ordered a draft. But Americans of that time thought the draft a violation of their liberties, and riots broke out in many Eastern cities. In addition, the law was enforced unfairly. Men could escape the Draft by paying a sum of money or finding someone to take their place. This last provision led in many cases to the kidnapping of innocent people who were forced to serve in the Army in place of the men originally drafted. There was open talk of running a peace candidate against Lincoln in the 1864 elections, someone who would bring the dreary War to a close and let the South go its way. Lincoln was well aware of the discontent, but had no intention of letting it dilute his determination to re-unite the Union. He appointed still another new general—George Meade on June 28, 1863—and sent him off to meet the Confederate Army, which was marching north.

For the first time since Antietam, Lee was invading the North. Nearly all of the War had been fought in the Rappahanock Valley, which was now ravaged and devastated. It was time that the fighting came north. He also wanted to get the Northern Army away from Richmond. Finally, Lee hoped that one stirring victory in the backyard of the Union capital would aggravate the North's war weariness, so that Lincoln would be unable to resist the pressure for peace.

Lee had the utmost confidence in his men, but he also knew that his men would want to retaliate on Northern property for the damage inflicted on their farms and homes. Therefore Lee issued orders that all private property was to be protected, saying, "I cannot hope that Heaven will prosper our cause when we are violating its laws. I shall, therefore, carry on the war in Pennsylvania without offending the sanctions of a high civilization and of Christianity." Lee always insisted that war—bloody business though it was—be conducted according to the moral law, staunchly opposing deliberate attacks on civilians.

Though his men were in high spirits as they marched through the Pennsylvania countryside, Lee had much on his mind. Jackson's corps had been reorganized with new men in command, and not everyone was yet accustomed to the methods of the men with whom they had to work. Taking Jackson's place as second-in-command was James Longstreet. Longstreet was an energetic commanding officer when he agreed with the overall strategy, but apathetic when his advice was not followed. And his advice was not being followed in the Pennsylvania campaign. Longstreet had urged a defensive strategy with a few minor raids to frighten the North. Lee disagreed, hoping for a major engagement and a smashing victory. As they rode through the June sunshine, Longstreet sulked and grumbled.

On June 30, Lee heard artillery fire in the distance. He rode to the small town of Gettysburg, an important road junction, to find a skirmish underway. A small detachment of Confederates had gone into town to purchase supplies, but had encountered federal infantry instead. Lee immediately took command and ordered more troops into battle. By evening, the Confederates had captured 5000 prisoners, and Lee decided to strike a major blow the next day before Meade could concentrate his forces. He directed General Ewell to take strategic Culp's Hill, then to move on to Cemetery Ridge, "if practicable," after which Longstreet was to concentrate the main body of the Confederate force to deliver the major blow. But Ewell had formerly served directly under Jackson, who gave very explicit orders. He was not used to exercising his own judgment. After taking Culp's Hill, he did not move, though he could almost certainly have taken Cemetery Ridge. Longstreet, meanwhile, delayed and dawdled, and the knockout blow was never delivered.

By early morning of July 2, the Federal Army had still not reinforced Cemetery Ridge, giving the Confederates another opportunity to seize a position which could well be the key to the battle. But Longstreet was nowhere to be seen. By 10:00, Lee was agonizingly asking his aides, "What *can* detain Longstreet? He ought to be in position by now." As Lee paced up and down, federal troops began to move onto Cemetery Ridge. At last Longstreet was discovered, and Lee ordered him to move immediately onto the Ridge. Longstreet waited forty more minutes, then finally began to move.

The Southerners fought with their usual valor, but met equally valorous opposition. Longstreet sent Hood's division to attempt a flanking movement. Hood saw the steep rocky hill known as Little Round Top and instantly realized its strategic value. If his men could reach the top, his guns could flank the whole Army of the Potomac. And the hill was unguarded. Immediately the Confederates began to move up Little Round Top. Meanwhile, Meade had sent Warren, his Chief of Engineers, to reconnoiter. Warren rode to Little Round Top for a better view and saw Hood's men coming. Instantly sizing up the danger, Warren rushed down the hill and snatched the 20th Maine Division out of formation, sending them to the top in a race against the Confederates. The Union troops barely won the race and were immediately plunged into a nightmare battle up and down the rocky slopes. The Maine farm boys were fighting hand to hand against three to one odds, but they never gave an inch, fighting on raw courage and love for the Union. They held the line. The attack was repulsed. The flanking movement had failed, and victory escaped the grasp of the Confederate Army.

And therefore, after two days of the Battle of Gettysburg, the Southern Army had failed to outflank the Union army on right and left. There remained the center, and on the evening of July 2, red-haired General Pickett arrived with his elite Virginia division. Lee reasoned that Meade must have taken troops and artillery from the center to reinforce the flanks. Therefore he planned an artillery barrage, then a direct charge at the center by 15,000 men. The objective was a little clump of trees on a high point of ground, which would give the South the victory it had sought. Longstreet was strongly opposed to the plan, but Lee resolved to smash the Union center come July 3.

The morning dawned bright and clear, and all was quiet as the guns were pulled into position. At 1:00 Lee nodded, and 160 guns let loose a bombardment. To everyone's surprise the Union guns returned the fire with greater force than ever. The artillery divisions had not been weakened, but were the best the Union had. As the minutes ticked by, the Confederate artillerymen were shocked to discover that they did not have enough ammunition to keep up the bombardment as long as planned: Longstreet had failed in his assigned task of ensuring a steady ammunition supply. Alexander, the Commander of Artillery, sent a message to Pickett: "For God's sake come quickly. The eighteen guns have gone. Come quickly or my ammunition will not let me support you properly." At 2:00 Pickett turned to Longstreet: "General, shall I advance?" Longstreet turned away; he refused to speak. Pickett turned to his men: "Up men, and to your posts! Don't forget today that you are from old Virginia!" Fifteen thousand men, in orderly ranks, stepped out onto the sunlit grass and marched straight ahead, looking into the muzzles of the Union guns.

For 200 yards they marched, heads held high and pride in their hearts. Then the Union guns opened fire. The march did not slacken. As men fell to the earth, others moved up to take their places. Man after man fell, the gray shirts stained red. Still the lines marched on, their ranks growing smaller but their courage never failing. Then with a rebel yell they began to run, to run faster toward the deadly fire that had laid low their comrades. They broke through the Union line and reached the copse of trees—the farthest north penetration of the Confederacy in the Civil War. Now it was hand-to-hand fighting, the decimated Virginians against the men of Pennsylvania and New England. The Northern Divisions outnumbered the Southerners. They launched a countercharge. The gray-clad men were killed, captured, driven back. The guns fell silent; the few survivors stumbled back to the Confederate lines. Lee's face turned ashen. "It's all my fault," he said and bowed his head.

Vicksburg

The federal troops were so shaken by the courage of the Southerners that Meade feared to order a counterattack, allowing the Southerners to withdraw through the mud and rain on July 5 back across the Potomac. In Washington, Lincoln was despondent because Meade had not followed up his victory. But in the afternoon of July 7, he received news which cheered him more than almost anything since the start of the war. General Grant—who dressed sloppily, drank heavily and refused to fill out forms properly—had just taken Vicksburg.

"The possession of Vicksburg is the possession of America," General William Sherman had once said. The Mississippi city controlled the Mississippi River. If it fell into Union hands, the Confederacy would no longer be able to use the Father of Waters to supply the States on the eastern side with the crops from the western side. The Confederacy would be cut in half to wither and die. The Union generals made the capture of Vicksburg of almost equal priority with the capture of Richmond.

But Vicksburg was not easily captured. Seven times, with seven different strategies, the Union forces moved against Vicksburg. Seven times they failed, miserably. Seven failures, and any other commander would have given up. Grant simply gathered his men together and decided to cross the Mississippi to high ground on the east bank. He would be cut off by the river from his supply lines, but he told his men that they would live off the land. In 17 days, he marched his men 130 miles, split the Confederate forces in half, won five battles, and cost the South 14,000 casualties. General Halleck in Washington sent Grant an order to return to the west bank. Grant stuck the order in his pocket and besieged Vicksburg.

His heavy guns bombarded the city and his trenches kept supplies from getting in. In Vicksburg the price of flour rose to $1000 a barrel and meat to $250 a pound. The men in the Union trenches were sick and hungry and infested with vermin, and it was a matter of which army—that inside the city or that outside—could hold out longer. The Northerners outlasted the Southerners, and on July 4 the Confederate flag came down from Vicksburg. Six days later the steamer *Imperial* ran unarmed from St. Louis to New Orleans, and Lincoln could say: "The Father of Waters once more flows unvexed to the sea."

The North Takes Charge

Lee could see as well as anyone the significance of the Union victory at Vicksburg. So he took the desperate step of weakening his own forces by sending Longstreet to the West to join General Bragg. The Confederates knew what was at stake, and on the first day of the Battle of Chickamauga (September 19), they broke the Union line and were only a quarter of a mile from cutting the road which would have prevented a retreat, thus trapping the Union army just south of Chattanooga. But the Union line re-formed and held, with terrific losses on both sides.

The next day the fighting resumed with equal ferocity. Union General Rosecrans surveyed the line and noticed that General Wood's regiment was out of place. He called Major Bond and told him to rush to Wood and have him close the gap. Major Bond confused the instructions, resulting in the famous "muddled orders of Chickamauga." He rushed to Wood and said: "The general commanding directs that you close up on Reynolds as fast as possible and support him." Reynolds was a quarter of a mile away. But Wood was used to obeying orders. He pulled his division out of formation and marched away. Longstreet immediately hurled 30,000 men through the gap, and the Union Army retreated in panic.

Longstreet and his men had a chance to capture the entire Union Army and pursued the Union troops. Union General George Thomas was ordered to cover the retreat. He formed his men against a superior force. Somehow he inspired them to hold. The Confederates had no more reserves. Thomas—known thereafter as the Rock of Chickamauga—held the line. The Union Army was saved. The Confederates won the battle, but they had lost thousands of men who could never be replaced, and—though they may not have realized it—they had lost their last chance to win the War. In November, Thomas took Chattanooga, and the Northern armies were in position to split the South horizontally by marching across Georgia to the sea.

The Road to Appomattox

On February 22, 1864, Ulysses S. Grant was appointed Commander-in-Chief of the Army of the Potomac. He and Lincoln together developed a strategy: Grant would harry Lee's army, wearing it down, while General William T. Sherman took the Western Army and split the Confederacy north and south by marching to Atlanta. On May 4, Grant's army broke camp. He had 122,000 men against Lee's 62,000, men whose equipment, clothing, food and ammunition were far superior to Lee's, as the Confederacy suffered from the combined effects of the sea blockade, the loss of Vicksburg and its general inability to manufacture and distribute supplies.

Lee knew perfectly well what Grant intended to do. His hope was that General Joseph Johnston could somehow stop Sherman while the Army of Northern Virginia inflicted enough losses on Grant to persuade the Union government that further loss of life was senseless. On May 5, Lee attacked the Union Army among the mass of trees known as the Wilderness, hoping that the tangle of growth would help to nullify Grant's numerical advantage. Clever strategy was impossible, and the battle settled down to murderous rifle fire. One hundred men were killed every minute. Dry leaves caught fire, and the woods were full of smoke. Lee tried several attacks, almost succeeding, but the Union Army held firm. By sunset of the second day, the Union losses were 17,000, twice those of the Confederate Army. In the darkness, Grant ordered his men out of the trenches. They started wearily down the road, soon coming to a crossroads. The road to the left led back to Washington, the road to the right led past the rebel front. Every other commander—from McClellan to Burnside to Hooker to Meade—would have been demoralized by Lee and would have turned his men back toward Washington. But Grant sat at the crossroads, silently pointing right as the men marched by. Their spirits began to revive. At last they had a commander who would not run from Lee, even when he had been beaten by him.

Lee quickly figured out what Grant was doing and rushed his men toward Spotsylvania. He had to get there first, or else Grant would have outflanked him, and the Union Army would be between Lee and Richmond. The Confederates won the race, and Lee had his men fortify an acute angle with Spotsylvania in the center, an excellent defensive position. On May 8, Grant attacked and captured a Confederate division. With his men starting to fall back, Lee mounted his white horse and rode to the front with uplifted sword to lead the countercharge in person. When his men realized what was happening, they pushed him back; they loved Lee too much to allow him to risk his life. "We'll take it for you," they shouted. They hurled the Union Army back. Then commenced a sixteen-hour battle over what came to be called Bloody Angle, as men fought with no rest or food, the Confederates outnumbered two or three to one through most of the battle. As both sides fought with by now legendary courage, separated only by the length of a bayonet, Lee had his men construct a new defensive line behind the old one. Finally, by midnight, the line was finished and his troops could fall back in orderly fashion. Seeing the Confederates in their new position, Grant ordered the Union Army to withdraw. So many bullets had been fired that 20-inch trees had been cut down by them. But the battle had served the Union purpose, wearing down Lee's army, killing men who could not be replaced. Though more Union troops than Confederates were killed, Grant had more men to spare and never hesitated to continue to pour the blood of Northern soldiers into the Virginia soil. But Grant's strategy—though often criticized—was neither senseless nor ineffective. For he *was* winning, and if he could just gain the victory in this campaign, the end of the War would be in sight, with the subsequent saving of many lives. So he never let up.

While Bloody Angle was earning its name, the Northern cavalry commander Philip Sheridan started toward Richmond. Jeb Stuart pushed his weary cavalrymen after him, heading him off just in time. But in the battle, Stuart went down with a bullet in his lungs, depriving Lee of his best scout, and Sheridan's cavalry cut the Southern supply lines, leaving Lee's ill-equipped men with almost no chance of getting the new supplies they desperately needed.

As the dead and wounded men from the Wilderness and Spotsylvania poured into Washington, Lincoln agonized: "I can't bear it. This suffering, this loss of life is dreadful." But he would not back down an inch. He was hotly criticized for putting Grant—a butcher they called him—into command. The Union dead at Spotsylvania had covered five acres of ground, and the Democrats nominated McClellan as a peace candidate for the 1864 elections, but Lincoln believed that only Grant could win the War. As the lines in his face grew deeper and his eyes hollower, he held to his strategy, urging Grant to "hold on with a bull-dog grip and chew and choke as much as possible."

Grant held on. His strategy was to keep swinging round Lee's left, forcing Lee to fight him, wearing down Lee's strength. In one month the Union lost 50,000 men, but the strategy was working. By June, the Union had new repeating carbines, giving Lee the impression that there were twice as many men opposing him as there really were, since they could now shoot twice as fast. They held off the Confederate Army while another force cut between Lee and Richmond and besieged Petersburg. The Northern Army exploded a huge mine, but when the Northern troops attacked, they ended up in the crater, where they were sitting ducks for the southern sharpshooters. Four thousand were killed.

Meanwhile Sherman defeated Johnston in a series of battles in Georgia, circling around Atlanta and coming in from behind to capture the city. Sherman received orders to march across Georgia to Savannah or Charleston, living off the land. Sherman made up his mind to spread as much destruction as possible, beginning by burning Atlanta. Then his 60,000 men turned toward the sea with the goal, "To make Georgia howl." They pried up railroads, burned the ties, heated the rails and wrapped them around trees, where they were known as Sherman's hairpins. They mixed kerosene with flour in stores and homes, poured corn meal over carpets and molasses over the cornmeal, kicked holes in windows, slashed mattresses. "I make war vindictively," said Sherman. "War is war and you can make nothing else of it." On December 22 he reached Savannah and the sea. His message to Washington: "General Sherman makes the American people a Christmas present of the city of Savannah with 150 heavy guns and 25,000 bales of cotton." He had cut the Confederacy in half and lost fewer than 400 men in the process.

In Tennessee, General Thomas cracked the Confederate line and ended the war in the West by taking Nashville. Jefferson Davis was now president of only three states. Abraham Lincoln was re-elected President of the rest of the States. The Union victories had silenced the opposition, and Lincoln had carried every state but Kentucky, Delaware and New Jersey. Because of this striking victory, Congress passed the Thirteenth Amendment to the Constitution, abolishing slavery. In his second inaugural address, Lincoln set what he hoped would be the tone of the peace settlement: "With malice toward none, with charity toward all, with firmness in the right, as God gives us to see the right, let us strive on to finish the work we are in; to bind up the nation's wounds . . ."

Sherman, meanwhile, marched his army through the Carolinas, slashing, burning and destroying. The best Johnston could do was rally his troops and launch a surprise attack at Bentonville, North Carolina. But Sherman's men were not green troops. They regrouped and drove the Confederates into the swamps.

Lee had said: "I shall endeavor to do my duty and fight to the last." His only hope was a desperation thrust. He concentrated his hungry troops on the east side of Petersburg, hoping that Grant would pull in his wings to meet the attack. Then the Army of Northern Virginia could be loaded on trains and rushed south to help Johnston. The Confederate charge broke the line, but was stopped with the loss of 6000 men. Grant then sent his troops out to cut the Confederate retreat and surround the Army. Lee scraped together all the men he could, putting 15,000 infantry and all his cavalry under Pickett, sending them to crush the Union left and roll up its line. But Sheridan led the counter-charge, beating off Pickett, then attacking. Lee lost 2500 casualties, 4500 prisoners, his artillery and his cavalry. Grant ordered an assault along the whole front. The Union broke through and Petersburg was taken on April 2.

Lee gathered his exhausted men together and started them down the road toward Amelia Courthouse where rations should be waiting. But when they arrived, there was nothing for his starving men to eat. Lee then marched them down the road toward Danville, hoping to meet a wagon train with rations. But after dragging along for several miles, they came to a federal entrenchment; their escape was blocked. The only hope was to move away fast, and Lee ordered a forced night march. The Union pursued, attacking all along the line. Lee himself picked up a fallen battle flag to rally his troops, but about half of his army was

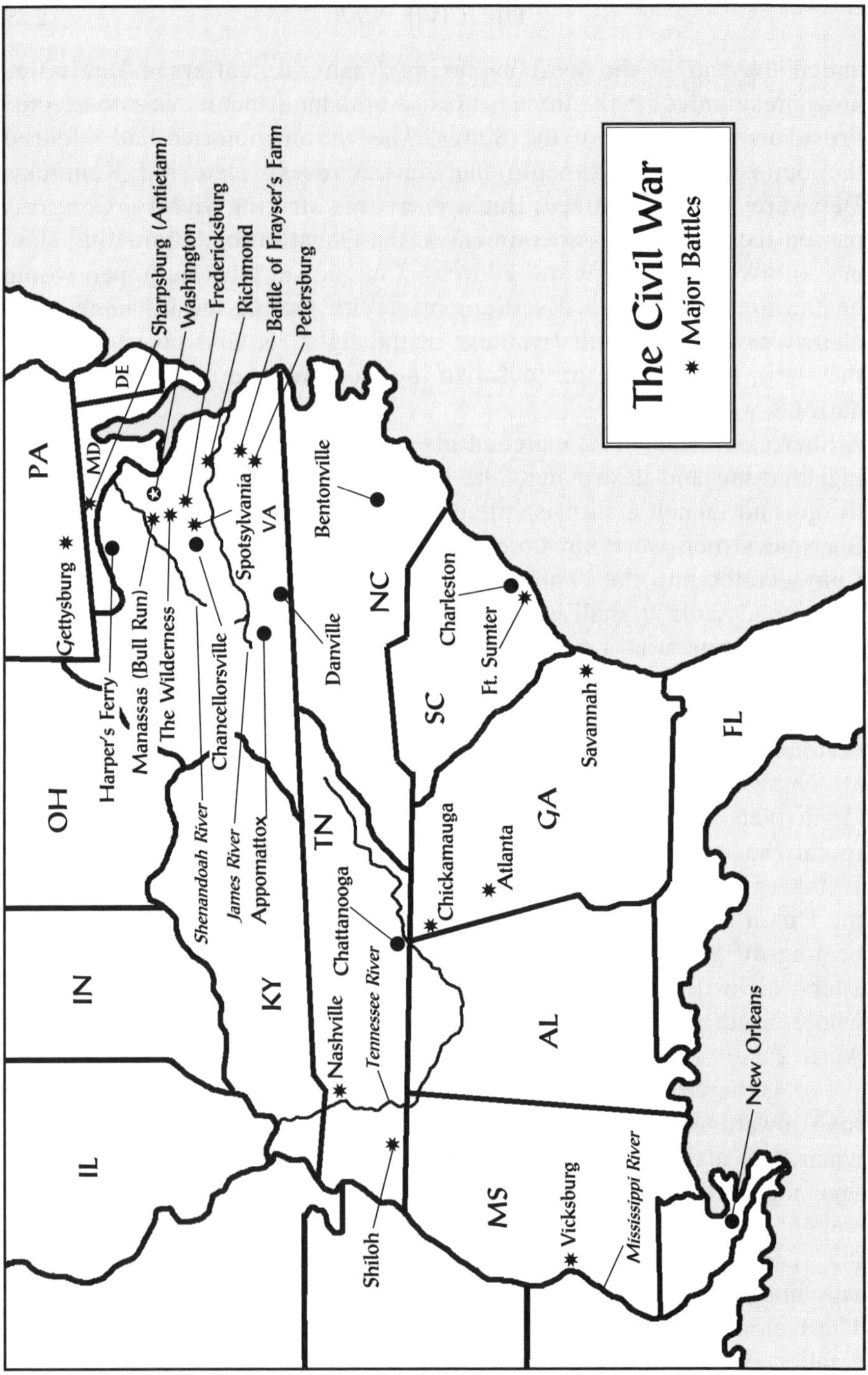
The Civil War
✱ Major Battles
PA
MD
DE
OH
IN
IL
KY
VA
NC
SC
GA
FL
AL
MS
TN
Gettysburg
Harper's Ferry
Manassas (Bull Run)
The Wilderness
Shenandoah River
Chancellorsville
James River
Appomattox
Sharpsburg (Antietam)
Washington
Fredericksburg
Richmond
Battle of Frayser's Farm
Petersburg
Spotsylvania
Danville
Bentonville
Charleston
Ft. Sumter
Savannah
Chickamauga
Atlanta
Chattanooga
Tennessee River
Nashville
Shiloh
Vicksburg
Mississippi River
New Orleans

lost. Lee marched on to Appomattox Station, still in hopes of finding his supply train. On April 8 he received a letter from Grant, suggesting a meeting to discuss surrender terms.

April 9 was Palm Sunday. The Confederate Army still had no supplies. The Union army had cut off all lines of march. Longstreet was fighting off two federal corps, trying to protect the Southern flank. Having received a full report of the situation, Lee wearily said, "Then there is nothing left for me to do but to go to see General Grant, and I would rather die a thousand deaths."

They met at the home of Major Wilmer McLean. Grant was in his dirty battle clothes. Lee—dignified to the last—had put on his full dress uniform and carried his gold sword. Grant began by wanting to talk about the Mexican War in which both men had learned the art of battle. Lee simply asked what terms he proposed. Grant agreed that prisoners would be allowed to return to their homes and officers to keep their side arms and horses. At 3:45, the surrender document was signed and the Army of Northern Virginia was no more.

Lee returned to the Southern camp, where his men greeted him with cheers and tears. Not once in a major engagement had Lee met the Union Army on even terms. He never had enough supplies or enough troops. Yet he had repulsed four major offensives against Richmond and by the invasion of Pennsylvania delayed another offensive five to ten months. From 1862-1864 he had fought ten major battles, winning six decisively and losing only one (Gettysburg), while Southern troops were losing everywhere else. He knew how to get the best from his men and his strategy was consistently daring. But he was never able to press his victories because he lacked the resources available to the North. Now, after the surrender, his true nobility shone forth. He urged the South to be conciliatory; he said that he would continue to pray for his enemies as he had done every day during the War.

On April 18, Johnston surrendered to Sherman; on May 10, Jefferson Davis was captured; and on May 26, the last Confederate forces surrendered.

Lincoln did not live to see the end of the War. On April 14, Good Friday, an actor named John Wilkes Booth had put a bullet into the head of the President, who died the next morning. Lincoln had begun his Presidency determined to do whatever was necessary to restore the Union and guarantee the survival of democratic government. If that goal took the violation of the Constitution (through the denial of *habeas corpus* without Congress's consent), the removal of any general who disagreed with him (such as McClellan), and the toleration of huge casualty totals, then he would take those actions without the slightest hesitation. His policy toward slavery early in the war—announcing that he had no intention or power of ending slavery in the South—was also aimed toward that end. When he later became convinced that slavery was so immoral that it must be ended everywhere, it was easier for him to act on that belief because he was now convinced that freeing the slaves would disrupt the South's war effort. But in everything, the Union came first.

Lincoln's greatest leadership quality was his ability to take a nation divided many ways—not just North and South, but within the North as well—and lead it in the direction he wanted. There was opposition to him in the press, the Congress, the Cabinet and the state governments, but his values triumphed. Overall, his values were good values. Though he was too much afflicted with American Messianism, though he violated more civil liberties than he should have, though he was too tolerant of battlefield slaughters, he persevered in the face of adversity. He loved his country and its people, he wanted freedom for the oppressed Negro people, and he wanted to forgive the South and heal the country's wounds. He thus earned the right to be ranked as one of America's greatest Presidents.

But Lincoln did not live to lead and perhaps heal the divided country after the War. Therefore the shape of the newly reunited nation was almost certainly not what he would have wanted it to be.

REVIEW QUESTIONS

1. How did the blockade help the North?
2. Why was it important to keep England neutral?
3. Why was Stanton a controversial choice for Secretary of War? Why was he a good choice?
4. What were the overall strategies for the North and for the South?
5. What was the result of the Seven Days Battle?
6. Why did Lincoln issue the Emancipation Proclamation? What were its results?
7. Show how the Battle of Chancellorsville was an "absolute masterpiece."

8. Summarize the Battle of Gettysburg. Why did the South lose? What were the results of the battle?
9. Why was Vicksburg important? How did the North finally capture it?
10. What was the significance of the Battle of Chickamauga?
11. Why did Lincoln appoint Grant commander-in-chief? What was his strategy?
12. Describe the battles of the Wilderness and Spotsylvania. What was their significance?
13. What role did Sherman play in ending the war?
14. Why did Lee surrender? Give the date and place.
15. Summarize Lee's achievements.
16. Summarize Lincoln's achievements.

PROJECTS

1. Do research and prepare a report on a Civil War general.
2. Choose a year of the Civil War. Put together a magazine in the format of a news magazine from that year.
3. Imagine that you were a soldier in either the Union or Confederate army. Write a diary of at least ten entries describing your experiences and your reactions to them.

Chapter 17

Traditionalists in Latin America

THE REBELLION AGAINST SPAIN had left a trail of wreckage in Latin America: unstable governments, inflation, violence, persecution of the Church, poverty and oppression of the Indians, lawlessness and disorder. But somehow through it all, the ordinary people held to their Catholic Faith, which gave them the courage to face each day. And even among the wealthier classes and the intellectuals, men emerged who rejected Liberalism, who professed traditional values, who were loyal Catholics, who wanted to help their countries rather than use them to gain wealth and power. In Guatemala, a traditionalist Catholic Indian named Rafael Carrera governed his country wisely for 27 years (1838-65). In Colombia a traditionalist intellectual named Miguel Antonio Caro (1843-1909) guided his country on the path of stability and sound moral values. But the most significant traditionalist movements were in Mexico and Ecuador.

Maximilian and Carlota

On July 27, 1857, Europe thrilled to a royal wedding. Maximilian von Hapsburg, the younger brother of the Austrian Emperor Franz Josef, wed the beautiful Princess Charlotte of Belgium. The blissfully happy young couple settled down in Trieste, a city in Italian territory governed by Austria where Max was governor. The royal couple were popular with their people, and it seemed the perfect beginning to a long and happy married life. But events far across the ocean and on another continent would bring first joy, then frustration, then tragedy to the Austrian Archduke and his dark-haired bride.

For forty years after the overthrow of Iturbide, Mexico suffered civil war. Liberals fought traditionalists; Mexico had 30 presidents in 30 years. By 1848 the Mexican government was heavily in debt and could neither control banditry nor restore order. Mexican traditionalists realized that in the Church and in traditional values was Mexico's only hope. Two leaders, José d'Estrada and José Hidalgo, conceived the idea of establishing a Catholic monarchy with a European prince on the throne. They discussed the idea in Europe and found a willing hearer in Empress Eugenie, the wife of Napoleon of France. Eugenie, Spanish-born and a dedicated Catholic, began to pressure her husband to use French troops and wealth to bring a Catholic emperor to Mexico.

Meanwhile, a Liberal revolution in Mexico overthrew Santa Anna in 1854. The leader of the new government was the Indian Benito Juarez. New laws confiscated Church property and sold it to wealthy speculators, who had no care for the Indians who lived on the property. The Church could no longer continue its educational and charitable activities, and the government did nothing to replace them. Rebellion broke out with the battle cry of *religión y fueros*—"religion and local rights." Juarez rallied the Liberals, with the help of weapons and money from the U.S., and thus began an intensely bitter civil war in Mexico.

In July 1859, Juarez issued the Laws of the Reform, confiscating all Catholic property for the government. Land, money, buildings, even works of art and sacred vessels were seized and sold for money to buy weapons. Marriage was made a civil contract only, and the government controlled all Church activities, except Mass and the Sacraments.

In 1860 the Liberal army defeated traditionalist general Miguel de Miramón. The liberals proceeded to strip and gut every church in the area, making a bonfire with sacred pictures and statues. On January 1, 1861, Juarez led his army into Mexico City. His slogan: "Nothing by force, everything by law and reason." The Mexicans must have thought he had a strange definition of law and reason.

Juarez had won only because of U.S. aid. But now the U.S. was in its own Civil War and unable to help Juarez further. His government was bankrupt, owing huge sums to France, Spain and England. In July 1861, Juarez declared a moratorium (delayed payment) on all foreign debts. The European countries were furious and thought seriously for the first time that a European prince on the throne in Mexico might be a good idea. Napoleon III began to envision France as a great civilizing influence in the Western Hemisphere; he also liked the thought of profits which might come to France.

Napoleon looked around Europe for a likely prince, and his mind fixed on Maximilian. Efforts were mounted to persuade Maximilian and Charlotte to go to Mexico, and both were attracted to the idea. Max was a romantic and an idealist; he liked to write poetry, to tend garden, to carry on discussions far into the night. The notion of a romantic rescue of Mexico appealed to him. He also thought that out from under the shadow of his brother the Emperor, he might be happier and more able to put some of his own ideas into practice. Charlotte, on the other hand, was a committed Catholic and saw the mission as one of service to Christ. She had a deep sense of the Hapsburg tradition into which she had married and felt that monarchy was the best form of government. She was also attracted by the thought of an imperial throne for Maximilian and herself, with all the ceremony and prestige that went with it. From the beginning, Charlotte made every effort to persuade Max to accept the throne.

The French army landed in Mexico in 1862. Supported by many Mexicans, they began to win victories. These successes worried the U.S., and Lincoln announced that "the liberation of the continent from European control has been a leading feature of American history in the past." But Lincoln was preoccupied with the Civil War and could not put his veiled threats into action. In May 1863, Puebla surrendered and Juarez fled Mexico City, leaving it in such a lawless state that the people welcomed the French army with a shower of flowers. In every city, an imposing list of signatures in support of Maximilian was collected. The traditionalist general Almonte convoked a national assembly, which voted to ask Maximilian to accept the throne. This Mexican support, added to Napoleon III's guarantee that the French army would remain in Mexico for three years, persuaded Maximilian to accept the crown of Mexico. Charlotte summed up her own reaction in a letter to her grandmother: "When one feels one is called upon to reign, then it becomes a vocation, like any other religious vocation. . . . For my part, I admit that, without putting too much store on the trappings of power, I have up to now known too little of life not to desire to have something to love and to strive for outside my own domestic circle."

In March 1864, the young Hapsburg couple made a state visit to Paris. Mexican flags were sold in the streets. The chefs of the royal palace created enormous sugar confections of Mexico's national emblem, an eagle devouring a serpent on a cactus plant. Charlotte and Maximilian were cheered and feasted. Their Mexican adventure was about to begin.

Glory and Disaster

On the morning of April 10, 1864, a Mexican delegation arrived at Trieste to present Maximilian with a list of Mexican towns swearing allegiance to him. Charlotte, who now adopted the Spanish form of her name, Carlota, was radiantly happy, but observers remarked that Max was pale and nervous. Max swore by the Gospels the following: "to assure by all the means in my power the prosperity and well-being of the nation and to defend the independence and integrity of its territory." The Mexican imperial flag was hoisted and the warships in the bay fired a 21-gun salute. The Mexican Empire was born, but the Mexican Emperor was on the verge of collapse. The departure had to be postponed three days because the awareness of the responsibilities he was assuming was too much for Max to absorb all at once. Carlota, on the other hand, was a tower of strength, and Max would rely on her more and more during the difficult days ahead.

At last they arrived in Mexico City. Max hardly knew where to begin. He was neither a good administrator nor a competent organizer, yet he had to cope with bankruptcy, banditry, instability and disorder. Max retreated by becoming dreamy and indecisive. But Carlota blossomed. She was quick and creative, giving Max by far the best advice he received. She dominated the decisions of the government, carrying on her thin shoulders the countless burdens of the Mexican Empire. Max's main value was as a symbol to the Mexican people. When he went on a tour of the outlying provinces, he was cheered everywhere and he enjoyed every minute of it. Meanwhile Carlota wrestled with financial reports, trying to bring some order to Mexico's economy.

By 1865 the financial problems became almost intolerable. In his comfortable palace in Paris, Napoleon III wanted some return on his investment in Mexico. He demanded repayment of French loans and threatened to withdraw his troops. Then, the end of the U.S. Civil War saw arms and ammunition smuggled across the Rio Grande to Juarez and his forces. The U.S. Secretary of State refused to receive Max's ambassador, referring to Maximilian as a "revolutionary." Faced with such monumental problems, even Carlota's energy and determination flagged and she had fierce headaches. The liberals stirred up antagonism against the royal couple, ridiculing Max for being dominated by his wife. Max's health deteriorated, and he became subject to violent changes in mood. Carlota, in spite of her administrative talents, began to feel herself a failure as a wife because she and Max had no children. Max himself added to her humiliation by bringing into the palace the grandson of Iturbide to prepare him to be the future heir to the throne. As the situation in Mexico worsened, Maximilian and Carlota became progressively less able to cope.

With winter, the crisis mounted. Sixteen thousand Juaristas terrorized the countryside, capturing the town of Hermosillo and massacring all 37 French inhabitants. Carlota was melancholy and distressed, Max nervous and frightened. Then came the news they had been dreading. On June 28, 1866 they received an official note from Napoleon stating that the French army was ordered to leave Mexico, on the excuse that he feared war with the U.S. They would be allowed to stay only if Maximilian would turn over all Mexican revenues to France, an impossible condition.

Napoleon's breaking his promise of three years of French army support was the final straw for Max. He began to talk seriously of abdicating and returning to Austria. At the first hint of abdication, Carlota snapped out of her melancholy. Never, she said, would a Hapsburg disgrace himself by abdicating under pressure. She summoned all her strength, reminded Max of all the Hapsburg tradition of honorable and courageous rule, of all their responsibilities to the Church and the Mexican people. Max must not abdicate. She persuaded him to write to Napoleon demanding that he continue his support. Napoleon's answer was embarrassed and apologetic but nonetheless a flat no. Carlota then determined that she herself would return to Europe, first to Paris to confront Napoleon with his broken promises, then to Rome to persuade the Pope that, without the Empire, Mexico would lapse into anarchy and atheism, and finally wherever necessary in Europe to raise money and obtain support.

At 4:00 a.m. on July 9, Carlota's mission began, as heavily loaded wagons moved slowly to the port of Veracruz. The trip was miserable. A wagon wheel broke; Carlota suffered splitting headaches. But nothing could stop her. The sea voyage was no more pleasant, as Carlota was constantly seasick. When the ship docked at St. Nazaire, she received no welcome befitting an Empress; the mayor of the town flew the Peruvian flag because he had no flag from Mexico. When Carlota arrived in Paris, no one came to greet her, an unbearable insult. Carlota sent frantic messages demanding an audience with Napoleon. Suffering from gall bladder problems, he was afraid to face her. He sent Eugenie to

Carlota's hotel on August 10, hoping that his wife could persuade Carlota to leave quietly.

As Carlota came to meet Eugenie, the contrast between the two women made onlookers gasp. Eugenie was twice Carlota's age, but the burdens Carlota had borne made her look the older of the two. Carlota was pale, her face was lined, her eyes wild with anger and anguish. Eugenie tried to soothe her. Carlota did not want soft words. She demanded an interview with Napoleon and the fulfillment of his promises. Nothing Eugenie could say or do would dissuade Carlota, who insisted so vigorously that Eugenie gave in and promised a meeting.

The next day, Carlota summoned every ounce of strength she had. She begged, pleaded, threatened, argued. But Napoleon could only weakly shake his head and say that his ministers would never allow him to leave his troops in Mexico. She paid the Emperor a second visit, and her passionate appeal was ended only when Eugenie pretended to faint. On August 21, Carlota received formal notification that Napoleon was finished with Mexico. A few days later, he wrote to Maximilian that "it is henceforward impossible for me to give Mexico another cent or another soldier." On the same day, Carlota sent her husband a telegram in Spanish: *Todo es inutil*—"All is useless."

Somewhere, somehow, in Carlota's inheritance and uprbringing and in her own free will, she had received great strengths. Throughout her marriage, throughout the overwhelmingly burdensome days of trying to govern Mexico, she had been a tower of strength. But when faced with utter failure, her strength left her. She collapsed into insanity.

She continued her journey, arriving in Rome on September 25 to visit the Pope. But she was no longer the self-possessed young Empress who knew what she wanted and how to get it. Now she was a crazed woman, afraid that everyone was trying to assassinate her, that everything she was offered to eat was poisoned. She fled to the Vatican, believing that only the Pope could protect her, refusing to eat anything that had not been prepared for the Pope himself, sleeping in the Vatican library because she believed that nowhere else would she be safe. When she was finally persuaded to return to her hotel, she would not eat anything that was not cooked in her room while she was watching, and she would often rush out of her room to drink from one of Rome's fountains because she feared to quench her burning thirst from any glass or bottle which could have been poisoned. At last the Hapsburgs brought her back to Trieste, where she was placed in total seclusion, having lost all touch with reality.

In Mexico, reality bore down ever more frighteningly on Maximilian. But as matters worsened, he grew stronger. Somewhere in his Hapsburg inheritance were strengths which began to emerge when all seemed hopeless. His first thought on hearing of Carlota's illness was to abdicate and rush to her side. But when he learned that she was totally and incurably insane, he decided that the best thing he could do for her, for himself and for Mexico was to stay and fight.

On February 5, 1867, the last French soldier left. Max turned to his aide and proclaimed, "At last we are free." On February 13, he left for Querétaro to take personal command of the loyalist army. He had 1600 men besieged in the city by an army of 40,000. But every single person in Querétaro rallied to his side. Max bore every hardship with his men, refusing any special comforts or privileges. He was loved and admired by everyone, and he was for the first time, perhaps, truly an emperor. But the situation was impossible. By May, the garrison had no food and almost no water, and suffered the threat of epidemics. Max and his best generals, Mejía and Miramón, decided on a desperate plan: to break through to the coast and rally support there. They knew the plan was almost hopeless, but at least it would enable them to go down fighting.

But Maximilian and his generals had not reckoned on treachery. Miguel Lopez, an officer angry because the Emperor had not made him a general, crossed over to the enemy. He opened the city gates and the Juaristas poured in. After 72 days of heroic defense, the Imperial army surrendered.

Juarez had won, and now he would take revenge. In spite of frantic appeals from all over the world to spare the Emperor's life, he was determined to execute Maximilian. For form's sake, he ordered a trial on June 12, but it was really a public spectacle to humiliate Maximilian. When it was completed on June 16, the death sentence was read aloud to the Emperor, Miramón and Mejía, with the execution set for the Hill of the Bells. On June 18, Maximilian wrote to Juarez: "I give my life willingly if the sacrifice will promote the welfare of my new country. But nothing good can grow on soil saturated with blood. Therefore I entreat you to let mine be the last blood you shed." Juarez was not moved by Max's plea.

On June 19 the condemned men heard Mass. The priest was so moved that he broke down. Then the men rode in closed carriages to the Hill of the Bells. They walked to the top of the hill, each carrying a crucifix. Maximilian said, "I forgive everybody. I pray that everybody may also forgive me, and I hope that my blood which is about to be shed will bring peace to Mexico. Viva Mexico! Viva Independencia!" The shots rang out, and Emperor Maximilian I crumpled to the ground.

Later the Hapsburgs were permitted to erect a small chapel on the dusty execution site, but the chapel was eventually dwarfed by a monstrously ugly statue of Benito Juarez. Carlota's sister-in-law took her home to Belgium, where she lived in a moated castle until her peaceful death in 1927. She never returned to the real world. Every spring she would go down to a little boat anchored in the moat and step into it, announcing in a clear voice: "Today we leave for Mexico."

From Juarez to Diaz

The United States had supported Juarez and denounced Maximilian because Juarez boasted of his adherence to Liberalism and democracy. But he set up a far tighter control over the country than the so-called autocrat, Maximilian, had done. The Mexican Congress did what he told it to do because the members knew that no pleasant fate awaited them if they refused. Juarez rigged local elections and put his own men in local offices. He tried and failed to build a secular education system to replace the destroyed Catholic system. He could not keep order. Juarez escaped being called to full account for what he had done to Mexico by dying of a heart attack in 1872.

Juarez was succeeded by his lieutenant Lerdo, but Lerdo was unpopular. General Porfirio Diaz marched on Mexico City and defeated the government forces, taking over in November 1876. Diaz was the first Mexican president able to keep order. His motto was *Pan o palo*—"Bread or the stick." He concentrated on material progress to keep the people from complaining. If trouble did break out, it was quickly suppressed, by force if necessary.

Diaz allowed no one group to gain too much power, instead balancing landowners and peasants, laborers and capitalists, soldiers and politicians. Mexico was no democracy under Diaz, but neither was it a tyranny. Diaz restored peace to the countryside by sending out strong forces to capture the bandit chiefs. The worst of them were executed. To the others, Diaz gave a choice: He would put five bullets in his gun and hold it in one hand, pointed at the chief; then he would extend the other hand. The choice: five fingers in a handshake of friendship or five bullets. The chiefs usually chose friendship, and some became Diaz's strongest supporters. Diaz also made peace with the Church. Though anti-Catholic laws remained on the books, Diaz did not enforce them. By the 1890's, the Church enjoyed considerable freedom and was displaying new strength. New dioceses were established and Catholic schools operated in many parts of the country.

But Diaz made serious mistakes. Though he brought railroads and electricity to outlying areas and developed industry, he did so with foreign money, making Mexico too dependent on other countries, especially the United States. The Indians' community lands were taken from them and given to wealthy landlords, called *hacendados*. The Indians had no choice but to work for the *hacendados* in peonage, a condition only slightly better than slavery. By the end of the century, at least half of Mexico belonged to a few thousand families and foreign investors.

Garcia Moreno in Ecuador

During the 1840's and 1850's, Eucuador suffered the usual post-revolutionary chaos. Sacrilege, theft, robbery and murder were all common occurrences. Church institutions had been secularized; convents were emptied and used for army barracks. A young Ecuadorian named Gabriel Garcia Moreno began publishing *The Nation*, a newspaper which defended Catholicism and traditional values. Moreno's newspaper was so critical of the government that his arrest was ordered; he escaped and fled to Paris, where the most important event of his life occurred. Heretofore he had believed firmly in Catholic doctrines, but his practice of his religion was sporadic at best. One day in Paris, while walking in the Luxembourg Gardens, Moreno became involved in a heated debate with some non-Catholic friends. His arguments in defense of Catholic doctrine were unshakable. But finally one of the men with him said: "You speak very well, but it seems to me that you rather neglect the practice of this beautiful religion. When did you last go to Confession?" Moreno could not answer that argument. He stood silently for a moment, then replied: "You have answered me by a personal argument which may appear to you excellent today, but which will, I give you my word of honor, be worthless tomorrow." His friend's words had cut straight to his heart. He realized that if he truly believed the doctrines of Catholicism, he should live a totally Catholic life. That same evening he went to Confession, and from that day forward he attended Mass and said the Rosary almost daily.

But even with prayer and worship added to belief, Moreno realized that he had not fulfilled his responsibilities as a Catholic. Since Moreno's main interests were politics and government, his new devotion to Christ meant that he must try to Christianize society. He returned to Ecuador, where he successfully ran for Congress in 1857. As a Congressman, he devoted his primary efforts to obtaining justice for the Indians and to curbing the activities of the anti-Catholic Freemasons. He again published a newspaper, but the first issue was so critical of government policies that the authorities forbade him to publish a second issue. He published it anyway, his arrest was once more ordered, and he fled to Peru.

He did not long remain exiled. On January 1, 1859 a traditionalist rebellion broke out in Quito. The leaders begged Moreno to return to command the patriot troops. To avoid capture, Moreno came into Ecuador through the forests and mountains, a path so dangerous that his guide almost died of snakebite and he himself was lost for two days without food. He reached Ecuador and took command of the traditionalist army. It was outnumbered and ill-equipped, and the government forces defeated Moreno's brave men. He was captured and his execution ordered for the next day. That night a single guard marched up and down in front of Moreno's cell. Moreno called to the young soldier, "Do you know who I am?" he asked. The guard shook his head, "No." "I am Garcia Moreno and I am fighting for the good of all Ecuadorians." The young soldier recognized the name of the man who defended all the values he believed in. Silently, he unlocked the door. Moreno escaped, rejoined the remaining troops and began working night and day to increase the size of the army.

The key city was Guayaquil. Moreno's men came upon it late on the evening of September 22. The inhabitants went peacefully to sleep, sure that the attack would not come until the next day. Moreno led his men on a secret night march through the marsh, working as hard as anyone to drag the heavy guns through the swamp. At 4:00 a.m. the army fell on Guayaquil. By 9:00 a.m. the battle was over, the enemy general had fled, and Moreno's men had triumphed.

Because the battle had taken place on September 24, the Feast of Our Lady of Ransom, Moreno decreed that "to thank the Mother of the Divine Liberator, as well as to merit her assistance in the future, the army of the Republic should be placed in future under the special protection of Our Lady of Ransom, and that every year on this great anniversary the Government and army should assist officially at the services of the Church."

But military victory was only the beginning. Ecuador desperately needed stable government. The National Assembly unanimously declared Our Lady of Ransom patroness of Ecuador, then elected Garcia Moreno president. His first major problem was the country's bankrupt economy. Moreno cut expenditures, insisted on honesty and efficiency in all officials, and restored half of his own salary to the treasury (donating most of the rest to charity). He restored discipline in the army. He established a Catholic school system throughout the country to protect children from Liberal doctrines. He put Ecuador's hospitals in the hands of the Sisters of Charity. He inaugurated the construction of new roads so that commerce could flourish. He signed a concordat with the Vatican which eliminated all government interference in the nomination of priests and bishops and gave the Church its full rights. On April 22, 1863, the concordat was solemnly promulgated at a Pontifical High Mass in the Quito Cathedral, where the Papal and Ecuadorian flags flew side by side.

As his presidential term came to an end, Moreno could look out over a country at peace, regaining the prosperity it had known under Spanish rule. He went to Chile on a government mission to arrange a treaty, but Moreno's efforts in defense of traditionalism and against Liberalism had earned many enemies. As he left the train in Santiago, Chile, two shots rang out, one piercing his hat and the other grazing his forehead. Always possessing quick reflexes, he grabbed the arm of the assassin and deflected the third shot, sustaining a wound in his hand.

But not even the threat of death could deter Moreno from fulfilling his God-given vocation. He returned to Ecuador and ran for the Senate, despite the personal tragedy of the death of his only daughter. The next year, revolution again threatened Ecuador, and the people turned to the only man who had been able to keep order. Once again Garcia Moreno was president of Ecuador. On July 30 in the cathedral, he took the oath of office: "I swear by God our Lord, and by these holy Gospels, faithfully to fulfill my charge as President of the Republic: to profess the Catholic, Apostolic and Roman Religion; to preserve the integrity and independence of the State; to observe and cause to be observed the constitution and the laws. If I keep my word, may God be my help and my defense: if not, may God and my country be my judges."

Ecuador now experienced six years of peace and prosperity. The people adopted a new Catholic constitution, beginning with the words, "In the Name of Almighty God, One and Three, Creator, Preserver, Legislator of the World," and proclaiming Catholicism the official religion of Ecuador. Great strides were made in education, including the establishment of a new Jesuit College in Quito with all the best equipment in the sciences and medicine. Though taxes were not raised and the government borrowed no money, Ecuador had a balanced budget. Moreno journeyed throughout Ecuador to hear the complaints of the poor and oppressed and to bring them justice. The leader of the bandits who plagued the country was captured and brought before Moreno, who promised him protection if he would change his life and assist the president in enforcing the law. The chief was so touched by Moreno's mercy that he agreed and thereafter was a devoted law enforcement officer. Crime became so rare in Eucador that no sooner had a new and more humane prison been built than it was no longer needed. Moreno visited the hospitals almost every day to ensure that the sick were receiving adequate care.

Moreno directed both the nation's affairs and his personal life in accord with Christian principles. He commissioned the Jesuits to minister to the Indians in the mountains and sent Redemptorists throughout Ecuador to bring fallen-away Catholics back to the Church. He was always in church by 6:00 a.m. for meditation and Mass. He cared nothing for personal glory and wealth, continuing to give away his salary. His motto: "God never dies. God is, that is enough." In 1873 came the climax of his presidential term. In a solemn ceremony in the cathedral, the archbishop consecrated Ecuador to the Sacred Heart.

In May 1874, Moreno was re-elected president without opposition. Furious, the Freemasons and other Liberals began openly plotting against him. Moreno refused to worry or change his policies in any way. His response to warnings: "I fear God, but God alone. I willingly pardon my enemies, and would do them good if I knew them or if I had a chance."

August 6, 1874 was the Feast of the Transfiguration and the First Friday of the month. Moreno attended 6:00 a.m. Mass and made an unusually long thanksgiving afterwards. Assassins had folowed him to the square outside the church. But the crowd leaving Mass prevented any action. Moreno returned home, where he talked to his family and worked on a speech. Then he set out for the Government House about 1:00 p.m. He dropped in to the cathedral to pray before the Blessed Sacrament. The conspirators, who had followed him all day, were becoming impatient. They sent a messenger to tell Moreno that he was wanted on urgent business. Moreno came out. Rayo, one of the assassins, drew a large cutlass, rushed at Moreno, and deeply cut his shoulder. Rayo then struck him on the arm, hand and head; the other assassins fired their revolvers. Bleeding from countless wounds, Moreno fell motionless to the steps. The assassins fled, as Moreno murmured his last words: "God never dies." The dying president was carried to the priest's house, where he was given absolution and the Last Sacraments. Fiteen minutes after the attack, he died. In his pocket, they found a note he had written that very day: "My Saviour Jesus Christ, give me greater love for Thee, and profound humility, and teach me what I should do this day for Thy greater glory and service."

Moreno's death was followed by civil war, lawlessness and economic depression, as six short-lived dictators tried to wield power in the country. Deprived of Moreno's intelligence and courage, the traditionalists could not defeat the Liberals. A revolution in 1895 put into power a radical liberal government. Religious orders were banished and the privileges of the Church curtailed. The Liberals promised free elections, but the promises were broken. Ecuador had 20 presidents in the next 50 years, falling into such disorder that to this day it has never again played a significant role in history.

Carrera in Guatemala; Caro in Colombia; Maximilian, Carlota and the traditionalists in Mexico; Garcia Moreno in Ecuador—all were attempts to restore to Latin America the achievements, progress, peace and order of the days of the Spanish Empire through applying the teachings of the Catholic Church to the public life. But wherever men seriously attempt to live the Gospels, they are in danger of attack from Christ's enemies. In both Mexico and Ecuador, the attempt to raise the standard of Christ the King ended in darkness and blood and the crack of gunfire echoing through the air.

REVIEW QUESTIONS

1. What was the background of Maximilian and Carlota? What motivated each of them to come to Mexico?
2. How had Juarez worsened conditions in Mexico?
3. What part did France play in Maximilian's assumption of the throne?

4. What problems did Maximilian and Carlota face?
5. What did Carlota try to do in Europe? Why did she fail? How did her failure affect her?
6. How did Maximilian respond to the worsening situation in Mexico?
7. Describe the circumstances of Maximilian's death.
8. What happened to Mexico under Juarez?
9. How did Diaz come to power? What was good and what was bad about his rule?
10. What was Garcia Moreno's background?
11. Summarize Moreno's political philosophy.
12. Summarize Moreno's achievements.
13. Describe the assassination of Moreno.

PROJECTS

1. Find out more about Empress Eugenie, especially her role in the Lourdes apparitions.
2. Do research and write a report on U.S. policy toward Mexico during the years covered in this chapter.
3. Prepare a dramatization of selected events from this chapter.

Chapter 18

The U.S. in the Gilded Age

BOTH LINCOLN AND his successor, Andrew Johnson of Tennessee, intended to carry out generous plans for the devastated South. Robert E. Lee also urged generosity for his former enemies, stating, "I have fought against the people of the North because I believed they were seeking to wrest from the South dearest rights. But I have never cherished toward them bitter or vindictive feelings, and have never seen the day when I did not pray for them." But the charity of Lincoln and Lee were to be ground underfoot by the vindictiveness of the radical Northerners and the race hatred of the radical Southerners; the wounds they inflicted on the country were a long time healing.

Reconstruction

Lincoln's original Reconstruction plan called for the re-establishment of state governments in the South when 10 percent of the qualified voters had taken an oath of allegiance to the Constitution. He refused to enforce the confiscation of property of Confederate supporters, though Congress passed a law authorizing it. Under Lincoln's plan, governments were re-established in Louisiana, Arkansas, Tennessee and Virginia before his death, but Congress would not seat the Senators and Representatives they elected. In his last public speech, April 11, 1865, Lincoln upheld these reconstructed governments.

After the assassination, Johnson intended to follow Lincoln's lead. His May 29 Reconstruction Proclamations offered full restoration of rights to all Southerners who took an oath to support the government, except for fourteen special cases which required a request for individual pardons; they provided for the President to appoint provisional governors for seceded states, which would then elect conventions to re-establish governments; and they required the returning states to proclaim the illegality of secession, repudiate Confederate debts, and ratify the Thirteenth Amendment, declaring slavery illegal. (Robert E. Lee was included in the special cases requiring an individual pardon. He immediately applied for a pardon, hoping thereby to encourage reconciliation. But he did not receive an official pardon—and one was granted only posthumously on July 22, 1975.) By April 1866 every Southern state had conformed to the provisions of the Proclamation; the Senators and Representatives of these states were awaiting admission to Congress.

But though the South accepted this plan and even the end of slavery, many Southerners were not prepared to accept the Negroes who had been freed. In 1866 the Ku Klux Klan was founded, first with the intention of frightening Negroes away from voting, later with the intention of doing Negroes bodily harm. The Southern state legislatures also enacted a series of laws known as Black Codes, which forbade any Negro to leave the farm or plantation unless he already had a job in the city; if he came to the city without a job, he would be arrested for vagrancy. Since most Negroes had no way of getting a job in the city without going to the city, these Codes in effect bound the Negro to the same agricultural job he had had before emancipation.

The leaders of the South had thus shown themselves unwilling to accept reconciliation. The leaders of the North were soon to follow suit.

The prime opposition in the North to a generous peace came from the radical Republicans, led by Theodore Stevens and Charles Sumner. Both men bore grudges, Sumner for being attacked on the floor of the Senate and Stevens for the burning of his farm during a Confederate raid. Sumner wrote that "clemency has its limitations," and Stevens referred to the Southern States as "conquered provinces." Stevens and Sumner dominated the 39th Congress, which convened in December 1865. They refused to accept Johnson's policies or to admit any southern delegates to Congress. Congress then began enacting policies of its own, designed more to punish than to heal. Congress dominated the government, despite the checks and balances in the Constitution.

In March of 1865 Congress had established the Freedman's Bureau to help the freed slaves. In July 1866, over Johnson's veto, Congress gave the Bureau the power to try by military commission anyone accused of depriving freedmen of civil rights. In April, over Johnson's veto,

Congress passed the Civil Rights Act, bestowing citizenship on the Negro and granting the same civil rights to all persons born in the U.S. (except Indians). In June Congress passed the Fourteenth Amendment to the Constitution, which defined national citizenship to include Negroes, denied national office to Confederate leaders, and declared that no state could "deprive any person of life, liberty, or property, without due process of law, nor deny to any person within its jurisdiction the equal protection of the laws." The last quoted clause was probably the most important item to come from Reconstruction. The vagueness of the wording lent itself to any interpretation which the Supreme Court might care to give, and in the years to come the Supreme Court would use the Fourteenth Amendment to justify, among other things, the killing of unborn children. The Radical Republicans had opened a Pandora's box which has not yet been closed.

According to the Constitution, three-fourths of the states must ratify a Constitutional amendment for it to become law. Except for Tennessee, all the Southern states rejected ratification. Therefore the Radical Republicans made ratification a condition for readmission to the Union. On March 2, 1867, Congress passed, over Johnson's veto, the First Reconstruction Act, dividing the South into five districts and sending the U.S. Army to occupy and govern the districts. In order to remove the soldiers from their soil, the States were required to call constitutional conventions to establish new governments guaranteeing Negro suffrage (voting rights) and ratifying the Fourteenth Amendment. Twenty thousand troops marched into the South. The troops were supported by some white Southerners derisively nicknamed **"scalawags"** by the more stubborn whites. Northerners who assisted the military governments were nicknamed **"carpetbaggers,"** as they were looked upon as coming with no more luggage than a carpetbag because their purpose was merely to gain power over the South, not to make their homes there.

Nevertheless, the Southern States still refused to call conventions. So Congress passed the Supplementary Reconstruction Acts of March and July 1867 and March 1868, empowering the military governments to enroll voters and hold elections. A total of 703,000 Negroes and 627,000 Whites were enrolled. Under the force of direct military rule, the newly enfranchised voters fulfilled the terms of the Reconstruction Acts; Southern States were admitted to the Union under governments consisting primarily of poorly educated Negroes and scalawags. The last Southern states were not readmitted until 1870; troops remained in the South to keep the Radical Republican governments in power.

These Radicals were not motivated solely by Christian brotherhood for the Negroes; they also hoped to eliminate the old Southern leadership so that the Republicans could dominate the South and the nation. Stevens himself said that former slaves must have the right to vote to guarantee the "ascendancy to the Party of the Union." The "Party of the Union," of course, was the Republican.

After the 1866 election gave the Radicals a more than two-thirds majority in both houses of Congress, they took further steps to establish Congressional dominance of the government. Legislation was passed denying the Supreme Court jurisdiction over Reconstruction cases. Johnson's constitutional power as Commander-in-Chief of the armed forces was restricted by legislation requiring him to issue all military orders through the General of the Army, U. S. Grant (March 1867). The Tenure of Office Act (March 1867) prohibited the President from removing without approval of the Senate any official appointed with approval of the Senate.

Johnson had attempted to fight a rear-guard battle by vetoing the **Reconstruction Acts** at every opportunity. But the Radical Republicans decided in early 1868 that they would show who was running the country by impeaching the President. According to the Constitution, a President may be removed from office only by impeachment and conviction. First the House of Representatives must indict him of charges, and then the Senate by a two-thirds vote must convict him. The House of Representatives obliged, impeaching Johnson by a vote of 126-47 on eleven charges, including attempting to bring disgrace and ridicule on Congress.

The emotion-charged Senate trial filled the chamber with tension. Many Senators knew perfectly well that Johnson was innocent. But they were more concerned with their political futures than with justice. They knew that if they voted for Johnson, the Radical Republican leadership would turn on them to destroy their political careers. But a few were braver than most. The bravest of all was Edward Ross of Kansas, who was under terrific pressure to vote for conviction. Ross knew that Johnson was innocent; he knew that the Radical Republicans had far too much power for the good of the country; he also knew that his political career could be at an end if he voted with his conscience. Facing the consequences of his actions, he said: "I look down into my open grave." But he was one of the few men in political life at that time to whom conscience was more important than political advancement. On May 16, facing the death of his political career, he voted no. The final tally was 35-19, one vote short of the two-thirds majority.

But Johnson's political career had been destroyed. Ulysses Grant, a competent general but an unknown quantity as a political leader, was elected in 1868, an election in which three Southern states did not participate and six others were under Radical domination. Grant, who endorsed Reconstruction, was opposed by Horatio Seymour of New York, who was against it. Grant's popular vote majority was only 300,000, as a Negro vote of over 700,000 decided the election. Grant was not a strong leader and allowed corrupt officials to dominate his administration.

Reconstruction continued under Grant. In February 1869 the Fifteenth Amendment to the Constitution was passed, stating that no one could be deprived of a vote because of race, color, or previous condition of servitude. In March 1875, Congress passed the Civil Rights Act, guaranteeing equal rights in public places (such as restaurants and hotels). This act was struck down by the Supreme Court in 1883 on the grounds that the Constitution prohibited states from infringing rights, but did not so prohibit individuals; that is, the Constitution protected political, not social rights.

Grant won re-election against Horace Greeley in 1872, but by 1876 even the Republicans were embarrassed by the corruption in his administration. They nominated Rutherford B. Hayes, governor of Ohio, to run against Democrat Samuel Tilden, governor of New York. Tilden won a 250,000 popular vote majority, but Republicans refused to concede the election on the grounds that the returns were in dispute in Florida, Louisiana, and South Carolina (the only three Southern States still under Radical rule), where two sets of electoral returns were reported because Republican election boards threw out Tilden votes on grounds of irregularity. Without these electoral votes, Tilden would be one short of the necessary majority.

Congress appointed an Electoral Commission to settle the dispute. The Commission was to have fifteen members: five each from the House, the Senate and the Supreme Court. Since the House was controlled by Democrats, they chose three Democrats and two Republicans. Since the Senate was controlled by Republicans, they picked three Republicans and two Democrats. From the Supreme Court came two Republicans and two Democrats. The fifteenth and deciding member was to be selected by those four justices, with the understanding that Justice David

Davis, an independent, would be chosen. But Davis was elected by the Illinois state legislature to the U.S. Senate. There was no choice left but another Republican. On every issue before it, the Commission voted 8-7. Hayes was President.

The Democrats agreed to accept the decision, but Hayes and the Republicans had to make some concessions in return. Hayes promised to withdraw Federal troops from the South, appoint at least one Southerner to the Cabinet, and make substantial appropriations to the Southern states. Thus was Reconstruction ended.

The South's reaction was to do everything possible to reverse the effect of Reconstruction. The majority of Southerners—even those not inclined toward the violence of the Klan—turned against the Negroes. Every state enacted Jim Crow Laws, enforcing a vicious segregation of the Negro from every place where Whites could go. And for the next 80 years, the Republican Party did not exist in the South, which became known as the solid South, because it always and everywhere voted Democratic.

Thus was the tragedy of the Civil War prolonged. Because charity and good will did not prevail, hatred and force did. White men turned against Black in the South, unleashing a brutality worse than that of the War. In the War, men could at least fight and die heroically. In the segregated South, the issue was a denial of the worth of another man's soul. Tragically, this denial was not confined to the South; the North was far from free from discrimination. Peace had brought not reconciliation, but bitterness.

U.S. Politics, 1877-1896

The main controversy of the Hayes administration was over the money supply. One faction advocated a gold standard: gold as the basis of the economy with all paper money convertible into gold. A gold standard limits the amount of money which can be put into circulation, and prices and wages stay relatively stable. A second position was bimetallism: both gold and silver as the basis of the economy. More money could be put into circulation, but the amount is still limited. Prices and wages will rise somewhat more than under the gold standard. A third position was unredeemable paper money. Those who held this position were usually debtors (because by the time they came to pay the debt, the amount they owed would be worth less in purchasing power than it was at the time they borrowed it), and farmers and wage earners who hoped that farm prices and wages would rise. But if wages and farm prices rose, then consumer prices would also rise. Then wage earners would demand still higher wages, resulting in still higher prices. This rise in prices (or decline in the value of money) caused by an increase in the money supply is **inflation**.

Corruption in government was another issue. Hayes removed some corrupt officials left over from Grant's administration. These officials and their friends did not take kindly to losing their jobs. So the primary issue in the 1880 election was patronage (appointing office holders because they are political friends) v. civil service (in which men are presumably appointed for merit, though this is by no means guaranteed). The Republican Party split into two factions: the "Halfbreeds," who opposed patronage and backed James G. Blaine of Maine, and the "Stalwarts," who were in favor of patronage and supported Grant. Neither faction would give in, and a compromise candidate was chosen on the 36th ballot, James Garfield of Ohio. To appease the Stalwarts, the vice-presidential nomination went to Chester A. Arthur, who had been involved in the Grant scandals. The November vote was close, with Garfield winning a narrow victory.

Then on July 2, 1881, President Garfield was shot in the Washington railroad station by Charles Guiteau, a mentally unstable and disappointed office seeker who boasted that he was a Stalwart and wanted Arthur for President. Garfield lingered until September 19, then died. As President, Arthur thought it prudent to be less friendly toward the Stalwarts than they had hoped, and he supported civil service reform and helped eliminate some of the corruption.

In 1884 Blaine won the Republican nomination. Although he had originally been a "Halfbreed," his past reputation was regarded as insufficiently clean, and a group nicknamed the **"Mugwumps"** appeared in order to reform the reformers. (They received their name because their enemies accused them of seeking support from both sides. They were said to have their "mug" on one side of the fence and their "wump" on the other.) The Mugwumps (an Algonquin word for "big chief," with the connotation of "bolter" or "dissenter") backed the Democratic candidate, Grover Cleveland, who thereby became the first Democratic President since before the Civil War. Blaine lost the key state of New York because of anti-Catholicism. On a visit with Blaine, a Protestant minister referred to the Democrats as the party of "Rum, Romanism and Rebellion" (meaning drunkenness, Catholics, and the Civil War). Because Blaine did not contradict the slur, the Irish Catholics in New York almost to a man voted for Cleveland, thereby throwing that state's electoral votes to the Democrats.

Under Cleveland, the first of the federal regulatory commissions (appointed groups to oversee and regulate some aspect of business) was established. This was the Interstate Commerce Commission (ICC), to regulate railroad rates and service. First the ICC was controlled by the railroads themselves; when it became more independent, it passed such unrealistic regulations that it helped contribute to the financial woes which afflicted the majority of American railroads.

Benjamin Harrison defeated Cleveland in 1888. The money controversy continued and led to the formation of the Populist Party in 1892. The Populists advocated an inflationary increase in the money supply and a curb on the power of banks and big business. Cleveland defeated Harrison in 1892, and money continued to dominate everyone's thoughts. A young Nebraska lawyer thought it provided a good opportunity to win the Presidency. William Jennings Bryan was an excellent orator and spent months rehearsing a speech against the gold standard for the Democratic convention. On July 8, 1896, he delivered his "Cross of Gold" speech, closing with these words: "You shall not press down upon the brow of labor this crown of thorns; you shall not crucify mankind upon a cross of gold."

This well-rehearsed speech won the "Boy Orator of the Platte," as he was known because of his youth and being from the Platte River Valley, the Democratic nomination, as well as the endorsement of the Populist Party. Bryan waged a vigorous campaign, traveling 13,000 miles in fourteen weeks. But America as a whole was prosperous and unimpressed. William McKinley, the Republican nominee, stayed home and waged a "front-porch" campaign, winning the election by almost half a million popular votes.

Business, Labor and The Gilded Age

The increase in the nation's wealth and the predominant role of wealthy families in American society gave the name "Gilded Age" to the last third of the 19th century when these families built highly ornate ("gilded") palatial mansions.

The Industrial Revolution came to America in the early 19th century and was speeded along by the drilling of the first successful oil well in the U.S. in 1859. Men moved from farms to crowded cities, no longer owning the means by which they could support themselves, becoming dependent on businessmen and factory owners. Capitalism—the system by which a few men control most of a country's wealth—became the dominant economic system. Most capitalists were Republicans, and Republican political ascendancy meant that the capitalists would not be much hampered in their drive to accumulate and retain wealth.

John D. Rockefeller's Standard Oil was the best example of the expansion of big business during the second half of the 19th century and also an example of the use of questionable means to drive out competitors. But rapid industrialization had a profound effect on America. The attention of everyone was focused on money; everyone was urged to spend money, which encouraged people to borrow unwisely. Success was equated with prosperity. Natural resources were ruthlessly consumed with no thought for their conservation. Since Christian moral principles frown on greed, religion had to be removed from daily life and confined to Sunday.

The only significant attempt by the government to check the concentration of wealth and power in the hands of a few was the Sherman Antitrust Act in 1890. Though its intentions were good, the wording of the act was vague, and those charged with its enforcement were lackadaisical. Hence the existence of the law did not prevent the continued growth of monopolies (control of almost an entire industry by a few men).

But some men outside government were aware of the evils of industrialization and the factory system, with its long hours, low wages and lack of job security. These men were the workers themselves, and America witnessed the birth of the labor union movement. Catholics formed the majority of union members, since the great influx of immigrants from Catholic Europe had provided the main work force for the factories. In 1878 the Knights of Labor were organized, calling for a general reform of working conditions and a just wage. At first the Knights were forced to be secret, since employers were more than ready to fire anyone known to belong to a union, or even resort to clubs and guns to discourage union membership. The first important leader of the Knights was Terence Powderly, at that time a strong Catholic (though he later abandoned the Church).

Though many members were Catholics, the Church at first had serious doubts about unions, for two reasons: they were secret; and in Europe Communists and socialists tended to dominate the labor movement. The bishops of Quebec condemned the Knights of Labor and sent the condemnation to Rome for approval. That the condemnation was not approved was primarily the work of one man, James Gibbons, an American Cardinal.

Gibbons was Archbishop of Baltimore for 44 years. He was the first American bishop to become widely respected and admired in anti-Catholic America. Gibbons' greatest service to the Church and to America was in labor relations. In an 1887 report to Pope Leo XIII, he pointed out the deplorable conditions under which people worked: long hours for women and children, as well as men, wages insufficient to support a family, the danger of losing a job for no good reason, the beatings and shootings of labor union members. Gibbons warned that if the Church did not help the workers, they might be driven into the arms of the Communists. Pope Leo XIII listened, reversed the condemnation of the Canadian bishops, and in 1891 issued his great encyclical letter, *Rerum Novarum* ("The Condition of the Working Classes"), which set forth Catholic principles of justice, pointed out the evils of both Communism and capitalism, and called for fair treatment for the workers.

The Knights of Labor, however, moved away from the Church's teaching and began to respond to violence with violence. After a bombing in Chicago's Haymarket Square, which was blamed on the Knights (although their guilt was never conclusively proved), the Knights of Labor were discredited in the eyes of most Americans. The leadership of the union movement passed to Samuel Gompers and the American Federation of Labor, which believed in peaceful political action. Their techniques would eventually bear fruit, but even many union men became too concerned with material advantage, so that neither business nor labor consistently followed Christian principles. Hence materialism remained strong in America, even when the labor unions had gained a dominant position.

With the growth of business and the spread of the population throughout the country, railroads were built to bring raw materials to factories and manufactured goods to markets. On May 10, 1869, the Union Pacific Railroad coming west and the Central Pacific coming east met at Promontory, Utah. It was now possible to travel from coast to coast by rail.

Bishop Lamy and the Southwest

Of all the groups in the United States, the one that emerged strongest from the sufferings of the Civil War was the Catholic Church. At the

Second Plenary Council of Baltimore (a meeting of all U.S. bishops) in 1886, the U.S. was treated to the sight of a united Church, bearing none of the wounds which divided the rest of the country. Irish and German Catholic immigrants were finding their places in society, making contributions in all areas of life, proudly handing on Catholic beliefs and traditions to their children. The Church had also won many friends during the Civil War. About 600 nuns, primarily Mother Seton's Sisters of Charity, virtually monopolized the nursing service during the War, and many a wounded or dying soldier had been deeply grateful for the charity and concern of these nuns. Now having served the suffering on both sides of the Civil War, the Church turned to the needs of the expanding Nation.

When it became necessary to appoint a bishop to administer the far-flung Southwest after the Mexican War, Pope Pius IX chose John Baptist Lamy, originally from France. For assistance, Lamy called upon his old friend, Fr. Joseph Machebeuf, to be Vicar General (chief assistant to the bishop). The boundaries of Lamy's diocese were indefinite but included the territory which is now the states of Colorado, Arizona and New Mexico.

The vastness of the area was probably the greatest obstacle facing the young Frenchman, who was destined to travel thousands of miles in service to his people. The primary problem was that during the years of chaos in the Mexican government and of war with the U.S., the priests in the New Mexico territory had become lax. Many led immoral lives, a scandal to the faithful. They were determined to hold their positions and opposed Lamy's reforming efforts. The leader of the rebellious priests was Fr. Martinez, who gathered his supporters into a schismatic church, encouraged prejudice against Lamy because he was French, and used gallons of ink to write to Rome and elsewhere to denounce Lamy. Sometimes the opposition was more than verbal. Once Fr. Machebeuf preached a sermon against murder which a parishioner thought was directed personally against him. He would have demonstrated his need for such a sermon by murdering Fr. Machebeuf if the men of the parish had not protected the priest.

Bishop Lamy early realized the necessity of Catholic education for the children in his diocese if the Faith were to be preserved and to grow. One of his first acts was to bring the Sisters of Loretto to staff a school in the cathedral city of Santa Fe. The long and dangerous journey did not deter the nuns, who willingly faced disease, exhaustion and

Indian attack. On one of these journeys, the wagon train was besieged by Kiowa Indians. Cholera broke out; one of the Sisters collapsed and died and the others nursed the sick in the midst of Indian attacks. The wagon train made its escape. When Bishop Lamy reached Santa Fe with the nuns, they found that newspapers carried reports of his death from Indian attack.

The nuns built a chapel which they patterned after St. Chapelle in Paris. But upon its completion, they discovered that the choir loft had no staircase and could be reached only by a rickety ladder. They made a novena to St. Joseph for help. A wandering carpenter appeared, barricaded himself in the chapel, and then disappeared. He left behind a staircase made of wood not native to New Mexico, a circular staircase with no central support. Engineers to this day do not know how the staircase stays up, but it has been safely used by the nuns ever since. The Sisters were convinced that St. Joseph himself had built their staircase.

In the 1850's gold was discovered in Colorado. Miners and other adventurers flocked to the banks of the Platte, and Fr. Machebeuf was appointed spiritual leader of the raw, untamed mountain area. While he was on a visit to Central City, Colorado, a supply train forced his buggy off the road. He broke his right leg at the hip, crippling him for the rest of his life. He used thereafter to conclude his letters, "Pray always for the poor cripple." But the injury did not noticeably slow his work.

Shortly thereafter, Bishop Lamy set off on a visit to Los Angeles. As he traveled higher in altitude, the weather turned bitter cold. His party rode through an ice storm, suffering frostbite and nearly losing the way. When they set up their tent at night, a helpful Mexican put a brazier of coals inside to keep the Bishop warm. But the coals gave off noxious fumes, and Bishop Lamy and his companions nearly asphyxiated before escaping to the fresh air outside. They celebrated Christmas Day Mass, 1863, in a miner's cabin with planks for an altar and most of the congregation kneeling outside in the snow.

As the Catholic population grew, Colorado was made a separate diocese with Fr. Machebeuf becoming its first bishop; Arizona was also separated. Bishop Lamy was now older and less vigorous, but he had one last task: the building of a beautiful new stone cathedral in honor of St. Francis of Assisi. In 1880 the railroad finally reached Santa Fe, bringing an end to the frontier life. The comforts of civilized life could be brought quickly and easily to formerly desolate regions.

Bishop Lamy retired in 1885 at the age of 73. His annual report to Rome listed 238 churches and chapels (when Bishop Lamy had arrived there had been only 66); 54 priests (instead of 12); two colleges, eight schools, many parish schools, and many Indian schools; a hospital, an orphanage, a novitiate and a seminary. Three years later, Bishop Lamy died peacefully and was buried beneath the high altar of the cathedral. A little over a year later Bishop Joseph Machebeuf died in Denver. The two men had given their lives to bring the message of Christ to the Southwest. They had civilized a vast, untamed territory. They had preserved the Spanish Catholic heritage and nurtured it to new growth. The deserts of New Mexico and Arizona and the mountains of Colorado were richly blessed by the presence of these two great and holy men.

The Indians, the U.S. and the Church

As the U.S. population expanded westward in the 19th century, conflicts with the Indians erupted. The main problem was that the Indians of the plains did not want to live in settled communities, but preferred the life of the hunter, roaming vast spaces in search of game. This preference conflicted directly with the westward expansion of the U.S., which filled the formerly open prairies. Some compromise between the needs of the two races should have been made. The Indians could have been given good, fertile land and instruction in farming and other trades, much as the Spanish and French did in the areas they colonized. The Indians could then have taken their places as citizens with special customs just as the European immigrants contributed their special cultures to America. Instead, the official policy of the U.S. government was to drive the Indians ever farther westward, breaking one treaty after another, finally forcing them onto reservations which contained the worst land and doing little to give them new skills.

It need not have been that way. An heroic Belgian priest pointed to an alternative, but unfortunately he was not heeded.

Jesuit priest Pierre-Jean De Smet arrived in the U.S. from Belgium in 1823. In 1838 he founded his first Indian mission at Council Bluffs, Iowa. His reputation for respect and love for the Indians spread rapidly among the far west Indian tribes. Representatives of the Flatheads and Nez Perce of the Rocky Mountains came to De Smet, begging him to come to them. On June 25, 1840, he crossed the Continental Divide at South Pass, and on Sunday, July 5, celebrated Mass at Green River, Wyoming, where thousands of Indians had come for fur trading. Fr.

De Smet left Green River on July 6, crossing 8000-foot Teton Pass through a snowstorm. He reached the main settlement of the Flathead Indians, who welcomed him joyously. In two months, he baptized 600. He established St. Mary's Mission, the first permanent white settlement in what is now Montana. By early spring in 1842, he could report that almost the whole Flathead Nation had been converted to Catholicism.

He decided to journey to the Oregon territory to investigate mission prospects there. His reputation preceded him, and he was met with many requests for Mass and Baptism. He could see the need for a permanent mission, so he returned to St. Louis for help. It was on one of his journeys that he discovered gold in a mountain stream. But as badly as he needed money, he refused to mention his discovery to anyone, because he knew that the gold would bring in a flood of white settlers, resulting in the extermination of the Indians. Father De Smet tried to persuade the government to adopt a constructive policy toward the Indians, advocating the gradual development of agricultural programs. But the government would not listen. When the Indians west of the mountains rebelled, the Army begged Fr. De Smet to make peace. But the Indians rebelled only because the white men had violated their treaties and taken away their land, shooting Indians and burning their homes. Nevertheless, he consented at least to travel among the Indian tribes to explain to them that violence would only worsen the situation. His efforts brought peace to the Pacific Northwest.

But the plains Indians fought on. In 1862 the Sioux went on a rampage, and again the government frantically called for Fr. De Smet. He went to Ft. Berthold, in the Dakota Territory, to be warmly welcomed by the Indians massed there for protection against the Sioux. On the afternoon of July 8, the Sioux appeared across the river, steadily increasing in number. Fr. De Smet announced that he would cross the river. Everyone begged him not to go, thinking it would mean certain death. The priest calmly climbed into a small boat, which he rowed across the river. He was immediately surrounded by the Sioux. For three hours the people at the fort kept vigil. They were sure that their beloved Blackrobe had been killed. As the sun began to set, they saw the little boat put out from the opposite shore. In it was Fr. De Smet.

Fr. De Smet had met with no difficulty. The Sioux had come only to visit him, whom they regarded as their friend. No other white man could have crossed the Missouri River that July day and survived.

Fr. De Smet told the government that he would not continue to negotiate with the Indians unless the officials would keep their promises. General Sully, speaking for the government, refused. He had been sent to punish the Sioux, and punish them he would. De Smet went back to St. Louis.

In 1867, again among the Indians, he compiled a list of grievances, which he sent to Washington with the admonition, "Peace could be brought about, if honest agents were employed." Finally he was persuaded to go among the Sioux to bring their leaders to a peace conference. Though ill and weak, he went deep into the wilderness, meeting with four chiefs: Sitting Bull, Four Horns, Black Moon and No Neck. As a result of his efforts, the Sioux and the Cheyenne signed a treaty with the government, giving up most of their traditional hunting grounds in return for a guarantee that they would always possess their sacred Black Hills.

But gold was discovered in the Black Hills. The government tried first to persuade the Indians to sell the land. But Chief Sitting Bull contemptuously declared that he would not sell the white men so much as a pinch of dust. So the Indian Bureau issued an order that all Indians must report to the nearest Indian agency within a certain time. As it was winter, the order was impossible to obey. Using this failure to report as an excuse, the U.S. Army launched a three-pronged invasion of Indian territory, planning to wipe out any Indians who would not peacefully accept the loss of their lands (the Second Sioux War). One of the generals was a flamboyant Civil War veteran named **George Armstrong Custer**. He sent his greatly outnumbered forces to attack an Indian encampment in broad daylight on June 26, 1876. Soon the Indian warriors massed and surrounded Custer and his men. Observers watching from a distance could see only clouds of dust and smoke as the day wore on. When the dust settled, every single U.S. soldier (264 men) was dead, including Custer.

But overall, the Indians were vastly outnumbered and not nearly so well-equipped as the U.S. forces. In May 1877, Crazy Horse was forced to surrender; and was killed a few month later, while Sitting Bull fled to Canada for a time. Elsewhere the Nez Perce War in the Pacific Northwest (1877) ended in the defeat of Chief Joseph and the banishment of the tribe to Oklahoma. The Apache War in New Mexico and Arizona (1871-1886) began with the massacre of over a hundred Apaches at Camp Grant, Arizona, and ended with the capture of Geronimo and the assignment of the remnants of the tribe to small reservations in the Southwest. And in 1889 the Ghost Dance War on the Black Hills Reservation came to an end with a massacre of Indians at Wounded Knee after the Army had tried to curb the religious rites of the Teton Sioux.

Father De Smet did not live to see these last bitter defeats. In 1870, while on his way to the East Coast, he had attended briefly a government conference on Indian missions. Later he was informed that of 43 missions authorized for the West, only four were to be assigned to Catholics. He wrote, "In the whole of this affair, the Indians have not been consulted as to the religion they desired to belong to." On May 23, 1873, he died peacefully in his sleep. Throughout the Indian territories, riders carried the sad news from village to village. Their beloved Blackrobe dead, the U.S government virtually prohibiting other Catholic missionaries from carrying on De Smet's work, the Indians were left with only desert land, broken promises and silent graves.

At the End of the Santa Fe Trail

Blandina Segale was a young Italian Sister of Charity (Mother Seton's order) just 22 years old in 1872 when she received a terse message from her superior: "You are missioned to Trinidad. You will leave Cincinnati Wednesday and alone." She had never heard of Trinidad; looking it up on a map, she believed that she was being sent to a Caribbean Island. Instead she was going to the Wild West, to Trinidad, Colorado, a primitive town of dugouts, Indians, outlaws—and young children needing a teacher.

Her adventures in Trinidad, and later in Santa Fe and Albuquerque, would provide ample material for a movie. Among the more spectacular of her experiences are the following:

A drunken quarrel between two men erupted in violence, one man shooting the other. As the wounded man lay dying, a lynch mob gathered outside the jail, ready to work instant vengeance on the man who had shot him. Sister Blandina rushed to the dying man's room and persuaded him to forgive his killer. She then received permission to bring the other man from the jail and walk with him to the room so that he could ask pardon and receive forgiveness. She forestalled the lynching, the man receiving ten years for manslaughter and owing his life to Sister Blandina.

An outlaw from Billy the Kid's gang was wounded in the leg. No doctor in Trinidad dared to treat him. Sister Blandina went to his room and cared for him, returning day after day. Then Billy the Kid himself arrived, the famous outlaw vowing to scalp every one of the four doctors in town for not helping his partner. When he arrived at the shack where his injured friend lay, he met Sister Blandina and learned of her acts of charity. In gratitude he promised her any favor she asked. She asked that he not take revenge on the doctors. He kept his promise and ever after had a soft spot in his heart for the little Sister of Charity who had not feared an outlaw's wrath, on one occasion sparing a party of travelers from the ravages of his gang simply because she rode with them.

In Santa Fe she opened a hospital for indigent patients, often building with her own hands the coffins for those who had died. The city granted her eight dollars for each burial, only about half her actual expenses. Finally, realizing that she needed more money to carry on her ministry to the poor, she asked the new County Commissioner to raise the grant to $15. He refused, telling her that he was sure she could manage. She told him that, if that were his attitude, she would bring the next body to his office and drop it on the floor. She received the money she had requested.

In 1892 the city fathers of Trinidad informed Sister Blandina that she would no longer be allowed to teach in the public schools of the town if she continued to wear her religious habit. They admitted all the good she had done for the children of the town, but they could not permit religious garb in a public school. Sister Blandina absolutely refused to abandon her habit. She lost her job, but soon had another, as principal of St. Patrick's School in Pueblo.

Through it all, she taught children and nursed the sick—Indian, Mexican, white—a vision of calmness, culture and charity in the midst of violence and sudden death.

While politicians worried about civil service and tariffs and bimetallism and winning elections, the real history was being made in Santa Fe and Denver and Green River. For it was in those places that souls were being won for Christ; and the Catholic Church, in spite of continued public hostility, was carrying on its mission of preaching the Gospel to all nations.

REVIEW QUESTIONS

1. Compare the attitudes of Lincoln and Lee with those of the Radical Republicans.
2. What is the significance of the 14th Amendment?
3. What were the provisions of the Reconstruction Acts?
4. Summarize the impeachment of Andrew Johnson.
5. How did the South react against the Negro?
6. How was Reconstruction ended?
7. Summarize the three positions regarding the money supply.
8. What were the issues and the results in the Presidential elections of 1876, 1880, 1884, 1890, and 1894?
9. Who were the Knights of Labor?
10. How did Cardinal Gibbons help the workingman?
11. What were the main achievements of Lamy and Machebeuf?
12. How did Father De Smet help the Indians?
13. What was U.S. government policy toward the Indians?
14. How did Sister Blandina's career show the possibility of holding to high moral values in the midst of a lawless society?

PROJECTS

1. Prepare a mural showing achievements of the Catholic Church in the West during this time.
2. Read Pope Leo's encyclical *Rerum Novarum* and note especially what he said about capitalism, socialism and labor unions.
3. Do research and prepare a report on the Industrial Revolution in the United States.

Chapter 19

The Age of Theodore Roosevelt

AS THE UNITED STATES became wealthier, the government pursued a policy of expansion and imperialism (domination of other countries). In 1866, Secretary of State Seward, an ardent expansionist, negotiated a treaty with Russia for the purchase of Alaska for $7,200,000. Acquiring this icy land was a bit much for many Americans, and Alaska was soon dubbed "Seward's Folly," while opposition to the treaty mounted in Congress. But pressure from the Administration, along with the Russian ambassador's judicious use of funds to buy votes, resulted in the ratification of the treaty. When gold was discovered in the Klondike in 1896, just 50 miles east of the Alaska border, hostility to the acquisition of Alaska melted away like the snows in summer.

In a very different climate, U.S. interest in Hawaii grew. After approval of an 1875 commercial treaty with Hawaii, U.S. businessmen soon controlled the island's sugar and pineapple plantations and moved to control the government as well. When Queen Liliuokalani came to the throne in 1891, she wanted no part of American domination and announced a new constitution, giving her absolute power. Under the leadership of Sanford B. Dole of pineapple fame, the Americans worked to overthrow the queen. Dole and his friends persuaded U.S. ambassador to Hawaii John L. Stevens that they were in danger from the queen, and he ordered in U.S. Marines. The Americans occupied the government buildings and raised the U.S. flag, as Stevens proclaimed Hawaii a U.S. protectorate and Dole became president of the new republic. President Cleveland was not pleased with this high-handed annexation, urging that Queen Liliuokalani be restored. But Dole refused to listen. Eventually Cleveland recognized the Republic of Hawaii as an independent nation (1894). Under President McKinley, pressure from imperialists within Congress brought about the annexation of Hawaii to the U.S. on July 7, 1898.

The U.S. also was interested in Cuba. An incompetent monarchy in Spain, despotic governors in Cuba, and the spread of Liberalism brought revolution to the island in 1868. The war dragged on for ten years, with neither side winning a decisive victory. Finally exhaustion drove the rebels to the conference table, and the Peace of Zanjon ended the Ten Years War on February 11, 1878. Taking advantage of the bankruptcy of Cuban enterprises after the war, U.S. capitalists acquired sugar estates and mines. The U.S. became the largest and most important buyer of the island's sugar crop.

Discontent remained below the surface until the rebels found a leader in the young poet and revolutionary, José Martí. Martí admired the U.S. but had remarkable insights into its weaknesses: "The Cubans admire this nation, the greatest ever built by freedom, but . . . they cannot honestly believe that excess individualism and reverence for wealth are preparing the U.S. to be the typical nation of liberty."

Martí trained a small army, rebellion breaking out on February 24, 1895. Martí was killed that same year, but the rebels fought on in spite of bitter repression by General Valeriano Weyler, nicknamed "The Butcher" because of his ruthless treatment of women and children as well as of military prisoners. In America, sympathy was with the rebels, and hostility toward Spain was further fanned by the so-called "yellow press" of William Randolph Hearst's New York *Journal* and Joseph Pulitzer's New York *World*, which invented Spanish atrocities to sell more newspapers.

President McKinley did not want to involve the U.S. in the Cuban revolt, but others in the Republican Party were not so peaceful, notably Secretary of the Navy Theodore Roosevelt. McKinley could not stand against intervention if the public demanded it. And two episodes ensured that it would be demanded. On February 9, 1898, Hearst's *Journal* published the "**DeLome Letter**" stolen from the Spanish ambassador, in which he called McKinley "weak and a bidder for the admiration of the crowd." Then on February 15, the U.S. battleship *Maine*, while at anchor in Havana harbor, was destroyed by an explosion which killed 260 Americans. The cause of the explosion was never conclusively found, and in fact evidence turned up later that Cuban revolutionaries may have ignited the explosion to bring America into the war. But everyone in the U.S. believed at the time that Spain had blown up the ship, and "**Remember the *Maine*!**" became the battlecry of the Nation. The pressure for war was irresistible and McKinley called for armed intervention, despite a last minute appeal from Spain that the Spanish government was willing to accept almost any peaceful settlement. War was officially declared on April 21, 1898.

The Spanish-American War was probably the easiest war the U.S. ever fought. Spain was in disarray. The U.S. was at a height of prosperity. The first major battle of the War was the sea Battle of Manila Bay, in which Spain lost 381 men and ten ships, while Commodore George Dewey's American fleet suffered no damage and not a single American was killed. On August 14, Spain surrendered in the Philippines and America proclaimed a military occupation of the Islands.

Theodore Roosevelt formed a volunteer cavalry regiment known as the Rough Riders. They rode into Cuba, along with a detachment of the Regular Army, and won the Battle of San Juan Hill on July 1. This victory was soon followed by the destruction of the Spanish fleet off the coast of Cuba. Spain's losses were 474 killed and wounded and 1,750 taken prisoner; U.S. casualties were one killed and one wounded. On July 26, the Spanish government asked for peace terms. The treaty that was finally concluded on December 10 granted independence to Cuba and ceded the Philippines, Puerto Rico and Guam to the U.S.

Cuba was in a state of chaos after the War. No one could keep order; disease was rife; people were hungry and homeless. The U.S. Army occupied the country, and Dr. Leonard Wood was appointed military governor of the island. He established order and called a constitutional convention in 1900 to begin preparing the Cubans to resume government of their island. The convention ultimately adopted a constitution based upon that of the U.S., but made no mention of a continuing relationship with the U.S. Wood made it clear to the Cubans that U.S. military forces would not leave the Island until Cuba made a proper acknowledgement of the U.S. The particular concessions which the U.S. wanted were embodied in the Platt Amendment, drawn up by Connecticut Senator Orville H. Platt. The most important provisions were as follows: Cuba would never enter into any treaty with any foreign power impairing Cuban independence; the U.S. was authorized to intervene to preserve Cuban independence and maintain law and order; and Cuba agreed to sell or lease to the U.S. lands necessary for naval stations. The Cuban convention added the amendment to the constitution, and

U.S. troops withdrew from Cuba on May 20, 1902. But Cuba remained under the shadow of the U.S. economically and politically. Of all the Latin American nations, it became the most Americanized.

Roosevelt as President

When the 1900 election rolled around, the Republicans again turned to McKinley. The country was prosperous, business was booming, farm output was increasing and the people were delighted with the outcome of the War. The Democratic candidate, **William Jennings Bryan**, charged that prosperity had been acquired by "big men" (industrialists and railroad magnates) at the expense of "little men" (farmers and small businessmen). Bryan had a strong moral point. Unrestricted capitalism was immoral. But the people, including many of the "little men," were prosperous and satisfied with their lot. Furthermore, the only solution Bryan could offer was the free coinage of silver. No American political leader could see that purely economic solutions to the materialism of America would not get to the heart of the problem. Materialism is a moral evil which can only be cured by a rejection of profits and wealth as the ultimate goal of life. Materialism, in other words, can only be cured by spirituality. And the free coinage of silver was not about to inspire a spiritual revival in the American people.

McKinley won by a million votes, but within less than a year was killed by an anarchist's bullet. On September 14, 1901, Vice President Theodore Roosevelt was sworn in as President of the United States.

Roosevelt in many ways echoed Bryan. But he was more capable than was Bryan of getting his beliefs accepted by the people. He had an appealing personality; he was a man of action in action-loving America; and he was a hero of the Spanish-American War. He began to act immediately. First he invoked the **Sherman Antitrust Act** against the huge Northern Securities Company, earning his nickname, "Trust Buster." He personally intervened to solve a major coal strike to the benefit of the miners, pushed through Congress the **Hepburn Act**, which gave the **Interstate Commerce Commission** rate-making powers over the railroads and created national parks and national monuments to preserve America's natural beauty.

The American people came more and more to applaud Roosevelt's attacks on big business because of the efforts of the "**Muckrakers**" journalists who exposed scandals in government and business; they were given their unflattering name because they were viewed as raking around in the muck of corruption and crime. Probably the best-known muckraking work was a novel, *The Jungle*, by Upton Sinclair. Sinclair's main purpose in writing the book was to propagandize for socialism, and he did so by describing the sufferings of his hero, a Lithuanian immigrant who worked for a meat packing company in Chicago. To paint his villain—the meat-packing industry—in the worst possible light, Sinclair told of meat from diseased cattle, waste from the floor, and mice and rats being mixed in with the meat sold to consumers. The book caused a sensation, but did not succeed in bringing thousands into the socialist movement as Sinclair had hoped. Instead, many people stopped eating commercial meat products and called upon the government to act against the meat industry. The meat packers, faced with sharply declining sales as a result of the novel and a government investigation which had confirmed many of the charges, supported federal legislation in the hopes that public confidence could be restored. The results were the Pure Food and Drug Act and the Meat Inspection Act, both passed in 1906.

By the end of Roosevelt's second term, business had less power, but government had more. Roosevelt saw no danger in the growth of government, stating, "I don't think that any harm comes from the concentration of power in one man's hands, provided the holder does not keep it for more than a certain, definite time, and then returns to the people from whom he sprang." Roosevelt would reluctantly return to "the people from whom he sprang," but the power which had now been given to the government remained with it. Though most of Roosevelt's policies were justifiable exercises of government power, correcting genuine evils, Roosevelt's presidency was the beginning of the move toward Big Government and toward a reliance on government for a solution to all ills.

The Progressive Movement

During the last decade of the 19th century and the first two decades of the 20th, the **Progressive Movement** rode high. The Progressives gave themselves that name because they claimed to have modern ideas of government. But like those who preferred more traditional ways of doing things, they put too much trust in governmental structures, thinking that the forms of a government would make a difference as to how good or bad it was. The Progressives were mainly active in the States rather than in the national government.

The main goal of the Progressives was to give the people more participation in the government. The **direct primary** was often the first step. Previously, candidates for office had been nominated by party meetings or conventions, attended by only a small proportion of the total population. A primary was an election for all voters to choose each party's candidates for the general election.

The **initiative**, **referendum** and **recall** were other popular innovations. By initiative, the people could initiate legislation. By referendum, the people could approve or disapprove laws that had been enacted by the legislature. By recall, the people could remove elected officials from office. Grove Johnson, a California Republican leader, pointed out the basic error in viewing these measures as a sure method for good government: "The voice of the people is not the voice of God." But California did not listen, pioneering in all of these changes.

The Progressives also worked for direct election of United States Senators. The Constitution had stipulated that Senators be elected by state legislatures. The authors of the Constitution saw the Senate as a body of experienced and knowledgeable men, less susceptible to popular pressure than the House of Representatives, the members of which were directly elected by the people. The efforts of the Progressives led to the Seventeenth Amendment to the Constitution, requiring the direct election of Senators.

Another area in which the reformers urged additional state action was in education. Most of the Progressive governors gave increased aid to schools or passed legislation more strictly regulating the schools. These laws increased state control over education, control which had become inevitable when the compulsory school attendance laws were passed in the 19th century. Although these laws appeared to be for the good of the children, they actually made it possible for a government to control every child living under its authority, as the state and federal governments would do in the second half of the 20th century. As long as the taxes to support a school came from the community where the school was located, the control of what was taught in the school was usually in the hands of the people most concerned: the parents. But if the state provided much of the money, it would also dictate what was to be done with it. Often parents would be the last to be allowed to influence what was being taught in the schools. Progressive governors also worked in close cooperation with the universities, and intellectual leaders at the universities became more influential throughout the country. Ideas which had formerly been discussed only in academic circles were now spread among the ordinary people. Many professors were atheists or agnostics, or at least thought that religion was a minor element of a person's life. Many of them adopted the new philosophy of **Pragmatism**, the belief that if an idea or action works, it must therefore be right, whether or not it conforms to the moral law. Some were socialists. Thus the universities, which in Catholic countries had helped governments to use their power wisely, would encourage government leaders to follow the dark and dismal road away from the light of Christianity.

The Supreme Court

The early years of the 20th century saw the U.S. Supreme Court begin to assume the unchecked powers which it now possesses. Earlier, the Court had prominence only on rare occasions: *Marbury v. Madison*, for example, or *Dred Scott v. Sanford*. All that changed around the turn of the century. As government and the Nation grew in wealth and power, more controversies would come before the Court, and its decisions became law. More importantly, the men now appointed to the Court had new and dangerous ideas as to the role of the Court in American life.

In 1901, Roosevelt appointed **Oliver Wendell Holmes, Jr.** to the U.S. Supreme Court. Holmes served for 30 years, until his retirement at the age of 90 in 1932. Because of his length of service, and the number of young lawyers who studied under him, his influence on the judicial system in America was enormous. He influenced it away from decisions based on moral principles and toward decisions based on the whims of the majority or the prejudices of the individual justices. His philosophy is summarized by his statement that the law "corresponds at any given time with what is understood to be convenient. That involves continual change, and there can be no eternal order." But law can be fair only if it is rooted in the eternal principles of the law of God, as reflected in the Natural Law (i.e., the order built into the nature of things) and Divine Positive Law (Revelation). If it is based on convenience, that will inevitably mean the convenience of those who are most vocal or have the most power and money.

Inevitably, the Constitution would be interpreted in accord with the views of whoever sat on the Court. Two cases, just three years apart, show how readily the Court could contradict itself. The first was the 1905 case of *Lochner v. New York*, in which the Court held that a New

York law regulating maximum working hours for bakers was invalid as an unreasonable interference with the right of free contract. But by 1908, the predispositions of the judges had changed. In the case of *Muller v. Oregon*, the Court upheld a law limiting maximum working hours. No matter how contradictory the decisions, they would be proclaimed as "The Law of the Land."

On the U.S. Supreme Court bench sat nine men, appointed for life and accountable to no one. If they chose one day to say that business should be free to do whatever it wanted, that was "the law of the land." If they chose the next day to say that business had responsibilities to employees, *that* was "the law of the land"—not because it was right, not because it was in accord with the moral law, but because the nine men had said so and no one had the authority to contradict them.

Foreign Policy Under Roosevelt

In foreign affairs, Theodore Roosevelt's motto was, **"Speak softly and carry a big stick."** He pursued an aggressive, imperialistic foreign policy, which was congenial to the American mood of the early 20th century.

Ever since the California Gold Rush had stimulated a desire for quick and safe transportation between the coasts, the U.S. had been interested in building a canal across Central America. The best route lay across Panama, which was then a province of Colombia. The U.S. concluded a draft treaty with Colombia, but it fell through because Colombia wanted $25 million for the rights to the Canal Zone instead of the $10 million offered by the U.S. Then on November 3, 1903, a group of Panamanians, aided by the New Panama Canal Company, revolted against Colombia and proclaimed the Republic of Panama. On several earlier occasions, the U.S. had assisted Colombia in restoring order in its unruly province. This time, the U.S. came to the aid of the Panamanians. U.S. warships prevented the landing of Colombian troops to quell the revolt. On November 6, the U.S. recognized the independence of the Republic of Panama, and on November 18 signed with the new government the Hay-Bunau Varilla Treaty, giving the U.S. a ten-mile strip for the canal in return for U.S. guarantees of Panama's independence, $10 million, and an annual fee of $250,000. Roosevelt took credit for the successful acquisition of the Canal Zone, saying, "I took Panama." He also believed that what he had done was in the best interests of both Panama and the United States, stating,

"Every action taken was not merely proper but was carried out in accordance with the highest, finest, and nicest standards of public and governmental ethics."

In 1904 the Dominican Republic was about to default on its debts to the U.S. and other countries. The government signed an agreement to permit the U.S. to administer its customs houses, the main source of income for the tiny island, and to manage its debt payments, which the U.S. did through 1907. When the debts payable to an American firm were paid before those owed to creditors of other countries, the other creditors protested and hinted at armed intervention from their governments. Thereupon, Roosevelt pronounced what came to be called the **Roosevelt Corollary** to the Monroe Doctrine, indicating that the U.S. did not merely give itself the right to prevent European nations from interfering in the affairs of Latin America, but to intervene actively on its own: "The adherence of the United States to the Monroe Doctrine may force the United States, however reluctantly, in flagrant cases of such wrongdoing or impotence, to the exercise of an international police power."

Also in 1904, a young American man named Jon Perdicaris was kidnapped by a Moroccan bandit chief named Raisuli. Roosevelt spent five weeks trying to obtain Perdicaris' release through diplomatic channels. When that seemed to have failed, he fired off a note with the words, "We want Perdicaris alive or Raisuli dead," and he prepared for military intervention by ordering the entire Mediterranean squadron to Morocco. But Perdicaris was released alive, and the big stick was only threatened, not used.

Roosevelt's firmness made an impression on other nations. In 1905, Russia and Japan called upon Roosevelt to mediate a settlement of the Russo-Japanese War. Roosevelt brought representatives of the two governments to New Hampshire for a conference, which was successfully concluded in a peace treaty. The U.S. was taking its place as a major nation in the world.

President Taft and the Bull Moose

William Howard Taft was Roosevelt's hand-picked successor and easily defeated the by then perennial Democratic candidate William Jennings Bryan in 1908. Roosevelt went off to hunt big game in Africa, and Taft continued his policies, though without Roosevelt's aggressive drive. Taft's most significant move was a 1909 special message to Congress urging a Constitutional amendment to permit **federal income taxes**. On July 12 Congress passed the Sixteenth Amendment, which was ratified by the required number of states in 1913.

Roosevelt returned to the U.S. in 1910, already beginning to regret his statement in 1904 that he would never again be a candidate for the Presidency. Yet if Roosevelt wanted to be President again, he would either have to wait until 1916, and six years is a long time in politics, or else challenge an incumbent of his own party, a man who had at one time been his close friend. Roosevelt made his choice. He destroyed a friendship, split his party, and contributed directly to the election of Woodrow Wilson in 1912.

By the time of the Republican convention in June 1912, Roosevelt still lacked about 70 committed delegates of the total needed for the nomination. His managers, however, had challenged 254 other delegates before the Credentials Committee. Some of the challenges were well-founded, but at least 150 were manufactured solely for the purpose of obtaining additional delegates for Roosevelt. Well-founded or not, the challenges had little chance for success because a majority of the members of the Committee were Taft supporters. Roosevelt refused to accept the decision of the Committee and took his case to the floor of the convention. In a wild scene, the convention voted down the Roosevelt challenges and then nominated Taft on the first ballot. The Roosevelt delegates refused to vote and marched out of the hall. In August, Roosevelt formed his own party, the Progressive Party (nicknamed the "**Bull Moose Party**"). Roosevelt urged his supporters to follow him as if on a crusade as he cried: "We stand at Armageddon and we battle for the Lord."

The Democrats nominated Woodrow Wilson on the 42nd ballot, and Roosevelt and Wilson ignored Taft and attacked each other in attempts to win the Progressive votes. Roosevelt and Taft split the Republican votes between them, giving Wilson a plurality, so that he became the first Democratic President since Cleveland. Taft retired from politics to teach at Yale University. But the damage was done. Roosevelt had split his party and caused the election of Wilson, who was to become one of the most important influences on history in the 20th century.

Italian Immigration and Mother Cabrini

On October 28, 1886, President Cleveland dedicated the 225-ton Statue of Liberty, a gift from the people of France to the United States. The statue was meant to symbolize the liberty for which the U.S. was famous and was one of the first sights that immigrants to the Country would see.

But not all of the immigrants received a cordial welcome. A good example is the fate of the Italians. At the peak of Italian immigration into the U.S., approximately 200,000 arrived each year. Those who came were mostly farm laborers from southern Italy, who were given the worst jobs with the lowest pay and treated with contempt. Wrote one Italian bishop, "I see those poor Italian immigrants in a foreign land, among people who do not speak their language, easily falling a prey to cruel exploitation." Help would have to come from someone who cared deeply about their welfare and was willing to make any sacrifice for them.

On July 15, 1850, that person was born. Francesca Cabrini was from Lombardy, the green and gold hills of Italy which had given Michelangelo to the world. Though her childhood dream was to be a missionary to China, Pope Leo XIII told her that her vocation was to her fellow countrymen in the U.S. Clutching a letter from Archbishop Corrigan of New York inviting her to come there, she and a few nuns boarded a ship for the long and dangerous journey to the New World. When she arrived, she had no money, could not speak English, and was told by the Archbishop that she had come sooner than he expected so that he had no house for the nuns. Frances and her nuns spent their first night in the U.S. in a rat and flea-infested boarding house.

But within a few months, she had opened an orphanage, started a day school in St. Joachim's Church (with no desks and few books), organized catechism classes, and begun visiting the homes of even the poorest Italians. Though Frances Cabrini was ill most of her life, she drove herself with seemingly boundless energy in the service of her people.

After only two years in New York, Frances received an invitation from a wealthy lady in Nicaragua to open a school there. Though Frances always believed her first obligations were to the poor, she knew that the wealthy also had spiritual needs, and off she went to Central America. The climate was miserable, there were snakes and earthquakes, and the people tried to tell her how to run her school; but she opened it nonetheless and it functioned from 1892 until 1894, when an anti-Catholic government forcibly ejected the sisters.

Once the school was started, Frances was back in the U.S. One of the greatest needs of the Italians was a hospital where they could be sure of obtaining good care at a cost they could afford. With $250 she started Columbus Hospital, using home-made mattresses. The sisters could not afford beds for themselves so they slept on the floor.

Meanwhile, her nuns from Nicaragua had gone to Panama and set up a school. Frances visited them and then went to Argentina, crossing the Andes on mule back. She bought a house in the center of Buenos Aires for a school, though everyone told her she should look for less expensive quarters since she could hardly expect more than six or seven pupils. Frances just smiled. The first day, 50 students arrived.

She spent 1899 founding schools in or near New York City for poor Italian children and establishing classes in Catholic doctrine for adults. She opened a boarding school for wealthy Italian girls, in danger of losing their Faith to the temptations of materialism. The school is now Mother Cabrini High School, where she is buried.

In 1900 she returned to Europe to establish convents, then back to the Argentine, where again she bought a house against all prudent advice, later to see its value skyrocket as the city expanded in exactly that direction. In Colorado, the children of Italian miners and the orphans of men killed in the mines were sadly neglected. Frances opened a parochial school, then a large orphanage. Her nuns climbed down into the mines to remind the miners of Christ's love for them.

Chicago needed a hospital. Frances bought the North Shore Hotel. But she suspected that the owners were cheating her. She gave two nuns a yardstick and sent them out at 5:00 a.m. to measure the entire property. She was in fact being cheated and forced the seller to adjust the contract. In 1909 she opened a second hospital in Chicago, this one strictly for the poor. When bigots in the neighborhood tried to sabotage the hospital, she simply ordered it to be opened earlier. In Seattle in 1909, she became an American citizen. Also in Seattle, she found a house she wanted to buy, but all she knew of the owner was that his name was Clarke and he lived in New York. She set her nuns to calling every one of the hundreds of Clarkes listed in the New York City telephone book, until they found the right one. Through it all, the money was always there when she needed it, but never earlier. As she said once, "We have nothing, but we spend millions."

In April 1917 she returned to Chicago, sick and exhausted. When she died on November 22, everyone knew that she had entered Heaven, and her canonization as the first American citizen to be declared a Saint confirmed this belief. She left a lasting legacy to the United States. To poor and rich alike, she brought the Good News of Christ, manifesting His love in her service of the least of Christ's brethren.

The Church Reaches Out

Mother Cabrini was the most spectacular example of the mission of the Church to the poor and neglected, but there were others in the Age of Theodore Roosevelt.

Mother Marianne Cope was the second Provincial Mother Superior of the Sisters of St. Francis of Syracuse. When the government of the Hawaiian Islands called for sisters to care for its sick poor, especially for the victims of leprosy, Mother Marianne was the first to respond to the appeal.

In 1884 the sisters established the first general hospital on the island of Maui. By 1888 she and her nuns were on Molokai, where Father Damien had pioneered the work of caring for the lepers. When her nuns expressed some fear of contracting the disease, Mother Marianne assured them that they were in the hands of Christ and that none of them would ever suffer from leprosy. None of them ever did.

For thirty years, Mother Marianne labored with compassion, self-forgetfulness and deep love for Christ. Upon her death in August 1918, the Honolulu *Advertiser* wrote, "Throughout the Islands, the memory of Mother Marianne is revered, particularly among the Hawaiians, in whose cause she has shown such martyr-like devotion. . . . She impressed everyone as a real 'mother' to those who stood so sorely in need of mothering."

Closer to home, the talented daughter of Nathaniel Hawthorne, Rose Hawthorne Lathrop, entered the Catholic Church in 1891. When a friend of hers died of cancer, she became appalled at the neglect and suffering that cancer patients endured.

Though Rose had been brought up in comfortable surroundings and had never known deprivation, she immediately plunged into volunteer work at the New York Cancer Hospital. She flinched the first time she dressed the open sores of a cancer patient, but that was the last time she flinched. Soon she withdrew her savings, sold her jewelry and purchased a home for the cancerous poor in the slums of the lower east side of New York.

At first the cancer sufferers of the area could hardly believe that this refined lady had come to care for them without compensation, but soon they flocked to her door. She treated them with dignity and respect. She would not wear rubber gloves when she dressed their wounds, and she adamantly refused to permit the dehumanizing experimentation that was allowed in many institutions.

Eventually she took the vows of a Dominican nun and established her own order to care for cancer patients. To this day the Hawthorne Dominicans, as they are known, follow in the footsteps of their foundress.

Another great foundress of this era was the wealthy Philadelphia heiress, Katherine Drexel. Deeply moved by the plight of the Negroes in the South, she obtained an audience with Pope Leo XIII and pleaded with him to help them. Leo, a wise and perceptive judge of human abilities, said to Katherine, "Why not become a missionary yourself, my child?"

Faced with the Pope's request, Katherine could do no less than comply. Katherine gave her entire fortune—$20,000,000—and her whole life, to her apostolate. She founded a new order of nuns, the Sisters of the Blessed Sacrament, whose sole purpose was to work among the neglected Negroes and Indians. She founded many schools for Negroes, often fighting the prejudice of the white neighbors. In New Orleans she founded Xavier University, named for the great Jesuit missionary Saint, Francis Xavier, where Negroes could receive a high-quality college education. She traveled into the poorest areas of the South to bring Catholic instruction and basic education to the Negroes.

She went to Bishop Lamy's Santa Fe to establish a school for the Pueblo Indians and to Arizona to set up a Navajo school. She founded five schools in Harlem and others in Columbus and Chicago. She came down with typhoid on a trip to Albuquerque, but that slowed her only temporarily. Her entire income went straight to her Order, while she lived in the strictest poverty, bringing her lunch on the train and sleeping in an upper berth to save money.

Just before her death in 1955, she wrote, "Let us give ourselves to real pure love. Devotion to the Sacred Heart is a devotion which alone can banish the coldness of our time. The renewal which I seek and which we all seek is a work of love and can be accomplished by love alone."

The Church in the United States was still struggling in the early days of the 20th century to establish its position in America when two young apostles determined that American Catholics should reach out to those in the rest of the world who had never known Christ. Thomas Price grew up in North Carolina, the state with the lowest percentage of Catholics in the Nation and where he had labored tirelessly to make converts. In 1904 he met Father James Anthony Walsh, the Director of the Boston Society for the Propagation of the Faith. The two men agreed that the way to get more vocations in the United States was to send missionaries abroad; in other words, the way to receive was to give.

With the help of Cardinal Gibbons, they gained the support of the U.S. bishops; then in 1911 they received permission from Pope Pius X to found the Catholic Foreign Mission Society of America. They established their first house in New York (not far from Rose Hawthorne's second cancer hospital), calling their small hill "Maryknoll." They soon came to be familiarly known as Maryknoll missionaries.

On September 7, 1918, the first group of five priests, including Father Price, joined with their brother Maryknollers to recite the Church's official prayer for travelers. They received their mission crosses from the hands of Father Walsh and were on their way to China.

Father Price died in China less than a year later. Another of that first group, Father Ford, became a bishop in China and was martyred by the Chinese Communists. Still another, James E. Walsh, became a bishop who spent years in a Chinese Communist prison camp before his eventual release.

Though the Maryknollers were driven out of China, the work they did there bore rich fruit in the souls of the Chinese. The founding of Maryknoll marked the beginning of America's generous support of overseas missionary efforts as selfless missionaries labored to fulfill Christ's command to evangelize all nations.

REVIEW QUESTIONS

1. How did the U.S. gain possession of Alaska and Hawaii?
2. What were the causes, events, and results of the Spanish-American War?
3. Summarize the domestic policies of Theodore Roosevelt.
4. What was the Progressive Movement? What political changes did the Progressives bring about? How did they influence education?
5. Who was Oliver Wendell Holmes? What was his philosophy?

6. What was Roosevelt's foreign policy? How did the U.S. gain control of the Canal Zone?
7. What was the Sixteenth Amendment to the Constitution?
8. Describe the Presidential election of 1912.
9. What was the attitude of many Americans toward immigrants during this time?
10. Summarize the accomplishments of Mother Cabrini.
11. Show how Marianne Cope, Rose Hawthorne, Katherine Drexel and the Maryknoll missionaries exhibited a spirit of self-sacrifice and how they met pressing needs in America and in the world.

PROJECTS

1. Prepare a mural showing the accomplishments of the Catholic Church during this time.
2. Prepare an exhibit on U.S. National Parks.
3. Do research and prepare a report on the suffragette movement, which began at this time.

Chapter 20

Woodrow Wilson and the First World War

FROM THE TIME he was barely old enough to understand the meaning of the words, Thomas Woodrow Wilson was taught that he was one of the predestined Elect, called to bring light and truth to a sinful world. Brought up by Scottish Presbyterian parents who still clung to many of the harsh doctrines of Calvinism, Tommy (as he was called until his early twenties) was firmly convinced that America was the City on a Hill. Wilson saw himself in a Messiah role: He would be one of the leaders of America and America would be the leader of the world. Ambitious, proud, brilliant, he settled for nothing less than the best in anything he did. He drove to the top in two fields. In education, he became president of Princeton University; in politics, he became President of the United States. Wilson had great charisma—the ability to attract dedicated followers.

What were his ideas? In his book *Congressional Government,* published in 1885, Wilson stated that *"power and strict accountability for its use* are the essential constituents of good government." Wilson at one time thought that the structure of American government might need to be changed in order to provide for a more free exercise of power, but after observing what a strong President—Theodore Roosevelt—could accomplish on his own, Wilson concluded that a chief executive could concentrate power in his own hands. His first principle then was the importance of the concentration of power in the hands of the government leaders.

What of accountability? His second principle was an unflagging faith in democracy, that sovereignty came from the people, that government was accountable to them and that most problems could be solved by elections. In a speech to Princeton alumni on April 16, 1910, he contended that the strength of the United States "comes from the great mass of the unknown, of the unrecognized men, whose powers are being developed by struggle."

His third principle was pragmatism, which led to a rejection of absolute moral values. In 1907, he said that "liberty fixed in unalterable law would be no liberty at all. Government is a part of life, and, with life, it must change alike in its objects and its practices."

His fourth principle was the belief that society was more important than the individual, that the individual person must surrender his hopes and ambitions and needs to the nation as a whole. In a 1909 lecture to the Princeton Club, Wilson had asserted: "There is nothing private in America. Everything is public; everything belongs to the united energy of the nation."

As governor of New Jersey, Wilson put his ideas into practice, becoming one of the leading Progressive governors in the nation. He based his Presidential campaign on his record as governor, formulating a "New Freedom," which called for stricter regulation of business, government control of the money supply, and enactment of an income tax to reduce the amount of money in the hands of the wealthy. His program was not without merit. Business did need the watchful eye of government to prevent its becoming too powerful, and Wilson was genuinely concerned with helping the poor and weak in our society. But Wilson was not content to curb excesses of power; he amassed power in his own hands. He was not content to assist the weak; he wanted to impose his view of righteousness on everyone, everywhere.

Soon after his election, Wilson made his plans clear, saying that the President "must stand always at the front of our affairs, and the office will be as big and as influential as the man who occupies it." In order to actualize the power that was potentially his, Wilson had to overcome the opposition of or gain the support of three groups: the Democratic Party, Congress and the American public. During the first months of his administration, he moved to win over all three groups.

Wilson, the party leader, was faced with a fundamental choice. He could either support Progressives whenever they struggled for control with old line Democratic leaders, or he could support the stronger faction to earn their indebtedness and support. On this issue, Wilson the idealist lost out to Wilson the power wielder. In party struggles, he usually went with the stronger faction, with the result that the Democratic

Party was strengthened and his leadership role enhanced. He also used the patronage available to him more skillfully than probably any other President since Jackson. He rewarded his friends and punished his enemies, and party members soon realized that if they wished to hold public office, they must be loyal to Wilson.

To extend his influence over Congress, Wilson introduced several innovations in the procedures of Presidential dealings with Congress. He formulated his own legislative program, made personal appearances at the Capitol, held many personal conferences with legislators, and delivered messages to Congress in person. He drove Congress as it had never been driven before. At his insistence, it sat for over a year and a half (April 7, 1913-October 24, 1914), the longest session in the nation's history. During this time all of the major planks in Wilson's New Freedom platform were enacted.

Wilson's ultimate weapon in his dealings with Congress was his ability to appeal to the people. He was a spell-binding orator who could inspire his audience with a belief that they were embarking on a crusade which only Wilson could lead. He was also skilled at using informal statements and press releases to influence the public. Wilson completed the work Theodore Roosevelt had begun. He made the President the most powerful man in America.

Wilson as President

From the beginning of his first term, Wilson pushed for a reform of the banking system and money supply. One problem the country faced was that the money supply was too rigid to allow for people's actual needs. For example, if a farmer or businessman needed to borrow money, he might be turned down, despite having good credit, just because the banks had loaned out their quota of funds for the year. The amount of money available was determined by the amount of United States government bonds that had been sold. This made for great monetary stability, but not for flexibility in the money supply. As a result, there were alternating periods of tight money supply, when business activity was high—resulting in hardship for businesses—and periods of surplus currency when business was slack—resulting in too much speculation on the stock market. Financial panics and crises became more frequent, but a solution to the problem was difficult because there was no central bank to co-ordinate the handling of the money supply. A more organized banking system was needed.

Because of current opinions against having one large central bank, a series of twelve regional banks was set up, united under the Federal Reserve Board. With this organization, the Federal Reserve banks were able to function as a central banking institution. Despite its not being a government agency, the Federal Reserve acts to a certain extent as a fiscal agent of the United States government.

The Federal Reserve system provided a mechanism for government borrowing which led to inflation. The government would receive loans from the Federal Reserve banks and then spend these funds, putting into circulation money which had not existed before. When the money supply is thus increased, the value of each unit in circulation—in terms of what it can purchase—decreases, because the increased money supply has not been the result of increased production. Since it takes time for the money to circulate through the economy and cause prices to rise, government and its selected beneficiaries get the full value of the money because they spend it first. The citizen suffers by eventually paying higher prices. But this process is difficult to understand and virtually impossible to track. If the government simply printed great quantities of paper money, which would rapidly fall in value, the citizen would know whom to blame. But not understanding the Federal Reserve system, the ordinary person will blame the seller for the higher prices he pays; he will not blame the government or the Federal Reserve. The worst effects of the Federal Reserve were not apparent at first because conservatives in Congress were able to amend the legislation to include the requirement that Federal Reserve notes be backed by gold or silver. But this requirement would not always exist, and Americans would eventually see the value of their money steadily decline.

Wilson brought about the enactment of the Federal Trade Commission Act, giving government more control over commerce; the Clayton Antitrust Act, giving the government more power to break up big business; the Underwood-Simmons Act, which enacted a modest income tax; the Federal Farm Loan Act, which provided loans to farmers; the Adamson Act, establishing the eight-hour day for interstate railroad workers; and the Child Labor Act, which prohibited children under the age of fourteen from working in factories. The last three laws were examples of **social welfare legislation,** laws enacted to assist individuals. Before Wilson, such laws were considered the prerogative of state governments. Wilson himself had not included these acts in his New Freedom program and had some doubts about the wisdom of involving the national government in such matters. But his advisers convinced him that that he must support social welfare legislation to win re-election.

Although the Supreme Court was eclipsed during Wilson's administration by the power of the Executive, Wilson made a significant appointment to the Court: Louis D. Brandeis. Brandeis was very much in the tradition of Oliver Wendell Holmes. He believed that law and morality were relative, saying on one occasion: "All judges should be made to feel, as many judges already feel, that the things needed to protect liberty are radically different from what they were fifty years back." The Senate must approve the nomination of Supreme Court justices, and opposition arose to Brandeis because of his socialistic and relativist tendencies. Though there were enough Democratic Senators who would support the nomination once it reached the Senate floor, the nomination first had to be approved by the Senate Judiciary Committee, where five of the ten Democrats on the 18-man committee refused to commit themselves to the support of Brandeis. But Wilson put pressure on the Senators, informing them that they need not expect much patronage if they failed to support Brandeis. This pressure worked, and in an eight-minute meeting on May 24, 1916, the Committee confirmed Brandeis' nomination.

The Election of 1916

Wilson based his 1916 re-election campaign on his record in domestic legislation and on the slogan, "He kept us out of war"—the war then slaughtering hundreds of thousands of young Frenchmen, Englishmen, Germans, Russians and Central Europeans in the mud and blood of the trenches and battlefields. The Republicans nominated Charles Evans Hughes, former governor of New York, who resigned from his post on the Supreme Court to accept the nomination. Hughes' views were similar to Wilson's. On the Supreme Court, he was nearly always on the side of increased government power.

Since the Republicans were the majority party and since Hughes was popular, many people expected Wilson to lose. But Hughes' campaign managers were incompetent, and he lost some states by narrow margins because of mismanagement. More important was the peace issue. Most of the leading Republicans, such as Taft and Roosevelt, supported a military build-up; and Roosevelt, not surprisingly, campaigned widely and almost exclusively for entrance into the European war. Hughes thus lost many votes in the heavily German cities of the Midwest. Further,

Hughes was made to appear less "progressive" than he actually was, and Wilson had the support of leading intellectuals and reformers. Finally, there was the so-called California incident. California was split between "regular" and "progressive" Republicans. Hughes did not support either side, believing that he needed a united party behind him. His attempt to achieve unity only widened the split. Several of his campaign managers displayed open sympathy with the regulars, thus alienating the other faction. Finally, Hughes did not meet with the progressive candidate for governor, Hiram Johnson, during his entire California campaign, although at one time they were in the same hotel for a day. Hughes probably knew nothing of Johnson's presence, while Johnson knew of his and refused to see him, but the story was widely circulated that Hughes had snubbed Johnson. On election day, Johnson was elected governor of California by nearly 300,000 votes, while Hughes lost the state and its crucial electoral votes by 3,775 votes.

Meanwhile Wilson made speech after speech advocating increased government power to remake society. He said on September 23: "The business of government is to see that no other organization is as strong as itself; to see that no body or group of men, no matter what their private interest is, may come into competition with the authority of society." Hughes could not demand more power for government than Wilson did, so he went to the other extreme and criticized Wilson as too collectivist. Business leaders united around Hughes, believing him to be their only hope. The Democratic Party therefore became known as the liberal party, the Republicans as the conservative, though this had by no means been true even a year earlier. The two major political parties thus began a realignment that would be completed under Franklin Roosevelt.

The election was extremely close. Early returns, from Eastern and Midwestern states, gave Hughes a lead, and he went to sleep election night confident that he had won. But then the gloomy totals began to come in from California. A phone call was placed to Hughes' home. His son answered: "The President has gone to bed." Said the voice at the other end of the line: "When he wakes up, tell him he is not the President."

Wilson won by 23 electoral votes. During his second term he would turn from domestic to foreign affairs. He would find world-wide scope for his Messianism. He slashed great, gaping wounds across Europe, and to this day the scars have not healed.

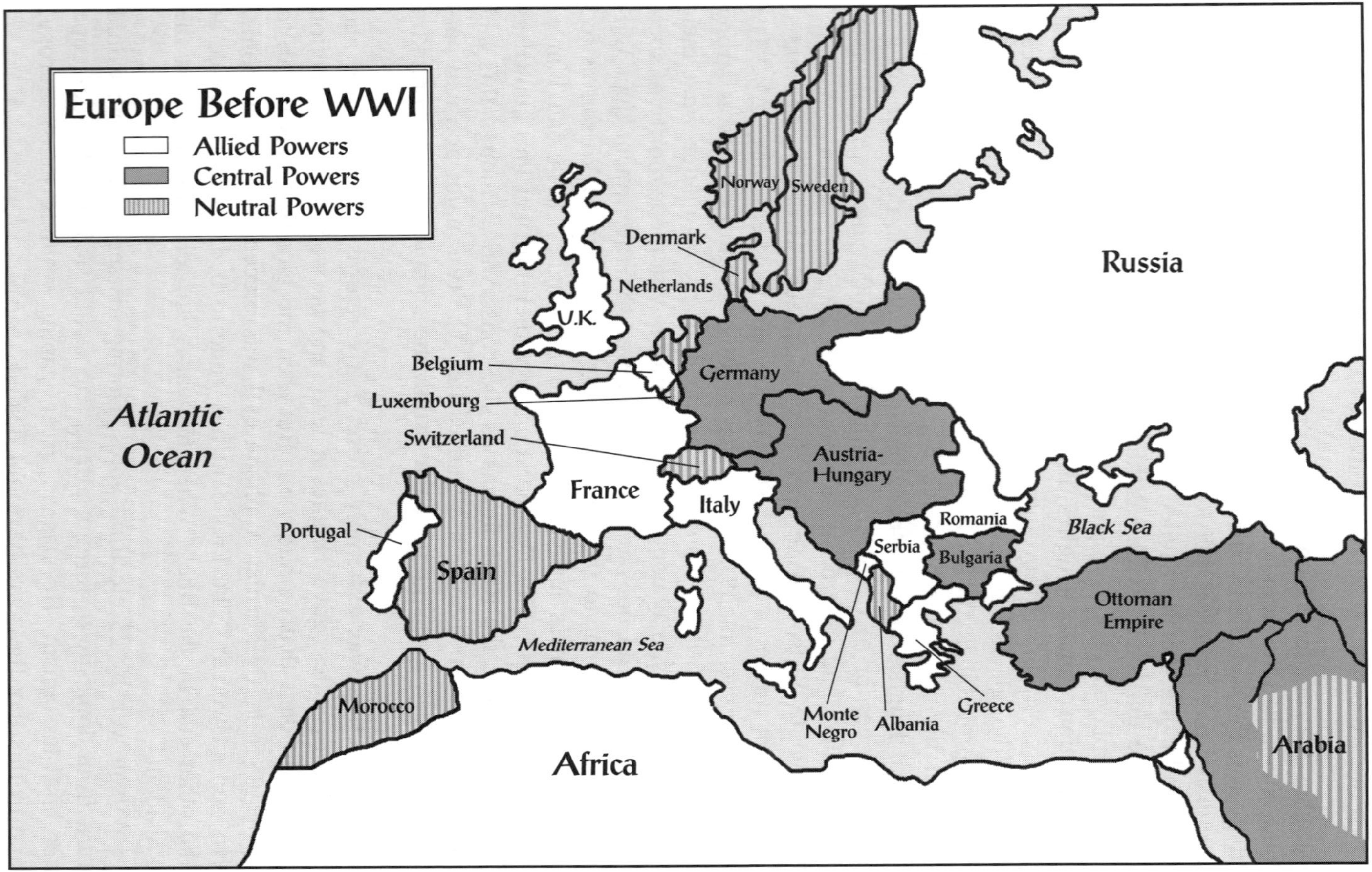
Europe Before WWI
Allied Powers
Central Powers
Neutral Powers
Atlantic Ocean
U.K.
Norway
Sweden
Denmark
Netherlands
Belgium
Luxembourg
Switzerland
Germany
Russia
France
Portugal
Spain
Italy
Austria-Hungary
Romania
Serbia
Bulgaria
Black Sea
Ottoman Empire
Monte Negro
Albania
Greece
Morocco
Mediterranean Sea
Africa
Arabia

America Goes to War

When the Germans crossed the Belgian frontier on August 4, 1914, in the great offensive which opened World War I, no one imagined the eventual consequences. It was generally believed that the War would be over in a few months, and throughout Europe, on both sides (the Allies: Great Britain, France, Russia, Italy, Belgium, Serbia and Romania; the Central Powers: Germany, Austria-Hungary, Turkey and Bulgaria), the attitude was excitement, confidence in righteousness and expectation of a quick victory. Young men paraded happily down the streets on their way to enlist, and young women handed them flowers and flags and cheered them on. The German offensive rolled to the outskirts of Paris, where it broke down in the first display of the extraordinary military incompetence on both sides which marked the whole course of the conflict. Because the Russians surprised the Germans by the speed with which they entered German soil in the east, the German General von Moltke sent two army corps from the army in France to the Russian front before he had even captured Paris, and for lack of these troops, his whole campaign ground to a halt.

For three full years, the lines of battle in the West, despite repeated offensives by both sides, remained within ten miles of the trenches dug at the end of the year 1914. During the whole time of Wilson's successful campaign for the U.S. Presidency, from July 1 to November 18, 1916, the British, French and Germans combined were suffering 1,100,000 casualties at the Battle of the Somme—to move just seven miles, as the generals sent Europe's young men into the mouths of blazing machine guns.

Each side made a tremendous effort to cut off as much as possible the flow of supplies to the enemy on the Western front. The British established a conventional blockade of Germany, in which all neutral ships sailing for German ports, or ports with access to Germany, were subject to search by the blockaders and seizure of goods the British defined as contraband. The Germans, unable to compete with the British surface fleet, retaliated by submarine attacks on ships sailing for British ports. The small size and slow speed of the submarine and its consequent dependence on the torpedo made it necessary for German submarines to sink or blow up ships in the war zone, rather than merely stopping them, searching them and seizing contraband.

On May 7, 1915, the British passenger liner ***Lusitania*** was torpedoed by a German submarine. The ship was carrying not only passengers but also war materials from America to Britain. The torpedo hit the cargo hold where munitions were stored, causing an enormous explosion and the consequent loss of 1,198 lives, including 124 Americans. Because the American public did not know about the munitions being illegally carried (in violation of America's neutrality), the casualty totals generated strong support in the United States for a declaration of war against Germany. For nearly two years, Wilson resisted the "war hawks" in his cabinet and, through a series of compromise agreements with the German government, kept the United States neutral and hence justified his campaign slogan, "He kept us out of war."

But on February 1, 1917, before Wilson had even been inaugurated for his second term, the Germans, desperate to break the stalemate on the Western front, opened unrestricted submarine warfare against all shipping in the northeastern Atlantic, neutral or otherwise. The German High Command estimated that enough British and Allied ships could be sunk in six months to knock England out of the War, even if America did come in. Wilson severed diplomatic relations with Germany but was not yet ready to ask for a declaration of war.

Two events made him ready. The first was the **Zimmerman Telegram**, a code message sent to the German minister in Mexico from German Foreign Secretary Alfred Zimmerman. The message encouraged an alliance with Mexico against the U.S., with Mexico to be rewarded in the event of a German victory with its lost New Mexico, Texas, and Arizona territories. The message was intercepted and decoded by the British and handed on to the Americans. The second event was the sinking of the ***Laconia*** on February 25, with two U.S. citizens dead.

The United States Senate declared war on Germany on April 4, 1917 by a vote of 82 to 6, and the House of Representatives followed suit on April 6 by a vote of 373 to 50. America was at war. Her citizens responded with the same enthusiasms as had the Europeans three years earlier, and the same hatreds for the "enemy" swept across the U.S. as had swept Europe (and led to such reactions as the killing of German dachshunds in England).

In his speech calling for a declaration of war, Wilson told Congress that the United States was fighting "to make the world safe for democracy." Rather than having the base motives of other countries, the U.S. was embarking on a moral crusade, supporting Europe's democratic nations against tyrannies. But it was not quite so clear-cut. Whatever Wilson thought, England was far from a democracy, power lodging in a Parliament still controlled by the wealthy classes, and France's anti-clerical government was clearly opposed to the deep Catholicism of the majority of its people. Then there was Russia. The Czar of Russia had just abdicated, leaving that great nation in the hands of Kerensky's Provisional Government. Wilson praised "the wonderful and heartening things that have been happening within the last few weeks in Russia . . . The autocracy has been shaken off and the great, generous Russian people have been added in all their naive majesty and might to the forces that are fighting for freedom in the world, for justice and for peace. Here is a fit partner for a League of Honor." In a few months, that fit partner would be under the iron rule of Lenin and the Communists, who ruthlessly stamped out freedom and justice and peace for the Russian people. One of the reasons Lenin and his Communists were able to come to power was the continuing devastation wrought by the War, which Wilson and the other Allies virtually forced Kerensky to continue. Wilson tried to keep up his spirits even after Lenin took over. It was not until the Czar and his entire family were brutally murdered that Wilson was forced to admit that Russia might not be as safe for democracy as he had hoped.

But that was in the future, and for now the people believed that they were fighting for democracy and went cheerfully off to war.

The President and the Emperor

In 1917, a compromise peace was still possible. Neither side was fighting for a great moral cause. The French and English governments were no more noble than the German. Each of the three, along with the Italian, was mainly interested in advantage for itself. If they could have been persuaded to stop the slaughter and come to the conference table, a compromise could have been worked out. The German government would have remained essentially unchanged, though the militarists who had pushed the country into war would have been discredited and forced out of power. There would have been no vacuum in Germany waiting for an Adolf Hitler to fill it. Pope Benedict begged all the governments in the War to come to the conference table. Heaven itself had answered Benedict's anguished pleas by sending the Queen of Heaven to Fatima with a plan for peace, but involving as it did prayer and sacrifice, it was not widely heeded. Besides the Pope, groups in England and Germany also urged their governments to sue for peace. Yet the bloodshed was increasing, not decreasing. Why did not the governments come to their senses? There were many reasons. Germany still wanted to inflict a crushing defeat on England and France. England and France had made secret promises of territory to Italy to get the Italian government to desert its alliance with Germany and come into the War, and the promises had not yet been fulfilled. Anti-German passion still ran high in the Allied countries. England and France were sure the U.S. would come into the War and lead them to a total victory.

Thus the U.S. was in a key position. If, instead of coming into the War, Wilson had instructed the U.S. Navy to protect U.S. shipping, then insisted that all parties involved begin peace negotiations, using diplomacy to play off both sides against each other until his insistence was met, peace negotiations might in fact have begun. Why Wilson did not even consider such a course of action and the consequences of what eventually he did do we can best discover by looking at the contrast between the President of the United States and the young Emperor of Austria-Hungary, Charles.

Charles came to the throne after the War had already begun when his uncle, Emperor Franz Josef, died in 1916. If Charles had been in power from the beginning, it is doubtful that Austria-Hungary would ever have been involved in a European-wide war, since he ardently desired peace. Charles was a Hapsburg in the tradition of Charles V (1500-1558). His greatest concern was the welfare of his people. He planned reforms which would have given greater rights and freedoms to the small nationality groups which made up his Empire, while at the same time preserving Austria's role of protector of these groups against outside aggression. But when the crown was placed on his head, Austria-Hungary was already deep in the War. So he worked tirelessly to bring the other nations to peace negotiations. The other nations were not interested. Charles expressed a willingness to give territory to the enemy powers as a sign of his great desire for peace. They ignored him.

Meanwhile, on January 8, 1918, Wilson issued a formal statement of **Fourteen Points**, which he hoped would be used as the basis of peace negotiations. Point One called for open agreements of peace, with no private understandings of any kind. England and France squirmed a little when they read that point, thinking of all the secret agreements they had concluded—most recently with Italy. Point Two called for absolute freedom of the seas. England squirmed a little more; the British Navy wanted freedom for itself but not necessarily for anyone else. Point Five called for free and impartial adjustment of colonial claims. England, France and Italy did not want anyone adjusting their colonies. But they pretended that the Fourteen Points were a good idea, and went on feeding young men to the machine guns.

It was Point Ten which brought Wilson and Charles into direct conflict: "Self-determination for the peoples of Austria-Hungary." Charles would have been the first to say that they could indeed have self-determination in their local affairs, which was all most of them had wanted before 1914, while retaining the Empire as their protector. But liberal ideas had spread their infection. It was now not enough to keep their own language and customs and traditions; they wanted to be independent. Wilson agreed; since Charles had not been elected, he could not be a rightful ruler.

In March 1918 Charles made a direct appeal to Wilson, asking for talks between a personal representative of each man to clear the way so "that nothing further might stand in the way of a world peace conference." Charles repeated earlier pledges he had made of territorial concessions. But he asked for clarification of what Wilson meant by self-determination and emphasized that the territorial claims of Italy, which Wilson had been supporting, could not possibly fit Wilson's guidelines since the people involved wanted to be ruled by Austria, not by Italy. Wilson received the request on February 25. On March 6 Charles received his reply: a flat no.

Charles was frustrated and angry. He wrote a cold reply to Wilson, repeating what he had already said. The note was probably colder than it should have been, and Wilson seized upon it as evidence that Charles had no interest in the freedom of his people—quite the opposite of the truth.

Winning the War

When the U.S. entered the war, its military was not prepared for major conflict. Men had to be drafted, rifles and machine guns had to be manufactured, and officers had to be trained. It was not until the spring of 1918 that any significant number of Americans arrived in Europe. But eventually the American Expeditionary Force would total over a million men, under the command of **General John J. "Black Jack" Pershing**.

On May 26, 1918, Germany's General Ludendorff launched a surprise attack against seven undermanned British and French divisions along the Chemin des Dames Ridge, overrunning the position in a single morning. By June 1, the Germans were just 37 miles from Paris, having reached the River Marne at Chateau-Thierry. Paris was in a state of panic. But the U.S. Seventh Machine Gun Battallion had just arrived after a 22-hour journey in overloaded trucks. They joined the French troops at the bridge. The disorganized, demoralized French troops were getting ready to retreat and asked the Americans if they were going to join the retreat. The Americans replied: "Retreat? We just got here!" The Americans proceeded to hold the position against the German onslaught and then attacked. Ludendorff's troops were exhausted and could not hold out. It was the Germans who ended up retreating.

Then the Fourth Marine Brigade arrived at Belleau Wood. On the other side of the wood were the Germans. Though the wood was a thick tangle of undergrowth, huge boulders and ravines, on June 6 the Marines launched an attack through the wood itself, a nearby village, and the German positions to the west of Belleau Wood. The battle took the rest of June, but by July 1 the Americans had won a major victory.

From July 18 to August 6, 85,000 Americans participated in the Second Battle of the Marne, which stopped another German offensive. Then the Americans joined the British and French in two offensives. On September 12, the first distinctively U.S. offensive began, successfully wiping out the St. Mihiel salient. Finally, the Americans launched the Meuse-Argonne Offensive on September 26, which was brought to a halt only by the Armistice on November 11. In both of the American offensives, U.S. air power played a significant role, as airplanes became a factor in war for the first time.

The Armistice was signed at 5:00 a.m. on November 11, and hostilities ceased at 11:00 a.m. The War was over.

Losing the Peace

Woodrow Wilson had proclaimed that the Great War (as it was then known) would be the "war to end all wars." When the Armistice went into effect, there were fourteen wars of various sorts going on throughout the world. Nevertheless, Wilson was supremely confident that peace could be guaranteed through the Versailles Peace Conference, which began in January 1919.

When Wilson landed in France, he received a tumultuous cheering welcome. American troops were rightly seen as the deciding factor that had finally brought the War to an end, and the European people wanted to show their gratitude to the President who had sent those troops. The European leaders, however, were much less enamored of Wilson and his peace plans. They had plans of their own.

Georges Clemenceau, France's prime minister, wanted to punish Germany and so weaken that country that France would dominate the continent. David Lloyd-George, England's prime minister, was more realistic about the long-term dangers of harsh punishments, but he knew that the English people wanted Germany punished; therefore, to stay in office, he went along with Clemenceau.

Wilson believed that the most important task of the Conference was to establish an international organization which would use the principles of American democracy to bring peace to the world. He called it the League of Nations. At one point Wilson said that the League would establish the brotherhood of man where Christianity had failed: "Why has Jesus Christ so far not succeeded in inducing the world to follow His teachings in these matters? It is because He taught the ideal without devising any practical means of attaining it. That is the reason why I am proposing a practical scheme to carry out His aims." Never was Wilson's Messianism so clearly revealed as in that statement.

But Wilson the Messiah was no longer Wilson the practical politician, and Clemenceau and Lloyd-George were able to outwit him on many occasions. Wilson opposed harsh punishments of Germany, but Clemenceau had merely to threaten an abandonment of the League and Wilson would give in. Wilson was not able to prevent one single punishment from being included in the treaty.

Clemenceau and Lloyd-George also allowed the American President to be in charge of "self-determination," to redraw the map of Europe to fit Wilson's ideas of how Europeans should be governed. He created the country of Czechoslovakia, putting Czechs and Slovaks together because they spoke the same language, though they had no other historical reason for being yoked. He created the country of Yugoslavia (Land of Southern Slavs), for Croatians, Serbians, Slovenes and Montenegrins, again using a common language as the only standard. He gave Austria's South Tyrol to Italy (though the area was German speaking) because the Italians showed him a map of the area containing a mountain with an Italian name, thereby "proving" that the province was part of "historic Italy." Romania, which had also come into the War by secret treaty, received Hungarian land, thereby making millions of Hungarians instant Romanians. Millions of Germans were put into the newly

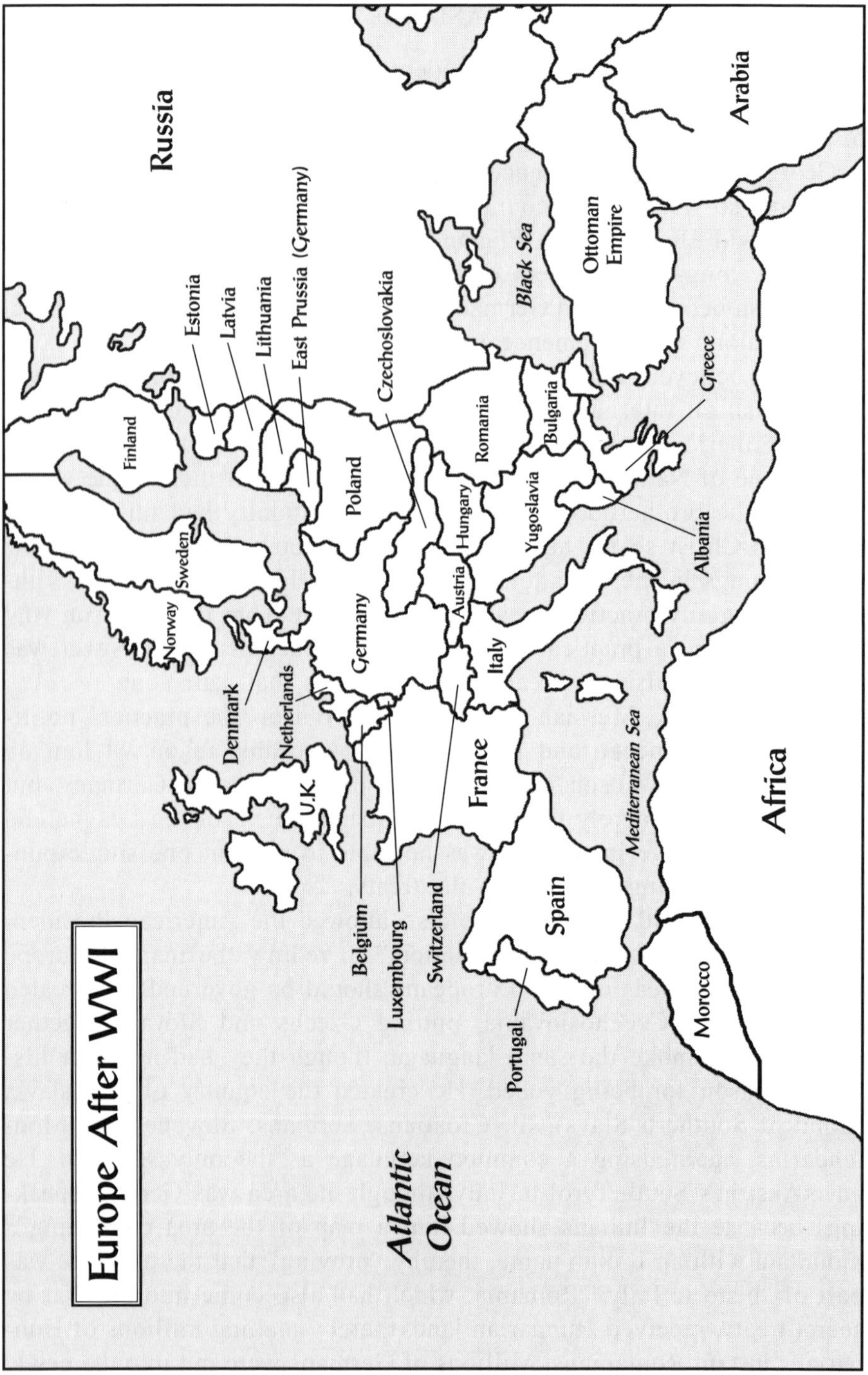

Europe After WWI

recreated Poland. But when the Christian Ukrainians asked that they be supported in their desire to be free from the atheist government of Communist Russia, Wilson told them to place their trust in the League of Nations. He also considered and then rejected the possibility of uniting Austria and Germany on the basis of common language, stating in one of his letters: "German Austria should go to Germany, as all were of one language and one race, but this would mean the establishment of a great central Roman Catholic nation which would be under the control of the Papacy." Wilson had principles, but they were applied at the wrong times and abandoned at the wrong times.

When the Germans were finally permitted to come to Versailles on April 28, they were told that they must sign the Treaty as it stood or face resumption of the War. The German delegates begged for negotiations on the harshest provisions. Lloyd-George agreed that some revisions were in order. Clemenceau said no revisions. Wilson listened to the German objections, then said that the whole thing made him tired and adjourned the meeting. There were no revisions. The Versailles Treaty was signed on June 28.

Woodrow Wilson's stated goals were democracy and self-determination. But just half a generation after Versailles, in 1934, we find Germany ruled by a Nazi dictatorship; Czechs oppressing non-Czechs; Yugoslavia ruled by a terrorist regime, which used assassination and execution as its main weapons; Russia in the grip of Communism. Worse was to come. Without the protection of Austria-Hungary, the small nationality groups that had composed their Empire fell under dictatorship—first Nazi, then Communist. If a just peace could have been concluded before the overthrow of the German Kaiser and the Austrian Emperor, Adolf Hitler would have had no place to go. There might never have been a World War II, and the Communists might have been checked in their westward drive.

After the Treaty

On July 10, 1919, Wilson came before the Senate to present the Treaty and the League of Nations Covenant for ratification. But he faced a Senate which had a Republican majority. Furthermore, the Senate was isolationist, believing that America should stay out of European affairs and that Europeans should not expect America to come to their rescue. The Senate majority leader was Henry Cabot Lodge of Massachusetts, strongly isolationist and violently anti-Wilson. Lodge told Wilson the

Senate would never accept the Treaty in its present form; Wilson told Lodge he would make no changes. The President tried to lobby individual Senators, but he had lost his master touch. He then decided, in spite of poor health, to take his case to the people.

Wilson began a nationwide tour on September 4, 1919. In 21 days he gave 37 major speeches in 29 cities on the theme that the "League of Nations is the only thing that can prevent the recurrence of this tragedy [the War]." This murderous schedule was too much for a man who had borne the double burden of domestic chief executive and commander-in-chief during three of the most tumultuous years in the history of the world. In Pueblo, Colorado on September 25, he had a stroke which almost killed him. Though paralyzed on his left side, he wanted to continue the tour. But his wife Edith refused to allow it, and the Presidential train turned east.

The full seriousness of the President's illness was not revealed to the press, to Congress, or even to Vice President Thomas Marshall. He was bed-ridden with almost no one allowed to see him. Edith was his only link to the outside world and virtually ran the country, telling Cabinet officers and other officials what was to be done.

Meanwhile the Treaty came up for a vote. Some of Wilson's advisers urged him to accept proposed reservations which might have enabled the Treaty to pass. But on this issue, Wilson did not need Edith to make his decisions for him. He would accept no reservations. On November 17 the Treaty was defeated. America concluded a separate treaty, and Americans retreated from the crusading idealism of the Wilson years.

Wilson regained enough strength to begin holding cabinet meetings in April of 1920 and even started thinking about running for a third term. But his friends refused to allow his name to be placed in nomination. The Republican victory in 1920 broke his heart, as he saw in it a repudiation by the American people of the League of Nations. Wilson was not to be the Messiah of the world after all, but for the people of Europe, the damage had already been done.

REVIEW QUESTIONS

1. List Wilson's four principles of government.
2. Summarize Wilson's domestic policies.
3. What factors contributed to Wilson's victory in 1916?

4. How did the U.S. come into World War I?
5. What role did the U.S. play in the military victory of the Allies?
6. How did Wilson frustrate Emperor Charles' efforts for peace?
7. How did Wilson have a wrong conception about the Russian Revolution?
8. What did Wilson do at the Versailles Conference?
9. What were the harmful results of the Versailles Conference?
10. How did Wilson try to gain acceptance of the Versailles Treaty in the United States? Why did he fail?

PROJECTS

1. Do research and prepare a report on some aspect of American involvement in World War I.
2. Choose a year from World War I. Put together a magazine in news magazine format for that year.
3. Find out more about Emperor Charles of Austria.

Chapter 21

Viva Cristo Rey!

TOWARD THE END of the 19th century, three governments in Latin America were reasonably stable: Colombia with its traditionalist President Nuñez, Brazil under Emperor Pedro II, and Mexico under Porfirio Diaz. Colombia continued to enjoy peace and prosperity as traditionalists ruled that small country until a Liberal government came into power in 1930. The closing years of the 19th century saw the overthrow of Brazil's emperor, ushering in the usual chaos and dictatorships. And in the early 20th century, Mexico entered years of violence, destruction and heroism.

Mexico: The Revolution Begins

In 1910, Porfirio Diaz was getting old. His rotting teeth caused him excruciating pain; he had lost the master touch which had enabled him to keep all the factions in Mexico in harmony and working together for the good of the country; he was mainly concerned with keeping himself in power until he died. But as he grew less able to cope with Mexico's problems, his earlier mistakes magnified the old problems and created new ones. New groups and leaders appeared who were opposed to Diaz and began working actively to bring about changes in Mexican society—some constructive, some destructive.

The most constructive group was young, intelligent, talented and Catholic. Young Catholics formed the National Catholic Party to advance papal teachings on social justice. The League of Catholic Students was formed as an auxiliary; its goals were to aid the political effort and to rally Catholic students to a more fervent practice of their religion.

In 1910, the Catholic Party supported Francisco Madera in the presidential election against Diaz because they believed that he would give them a chance in a new government to apply Catholic principles. Madera campaigned all over Mexico and drew huge crowds. Diaz had agreed to this election, Mexico's first since he took power, but he was not too concerned about losing. When he saw the popular support Madera was receiving, Diaz simply put him in jail for inciting riots. The election was held in July, but Diaz did not announce the results until September 16, when he casually mentioned that he had received 99 percent of the votes. This obvious falsehood made Mexico look ridiculous and turned more people against Diaz.

Madera escaped across the border to Texas on October 6, proclaimed the election a fraud and himself president, and called for an uprising on November 20. The revolt was unplanned and failed miserably. But the obvious incompetence of Diaz's army—the generals had an average age of 80 and the lieutenants were mostly over 60—led to the formation of guerrilla-bandit bands. The leader of these bands was the brave but cruel Pancho Villa, a brilliant general popular among the men he led. The outbreak of violence marked the beginning of what is known in Mexico as **The Revolution**.

Still another group rose against Diaz. In early 1911 Emiliano Zapata, a mestizo farmer in the sugar state of Morelos, organized the Indians and attacked wealthy land-owners who had stolen the Indians' land with Diaz's blessing. With pictures of Our Lady of Guadalupe pinned to their sombreros, Zapata's Indians drove off landlords, seized estates and divided the land among the Indians. By Holy Week, Mexico City's residents could see the fires of burning mansions across the lava flow. Zapata was a rarity among revolutionary leaders. He wanted nothing for himself, not wealth, not power, not fame. He wanted only justice and land for the poor Indians he led.

Driven mad by the pain from his teeth, fearful of Zapata's Indians and unable to cope with the rising chaos, Diaz resigned and left Mexico for Paris, where he lived until his death in 1915.

Madera became the new president, but he was neither strong enough nor wise enough to solve the problems which had led to the uprisings in the first place. His only solution to any difficulty was to hold an election. In less than two years, Victoriano Huerta seized power, kidnapped and murdered Madera, murdered almost everyone else in his way, and ruled the country from a bar, drunk half the time. Rebellions broke out in the north, led by Alvaro Obregon, Plutarco Calles and Venustiano Carranza.

In March 1913, Pancho Villa rode back across the Rio Bravo from Texas, calling for vengeance against Madera's murderers. He raised an army, a wild band with horses, goats, cooking pots and *soldaderos*—the wives and sweethearts who did the cooking, the laundry and even some of the fighting. Villa attracted to his cause many Indians and mestizos who were hoping for land and justice, but Villa's idea of social justice was to seize the haciendas and drive off the livestock to sell in Texas for money to buy guns and ammunition. Villa's band was cruel and capricious and spread a reign of terror wherever it went, killing and robbing from the poor as well as from the rich, shooting helpless prisoners, inflicting horrible tortures. The United States newspapers made Villa into a Mexican Robin Hood, and he had no trouble getting the guns and bullets he needed in the United States. Villa and the other revolutionary leaders (with the exception of Zapata), had no respect for the Church; they seized Church property, harassed Catholics, jailed or exiled bishops and religious.

By 1914, the North was in full-scale revolt, Zapata was active in the South, and Villa was spreading terror wherever he rode. But Huerta had the army, the power structure and superior weapons. A key role in the Revolution would be played by Woodrow Wilson and the United States.

Wilson Gets Involved

Woodrow Wilson's attitude toward Mexico was in line with his attitude toward Europe. He saw his role as enforcing democracy throughout the Western Hemisphere, stating in 1913: "I am going to teach the South American republics to elect good men." Wilson informed Huerta that the U.S. would not recognize Huerta's government, telling his friends that he would destroy it by every means short of actual invasion. Wilson had an embargo (prohibition) placed on the selling of arms to Huerta (a wise policy), but gave U.S. aid openly to the revolutionaries, especially to Villa, who was Wilson's favorite general (an unwise policy).

U.S. meddling in Mexico led to the **Vera Cruz Incident**. In April 1914, a few U.S. sailors inadvertently entered a restricted area in the port of Veracruz. They were arrested but quickly released by authorities, along with apologies. But U.S. Admiral Mayo insisted that Mexico publicly apologize with a ceremonial salute to the U.S. flag, a humiliating gesture. The Mexican authorities were so angry that they refused even to issue a simple apology. In retaliation, Wilson ordered the U.S. fleet to Veracruz to intercept any arms shipments coming into Mexico. It happened that the German freighter *Ypiranga* was about to land with arms for Huerta's government. Admiral Mayo did not want to anger Germany, so he conceived the idea of landing his men on shore, where they would seize the port and customs house and confiscate the arms shipment *after* it had been taken off the German ship. When U.S. troops landed, the Mexicans understandably opened fire. In response, the U.S. fleet bombarded the town, killing hundreds of innocent people. In the confusion, the *Ypiranga* quietly went to another port and landed its cargo. The U.S. commanders, furious, occupied Veracruz, to the accompaniment of much property damage and personal injury. Both the Mexican government and the Revolutionaries were outraged at the U.S. and for once united in protesting indignantly. Of the rebel leaders, only Villa kept silent, because he was getting guns from the U.S. For a few days Mexico and the U.S. were on the verge of war. Finally, Argentina, Brazil and Chile offered to arbitrate the dispute, and both sides—eager to avoid war—accepted. But during the negotiations, the U.S. held Veracruz, cutting off Huerta's supply line and customs receipts, resulting in damage both to Huerta's cause and to the reputation of the U.S. in Mexico.

The Constitution of the Revolution

Finally, Obregon took Mexico City in August 1914. Huerta fled, but the bloodshed had only begun, as the Revolutionary leaders now turned against each other. Villa was enraged that he had not captured Mexico City, Zapata was mistrustful of the other leaders because they seemed more concerned with power for themselves than with land for the Indians, Carranza was self-centered and primarily concerned about taking over the government and Obregon sat quietly aside with his well-trained, battle-tested army. Finally at the risk of his life, Obregon went to Villa and arranged a truce between Villa and Carranza, setting up a convention of all factions to decide on a government.

The convention met in October 1914 and quickly collapsed into chaos because no one knew anything about government. Carranza and Obregon withdrew in disgust to Veracruz. Villa and Zapata marched on Mexico City. Zapata's Indians were bewildered in the big city. Villa took over the government, though he did precious little governing, concentrating on executing anyone he did not like. Money was worthless. No one worked. When Mexico City ran out of food, Zapata and his men went back to Morelos. Villa and his army sought forage in the nearby Bajio area. Then Obregon quietly reoccupied Mexico City. He took his men to the Bajio, where they dug trenches and strung barbed wire in the fields, in imitation of the tactics being used in the war in Europe. He commanded the approaches with machine guns. When Villa realized what was happening, he attacked. Fifty thousand Mexicans were killed. His men died on the wire, chopped down by machine gun fire. By summer Villa had been driven back to Chihuahua in the North.

Mexico now cringed under worse horrors than ever before. Carranza had the title of president but could not keep order. No one's life was safe. Bandit gangs pillaged homes and burned churches. An estimated two million Mexicans were killed or fled the country.

In October 1915, Wilson finally withdrew his support from Villa. Villa cold-bloodedly declared open season on U.S. citizens in Mexico. In March 1916, he even raided the border town of Columbus, New Mexico, hoping to provoke the U.S. into declaring war on Mexico and thereby bring down the Carranza government. Wilson was running for re-election and could not let Villa get away with it. With Carranza's permission, he sent General John Pershing and U.S. troops into Mexico. Pershing could not catch Villa, but the bandit leader was forced into hiding, thereby making it possible for Carranza to get control of Chihuahua for the first time. By 1917 Villa was only a minor nuisance, engaging in occasional banditry. (A later Mexican government gave him amnesty and a hacienda in return for his settling down, and Villa became a wealthy landowner. In 1923 he was gunned down in revenge by the families of men he had killed.)

With Villa out of the way, Carranza had enough control of the country to proclaim the Constitution of the Revolution and to be inaugurated as President in March 1917, though the country was still far from peaceful. (Men were married with weapons at their side in case they were attacked in church.) The new constitution lodged most of the power in the president, who was to be elected for one term only. Most importantly, the Constitution gave the government complete power over the Church. But Carranza was not yet strong enough to enforce these provisions.

About the only thing that was enforced under Carranza was the destruction of Emiliano Zapata. General Pablo Gonzalez longed to be president himself, so he thought to achieve glory and fame by eliminating Zapata. He persuaded one of his colonels, Guajardo, to pretend to defect to Zapata. Zapata, of course, would be very suspicious of any such defection; therefore, to allay the suspicions, Gonzalez allowed Guajardo to attack a detachment of his own soldiers—who were not aware of the plot—and to slaughter 59 of them. Zapata therefore came to a meeting with Guajardo. He rode into the fire of 600 rifles. Zapata died instantly and his movement collapsed.

By 1920 everyone was sick of Carranza and eager for the end of his term, ready to vote in Obregon as his successor. Carranza intended to manipulate the election so that a friend of his would be elected instead, so Obregon and Calles marched on Mexico City. When Carranza realized that he had no support left, he grabbed bags of gold from the country's treasury and fled to the mountains, leaving a trail of coins behind him. A local bandit chieftain pretended to be his friend and allowed Carranza to sleep in his hut. Then his men surrounded the hut and killed Carranza.

The Cristero Rebellion Begins

Obregon's government was quickly recognized by the U.S., but Catholics were less ready to approve. They could not forget that during the Revolution Obregon had imprisoned priests and nuns, seized churches and convents and closed Catholic schools. Their suspicions were not long in being fulfilled. In February 1921, dynamite exploded at the door of the archbishop's palace in Mexico City. In June a bomb exploded at the archbishop's residence in Guadalajara. Then on November 14, a man carried a bouquet of flowers toward the miraculous picture of Our Lady of Guadalupe. Those who hated the Church had one thought: destroy the portrait and they would destroy the faith of thousands of Mexicans. Therefore, a time bomb was concealed in the flowers placed before Juan Diego's tilma.

The bomb exploded. The shattering concussion ripped out large sections of the stained-glass windows around the basilica and plunged them to the floor of the church. On the altar itself, a heavy crucifix was twisted into a semi-circle. Mexicans fell to the ground in fright. Then they slowly looked up. The portrait was unharmed. Not even the glass in front of Juan Diego's tilma was cracked.

Instead of destroying the faith of the Mexicans, the bomb increased it. Our Lady's portrait had been preserved by a miracle. To show their gratitude, the Catholics of Mexico City began daily Eucharistic adoration at the basilica in reparation for the wrongs committed by the Obregon government.

Furious that violence had failed, the Obregon government prohibited public religious ceremonies. On January 11, 1923, the bishops, with the Pope's representative Filippi officiating, dedicated a monument to Christ the King. The government responded by expelling Filippi from the country and bringing criminal charges against several bishops. In 1924, Mexico was host to Catholics from around the world at a Eucharistic Congress. Obregon dispersed the Congress and fired any government employee who had participated.

But the worst was yet to come. On December 1, 1924, Obregon's hand-picked successor, Plutarco Elias Calles, took office as president of Mexico. He was even more anti-Catholic than Obregon. He announced, "I have a personal hatred for Christ," and declared his intention of enforcing the 1917 Constitution to the fullest extent. On January 30, 1925, the state of Tabasco limited the number of priests to six (one for each 30,000 Catholics). On February 18, a priest was jailed for wearing clerical garb and a seminary closed. Later in February, the government tried to promote a schism by installing a renegade priest in the Church of La Soledad in Mexico City's working class district. But the people forced the priest to flee.

Mexico's Catholics were not about to sit by quietly as the government attempted to destroy their Church. On March 9, Catholic lay societies in Mexico formed the National League for Religious Defense (NLDR), declaring, "We must unite [to] make an effort that is energetic, tenacious, supreme, and irresistible, which will uproot once and for all from the Constitution all its injustices of whatever kind and all its tyrannies whatever their origin."

But persecution continued. In July two seminaries were closed; in August the government took over a Catholic orphanage and home for the aged; in late October Tabasco passed a law that only married priests over 40 could exercise the ministry. By the middle of March 1926, 200 foreign-born priests had been sent out of the country, and 83 convents and monasteries had been closed.

On July 2 the government announced that as of July 31 all priests must be registered, with the intention of driving them out of the country or forcibly preventing them from practicing their priesthood. The bishops decided that no priests would register; instead they would practice their ministry in secret, avoiding the clutches of the government as long as possible. The bishops put the country under interdict, ordering the suspension of all public worship as of August 1, to put pressure on Calles to back down.

At the same time, the NLDR leadership came to the conclusion that their only hope to restore Catholicism to Mexico was to take up arms against the government. The leaders met secretly with the bishops, who told them to go ahead with their plans, that they would be fighting in a just cause. In the fall, NLDR leader Capistrán Garza and two friends began crossing the U.S., sleeping outdoors to save money, to beg funds to buy arms and ammunition for the rebellion. Their cause received little sympathy. Though Catholics were dying in Mexico (the first martyrs were Father Luis Batís and two laymen, who cried, *Viva Cristo Rey* —"Long live Christ the King"—as they were shot), American bishops and Catholic leaders did not want to get involved in the rebellion. The bishop of Corpus Christi, Texas would give no money because, he said, the people in his diocese did not like Mexicans. The bishop of Columbus, Ohio would not even listen to the men. The bishop of Boston suggested to Garza that he get a job. But though he had been able to raise practically no money, Garza felt that the rebellion could not wait because every day the persecution grew fiercer. The last week of December, Garza sent a formal call to arms to the NLDR leaders, condemning the "implacable rule of a regime of armed bandits." He appealed to "the sacred right of defense" which justified "the necessity of destroying forever the vicious rule of faction in order to create a national government. The hour of battle has sounded! The hour of victory belongs to God!"

In Jalisco, Anacleto Gonzalez Flores—a brilliant young lawyer and a daily communicant—decided to join the rebellion. He told his followers: "I know only too well that what is beginning now for us is a Calvary. We must be ready to take up and carry our crosses. . . . If one of you should ask me what sacrifice I am asking of you in order to seal the pact we are going to celebrate, I will tell you in two words: *your blood*."

During the first week of January, the rebellion broke out in a dozen Mexican states. Capistrán Garza remained in the U.S., now trying to raise money from U.S. businessman William F. Buckley, president of Patempec Oil Company. Buckley was an exemplary Catholic and sympathetic to the cause in Mexico. But before committing himself and some of his friends to financing the rebellion, he visited Pascual Diaz, exiled bishop of Tabasco. Diaz refused to endorse the uprising. Buckley turned down Garza's appeal. And the rebellion lost its last chance for the major financial support it desperately needed.

Without money, the rebels, who had been given the name *Cristeros* from their *Viva Cristo Rey* battle cry, could not wage a major military campaign. They settled into guerrilla warfare, harassing the government but unable to win a decisive victory. By early 1927, it was clear that Gonzalez Flores was the mainspring of the Cristeros. As chief of military operations, he was driving the Calles government insane. At midnight on March 31, government forces raided his home, taking Gonzalez Flores and three others prisoner. The four were interrogated under torture, alternately whipped and slashed with bayonets. Under Gonzalez Flores' encouragement, the men remained silent, refusing to reveal their military plans or the hiding places of their comrades. Frustrated, the government ordered their execution. The four were shot on Monday, April 1. Gonzalez Flores' last words echoed Garcia Moreno: "I die, but God does not die. *Viva Cristo Rey*!"

Blessed Miguel Pro

Gonzalez Flores was far from the last martyr, as the government began ruthlessly hunting down priests. Father José Genaro Sanchez was hanged for refusing to tell where his pastor was hiding. Father David Uribe was shot for saying Mass. Father Mateo Correa Magallanes was killed for not revealing the confessions of Cristeros. But the greatest martyr was Padre Miguel Pro.

Miguel Pro had been a lively, happy young man, noted mainly for his practical jokes. His family barely suspected the deep spirituality under the laughter, but in August 1911 he entered the Jesuit order. He was in the novitiate when revolutionary troops forced the novices to flee. Miguel went first to California, then to Spain, then to Nicaragua, then to Belgium. Through all his travels, Miguel was a ray of sunshine to his friends and deeply concerned for the poor. But he was also so ill that finally the Jesuit superiors decided that perhaps the only cure would be a return to his native Mexico, as dangerous a place as that had become. Padre Pro was delighted. He wanted to see his country again, but even more he wanted to minister to the persecuted Catholics there. The danger to his life counted for nothing.

In 1926 Padre Pro returned to Mexico City and immediately plunged into work. He brought Communion to Catholics at secretly arranged meeting places. He directed a group of young men who gave religious instruction. Disguised as a worker, he rode his bicycle throughout the poorest parts of the city, bringing the Sacraments to the people. He lived with his father and younger brothers and sisters; his brothers Humberto and Roberto were members of the NLDR and active in its political work. On one occasion they released balloons over the city which floated to earth carrying leaflets attacking the government and encouraging the people to hold fast. Calles was furious and sent 10,000 people running about the city chasing the balloons. Padre Pro was arrested after this episode and taken to the police station, where he kept his sense of humor in spite of the danger, describing his sleeping accommodations thus: "An extensive bed of cement, which is to say the whole patio, was placed at our disposal, together with some enormous pillows, otherwise serving as walls." Soon after he was released, he and his family went into hiding.

But he could not stand the inactivity and requested from his superiors permission to go back into Mexico City. His begging was so insistent that the Jesuit superiors relented, and Padre Pro was again plunged into work. Calles had declared in 1924 that he stood for "dictatorship of the proletariat; suppression of private property; total submission of the family to the state; the uprooting of religion." Padre Pro proclaimed that his goals were to enable the people to practice their faith and to control the education of their children. He and Calles were on a direct collision course.

On November 13, a car formerly belonging to his brother was used in a failed attempt to assassinate Calles. Again the family went into hiding. But Calles was not to be denied this time. A young boy who had gone to Padre Pro for Confession revealed under torture his hiding place.

On the morning of November 17, Padre Pro said Mass in Señora Valdez's house, where he was hiding. Señora Valdez said later, "At the moment of the Elevation, I saw [Padre Pro] seemingly transformed into a white silhouette and plainly raised above the level of the floor. I became aware of great happiness. Later, my servants told me spontaneously that they had observed the same phenomenon, and, simultaneously, had experienced an exceptional consolation." Padre Pro was indeed very close to God.

That very night, police surrounded the house. At 3:00 a.m. they broke in. Said Padre Pro to his brothers: "Repent of your sins as if in the very presence of God." He gave them absolution. "From here on, we're offering our lives for the cause of religion in Mexico. Let us all three do it together, that God may accept our sacrifice." As the soldiers led him out of the house, he turned and shouted, *Viva Dios! Viva la Virgen de Guadalupe*!

It was clear from all the evidence that the Pros had nothing to do with the assassination attempt, but Calles ordered their execution. On November 23, 1927, Padre Pro was taken from his cell. Carrying his rosary and a crucifix, he walked calmly to the outside plaza and stepped up to a wall on which were drawn life-size outlines of men to serve as targets. The soldiers asked: "Is there anything you wish?" Padre Pro replied: "That I may be permitted to pray." He knelt, prayed and then rose. He stretched his arms in the form of a cross and said softly, *Viva Cristo Rey*. Shots rang out. He crumpled to the ground. Padre Pro had once prayed to be a martyr for Christ. His prayer had been answered.

The Rebellion Ends

Inspired by the martyrdom of Padre Pro and of other priests, the Cristeros fought on, and the pressure was beginning to tell on the government. The Catholic haters were discovering that the Church was not so easily crushed. The government was therefore willing to listen to the new U.S. ambassador, Dwight Morrow, who, believing the Cristeros were mindless revolutionaries, wanted to end the revolt in order to preserve Calles' government in power. He arranged meetings between President Calles and Father Burke of the U.S. National Catholic Welfare Conference (the official organization of the U.S. hierarchy); Calles refused to change any laws but conceded that he would be somewhat more cordial to the Church if the bishops would resume public worship.

Calles' term of office was near an end, and in July 1928, Obregon was re-elected President, as he and Calles continued their trade-off arrangement. Obregon told Morrow that he agreed with Calles regarding the Church, and Morrow was hopeful that he could soon negotiate a settlement. Then, on July 16, while Obregon was at a luncheon, an unbalanced young man named José de Leon Toral fired a revolver into Obregon's face, assassinating the president-elect. The first inclination of Obregon's supporters was to think that Calles was in on the killing as a means of getting himself back into power. To protect himself, Calles renewed his attacks on the Church, blaming it for Obregon's murder.

But that was not enough to satisfy Obregon's supporters. Calles might well have been assassinated himself if he had not promised to step down from office and hold new elections. He kept his promise, and the new president, Emilio Portes Gil, reopened negotiations with the Church through Morrow.

The Cristeros were not interested in negotiations. In the summer of 1928, they mounted new attacks, continuing into 1929. Afraid that his government would be overthrown before he could negotiate a settlement, Portes Gil ordered an all-out drive against the Cristeros in April 1929. The Cristeros responded by a bold stroke. They would capture the Mexico City-Guadalajara train, put a task force aboard, and rush to Guadalajara to capture the government garrison there. But the train turned out to be a troop convoy. The Cristeros fought valiantly through an entire day. By nightfall the brave Catholics had only 20 rounds of ammunition per man. They were forced to retreat.

The government ordered a ranch-by-ranch search for Cristeros. More innocent people died. On June 4 and 5, hymn-singing Cristeros fought government troops to a standstill in the bloody battle of El Borbollon. By the middle of June, it was clear that the government could prevent the Cristeros from winning a victory but they could never destroy them.

Finally, in June, representatives of the bishops and Portes Gil issued a statement that the government did not intend to "destroy the Catholic Church or any other, nor to intervene in any way in its spiritual function." The bishops believed this a sufficient compromise and announced the resumption of public worship. With this agreement reached and the hunting down of priests ended, the Cristeros could no longer muster enough support to continue the rebellion. The leaders voted to end the rebellion if the government would grant amnesty for all past and present offenses. Portes Gil agreed. The Cristero rebellion was over.

But the government broke its promises, arresting Cristero leaders. On February 14, 1930, 41 ex-Cristeros were executed. Even into the 1950's, Cristeros were still in danger. In 1931 the government restricted priests once again. By 1935 many states closed almost every church. No Catholic could teach in the schools. It appeared that the Cristeros had died in vain.

But no sacrifice is ever wasted. In 1936 a new president, Cardenas, came into power and the persecution relaxed. Then in 1940, another president, Manuel Avila Camacho, could announce: "I am a believer." And in 1979, the Pope himself, John Paul II, traveled to Mexico, where he cheerfully disobeyed still-existing laws prohibiting the wearing of clerical garb on the streets and the public celebration of the liturgy by foreign priests. The Holy Father was greeted by cheering millions, as he paid homage to the Virgin of Guadalupe. Clearly the Catholic Church in Mexico was alive and strong. The blood of the martyrs of the Revolution had borne fruit.

REVIEW QUESTIONS

1. Summarize the characters and goals of Diaz, Madera, Villa and Zapata.
2. How was Diaz overthrown? How did Huerta come to power? Describe his rule.
3. What happened in the Veracruz incident?
4. Describe the Carranza regime.
5. How were Villa and Zapata defeated?
6. How did Obregon and Calles come to power?
7. What events led up to the outbreak of the Cristero rebellion?
8. Why did the Cristeros fail to gain support in the United States?
9. Summarize the role of Gonzalez Flores.
10. How did Padre Pro practice his ministry?
11. Describe the martyrdom of Padre Pro.
12. How was the rebellion ended?
13. How did religious peace come to Mexico?

PROJECTS

1. Prepare an exhibit showing the life and accomplishments of Padre Pro.
2. Do research and prepare a report on the history of Mexico from 1940 to the present.
3. Find out about the new Basilica of Our Lady of Guadalupe.

Chapter 22

Boom, Depression and The New Deal

AS THE AMERICAN PEOPLE entered the decade of the 1920's, they were exhausted. They had been shaken by their firsthand experience with the sufferings of war; they were tired of the Progressive urgings to reform; they had been shattered by a severe influenza epidemic which raged throughout the world, striking down old and young and weak and strong alike, leaving scarcely a family untouched. The desire of many Americans was to be left alone: to be left alone by Europe, to be left alone by reformers, to be left alone by religion. They wanted to make money and to spend it; they would rather listen to the radio than to sermons. This new mood in America could be seen in every area of life.

In foreign policy, America was isolationist. Neither the men in power nor the majority of the people wanted to get involved in Europe's troubles. There had been enough bloodshed in the Great War just ended. Americans wanted nothing to do with the countries that had started the War. Hence the Senate decisively voted down the Versailles Treaty, and America never joined the League of Nations. Because they wanted never to go to war again, Americans (and Europeans) believed that if they wished hard enough, they could make war go away. Hence in August 1928, 15 nations signed the Kellogg-Briand Pact (named after the U.S. Secretary of State and the French foreign minister), promising to renounce war as an instrument of national policy.

In politics, the keynote for the 1920's was set by the Republican Presidential nominee in 1920, Warren G. Harding, who said: "America's present need is not heroics, but healing; not nostrums, but normalcy; not surgery, but serenity; not the dramatic, but the dispassionate;

not experiment, but equipoise; not submergence in internationality, but sustainment in triumphant nationality." His newly coined word "normalcy" entered the vocabulary to characterize the American mood.

Harding's nomination and election illustrate clearly that Americans were no longer in the mood for crusaders. Going into the Republican convention, Governor Frank Lowden of Illinois, a moderate Progressive, and General Leonard Wood, a hard core Progressive, were the front-runners. Hiram Johnson of California, even more of a Progressive than Wood, also had a sizeable block of delegates. Harding, a Senator from Ohio who had done poorly in the primaries, was a very distant fourth. But several factors were working for Harding. He was a loyal follower of the Senate Republican leadership. He had taken no part in Progressive crusades. His campaign manager Harry Daugherty had made friends with individual delegates. Thus, when a deadlock developed between Lowden and Wood, convention chairman Henry Cabot Lodge and other Senate leaders decided to choose a compromise candidate to avoid a knock-down fight which would weaken the Party. They settled on Harding because he was from Ohio, a state with a sizeable number of electoral votes. He was nominated on the tenth ballot. Then the Senate leaders agreed that a Progressive vice-presidential candidate was needed to balance the ticket and selected Senator Irvine Lenroot of Wisconsin. But Lenroot was not popular with the delegates. A delegate from Oregon, acting on his own initiative, nominated Massachusetts Governor Calvin Coolidge, and immediately the delegates began chanting "We want Coolidge!" Coolidge received 674 votes to Lenroot's 148. Thus one man became President of the United States because he was from Ohio and another because a delegate from Oregon could shout louder than Henry Cabot Lodge.

As the campaign between Democrat James M. Cox and Harding developed, there were no clear-cut issues. The League of Nations did not assume that role, both men were economic conservatives, and both were former newspaper editors from Ohio. Their images therefore played a role in the campaign, and since Harding was described as "the man who looked like a President" and represented "normalcy," he won the election by the highest percentage of the popular vote of any candidate since before the Civil War.

In morality, traditional moral standards were ignored or ridiculed. The 1920's were the age of the criminal gangs, in which a murderer and thief like Al Capone could control an entire city (Cicero, Illinois) and terrorize others to make himself and his henchmen rich. Rival gangs fought full-scale wars with each other, virtually untouched by the police. In the notorious St. Valentine's Day Massacre, for example, members of one gang walked into an auto repair garage, lined up seven rival gangsters and mowed them down with machine guns. No one was ever convicted for this murder.

An attempt to impose a false morality on the entire Nation contributed to the crime wave. On January 16, 1920, the Volstead Act went into effect, implementing the 18th Amendment to the Constitution, which prohibited the sale of alcoholic beverages. Foisted upon the country by rural fundamentalist Protestants, who regarded alcohol as the world's worst evil, Prohibition soon became the most widely disobeyed law in the nation's history. Anyone who wanted a drink would either manufacture his own or go to the nearest "speakeasy" (a clandestine bar). The field was wide open for criminal gangs to go into the liquor business to make fantastic profits. Respect for the law plummeted as tens of thousands of people became lawbreakers, including people who might normally never have been heavy drinkers but were attracted by the excitement of getting an illegal drink.

By being told that alcohol was the worst evil, Americans were distracted from far more serious moral problems. By 1929, there were 200,000 divorces a year in the United States, double the number of 1915. Sunday was no longer regarded as a day for church but as a day for entertainment. Immoral movies attracted large audiences. Margaret Sanger led a movement for the legalization of contraceptives, arguing that the way to help the poor was to prevent their having children. At the beginning of the decade, every religious denomination in the United States and even people who belonged to no church had regarded contraception as evil because it struck at the heart of marriage and the family. By the end of the next decade the Catholic Church was almost alone in its defense of the union between love and life.

In education, new theories took hold. **Pragmatism**, developed primarily by John Dewey, denied that the purpose of education was to discover and transmit truth or to make the student a better person. Instead an idea was valuable only if it worked, if it helped a man get what he wanted, whether or not the end or the means were moral in themselves. **Permissiveness** ridiculed discipline as hampering freedom. The permissiveness in the schools would gradually filter down to parents, who would be told that they must be permissive in their homes, or else their children would grow up emotionally disturbed.

In society, many Americans reacted violently against anything that differed from the dominant American culture: White Anglo-Saxon Protestant (or WASP as it was nicknamed). The Ku Klux Klan had been revived in 1915 and reached its peak in the 1920's, with five million members and dominant political power in the states of Indiana, Oklahoma and Texas, and the cities of Chicago, Denver and Detroit. In Oklahoma a Klan-controlled legislature impeached a governor who had fought the Klan. In Oregon, the Klan elected a governor and put through a law requiring all children to attend public schools. Not just persecuting Negroes, the Klan also hated Catholics, Jews and immigrants. They lynched hundreds of people, destroyed property, burned crosses in front of homes and churches, held mass meetings dressed in white sheets and hoods, and tried to terrorize others into condoning their bigotry and hatred. Finally the Baltimore *Sun* and the New York *World* newspapers exposed the Klan's reign of terror. The Grand Dragon (leader) David C. Stephenson was convicted of second degree murder, and by 1930, the Klan was down to only 9,000 members.

But the Klansmen were not the only bigots. There was a general attitude that America did not need immigrants, especially from southern and eastern Europe and the Orient. Laws restricting immigration were passed, and the general feeling toward immigrants was hostile. In addition, anti-Negro feeling became strong in the North, and Negro-white riots erupted in Northern cities. The worst was in Chicago, where an incident at a beach led to week-long violence in which 40 were killed and 500 injured.

In entertainment, Americans had more leisure time because of continued mechanization of farming and industry. They used it to listen to the new invention, radio, and to attend the new invention, movies. Professional sports became big business with the heroics of Babe Ruth, Lou Gehrig, Bobby Jones, Bill Tilden and Red Grange. But the greatest hero of the 1920's was not a sports figure, but the young aviator, Charles Lindbergh, who became the first man to make a solo flight from New York to Paris. He and his plane, the *Spirit of St. Louis*, captured the heart and the imagination of the entire world.

In economics, America went all out for materialism. In the April 1921 issue of *The Independent* magazine, the following appeared: "What is the finest fame? Business. The soundest science? Business. The truest art? Business. The fullest education? Business. The fairest opportunity? Business. The cleanest philanthropy? Business. The sanest religion? Business." Said Calvin Coolidge, "The man who builds a factory builds a temple. . . . The man who works there worships there." People with money invested in the stock market, buying on margin, which means that they would only pay for part of the stock, hoping to sell it for a profit before the rest of the payment became due. People with less money spent it on cars and other consumer goods, buying on credit. By 1929, installment buying was up to $7 billion a year, in a nation which had formerly regarded any kind of debt as a national sin. More people than ever before wanted to get rich or at least appear to be rich by owning as many things as possible. But everything America was doing had a price, and it would be paid many times over.

Politics of the 1920's

Warren G. Harding was once quoted as saying: "I am not fit for this office and should never have been here." He was not far wrong. In the words of one historian: "Harding's conception of public service was to give a friend a job." He appointed one friend as Attorney General, Harry Daugherty, now almost universally recognized as both an incompetent lawyer and a dishonest man. Daugherty and other Harding friends—Edward N. Denby, Secretary of the Navy, and Albert B. Fall, Secretary of the Interior—wanted to get rich and saw nothing wrong with using their positions to achieve this goal. As the year 1923 wore on, rumors of serious scandals in the Harding administration began to circulate throughout Washington. Harding himself appeared nervous and worried. He left on a speaking tour across the United States. On the trip, both his physical and mental health deteriorated and on August 2, he suffered a stroke and died the same day. The next day, Vice President Calvin Coolidge was sworn in as President. Under Coolidge, the full scope of the Harding scandals came to light.

The best known scandal involved the Teapot Dome oil reserves in Wyoming. Albert Fall had induced Harding to transfer control over Navy oil reserves from the Navy to the Interior Department. Fall then proceeded to lease the rich reserves to Edward Doheny of Pan American Petroleum and Harry Sinclair of Continental Trading Company, receiving money and stock in return.

The other major scandals revolved around Attorney General Daugherty and his cronies, known as the Ohio Gang. The Gang involved itself in protecting bootleggers, selling offices, selling pardons and paroles, and various other illegal dealings.

Historians agree that Harding played no actual part in the scandals, and he did take action against those men whose dealings were brought to light before his death. Coolidge had high personal standards and swept out of office all those involved with the Ohio Gang, replacing them with men of good reputation. But the materialistic attitude the scandals symbolized continued to pervade both the government and the Nation as a whole.

Coolidge was easily nominated to run for the Presidency in 1924, but the Democratic convention was chaotic. That party was deeply divided between urban and rural, wet and dry, Catholic and Protestant, North and South. The rural, more conservative wing of the party supported William Gibbs McAdoo, former Secretary of the Treasury. The city wing supported Al Smith, Governor of New York. Neither faction would yield to the other, and the American people, for the first time listening to a convention by radio, were treated to the spectacle of a party tearing itself apart. Finally on the 103rd ballot, the weary delegates turned to a compromise candidate and nominated a Wall Street lawyer, John W. Davis of West Virginia. The Vice Presidential nomination, in a concession to the Progressives, went to Governor Charles W. Bryan of Nebraska, brother of William Jennings Bryan. Yet Davis' Wall Street connections alienated him from the Smith wing of the party and the name of Bryan was enough to frighten the conservative wing, leaving the nominees with little support.

The issue was never in doubt. The Democrats had created such an unfavorable impression that it is unlikely that any candidate could have overcome the handicap. Said Davis after the election: "I went around the country telling the people I was going to be elected, and I knew I hadn't any more chance than a snowball in hell."

The Great Inflation

In his message to Congress on December 3, 1924, the newly elected President Coolidge called for tax reduction and economy in government spending. He made no mention of a policy that had been pursued since the end of the 1921 depression: artificial inflation of the economy, primarily through policies of the Federal Reserve System. This inflation created the artificial boom of the 1920's.

A boom—and the United States had experienced many before the 1920's—is created by bank credit expansion. When banks have more money to lend, interest rates will be lower and businessmen will borrow more for investment purposes. If the new money available comes from increased savings by the consuming public, the results of business investment will be good. The fact that consumers are saving money instead of spending it indicates that they wish to have goods later, instead of immediately. Therefore business investment to produce those goods later is wise.

This was not the case in the 1920's. No one was saving. Everyone was spending. And many were spending more money than they had by borrowing and buying on credit. Businessmen were so eager to make more money that they overexpanded their businesses, also borrowing huge sums of money. Investors were so eager to get rich in the stock market that they bought wildly, also on credit. The extra money to make all these loans came, not from savings, but from the inflationary policies of the Federal Reserve System.

The Federal Reserve System lulled bankers into a false sense of security because it had been touted as a means of ending bank failures. The banks lent money to investors in stocks and bonds, provided backing for installment buying, underwrote long-term real estate investments and made loans to Europeans (so that the inflation was world-wide). Especially during 1927, the U.S. government played a direct role in stimulating the stock market by adopting a policy of keeping call loan rates (interest rates on bank loans to the stock market) especially low. Whenever stock prices started to fall, Coolidge and Secretary of the Treasury Mellon made optimistic statements designed to spur the market upward again. In March, for example, Mellon said: "There is an abundant supply of easy money which should take care of any contingencies that might arise." Such irresponsible statements clouded the judgment of investors, who believed that there could never again be a stock market crash because of the Federal Reserve and its "abundant supply of easy money."

Late in 1927, the Federal Reserve authorities began to be worried by the monster they were creating (as stock prices rose 20 per cent in the latter half of that year), and in the spring of 1928 tried to slow down the boom. The deflationary effect worked for a time and could have brought an end to the boom before it did any more damage. But with an election coming up, and with loud pleas for financial help from Great

Britain, the Federal Reserve resumed its inflationary policies during the last half of 1928.

Americans were riding on the crest of an economic wave and they could not believe that the wave would ever break. After all, wages were higher than ever, everyone was able to buy new appliances, cars were rolling off Henry Ford's assembly lines, stock prices were high, business was expanding and there was plenty of bootleg whiskey in the local speakeasy. Herbert Hoover's 1928 campaign slogan, "A chicken in every pot and two cars in every garage," sounded like paradise.

The Depression Strikes

Neither major party convention in 1928 presented much of a contest. Ever since Coolidge's statement in 1927, "I do not choose to run for President in 1928," Secretary of Commerce Herbert Clark Hoover had been quietly rounding up delegates. His platform sang the praises of Coolidge and gave the Republicans credit for prosperity. Among the Democrats, Al Smith's supporters had finally captured control of the party, and he was nominated on the first ballot.

The general prosperity for which the Republicans received credit and Smith's handicaps of being urban, anti-prohibition and Catholic decided the election. The Ku Klux Klan and other bigots were out in force, warning the people that if Smith were elected, a direct telephone line would be established to Vatican City and the Pope would dictate American policy. Hoover won overwhelmingly, receiving 444 electoral votes to Smith's 87. Hoover even carried some Southern states for the Republicans (where anti-Catholicism was highest), the first time since Reconstruction. Though the big cities, because of their large numbers of Catholic immigrants, gave decisive majorities to Smith and the Democrats, that was not enough to offset the votes of rural Protestants.

The confidence in the American economy and the Republicans was to be short-lived. By July 1929, signs had appeared that the great boom had finally ended. Businessmen realized that their investments in capital goods had not been made in response to consumer demands and began to cut back on expansion. Business inventories more than tripled, as markets became unavailable. Consumer spending slowed as did industrial production.

By autumn, stock market investors realized that the boom was over. On October 24, more than 13 million shares of stock changed hands on the New York Stock Exchange; on October 29, another 16 million, as investors frantically tried to rid themselves of what were by now obviously unsound investments. By November 13, no less than $30 billion in the market value of listed stocks had been wiped out. It had not been spent; it had not been wasted; it had simply vanished, because it had never really existed in the first place. The first effect of the stock market crash was felt by the speculators, a number of whom committed suicide, unable to face their loss of wealth. But the shock waves would extend throughout the country, leaving no one untouched.

Without investment capital, businesses had to cut back or close down. Employees lost their jobs. Debtors were unable to pay their debts and lost homes and possessions purchased on credit. Since they could not collect debts, businesses were forced to cut back still further, throwing more people out of work. Farm prices dropped drastically because consumers had less money to purchase farm products. Throughout the United States people began to know poverty when they had thought they would never know anything except prosperity.

This new experience could have been healthy for Americans. It could have been God's way of telling them that they needed to be less materialistic and more spiritual. Some Americans did respond to this experience by learning to get along without material things and to accept the sufferings of poverty as a means of coming closer to God. But most Americans begged the government for action. But the men in the government did not know what to do, any more than the people they governed.

They tried. Hoover and his Cabinet and Congress tried to do something about the misery mounting all about them. Hoover personally called a series of White House conferences with leaders from business and industry to urge them to maintain wage rates, expand investments and increase construction. He sent telegrams to all state governors, urging expansion of state public works. The Department of Commerce established a Division of Public Construction to stimulate public works planning. The Federal Reserve lowered its loan rates, thus pumping more artificial credit into the economy.

Unfortunately, these measures did more economic harm than good, because they were inflationary when the economy needed the opposite. But deflation would have caused more short-term suffering because businesses would have had to cut back, the government would have spent less, and more people would have been out of work, until the economy could get back onto a sound footing. If the government and the American people had known how to handle suffering, and if enough community spirit could have been created so that those who still had more than they needed (and there were many) would have helped those who did not, a deflationary policy could have succeeded. Instead, the country tried to relieve suffering caused by too much spending of money by spending more money.

An act of nature brought new anguish in the summer of 1930. A severe drought struck the Midwest and Southwest. Because farmers had not followed conservation practices, the good topsoil dried up and blew away, creating the **Dust Bowl**, and hurling thousands of farmers into abject poverty. Farmers in the South were especially hard hit because many of them had been working as sharecroppers—not owning their own land but paying a large share of their crops for the privilege of leasing the land. When the crops burned up and the soil blew away, they were driven off the land and forced to migrate. Many of them packed all of their possessions into Model T Fords and went west, often to California, which was regarded as the land of opportunity. In the space of a single year, farm income fell $3 billion.

In May 1931, Austria's largest bank, the Credit-Anstalt, failed, precipitating a general panic throughout Central Europe. The heavy American investments in those countries were lost, and the U.S. economy suffered serious shocks. Later in the summer, the Bank of England defaulted on payments to foreigners, and England went off the gold standard. Since the U.S. had upset its own economic system in an attempt to keep Britain on the gold standard, U.S. investors and financial institutions suffered gravely. Now the Depression was world-wide.

By the end of 1931, the U.S. government had the largest peacetime deficit in history—$2.2 billion—and still the tide of the Depression had not turned. In his December message to Congress, Hoover called for a Reconstruction Finance Corporation to loan money to banks, industries, agricultural credit agencies and local governments; a Home Loan Bank to encourage construction; expansion of Federal Land Banks to aid farmers; a Public Works Administration to put men to work for the government; and direct loans for relief. But none of it worked. Bank failures continued at an undiminished rate. Farm prices stayed low. Foreclosures and bankruptcies continued.

By the summer of 1932, the Nation had been in the Depression for nearly three years, and conditions were steadily worsening. The people became desperate and hungered for someone who would promise new and decisive action. The desperation found outlets. Hunger marches filled the city streets. Friends of farmers facing foreclosure would buy the farm at foreclosure sales for a penny and use threats and force to prevent anyone's bidding higher. Communist agitators gained new followers, and Communist Party membership in the U.S. doubled between 1930 and 1932. Influential people called for a dictator.

In this atmosphere of fear and frustration, the Presidential campaign was waged: between Herbert Hoover, the completely discredited Republican incumbent, and the challenger, a man with compelling charisma, enormous powers of persuasion and an unquenchable thirst for power, Franklin Delano Roosevelt.

The Election of Roosevelt

The Republican convention met first and routinely (almost despairingly) nominated Hoover on the first ballot. In the Democrat convention, the contest was between Al Smith—the son of Irish immigrants, who had worked his way to the top—and Roosevelt, the son of a wealthy father, who had previously been Assistant Secretary of the Navy, vice-presidential candidate in 1920, and then governor of New York, having fought his way back from a severe attack of polio. Roosevelt gathered around himself a highly talented campaign organization, headed by James Farley, an astute politician. Primarily through Farley's work, Roosevelt went into the convention with a large bloc of delegates, but not the two-thirds majority then required by the Democrats for nomination. Smith, John Nance Garner of Texas and William Gibbs McAdoo also had delegates. After the first few ballots, it became obvious to Garner and McAdoo that neither of them had any chance and that the hostility between Smith and Roosevelt could well lead to a repeat of the 1924 disaster. The two men threw their delegates to FDR, who was nominated on the fourth ballot.

After a convention had chosen its nominee, the tradition was for a committee to "notify" him at a time set a few weeks later. The nominee would then deliver a formal acceptance speech, usually at his home or near it. But Franklin Roosevelt was never one to abide by tradition. In a stroke of genius, he flew to the convention to give his acceptance speech on the spot, thus impressing the people as a man of action who was not bound by old ways of doing things. In that speech, he uttered the phrase which would be ever after applied to his programs. Said Roosevelt: "I pledge you, I pledge myself to a **New Deal** for the American people."

During his campaign, Roosevelt was all things to all men. At times he sounded more conservative than Hoover; at other times he advocated government regulation and welfarist programs as the Progressives did; at still other times he spoke in favor of government economic control along collectivist lines. He could make almost all the voters think that he supported policies they would favor. And whether he was being conservative, Progressive, or all-out collectivist, Roosevelt attacked Hoover: "I want to say with all the emphasis that I can command, that this Administration did nothing and their leaders are, I am told, still doing nothing." This statement was not true, but the American people, frustrated and desperate, could easily believe it.

They elected FDR by over 12 million votes.

The New Deal

In their desperation the people had overwhelmingly called upon Roosevelt, but his election by no means eliminated fear. Economic conditions in the country reached crisis proportions. At this time the President was not inaugurated until March 4. Therefore, from the November 8 election's repudiation of Hoover until Inauguration Day—almost four months—the country was leaderless. Hoover refused to do anything without Roosevelt's endorsement, and Roosevelt not only refused to endorse any program suggested by Hoover but refused to give even a hint as to what he himself intended to do. During the election campaign, Roosevelt had endorsed contradictory programs for handling the Depression. Now all of these contradictions added to the uncertainty. Since no one could be sure what Roosevelt might do, and since Hoover was doing nothing, many people took matters into their own hands. Runs on banks became increasingly frequent; citizens held on to their money and spent as little as possible. Without assets, banks closed down. On February 4, Louisiana declared a one-day bank holiday (on which no banking business could be transacted). In Michigan, the governor proclaimed an eight-day bank holiday on February 14. By March 2, 21 other states had suspended or drastically restricted banking operations. As Inauguration Day dawned, virtually every bank in the Union had been closed or placed under restrictions by state proclamations.

Roosevelt was nothing if not an astute reader of the public mood. He knew that what Americans needed more than anything else at this point was confidence, and they expected the new President to provide it. Roosevelt took the first step toward restoring that confidence in his inaugural address. Promising vigorous leadership, he told the people that "the only thing we have to fear is fear itself." Then, as soon as the last float of the inaugural parade had passed his reviewing stand, Roosevelt met with his advisers (nicknamed the Brain Trust, because many of them were from colleges and universities). The next day Roosevelt prepared a proclamation declaring a four-day national banking holiday and forbidding the export of gold, silver and currency. His action was of doubtful legality since he had no clear authority to take such action, but no one was in the mood to quibble. The President then called a special session of Congress to convene on March 9. Working round the clock for the next four days, Roosevelt's advisers prepared an Emergency Banking Relief Act to present to Congress on the ninth. When Congress convened, only one copy of the act was available, and most Congressmen did not have time to read it. But it was introduced, passed by both houses of Congress and signed by the President within seven hours (instead of the usual months most legislation takes). The Senate vote was 73-7, the House vote unanimous. The act endorsed the President's March 6 proclamation and extended government powers over banking and currency with the goal of keeping money in the country and getting the banks open.

This rapid-fire action worked. Americans' confidence in the government and the economy was restored. Somebody was doing something at last. When the banks reopened, people began putting their money back. This restoration of confidence, far more than the actual legislation, brought the bank failures to an end and made it possible for people to carry on business calmly rather than in panic. On March 12, Roosevelt took another step which helped restore confidence. He held a **Fireside Chat**, the first of many radio broadcasts to explain his programs to the people. Beginning his speech with the greeting "My friends," Roosevelt's magnificent speaking voice captivated the American people and convinced them more than ever that Roosevelt was their saviour.

Congress had only begun its work. This special session would last until June 16 and be known as the "Hundred Days," a time of almost constant legislative action, all generated by Roosevelt. During the Hundred Days, Roosevelt sent 15 messages to Congress, pushed through 15 major laws, made 10 speeches, and held press conferences and cabinet meetings an average of twice a week. Some of the new programs were beneficial, some were of little effect, some were harmful; but the image of action restored the confidence of the people in their government and in the economy.

Among the more significant programs of the Hundred Days were the following:

The Civilian Conservation Corps Reforestation Relief Act, passed March 31, established the **Civilian Conservation Corps (CCC)** to provide work for jobless men between the ages of 18 and 25 in reforestation, flood control, national park improvement and other conservation projects. The youths received $30 per month, part of which went to their families, and room and board in work camps in the forests and mountains. The CCC was one of the most useful of New Deal programs, doing needed conservation work which had been neglected since the days of the first President Roosevelt and providing many city-dwellers with their first experience with the countryside and hard work in the open air.

Abandonment of the gold standard on April 19 meant that U.S. currency was no longer redeemable in hard money. This inflationary measure was taken by Roosevelt in order to raise prices and stimulate business. Since the value of the dollar was no longer determined by specie, Roosevelt and his advisers set the value, changing it from day to day, usually with no logical reason. This tampering with the value of the dollar lessened the confidence which foreign nations and businessmen had in the U.S. and ultimately prolonged the Depression by reducing the value of money which people had been saving.

The Federal Emergency Relief Act (May 12) created the **Federal Emergency Relief Administration (FERA)** to provide direct federal relief payments to the states for the destitute. The administrator was Harry L. Hopkins, a former social worker from New York, who was one of the New Deal leaders. This legislation marked the real beginning of one of the most important long-lasting effects of the New Deal: the abandonment of the **Principle of Subsidiarity**. The Popes in their social teachings have stressed this principle, that those closest to a situation should make the decisions regarding it. They best understand the problem; they are more likely to care about the people involved, rather than wanting power for themselves. FERA violated the principle of subsidiarity by giving the federal government power to perform actions which would be better performed on the local level. The excuse for the Act was that the local communities had run out of relief funds, but it would have been far better for the federal government to have reduced taxes to leave more money in the local communities to meet these needs.

The Agricultural Adjustment Act of May 12 was aimed at helping the farmers. Even during the 1920's, American farmers had not been prosperous because prices they received for their products did not rise as fast as the prices they had to pay for items they bought, this problem being aggravated by the fact that farmers were now less self-sufficient and more dependent on things they had to buy, rather than on things they could make or grow themselves. The Act established the **Agricultural Adjustment Administration** (AAA), which made payments (called subsidies) to farmers who reduced their production, hoping that the prices would rise. Under the leadership of Agricultural Secretary Henry Wallace, farmers deliberately plowed under crops and slaughtered animals in order to receive subsidies. Although some farmers benefited, the overall effect was harmful. Deliberate waste was encouraged at a time when people were going hungry; cutbacks in production were not sufficient to increase prices; sharecroppers in the South were hurt especially hard by having to plow under their cotton crops; larger, more mechanized farms tended to drive out the smaller family farms. The Roosevelt Administration tried many different remedies for the farm problem, but none of them worked, and the farm problem is still very much with America as this is being written.

On May 18, the **Tennessee Valley Authority** (TVA) was established to construct government-owned dams and power plants in the Tennessee Valley (Tennessee, North Carolina, Kentucky, Virginia, Mississippi, Georgia and Alabama) and to inaugurate a comprehensive program of social and economic planning, with the goal of improving the lives of the Valley residents. For the first time, the federal government entered the electricity business in a big way and was attempting total control of the environment in which large numbers of people lived. The production of electricity worked rather well; the attempt at social reconstruction did not. As the Roosevelt Administration would learn several more times, it is impossible for a government to blueprint the lives of a community; human beings are not that easily managed.

On June 5, Congress passed the **Gold Repeal Joint Resolution**, which canceled the gold clause in all contracts and required all debts to be paid in currency. Many people had included in contracts a clause requiring payment of the debt in hard money rather than currency, on the assumption that the value of paper money could fluctuate while the value of gold remained the same. Since the government had gone off the gold standard, paper money was worth less than ever, and its value would continue to decline so long as individuals were allowed to trade in gold. By canceling the gold clauses, the Roosevelt Administration hoped to make paper money more secure. But they were in effect committing theft by depriving people of what was rightfully theirs. Since paper money had declined in value, creditors were getting back less than their contract had originally specified, even though the face value of the paper money was the same.

The Glass-Steagall Act (or Banking Act of 1933, passed June 16), created the **Federal Deposit Insurance Corporation** (FDIC), providing government guarantees of individual bank deposits under $5,000. This act was beneficial, making it less likely that individuals would lose their money when banks failed.

The final act of the Hundred Days was intended to be the most far-reaching of all: the National Industrial Recovery Act, which created the **National Recovery Administration** (NRA) under the leadership of General Hugh S. Johnson. NRA was founded on the principle of total economic planning by government, and attempted to establish wage, price and employment condition codes for every major business in the United States. Obviously such a goal could never be reached. Many businesses refused to subscribe to NRA codes; many of those that did subscribe violated them right and left. Johnson tried to bring public pressure to bear on businesses by encouraging the public to buy only from enterprises displaying the NRA symbol, a blue eagle, and by holding a massive parade on New York's Fifth Avenue. Enthusiasm for the parade ran high, but enthusiasm for the NRA itself was far less. The NIRA also established a **Public Works Administration** (PWA) for the construction of roads and public buildings as a means of putting more men to work. The director was Secretary of the Interior Harold L. Ickes, who spent most of his time in a power struggle with Johnson and Hopkins.

With the passage of the NIRA, Congress adjourned and its members went wearily home, but the mood of the country had been drastically changed. Money was flowing from Washington into the pockets of citizens, who were being encouraged to spend it to bring business back onto its feet. The fear and frustration had largely been dissipated, and for the first time in almost four years, people were convinced that "prosperity was just around the corner," as the saying went at that time.

The Second New Deal

Congress returned in October, but without the frantic urgency of the Hundred Days. During the next year laws were enacted financing more public programs, increasing government control over agriculture and establishing the Securities and Exchange Commission to control the stock market. By the Gold Reserve Act of 1934, the government was given full control over dollar devaluation. On January 31, Roosevelt fixed the value of the dollar at $.5906, meaning that people who had been trying to save money saw its value cut almost in half. But the massive public confidence in Roosevelt continued, and the November 6 Congressional elections saw a Democratic gain of 10 in the Senate and 10 in the House, reversing the usual tendency in off-year Congressional elections to reduce the strength of the party in power.

The First New Deal had been an attempt to plan the entire economy from Washington, to bring about prosperity by government dictation. But with the failure of the NRA, Roosevelt developed a new policy, which came to be called the Second New Deal, based on social reform of existing institutions rather than on an attempt at total government direction. During 1935, Congress passed three major pieces of legislation for the Second New Deal.

The Emergency Relief Appropriation Act of April 8 established the **Works Progress Administration** (WPA), with Harry Hopkins as administrator (much to the dismay of Ickes who saw the WPA as a rival to his PWA). The goal of the WPA was to put people to work, on useful projects if possible, otherwise on anything, so long as they were working. The obvious result, in cases where the work was not really needed, was sloppy work and wasted effort.

On July 5 the National Labor Relations Act created a **National Labor Relations Board** (NLRB) to assist labor unions in gaining recognition by employers. Because of this New Deal boost to labor, unions gained strength until they became one of the major political forces in America.

Probably the most long-lasting and far-reaching of all New Deal programs was enacted on August 14: the **Social Security Act**. Financed by compulsory deductions from pay checks and by matching compulsory collections from employers, the Social Security program was to provide payments to the unemployed and to the elderly and disabled. The Social Security Act seemed like such a perfect solution to the problem of helping people who cannot help themselves that hardly anyone has ever dared criticize it. But it has several flaws. For one, the payroll tax meant that even very poor people had to have their wages reduced to pay into the fund. Since employers had to make a matching payment, they would naturally deduct this from the salary they would otherwise have been able to pay, thus further reducing wages, or they would raise prices to cover the cost. The notion that Social Security would take care of the elderly led to increased irresponsibility on the part of those who should have taken care of them—their own families or communities—resulting in a situation where many old people have been virtually abandoned by their relatives. Too many people count on Social Security to meet all their needs when they are old and therefore do not exercise care and thrift in saving for their old age. More is paid out in benefits than was originally paid into the fund by the recipients, frequently leaving the fund on the verge of bankruptcy and leading to increases in the Social Security tax for current workers.

As 1935 wore on, it became increasingly obvious that the Depression was far from over. Ten million people were out of work. National income was $40 billion below 1929 and even $10 billion below 1931, the first Depression year. Little improvement could be seen over 1934. For the first time, serious opposition to Roosevelt and the New Deal began to emerge.

The **Liberty League** drew its following from industrialists, financiers, corporation lawyers, conservative Democrats and others who thought Roosevelt far too collectivist. The members of the Liberty League had money and were able to publicize their views, but precisely because they were wealthy they never attracted a large popular following. At the other political extreme were those who did not think Roosevelt liberal enough: left-wing radicals such as Governor Floyd Olsen in Minnesota and gubernatorial candidate Upton Sinclair (author of *The Jungle*) in California. Communism attracted new adherents. From 1931 to 1933 its membership in the U.S. doubled, then doubled again, though the Party was unable to get much above 30,000 members.

Three movements during the mid-1930's did gain fairly wide support. The first was founded by Dr. Francis Townsend and real estate speculator Robert Earl Clements. They set up Townsend Clubs all over the country to agitate for Townsend's Old-Age Revolving Pension Plan. Townsend's plan would have given everyone over 60 a federal pension of $150 month, financed by a national tax on every sale or business transaction. Under Clements' leadership, the movement gained an almost religious character, as many elderly people, who had cruelly suffered during the Depression, looked upon Townsend as their saviour. But the plan would have cost half the national income to support 11 per cent of the population, and the transactions tax would have been an especially heavy burden on the poor. But Townsend had called attention to the needs of the elderly; Roosevelt's Social Security Act was in part an attempt to defuse the Townsend movement.

Far more sinister was the **Share Our Wealth Movement** led by Louisiana Governor Huey Long. Long rode to power in Louisiana on the support of the poor because of his plan to confiscate all income over one million dollars and give everyone else a homestead allowance of $5000 and an annual income of at least $2000. His slogan was "Every man a king, but no one wears a crown." In practice, Long's government was a dictatorship, kept in power with threats, beatings and kidnappings. The state legislators had to do what he said or see their careers destroyed; once the legislature passed 44 bills in 22 minutes. He was elected to the U.S. Senate and announced his intention of running for President in 1936. But on September 8, Long was killed accidentally by bullets from his bodyguards' machine guns as he was leaving the Louisiana Assembly House. The guards were shooting at an armed doctor who had struck Long on the face. (The doctor himself was killed, his body being riddled with machine gun bullets from Long's bodyguards.) Long's Share Our Wealth clubs (though not Long's political empire) were taken over by Rev. Gerald L. K. Smith, a rabble-rousing speaker more interested in power than in religion.

The most significant new political force was led by an Irish American priest, **Fr. Charles Coughlin** of Detroit. On weekly radio broadcasts, drawing as many as ten million listeners, he attacked both Communism and capitalism. He showed how the failure of the rich and powerful to work for social justice had helped bring on the sufferings of the Depression. Coughlin was an expert on the social encyclicals and opposed to banks and the charging of high interest. He backed Roosevelt at first, though opposing the AAA because it slaughtered pigs while people starved. But when Roosevelt did not follow Coughlin's advice on the free coinage of silver, the priest turned against the President. On Nov. 11, 1934, he announced the formation of his own movement: **The National Union for Social Justice**. As the 1936 Presidential election neared, Smith, Townsend and Coughlin formed a coalition called the Union Party and endorsed William Lemke (a Republican Congressman from North Dakota) for President. As time went on, however, Coughlin became increasingly controversial. His bishop eventually censured him, and his following dwindled.

Hoping to capitalize on the discontent, the Republicans nominated Kansas Governor Alfred Landon, the only Republican governor west of the Mississippi elected in 1932 and the only Republican governor anywhere re-elected in 1934. Landon tried to find a middle ground between old-fashioned Republican laissez faire economics and the New Deal. But he lacked style and appeared to be just another New Dealer, whose only novelty was wanting a balanced budget. His speeches contained such memorable lines as, "Wherever I have gone in this country, I have found Americans."

Roosevelt, on the other hand, accepted the nomination with the cry: "This generation of Americans has a rendezvous with destiny!" Under the leadership of Farley, he had broadened the base of the Democratic Party to include Negroes and Southerners, big city immigrants and farmers, intellectuals and working men, Jews and Catholics. But more importantly, almost every voter in the United States had received some assistance from the New Deal. Though the Depression had not been ended, everyone either was or thought he was better off than he had been under Hoover. Before the election, Farley handed Roosevelt a sealed envelope with his prediction as to the outcome of the election. When Roosevelt opened it after Election Day, he found that Farley's prediction had been exactly correct. The only states Landon carried were Maine and Vermont. Roosevelt had 27,751,621 popular votes to Landon's 16,680,913 (Lemke had less than 900,000) and 523 electoral votes to Landon's eight. The old political saying, "As Maine goes, so goes the Nation," had henceforth to be changed to "As Maine goes, so goes Vermont."

Roosevelt v. the Supreme Court

Roosevelt's second inauguration was the first to be held on the new date of January 20 (changed from March 4 by the Twentieth Amendment to the Constitution). In spite of his landslide victory, his second inaugural address implicitly recognized that scarcely a dent had been made in the Depression. The challenge to American democracy, he said, is the "tens of millions of its citizens . . . who at this very moment are denied the greater part of what the very lowest standards of today call the necessities of life. . . . I see one-third of a nation ill-housed, ill-clad, ill-nourished. . . ." He pledged to continue his social reform program.

But Roosevelt's attention was primarily occupied by the Supreme Court, which had been his greatest opponent during his first term. At this time, the Court was sharply divided. Four of the justices were laissez faire conservatives (James McReynolds, Willis VanDevanter, George Sutherland and Pierce Butler) and three were collectivists in the Holmes tradition (Louis Brandeis, Benjamin Cardozo and Harlan Stone). The other two were swing votes, not committed to any ideology (Owen Roberts and Charles Evans Hughes). Hughes, Wilson's Presidential opponent in 1916, was Chief Justice. His goal seemed to be to keep the Court from following either the laissez faire or the collectivist position exclusively, and he moved back and forth from one side to the other. Hughes had once said, "We are under a Constitution, but the Constitution is what the judges say it is." This statement was proved true during the fight between the Court and Roosevelt, as the justices switched back and forth from one reading of the Constitution to another, depending on what the judges decided to say that the Constitution was.

The first major New Deal cases to come before the Court were the Gold Cases in early 1935, which involved the constitutionality of the Congressional Joint Resolution which had nullified the gold clause in private and public contracts. There were four cases, all decided at the same time. Roosevelt had been virtually certain that the conservatives would win out, and had in reserve a set of proclamations and orders nullifying an adverse decision. He had intended to refuse to obey the Court's decision and to enlist the people on his side. Hughes may have been aware of Roosevelt's plans, or at least suspected them. He voted with the liberals in upholding the government and avoided a major confrontation with Roosevelt.

But the confrontation was only delayed. Later in 1935, the constitutionality of the NIRA came before the Court, in the case of *Schecter v. U.S.*, known as the Sick Chicken Case, since it involved NRA authority over a poultry dealer. Hughes this time voted with the conservatives, invalidating the NIRA. In December 1935, in the case of *U.S. v. Butler*, Hughes and Roberts again joined the conservative four to invalidate the AAA, and on May 18, 1936 the Court declared unconstitutional the Guffey Coal Act, in which the government had regulated prices and wages in the bituminous coal industry.

The Court itself was far from harmonious. Stone said that there had never been "a time in the history of the Court when there has been so little intelligent, recognizable pattern in its judicial performance as in the last few years." After the Court's term ended, he wrote, "We finished the term of Court yesterday, I think in many ways one of the most disastrous in its history." With Roosevelt insisting that "nine old men" should not be allowed to dictate policy, public outcry against the Court was violent. Said Senator George Norris: "The people can change the Congress, but only God can change the Supreme Court." Judge Hugo Black wrote: "This means that 120 million are ruled by five men." Near Ames, Iowa, six figures in black robes, representing the justices who voted against AAA, were hanged in effigy.

Spurred by his landslide re-election, Roosevelt challenged the Court head on. On February 5 he submitted to Congress a plan to increase the membership of the Supreme Court from nine to a maximum of 15, if judges reaching the age of 70 declined to retire, and to make various other changes in the judicial system which would make it easier for his programs to be upheld. But Roosevelt had made his first major tactical mistake. He was accused of trying to "pack" the Supreme Court, of wanting to give the President too much power, of destroying judicial independence and integrity. Even some Democrats in Congress spoke out against the court-packing scheme. Congress voted no.

But though Roosevelt had lost the battle, he won the war. At the very time the proposal was being debated in Congress, Hughes and Roberts permanently switched to the liberal side on the Court, which then upheld a series of important New Deal measures, including the National Labor Relations Act and the Social Security laws. The Court had proven susceptible to public pressure. And then, within the next four years, seven justices died or retired, so that Roosevelt was able to put a New Deal majority on the Court, including Hugo Black, Felix Frankfurter and William O. Douglas, who all remained on the Court for many years.

In 1938 Congress passed the **Agricultural Adjustment Act of 1938**, which for the first time assigned acreage allotments to farmers and guaranteed "parity payment," that is, a selling price based on farm purchasing power in 1909-1914. In June of that year, the Fair Labor Standards Act was enacted, establishing the first federal minimum wage, of 40 cents an hour.

But the split in the Democratic Party over the court-packing fight, along with a serious business recession in 1937, weakened Roosevelt's position. In the 1938 Congressional elections, the Republicans made their first gains since 1928. It was becoming obvious to some people that the New Deal had not ended the Depression.

The Presidential election year of 1940 arrived. Since George Washington had declined to stand for a third term of office, no President had ever run for more than two terms. But Roosevelt, as he had done so often, broke precedent. He was nominated by the Democratic convention. His opponent was Wendell Willkie, who supported the New Deal but said that it should be better administered. The most important issue, though, was not the New Deal, in spite of its failures, but the war that had broken out in Europe when Hitler's tanks rolled into Poland. New production, needed to send aid to Great Britain, was stimulating business and manufacturing as no New Deal program could, and Americans felt that they should retain the President they had come to know and trust since the whole world might be about to explode. Roosevelt won by 5,000,000 popular votes, carrying 38 states to Willkie's 10.

The New Deal in Retrospect

Though most Americans still do not realize it, the New Deal did not end the Depression. America's economic illnesses ran too deep; they had been caused by inflationary spending by both government and private citizens. They could not be cured by more such spending. World War II is what ended the Depression, by starting the factories humming and putting everyone back to work.

But Roosevelt and his New Deal had a profound effect on America. Social Security became deeply entrenched in America, eroding family responsibilities and discouraging thrift. Labor unions became a dominant force in American politics; demanding ever higher wages, they contributed to inflation. The Democrats became the majority party, replacing the Republicans, who had been the majority since Lincoln. The Republicans came to be almost exclusively identified as the party of big business, with the Democrats absorbing what remained of Progressivism. Most importantly, the principle of subsidiarity was virtually destroyed, with Americans coming to depend on the federal government, so that henceforth problems would be referred to Washington.

The Depression had offered Americans a chance for spiritual renewal. But spiritual leadership was not forthcoming. More than ever, Americans saw their problems in material terms. Roosevelt rode this preoccupation for all it was worth, amassing more power than any other American before or since.

REVIEW QUESTIONS

1. Characterize America in the 1920's in the areas listed in this chapter.
2. What kind of President was Harding? What caused the scandals of his term?
3. What caused the boom of the 1920's? Why could it not last?
4. What were the issues in the election of 1928? Why did Hoover win?
5. What was the Stock Market Crash of 1929? Summarize the chain reaction that led to the Depression.
6. What was Hoover's response to the Depression? Why did it fail?
7. Why did Roosevelt win in 1932?
8. What happened between the election and the inauguration? How did Roosevelt contribute to the fear and despair? How did he end it?
9. Summarize the most important legislation of the Hundred Days.
10. What was the Second New Deal? What programs were enacted?
11. Summarize the opposition to Roosevelt by Townsend, Long, and Coughlin.
12. Why did Roosevelt win by a landslide in 1936?
13. Summarize the conflict between Roosevelt and the Supreme Court.
14. Why is it true to say that Roosevelt lost the battle with the Supreme Court but won the war?
15. Why did Roosevelt win in 1940?
16. Why did the Depression end?
17. Summarize the most important effects of the New Deal on America.

PROJECTS

1. Prepare a mural on America in the 1920's.
2. Research one of the areas of life in the 1920's and prepare a report.
3. Interview someone who remembers the Depression and New Deal.

Chapter 23

The United States in World War II

IN 1937 THE U.S. CONGRESS had enacted a neutrality act which forbade the selling of arms to any belligerent nation. On September 1, 1939, the Nazi blitzkrieg smashed into Poland, and the world was once again plunged into total war. In a Fireside Chat on September 3, President Roosevelt declared: "This nation will remain a neutral nation, but I cannot ask that every American remain neutral in thought as well." In the early weeks of the War, American thoughts probably were neutral, as the country painfully remembered the sufferings of World War I, and there was strong isolationist sentiment led by aviation hero Charles Lindbergh and his **America First Committee.**

On November 4, 1939, Congress repealed the arms embargo and authorized the export of arms and munitions under a "cash and carry" arrangement that required the purchasing nation to pay cash and to carry the weapons in its own ships. In his January 1940 budget, Roosevelt requested $1,800,000,000 for national defense and in May an additional $1,300,000,000. After Dunkirk, FDR began extending credit to the British, and in June the War Department released to them surplus stocks of arms, munitions and aircraft. Throughout the summer, the U.S. continued building up its own armed forces. In September the U.S. transferred 50 destroyers to Britain, in exchange for 99-year leases on bases in British territory. In October, the U.S. instituted its first-ever peacetime draft. In December Roosevelt set up the Office of Production Management to coordinate defense production and to send all possible aid "short of war" to Great Britain. In a Fireside Chat that same month Roosevelt called for maximum production to make the U.S. an "arsenal of democracy."

In his annual message to Congress on January 6, 1941, President Roosevelt recommended Lend-Lease, to enable any country whose defense the President deemed vital to that of the U.S. to receive arms and other equipment and supplies by sale, transfer, exchange or lease. On March 11, the **Lend-Lease Act** was signed into law. Germany invaded Greece and Yugoslavia; Rommel rolled through North Africa; British ships sank in the North Atlantic. In May, Roosevelt proclaimed an unlimited national emergency and in June broke off diplomatic relations with Germany and Italy. Hitler turned on Russia and sent his troops pouring across a 2,000 mile front from the Arctic to the Ukraine. The U.S. granted Lend-Lease credit of $1 billion to the Soviet Union.

In August, Roosevelt and Churchill met off the coast of Newfoundland and issued the **Atlantic Charter,** which, among other things, declared opposition to the imposition of any government against the will of the people and to territorial changes contrary to the will of the people involved. The Charter also enunciated "four freedoms," which Roosevelt had expressed in his January 6 message: freedom from want, freedom from fear, freedom of speech, and freedom of religion. The Charter as a whole was rather vague, but 15 nations endorsed it, including the Soviet Union, which had broken, was breaking and would break almost every provision in it.

By the fall of 1941, the U.S. and Germany were fighting an undeclared sea war, as the U.S. defended what FDR called its "sea frontier"—actually two-thirds of the way to Great Britain. In May, the U.S. secretly helped the British navy find and sink the great German battleship *Bismarck.* In October, three U.S. destroyers were sunk. Roosevelt issued orders to shoot on sight.

Day of Infamy

Japan, which had signed a mutual assistance pact with Germany and Italy, occupied French Indochina on July 24, 1941. President Roosevelt nationalized the armed forces of the Philippines, placing them under the command of General Douglas MacArthur, who was named commander-in-chief of U.S. forces in the Far East. On October 18, General Hideki Tojo became Prime Minister, and Japan began preparing an all-out assault on Eastern Asia. U.S. Ambassador Grew warned Washington of the possibility of a sudden attack by the Japanese, because the U.S. fleet presented the only obstacle to Japan's ambitions. On November 20, discussions began in Washington between Secretary of

State Cordell Hull and a special Japanese envoy, Saburo Kurusu. Each side made proposals which were unacceptable to the other, and the talks dragged on. On December 6, President Roosevelt made a direct appeal to Emperor Hirohito, asking him to preserve the peace and to withdraw troops from French Indochina.

At 8:00 a.m. on the morning of Sunday, December 7, Kurusu received a message from Tokyo, ordering him to break off negotiations with Hull at 1:00 p.m. Since U.S. intelligence had broken the Japanese code, we knew exactly what the message said, and that obviously something important would happen at 1:00 p.m. Washington time, which happened to be dawn at the U.S. naval base in Pearl Harbor, Hawaii. But it was Sunday; most personnel were off work; and Army Chief of Staff George Marshall was horseback riding and could not be reached. Finally a message was sent to Pearl, calling for an alert. The message was sent by regular telegraph and not even on priority status. It was received at the Hawaii telegraph office, and a young boy set off to deliver it to Admiral Kimmel, who finally received it—after the attack was over and his entire fleet in flames. Meanwhile, a private manning a radar station was turning the radar screen while waiting for the breakfast truck to arrive. He was shocked to see airplane after airplane coming in on the screen. He called in an alert—but no one would believe him.

At 7:55 a.m. Hawaii time, bombs began dropping from Japanese planes onto the American battleship fleet in Pearl Harbor. Flames, smoke and the anguished cries of dying men filled the air, as the *Arizona, California* and *Utah* sank to the bottom of the harbor. Fifteen other ships were sunk or disabled, 120 planes were destroyed, and 2,408 human beings died. On December 8, with only one dissenting vote, Congress declared war on Japan.

Three days later, Germany and Italy declared war on the U.S., which then recognized a state of war with these nations as well. Why Hitler made this decision is incomprehensible, since Congress would have found it very difficult to enter the war against Hitler if he had not declared war first. Perhaps Hitler was fooled by the small size of the U.S. Army and the apparent destruction of the Navy by the Japanese. But the U.S. had one tremendous asset, which no one fully appreciated until it was brought into play: its enormous industrial potential. Once into the War for keeps, the U.S. turned its factories loose and simply outproduced the rest of the world.

The young men lined up at the enlistment centers. America had been attacked and America would fight back, with all the heroism and determination characteristic of American fighting men in many an earlier war.

War in the Pacific

On the same day as they attacked Pearl Harbor, the Japanese also bombed the U.S. base in the Philippines. The bombs did extensive damage because General MacArthur, though knowing of the Pearl Harbor raid, had unaccountably left his airplanes on the ground. On December 13, the Japanese took Guam; on December 22, Wake Island; and on December 25, Hong Kong. From December 10 to December 23, the Japanese made landings in the Philippines. In accordance with a plan earlier devised, MacArthur's small force retreated to the more easily defensible Bataan Peninsula, while he himself took refuge in the heavily fortified underground bastion at Corregidor. For two months his greatly outnumbered troops, under command of General Wainwright, held out, inflicting heavy losses on the Japanese. In early March, with defeat imminent, MacArthur was secretly removed from Corregidor by direct order from President Roosevelt and taken to Australia to prepare a counterattack. After a siege of more than three months, Bataan fell on April 9. A month later Corregidor and 11,500 men surrendered to the Japanese. Since the Japanese war code had no provision for surrender, they did not know what to do with prisoners. They finally took the men on a march to another part of the island. The treatment was so bad on the march and so many men died that it is known as the **Bataan Death March.** At the same time, another Japanese force occupied the Netherlands East Indies, Malaya and Indonesia. In April at the Battle of the Java Sea, the Allies lost an entire fleet of U.S., British and Dutch ships. The last ship was the U.S. *Houston,* which refused to surrender and sank with its guns still firing.

In the midst of the disasters, Roosevelt decided to let the Japanese know that the Americans would never give up. On April 18, General James H. Doolittle led a bombing raid over Tokyo. Sixteen B-25 bombers took off from the carrier *Hornet,* which had managed to get within 750 miles of Tokyo. The crews knew that they could carry enough fuel to reach Tokyo but not enough to get back. If they were lucky they would be able to fly into China and land there. The bombs were dropped, but most of the planes crashed. Nevertheless, the raid gave the Americans a tremendous psychological boost.

Still the Japanese rolled on. By May 1, 1942, Japan had seized control of almost the whole of East Asia at little cost to itself. The Japanese leaders now had unlimited confidence in their carrier force, victorious at Pearl Harbor, Darwin (Australia) and Ceylon. They decided to attack New Guinea, which had not been on their original list of targets. The U.S. knew that if New Guinea fell, Australia would be next, and sent out its carriers to engage the Japanese. The engagement was the Battle of the Coral Sea, but it was also known as the "Battle of Naval Errors." The two fleets were only eighty miles apart, yet spent an entire day looking for each other without success. When the battle was finally fought (May 7-8, 1942), it was the first naval engagement in history in which surface ships did not engage each other. All fighting was done by carrier-based planes. One Japanese carrier was sunk and two damaged, while the U.S. carrier *Lexington* was lost. It was not a decisive victory for either side, but the Japanese abandoned the attack on New Guinea.

The Japanese chose a new objective: the U.S. occupied island of Midway. Convinced that most of the American carriers were far away or damaged, Admiral Nagumo loaded Zeroes (Japanese fighter planes) and bombers on board carriers and steamed toward Midway. But the U.S. had broken the Japanese code and knew the attack was coming, so the *Enterprise* and *Hornet* were in a position to launch a counter-attack, and the *Yorktown,* one of the carriers the Japanese believed out of action, had been repaired in 48 hours by 1400 men working around the clock. Nagumo's first air strike against Midway was successful, destroying over half the U.S. planes. But at 8:35 on the morning of June 4, as the Japanese bombers were returning to their carriers to refuel and reload, U.S. planes were already on their way toward the Japanese ships.

By 9:00 a.m. the Japanese carriers were in perfect position for a U.S. attack. All of their bombers were on board, re-arming and refueling. Admiral Spruance sent off Torpedo Squadron 8: fifteen old planes armed with one torpedo each, torpedoes which often would not explode, and two crewmen on each plane. Their chances of survival were slim, but the men were ready. The night before, Lt. Commander Waldron had written: "I want each of us to do his utmost to destroy our enemies. If there is only one plane left to make a final run in, I want that man to go in and get a hit. May God be with us all." Torpedo Squadron 8 found the enemy about 9:25 a.m., and the enemy found them. Waldron led his men low over the Japanese carriers, as the Zeroes attacked on all sides. Plane after plane went down, but the other pilots kept coming and dropped their torpedoes. Then they too were shot down, hitting the

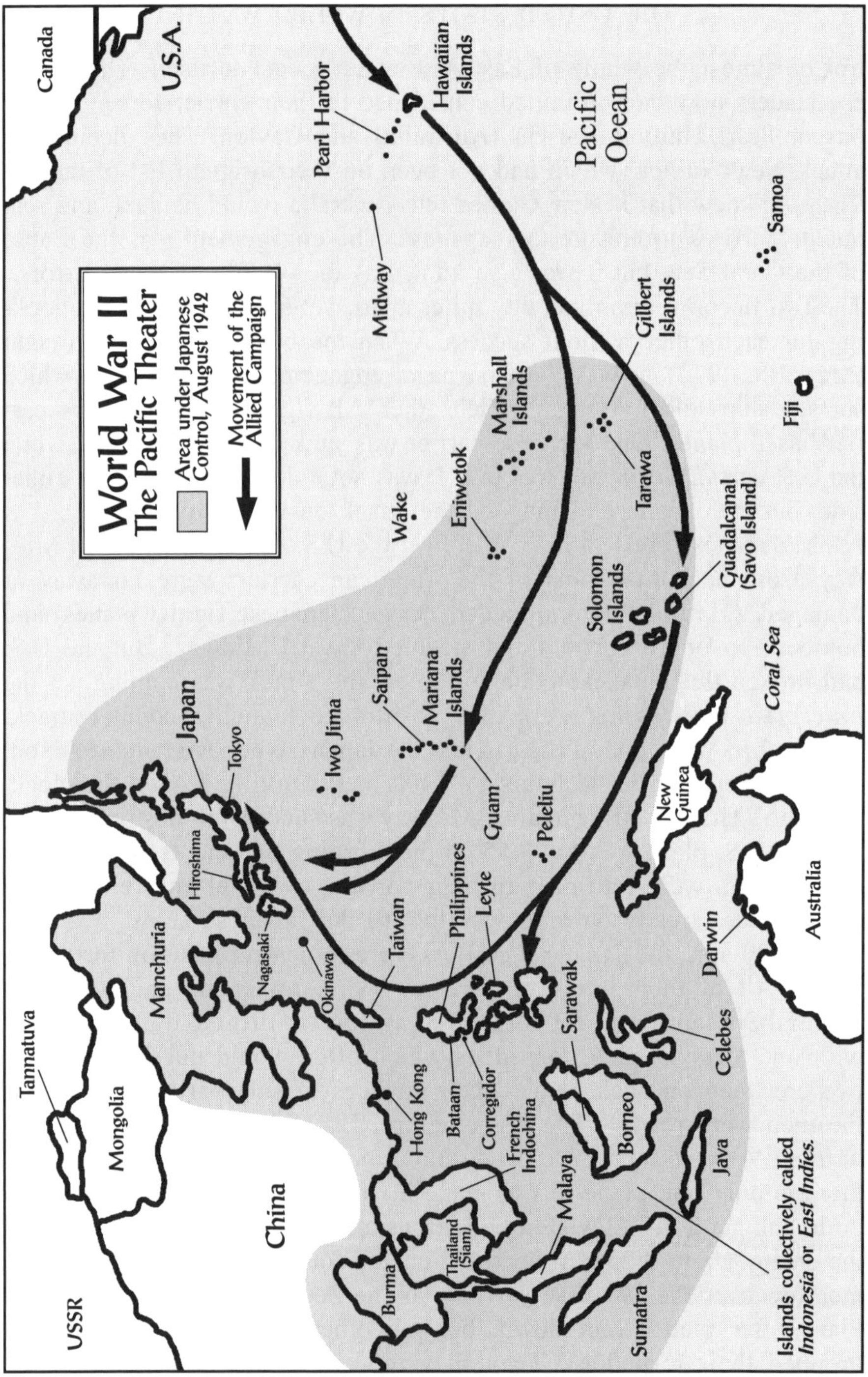

World War II
The Pacific Theater
Area under Japanese Control, August 1942
Movement of the Allied Campaign
Canada
U.S.A.
USSR
Tannatuva
Mongolia
China
Manchuria
Japan
Tokyo
Hiroshima
Nagasaki
Okinawa
Iwo Jima
Taiwan
Hong Kong
Burma
Thailand (Siam)
French Indochina
Malaya
Philippines
Bataan
Corregidor
Leyte
Sumatra
Java
Borneo
Sarawak
Celebes
New Guinea
Darwin
Australia
Coral Sea
Peleliu
Guam
Saipan
Mariana Islands
Solomon Islands
Guadalcanal (Savo Island)
Eniwetok
Wake
Marshall Islands
Tarawa
Gilbert Islands
Fiji
Samoa
Midway
Pearl Harbor
Hawaiian Islands
Pacific Ocean
Islands collectively called Indonesia or East Indies.

water at high speed, with the impact of hitting a stone wall. Their torpedoes made not one single hit. Out of thirty pilots and crewmen, only one man survived.

Two more torpedo squadrons came in from the other carriers, 26 more planes. Only six returned. But the pilots' heroism had won the day. The Japanese were forced to maneuver their ships to avoid the torpedoes and could not launch more planes. A few minutes after the last torpedo plane had been shot down, U.S. dive bombers dropped their bombs on full deckloads of planes. Three of the four enemy carriers were severely damaged, all sinking the next day. The fourth carrier was hit by an air strike on June 5 and also sank.

For the Japanese, the Midway operation was meant to draw out the U.S. Navy and destroy it. Midway Island was selected because, had it been taken, it would have posed the greatest threat to American Naval power in the Pacific. But instead of destroying the U.S. Navy, the Midway operation marked the beginning of the end for Japan.

The Japanese lost 3,500 men, four carriers and a cruiser, and 332 aircraft. The Americans lost 307 men, one carrier, one destroyer and 150 aircraft. The Americans had beaten the same Admiral, the same carriers, the same planes and the same pilots that had attacked Pearl Harbor. In just six months, the Day of Infamy had been avenged.

Now the U.S. could go on the offensive. The first objective was Guadalcanal in the Solomon Islands, an ideal location for a U.S. airbase. The U.S. Marines landed virtually unopposed on August 7, 1942. But if anyone thought it would be easy to hold Guadalcanal, he soon reached a different conclusion. The very first night of U.S. occupation, the Japanese steamed in and sank four U.S. cruisers at the Battle of Savo Island. As daylight came, the Japanese steamed out again, fearful of U.S. air power. For three months, control of the sea changed hands every twelve hours. By night, the Japanese would dominate because U.S. planes could not see in the dark. By day, the U.S. Air Force would prove its superiority. On land, the troops disembarked by the Japanese at night would fight bitter and bloody battles with the First Marine Division, neither side giving an inch.

By the beginning of September, the Japanese knew that they must seize control of the airfield to stop the invincible U.S. planes, planning a massive offensive against the Marines guarding the field. Colonel M. A. Edson took 700 Marines and dug in on a grassy ridge which ran south from the airfield. On the night of September 12, the Marines fought off Japanese bayonet attacks. But the big assault was the next night. At 10:30 p.m., 2000 screaming Japanese charged at Edson's left flank. His men were pushed out of position, but Edson pulled them back to the last knoll of the ridge, only 1500 yards short of the airfield. Attack after attack crashed against the Marines. They held. The sun rose next morning over a ridge littered with dead Japanese. Six hundred Japanese soldiers had died on the ridge and hundreds more of wounds when retreating. The Marines had lost only 40 men. The field had been saved against 3-1 odds, and the ridge had a new name: "Bloody Ridge."

But the Battle of Guadalcanal was far from over. The Japanese continued to win at night, the U.S. during the day, until so many ships lay at the bottom of the bay that it was nicknamed Ironbottom Bay. The Marines were called again and again to heights of heroism, so that on one of the crosses in the cemetery was the following epitaph: "And when he goes to Heaven / To St. Peter he will tell, / Another Marine reporting, Sir; / I've served my time in Hell!"

By the end of October, both sides were frustrated by the seemingly endless struggle. The Japanese planned an all-out bombardment of the airfield and the landing of a huge new striking force. Just after midnight on Friday, the 13th of November, the Japanese steamed in, their big guns ready to bombard Henderson Field. The U.S. sent out its fleet hoping to surprise the Japanese. The enemy were not the only ones surprised. The leading U.S. ship suddenly discovered that it was only 3000 yards from a Japanese ship. Making a sharp left turn to avoid a collision, it forced all the ships following to turn as well. All was confusion, and the Japanese opened fire. Within minutes the *Atlanta* was dead in the water. U.S. ships fired on other U.S. ships. When daylight came, five U.S. and three Japanese ships floated crippled on the sea. But the Japanese had been unable to carry out their bombardment and Henderson Field was safe.

The next night the Japanese succeeded in a minor bombardment of the field, but during the day of the 14th, the Japanese troop transports were hit by U.S. planes, which sank seven. Japanese Admiral Tanaka shifted as many troops as he could to destroyers and kept coming. That night Admiral Lee led the U.S. fleet against the Japanese. This time there was no confusion. Tanaka was able to land only 2000 men. Two battleships and eleven troop transports had been sunk. The Japanese gave up trying to land more troops on the island, and within ten weeks, Guadalcanal belonged solely to the U.S.

The War in Europe

By the fall of 1942, the U.S. was ready to contribute substantially to the war against Germany. The U.S. and Great Britain prepared "Operation Torch," an amphibious landing in North Africa. The Supreme Allied Commander was U.S. General Dwight D. Eisenhower, and Morocco and Algeria were chosen as the site of the first major Allied counteroffensive against Germany, because they were the most lightly held and easily reached of the Axis-occupied territories. Most of the troops there were from Vichy, France, the southern part of France which had made terms with Germany rather than carry on the fighting. They did not make an all-out resistance to the landing on November 8, and on November 11 an armistice was arranged with Admiral Darlan, Vichy representative in North Africa. About the same time, the British defeated the brilliant German tank commander **General Erwin Rommel ("The Desert Fox")** at the Battle of El Alamein in Egypt. The Germans coalesced in Tunisia and successfully counterattacked at the Battle of Kasserine Pass, routing the green American troops on February 14, 1943. But the Americans retook the position on February 19. The Americans and British won a string of victories, and by May 13 the Germans were driven out of North Africa.

The next logical step for the Allies was an invasion from North Africa to the island of Sicily off the coast of Italy. To try to fool the Germans, the British invented the "Man Who Never Was." The body of an unidentified soldier was given a fictitious identity as Major David Martin and a fictitious set of documents indicating a landing in Sardinia. The body was dropped off the coast of Spain. "Major Martin" was found by an Axis agent and his documents rushed to Berlin. Hitler was convinced that Martin was real and ordered Sardinia reinforced. On July 10, General George Patton and the Allied troops landed in Sicily. The conquest of the island was completed by August 17.

The successful invasion of Italian soil led to the fall of the Italian dictator Mussolini. King Victor Emmanuel formed a new government under Marshal Badoglio, who opened secret negotiations with the Allies. On September 3 the British Eighth Army invaded Italy from Sicily across the Straits of Messina, and on September 8 the Italian government surrendered unconditionally.

But the battle for Italy had only begun. The Germans took control of the Peninsula, sending their best troops to Salerno to stop Operation Avalanche, the landing of the U.S. Fifth Army. The Germans fought

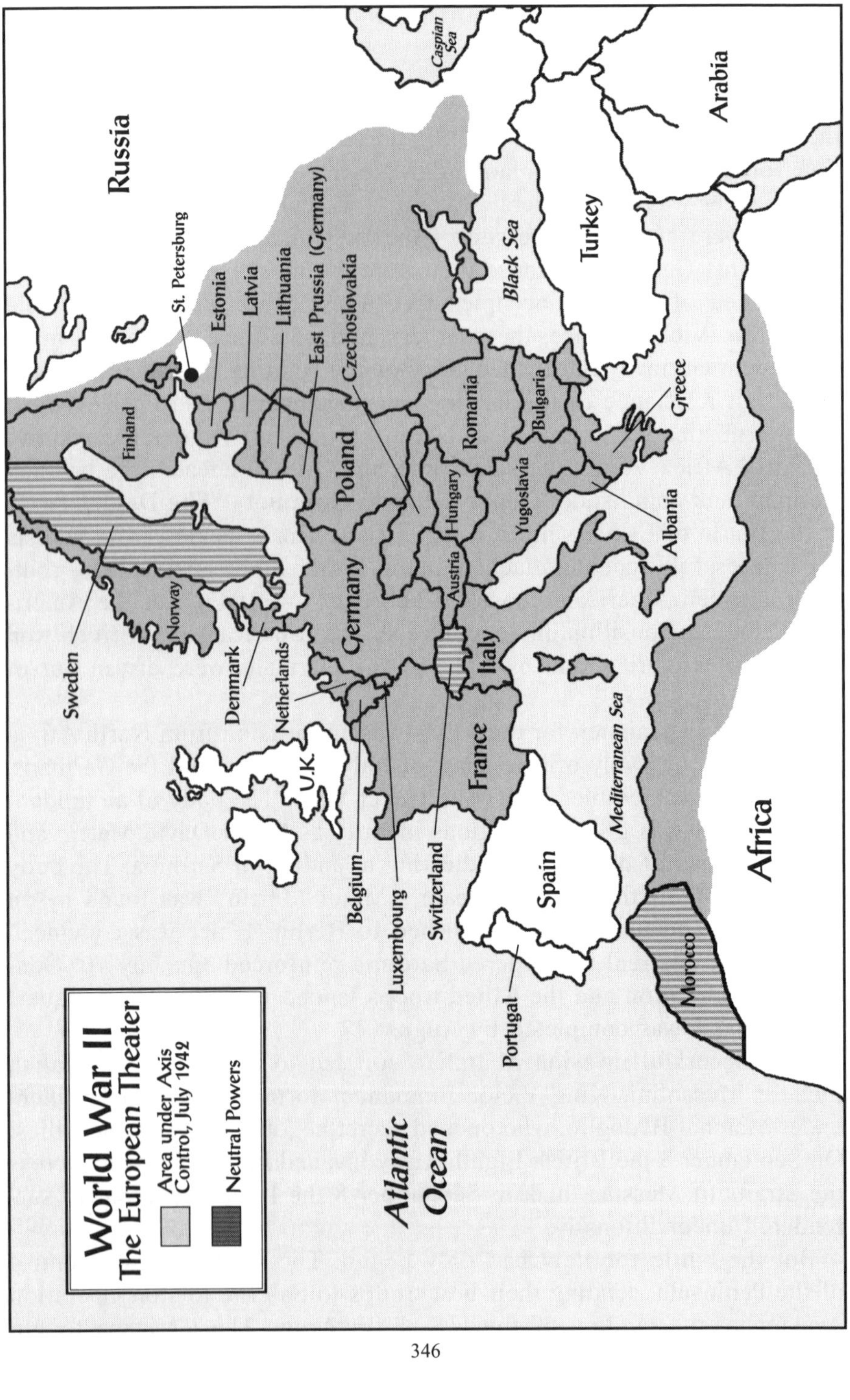
World War II
The European Theater
Area under Axis Control, July 1942
Neutral Powers
Atlantic Ocean
Russia
St. Petersburg
Finland
Estonia
Latvia
Lithuania
East Prussia (Germany)
Czechoslovakia
Poland
Sweden
Norway
Denmark
Netherlands
Germany
U.K.
Belgium
Luxembourg
Switzerland
Austria
Hungary
Romania
Bulgaria
Yugoslavia
Albania
Greece
Italy
France
Spain
Portugal
Morocco
Mediterranean Sea
Africa
Black Sea
Turkey
Caspian Sea
Arabia

ferociously and almost destroyed the U.S. landing force. The U.S. had to throw every available man into the line, from the cooks and supply personnel to the walking wounded. The resistance was broken and Salerno secured on September 18.

But it is a long way from the Bay of Naples to the northern border of Italy or even to Rome. The Germans set up a defensive line anchored at the centuries-old Benedictine monastery of Monte Cassino. The line held through some of the most ferocious fighting of the War. The end of 1943 saw U.S. and British soldiers dying in the hills of Italy and the Peninsula still under German control.

Unconditional Surrender and Terror Bombing

Wars are won by soldiers, but the policies which will determine what is done with the victory are made by politicians. The Allied soldiers fighting in World War II need make no apologies for their courage. But the Allied politicians have much to answer for.

On January 14, 1943, President Roosevelt and British Prime Minister Winston Churchill met in Casablanca in recently re-won Morocco. They discussed overall strategy for the War and agreed on the invasion of Sicily. The invasion was successful and contributed to Hitler's ultimate defeat. But they also agreed on two other policies, which, though equally successful, had disastrous consequences. The first policy was **unconditional surrender**: that the Allies would not even consider negotiations or compromises if the Germans sought them as a means of ending the War. Germany would have to surrender without asking any special treatment and place itself under the domination of the Allies. In view of the evils of the Nazi regime, this policy seemed reasonable to Americans. But there were many pitfalls beneath the surface. Even if Hitler were overthrown and a moral government replaced his, the Allies would have refused to negotiate with it. This policy had already been invoked in June 1942, when Louis P. Lochner, a former newspaperman acting for the anti-Hitler movement in Germany, had sought an interview with Roosevelt to get U.S. assistance for an attempt to overthrow Hitler and establish a new German government. In the movement were army officers, government officials, priests, ministers, and labor leaders, all risking death if caught. Yet Roosevelt refused even to speak to Lochner.

Without unconditional surrender, the War could have been ended earlier with the saving of many lives. By 1944, many German leaders could see that Germany was going to lose. If the U.S. and Great Britain had been willing to negotiate with them and offer them some hope for their country, they might have brought an earlier end to the War. But the Allies had come to regard all Germans as evil. No negotiations were considered. The War had to continue and more men had to die. Even worse in the long run, delaying an end to the War gave the Soviet Union more opportunity to take over territory in Eastern Europe and enslave those people under Communism.

Churchill and Roosevelt adopted another policy at Casablanca which led to many deaths, of women and children as well as fighting men. That was the policy of **strategic** or **terror bombing**: the bombing of cities rather than military targets as a means of destroying the morale of the people.

Great Britain's Royal Air Force had already engaged in some bombing of civilians even before Casablanca. But Casablanca, though it did not begin strategic bombing, accelerated it and involved the U.S. Air Force. For five months, beginning in March 1943, bombers flew over the Ruhr area of Germany. Though this was an industrial area, the bombers were ordered to aim at the center of the cities because they would burn more easily. Dusseldorf, Essen, Cologne—beautiful old cities went up in flames. In July, night raids with incendiary bombs destroyed half the homes in Hamburg. In November, the RAF began the night bombing of Berlin, joined by the USAF during daylight hours. The bombers destroyed three and one half square miles of the city. In many raids, the bombs never touched a single military or industrial target, only homes and the people who lived in them.

Another major conference occurred at the end of November 1943 in Teheran. This was the first conference in which Soviet dictator Josef Stalin joined Churchill and Roosevelt. The supposed purpose of the conference was to discuss the conduct of the War, but Stalin was less interested in the War than in greater power for the Soviet Union. Unfortunately, he was assisted in his power grab by Roosevelt, who said before the conference: "I think that if I give him everything I possibly can and ask nothing from him in return . . . he won't try to annex anything and will work with me for a world of democracy and peace." Roosevelt thought he could appease Stalin. On another occasion, he told an adviser that he could charm Stalin into friendly cooperation with Great Britain and the U.S. But Stalin was one of the least likely candidates on the face of the earth for either appeasement or charm.

World War II had begun when England and France had come to the assistance of the Poles to help them preserve their independence. At Teheran, Roosevelt and Churchill endorsed the Soviet absorption of Eastern Poland, which the Communists had seized in the early days of the War. Roosevelt asked one favor of Stalin, however. He asked that the agreement be kept secret until after the 1944 Presidential elections, because he was afraid of losing the Polish vote in that election.

1944 in Europe

During the early months of 1944, the bloody battle for Italy continued. To enable the forces at Cassino to make a breakthrough, Eisenhower and British General Montgomery planned a landing on the coast north of Cassino, at Anzio. They expected that the Germans would fall back to stop the landing, weakening the lines at Cassino so that the Fifth Army could break through. On January 22, the Anzio landings took place against almost no opposition. But General Lucas made no attempt to advance. Overly cautious, he dug in to secure the beachhead and concentrated on bringing supplies and vehicles ashore. The Germans therefore had the time to move troops to Anzio from a reserve force which the Allies had overlooked. They had no need to weaken the Cassino lines at all. Meanwhile, an attack (known as First Cassino), launched on January 17 to coincide with the Anzio landings, went nowhere. The British, Americans and French had attempted to cross the Rapido River, break into the Liri Valley and move on to Rome. But a heavy fog and murderous fire from the Germans decimated the attacking force. Two companies got across, but the Germans kept pounding them. Finally, a few who were able to swim made it back across the Rapido to the American lines. The rest were captured, wounded or killed. So instead of a breakthrough in two places—Anzio and Cassino—the Allies were now bogged down in two places—Anzio and Cassino.

Second Cassino was planned for February, involving mainly troops from India. In frustration, the Allies bombed Monte Cassino, obliterating the beautiful and historic monastery that dated in part from the 5th century. The Allies found out later that the Germans had not been using the monastery itself for troops, or even as a headquarters; they had respected the religious and cultural value of the place. The bombing had no strategic or tactical significance, and Second Cassino failed.

By mid-February, the beachhead at Anzio was under heavy German attack, so an order was given to launch Third Cassino to relieve the pressure on Anzio, though Anzio's original purpose had been to relieve the pressure on Cassino. Cold, wet weather delayed the assault until March, by which time the German Anzio assault had been repulsed. But Third Cassino went on anyway, with New Zealand troops and Gurkhas from Nepal. There were heavy losses on both sides, and the attack was finally called off.

At last British General Alexander developed a strategy of something other than frontal assaults on an impregnable position. He secretly brought up seven divisions of reinforcements, using camouflage and night movements to completely fool the Germans. Fourth Cassino, involving Americans, French, Moroccan, British and Polish troops, began on May 11, and the breakthrough finally came on May 17, when German Commander Kesselring withdrew his men to the Adolf Hitler Line farther north.

On May 23, the Americans broke out of Anzio, and on the same day the Eighth Army attacked the Adolf Hitler Line. Realizing that they were going to lose that line also, the Germans quickly changed its name to the Dora Line and went into full retreat. At this point, the German Army in Italy could have been destroyed, but U.S. General Mark Clark wanted his Fifth Army to be the first Allied troops into Rome. Therefore, instead of pursuing the Germans, he marched his men into Rome on June 4, liberating the Eternal City.

While the fighting raged in Italy, the Allied High Command planned the most important operation of the War: Operation Overlord, the invasion of Normandy, France. The U.S. poured men and supplies into England. The Germans knew what was coming and put General Rommel in charge of defenses. To decoy the Germans, General Patton was sent to Kent in southeastern England, and messages went back and forth to persuade the Germans listening in on the radio that the invasion would be launched from Kent to Pas de Calais. The invasion day, D-Day, was set for early June, but the weather was stormy and could pile up the landing craft, which needed smooth seas. General Eisenhower studied the weather reports. A two-day clear spell was forecast for June 6-7, but Eisenhower's advisers recommended against launching the invasion since the reports could easily be wrong. But because the British could read the German codes, the Allies knew that the Germans did not expect an attack and that Rommel had gone off to Berlin for a rest. Eisenhower ordered the attack. The weather held. A force of 176,000 troops on 4,000 invasion craft, supported by 600 warships and 11,000 planes, landed along a 60-mile line on the coast of Normandy on June 6, the largest amphibious operation in all history.

The U.S. troops were assigned two beaches, code-named Utah and Omaha. On Utah, the 4th Infantry Division made good progress and by the end of the day had a 4000-yard beachhead. On Omaha, the fighting was much heavier with severe casualties, but the 1st Infantry managed to win a beachhead of about a mile. The fighting continued hard at Normandy with the Germans resisting fiercely, even though Hitler kept reserves pinned down at Pas de Calais because he was sure Normandy was a diversion. It was not until the end of June that the original D-Day objectives were reached.

The invasion succeeded just in time. In 1942, Werner von Braun, the brilliant pioneer in rocket technology, told Hitler that he had developed a missile which could travel faster than sound to drop bombs on England, with no possible defense. Hitler was not interested and sent Von Braun away. But in 1943, the dictator called Von Braun back and told him to give top priority to the rockets. For the first, last and only time in his life, Hitler admitted he had made a mistake, apologizing to Von Braun. But Allied intelligence, as usual, knew what was going on. The rockets were being constructed at a factory in Pennemunde on the Baltic Sea. The Allied High Command ordered massive bombing raids on the factory. The program was set back an entire year and not until 1944 were any fired. The first V-1 missile hit London on June 13, the first V-2 on September 8. They were terrifying and could not be stopped. But because of the Normandy landings, the launching sites were one by one taken over by the Allies. Although about a thousand V-1 and V-2 Rockets were eventually fired, doing much damage, they had come too late to help Germany win the war.

Now it was only a matter of time before the huge Allied force would invade Germany itself. General Rommel sent messages to the Allied leaders, calling for a surrender on the Western Front so that Germany could concentrate its remaining resources on stopping the Soviet troops coming from the east. But the Allies, holding to the policy of unconditional surrender, refused to talk to Rommel. In Germany itself, the Stauffenberg conspiracy failed in its attempt to assassinate Hitler and seize the government. In his insane rage, Hitler ordered the execution of all those who had any part in the plot or who had ever opposed him in any way. Altogether about 5000 people were executed. U.S. newspapers dismissed Stauffenberg's heroic attempt. Wrote the New York

Herald Tribune: "American people as a whole will not feel sorry that the bomb spared Hitler for the liquidation of his generals. Americans hold no brief for aristocrats as such and least of all for those given to the goosestep . . . Let the generals kill the corporal [Hitler] or vice-versa, preferably both."

After D-Day, the going through France was difficult, as the hedgerows slowed progress and land was taken almost yard by yard. But on August 1, General Patton arrived on the Continent and led a breakout, moving 75 miles in three days. On August 25, Paris was liberated and on September 4, Brussels. But then the Allies bogged down in the watery maze that was Holland. General Montgomery planned Operation Market Garden, whereby paratroopers would land behind the German lines, secure the bridges over the canals and rivers, and enable XXX Tank Corps to cross the Rhine and enter Germany. The U.S. 82nd Airborne took Nijmegen and the 101st took Eindhoven, but the fighting was bitter and everything took much longer than expected. British paratroopers who were dropped at Arnhem, the farthest bridge to be taken, ran right into the German Fifteenth Army, which had been sent there for recuperation. XXX Corps was stopped before Arnhem, and Market Garden failed, at a cost of more casualties than the Normandy invasion.

The failure of Market Garden meant that the Allies had to go the long way around, entering Aachen on October 21, the first large German city taken by the Allies. The Russians were in Poland and pushing against Germany from the east. The Germans had to make one last desperate counterattack and secretly concentrated their forces in the Ardennes. Though the Germans had attacked through the Ardennes many times before in history, Eisenhower had no thought that they would do it again and put his weakest troops there. The German commander, General von Rundstedt, was old-fashioned. He did not use radio to direct his preparations, so that the Allies could not pick up and decode signals. Lulled into a false sense of security, the U.S. was caught flat-footed when the Germans attacked on December 16. They advanced 50 miles, making a huge bulge in the Allied lines, so that the battle was known as the **Battle of the Bulge.** The Germans reached their high point on December 24 and could not go on, but they still had surrounded the 101st Airborne under General McAuliffe in the fortress of Bastogne. When the Germans ordered McAuliffe to surrender, he replied: "Nuts!" General Patton came to his rescue and the siege was raised on December 26. By January 20, the Germans were back to their starting points. They had lost 100,000 men, the U.S. 81,000. But the U.S. could replace its losses in 15 days; the Germans had no replacements.

1944 in the Pacific

After Guadalcanal, the U.S. began a long counterattack across the Pacific. The Japanese fought ferociously, having been ordered never to surrender. If all else failed, they would strap grenades to their bodies and make a ***Banzai*** charge into the American troops, killing themselves along with the Americans. By June, the Americans had re-won the Marianas, Guam and Saipan and were now within bombing range of Japan. On June 16 the first U.S. B-29's flew a raid against the Japanese home islands. Tragically, as in Europe, many of the bombs were dropped on cities and innocent civilians.

The most important battle in this U.S. drive was the Battle of the Philippine Sea, June 19-20. Admiral Ozawa had orders to search out the U.S. fleet near the Marianas and defeat it, and he concentrated what was left of the Japanese carrier fleet, telling his men, "This operation has immense bearing on the fate of the Empire. It is hoped that the forces will exert their utmost and achieve magnificent results . . ." But the U.S. had more ships, more planes and better trained pilots; they were ready for anything the Japanese could throw against them.

Between 10:00 a.m. and 2:50 p.m. on June 19, Ozawa launched four massive air raids. But several carriers sent wave after wave of fighter planes against them. The U.S. Hellcats took the measure of the Japanese, and over half of Admiral Ozawa's planes went to the bottom of the sea. But the biggest prize of the day belonged to a submarine. The Japanese had been pumping crude oil from Borneo into their ships without refining it first because the U.S. subs had been sinking too many of their tankers. The Japanese carrier *Taiho* had just completed launching 42 planes, when the submarine *Albamore* sent a torpedo into her starboard side near the forward fuel tanks, rupturing at least one of them. As the ship steamed ahead, deadly vapor spread throughout the ship, the fumes from the unrefined petroleum being especially volatile. At 3:32 p.m. a terrific explosion heaved up the armored flight deck, blew out the sides of the hangar and blasted holes in the bottom. The ship was bathed in flames, and no other ship could get close enough for rescue. The *Taiho* capsized and sank in 15,000 feet of water.

Despite his losses, Admiral Ozawa ordered new strikes the next day, June 20. But it was hopeless. U.S. fighters attacked and attacked again, sinking another carrier and losing only a few of their own planes. By the end of the day, Ozawa had exactly 35 aircraft still operational, out of the 430 which had proudly lined up in his hangars and on flight decks on June 19.

On October 20, U.S. forces under General MacArthur returned to the Philippines, using the islands of Leyte Gulf as stepping stones to its reconquest. In the days that followed, more ships fought in **The Battle of Leyte Gulf** (October 23-25) than in any other naval battle in history.

The Japanese, who were badly outnumbered, sent Ozawa with planeless and virtually useless aircraft carriers in a feint to the north of the Philippines. Admiral William "Bull" Halsey fell for the ruse and pursued the carriers with the largest part of the U.S. force.

On October 23, U.S. submarines drew first blood against Admiral Takeo Kurita's Japanese fleet. The following morning air strikes began and continued almost non-stop for the rest of the day. Shortly after midnight, Kurita turned his fleet away from the battle. Meanwhile, far to the south, U.S. forces were attacking a 42-ship Japanese Support Force. By dawn, every ship but one had been destroyed.

Kurita turned his fleet once again toward Leyte Gulf, hoping to wipe out MacArthur's land invasion force. But first he met U.S. Admiral Sprague's 13 small ships, which lay off the shore of Samar. When Sprague's men saw Kurita's battle-ready fleet come steaming in, they did what Americans have often done in similarly hopeless situations: they attacked. Seven of the ships were sunk, but the men kept fighting. Suddenly, for reasons still unknown, Kurita turned his fleet around and sailed away from Leyte Gulf, abandoning his pursuit of MacArthur's land force, which would have been helpless before his still mighty fleet. Not a single ship of MacArthur's supply and transport fleet was touched, while the damage inflicted on the Japanese had been enough to effectively eliminate their Navy for the rest of the war.

Yalta

As victory over the Axis powers neared, Stalin's ultimate goal of the War—extending Communist power—became increasingly obvious. In October 1944, Stalin informed Churchill that he expected the Polish Communist committee to have a majority in the new Polish government as soon as Germany was defeated. In late December, Stalin recognized a Communist regime (controlled from Moscow) as the official government of Poland. Roosevelt and Churchill did not try to stop this takeover of Poland by a dictatorship more ruthless than the Nazi regime against which Britain had gone to war. Soon Bulgaria was occupied by Soviet forces, and Communists in Hungary and Yugoslavia moved toward control.

On February 4, 1945, the Yalta Conference convened, attended by Roosevelt, Churchill and Stalin. Roosevelt, only weeks away from his death, was so ill that he relied on his advisers to direct the conference, especially on Alger Hiss, later proved to be a Communist. Roosevelt's main concern, as Eastern Europe slipped under the shadow of the hammer and sickle, was to gain Stalin's support for the United Nations to be set up after the War. Newspapers and magazines in the U.S. heralded this new organization with the typical American attitude that all problems could be solved by voting, ignoring the failure of the League of Nations to prevent World War II.

At Yalta, Stalin agreed to allow Russian delegates to attend a conference to set up the United Nations. In return, Roosevelt and Churchill agreed to permit the Soviet Union to control the Manchurian railroad and the port of Darien, the naval bases at Port Arthur, the Kurile Islands and Southern Sakhalin, all in Asia; to have three votes in the United Nations by giving the Soviet states of Ukraine and White Russia equal status with the Kremlin government in the new organization; to dominate the government in Poland; and to use Germans in forced labor for ten years after the War.

Most of these agreements were kept secret for months. The Yalta Conference was described to the press as guaranteeing permanent peace through the U.N. In response to inquiries, reporters were told that the "Polish question" was agreeably settled. It had been: The Poles had been consigned to Communist tyranny.

But Stalin still was not finished. By February 27, the Soviet Union demanded that the King of Romania install a Communist-dominated regime; four days later the Communists were in control of Romania. A group of Polish non-Communist leaders disappeared in March after traveling to Moscow to confer with the Soviets; they were later executed for treason. When the U.S. protested, Moscow promised that the Polish Communist government would later hold "free elections." When they finally held elections in 1947, all non-Communist influence had been extinguished by terror and murder. One by one, the countries of Eastern Europe fell under Communist control, and the lights of freedom, human dignity and Christianity were extinguished.

Dresden

From the west, the Allies drove toward Berlin; from the east, the Soviets. American and British forces were ordered to allow Russian troops to reach Berlin first and to press on to the Oder River, giving the Communists control over eastern Germany and Czechoslovakia. In the meantime, the Allies made a decision to bomb eastern European cities filled with refugees to hamper German troop movements and to make it easier for the Russians to seize more territory. A prime target was Dresden.

Dresden was a beautiful, baroque city in eastern Germany. In the early days of 1945, it was filled with hundreds of thousands of refugees fleeing Russian troops. The city was undefended by the Germans; it had not a single anti-aircraft gun. An incendiary attack was ordered for the night of February 13. The target was the center of the city. The first planes dropped flares to indicate targets for the bombers. The first indicator was dropped on the largest hospital complex in Germany. Then the bombers came. Bombs crashed into buildings, starting fires all over the city. The air heated to a temperature as high as 1100 degrees, creating a violent updraft which sucked fresh air into the center of the fire and created a wind of tremendous velocity. The result: a roaring inferno.

The bombers flew away. Fire-fighting brigades and relief suppliers from other cities rushed toward Dresden. Three hours after the first raid, just as help had arrived from other cities, a second raid dropped more fire bombs, sending up a glare which could be seen for 150 miles. The firestorm picked up crowds of people and hurled them along the streets. In one hospital, 200 people died, including 45 expectant mothers. Some sections of the city could not be entered for days, so fierce was the fire. Close to 135,000 innocent human beings died as American and British pilots destroyed a city which had no military significance whatsoever.

Dresden was the worst senseless destruction, but it was not the last, though many members of Britain's Parliament registered outrage against firebombing. At the end of March, when Germany was in utter ruin, giant raids were ordered for all available bombers, with the aim, according to the official USAF history, "to produce a stupefying effect on morale." There was little opposition; most of the targets were small towns that had not been bombed before. Even small villages which had stood since the Middle Ages were destroyed.

On March 7, American troops crossed the Rhine at Remagen, the only bridge the Germans had not destroyed, and by March 24 had control of the west bank of the Rhine. On April 16, an offensive of 1,600,000 men began against Berlin. On April 30, Hitler committed suicide. On May 2, Berlin fell and German forces in Italy surrendered. On May 7, Field Marshal Jodl signed the document of unconditional surrender. May 8 was officially designated V-E Day—Victory in Europe, the formal end of the War against Germany. The Nazi regime had ended. But the red flag of Communism waved over Eastern Europe as a new and more terrible tyranny settled its iron grip upon Europe's suffering people.

Operation Keelhaul

The Yalta agreements contained one more secret clause. Roosevelt and Churchill agreed with Stalin that all citizens of an Allied country who were liberated by another Allied country would be sent back to their homeland. On its face, the clause sounded harmless. Why not help people to return to their homeland? But the agreement included sending back even those persons *who did not want to return.* And where Communist Russia was concerned, many people did not want to return because they knew that slavery, imprisonment or even death awaited them.

One group that did not want to return were the Russian soldiers known as Vlasov's Army. General Vlasov had been an heroic leader of the Russian defense of Moscow against the Germans. But in the fighting around Leningrad, he was captured and put into a prison camp, along with other Russians. Many of these men, while violently opposed to Nazism, also rejected Communism, and began to formulate plans for an army to liberate Russia from Communist tyranny after the War. Many worked in German labor battalions in exchange for better food and improved living conditions. When the German Army started to disintegrate, these Russian soldiers were forced to fight for Germany, mostly in France.

After Germany surrendered, Stalin demanded the return of all the members of Vlasov's Army to the Soviet Union. They begged the U.S. not to force them to return; they knew that because of their anti-Communism they would be executed. The U.S. forced them into trucks, trains and boats for the return trip to Russia. Some of them jumped overboard or committed suicide rather than return to the Soviet Union. But the U.S. refused to listen to their pleas. All were returned. Vlasov was hanged; many of the soldiers were machine-gunned by Soviet troops almost as soon as they left the boats; others were sent to slave labor camps.

Another group of Russians who did not want to return were the Cossacks, a people from central Russia who had traditionally held independence under the Russian Czar. So opposed to Communism were they that 20,000 of them fought with the German Army in the hope of overthrowing Stalin's government. When they came into the custody of the Americans, they too begged to be allowed to remain in the West. Most of the Cossacks had their wives and children with them, and could not bear the thought of sending their children to Russia, since as Christians they did not want their children poisoned by Communist atheism. But American and British soldiers, many of whom did not relish their task but felt that they must obey orders, forced the Cossacks, women and children included, into railroad cars at bayonet point.

Other groups were also forced to return—over two million human beings in all were sent back at gunpoint. The name given to this episode was **Operation Keelhaul,** a particularly appropriate choice. Keelhauling was a punishment in the British and Dutch navies, by which a man who had committed some offense was tied with ropes, then thrown overboard and hauled under the boat's keel from one side to another. Most men were already dead by the time they were pulled out of the water. Thus were the Russians who wanted to remain in the West returned to the Soviet Union. As they were forced onto trucks and trains and boats, most of them knew that they were as good as dead already.

The Atomic Bomb

On April 12, 1945, Franklin Roosevelt died in Warm Springs, Georgia, and Harry Truman became President of the United States. That same evening he was told that the U.S. possessed a new and devastating weapon.

On October 11, 1939, Albert Einstein (a German Jew who had left Germany because of Hitler's racist policies) and other scientists had informed Roosevelt that the splitting of the atom could be used to manufacture a bomb with more destructive capability than any other weapon in history. Since that time, thousands of people, most of them without any idea of what they were doing, had been working on various aspects of manufacturing an atomic bomb. The overall name of the project, to hide its true nature, was the **Manhattan Project,** and its influence was felt all over the country. The first sustained nuclear chain reaction took place in a lab under the football field at the University of Chicago. At Oak Ridge, Tennessee, giant plants separated Uranium 235 from Uranium 238. On the Columbia River in Washington, nuclear reactors produced radioactive plutonium. At Los Alamos, New Mexico, the bomb was being assembled. At Wendover Field in the Utah desert, the 509th Composite Group, a picked crew of airmen and bombardiers, made last-minute preparations for going overseas, after rehearsing the dropping of a secret weapon nicknamed "The Gimmick," about which they knew almost nothing.

By the time Truman was sworn into office, U.S. forces in the Pacific had reconquered the Philippines, had raised the flag on Iwo Jima and had retaken Okinawa in spite of the suicide dives of the Japanese *kamikaze* pilots. Now U.S. planes were firebombing Tokyo, with such devastation that 56 square miles were destroyed and 85,000 persons killed. The U.S. announced an unconditional surrender policy toward Japan also, even though some members of the Japanese government had sent out tentative diplomatic feelers for a negotiated peace. Because the U.S. would not budge from unconditional surrender, our government believed that an invasion of Japan would be necessary. After experiencing the enormous casualty rates on Iwo Jima and Okinawa, American political and military leaders shuddered at the number of lives that would be lost in any such invasion. Therefore Truman appointed an Interim Committee to consider using the atomic bomb against Japan as a means of bringing about unconditional surrender without an invasion. On June 1, the Committee recommended "that the bomb should be used against Japan, without specific warning, as soon as possible, and against such targets as to make clear its devastating strength."

Sunday night, July 15, saw rain and lightning near Alamagordo, New Mexico as scientists looked at the tower out on the desert and tried to decide whether to go ahead with the planned 4:00 a.m. test of the atomic bomb, the first time such a weapon would ever have been exploded. They postponed the test until 5:30, and then—in the words of General Thomas Farrell—"There came this tremendous burst of light. The whole country was lighted by a searching light with the intensity many times that of the midday sun." In the town of Carrizozo, 30 miles away, people jumped out of bed awakened by a deafening roar and looked out their windows to see a six-mile-high pillar of fire. In Potsdam, near Berlin, where Truman was meeting with Churchill and Stalin, a cable arrived reading "Babies satisfactorily born." On July 24 an order went out to the commander of the 509th Composite Group, now based in the Pacific, to drop the bomb on Japan on the next clear day.

Truman had made his decision. But it was by no means unanimously supported in the government or the military. A group of scientists had submitted a petition asking that the bomb not be used. Fleet Admiral William Leahy had said that the dropping of the bomb bespoke "an ethical standard common to the barbarians of the Dark Ages . . . these new and terrible instruments of uncivilized warfare represent a modern type of barbarism not worthy of Christian man." Their pleas were ignored.

On July 26 the Potsdam Proclamation was sent to the Japanese government: "We call upon the government of Japan to proclaim now the unconditional surrender of all Japanese armed forces, and to provide proper and adequate assurances of their good faith in such action. The alternative for Japan is prompt and utter destruction." When Stalin had arrived at Potsdam, he had brought word that the Japanese had asked him to raise the question of a negotiated peace. But the three Allied leaders agreed to ignore the Japanese request. When the Japanese received the July 26 message, they replied, "No comment."

The weather report for August 6 was for clear skies over Japan. At 1:45 a.m. that day, the B-29 bomber ***Enola Gay*** lifted off. In its bomb bay was "The Gimmick," though its crew still did not know exactly what they were carrying. At 8:15 the plane was over Hiroshima, a city of little military significance to Japan. At 9:11 the ship leveled into a bomb run. At 9:15 it was dropped. The plane turned. Fifty seconds later light filled the sky, and the plane felt a terrific shock. In Captain Robert Lewis' log was an entry just before the bomb fell: "There will be a short intermission while we bomb our target." The next entry: "My God." One hundred thousand people were killed, many of their bodies burned into the walls of the buildings in which they had stood. When he received word, Truman exulted: "This is the greatest thing in history."

The Japanese Council met at midnight on August 9. It was evenly divided between those who wanted to surrender and those who still could not accept unconditional surrender. As they met, they received word that a second bomb had been dropped, this one on Nagasaki (the most Catholic city in Japan). The Emperor intervened in the conference. Throughout most of history, the Japanese Emperor had been a mere figurehead, while others ran the government. Now he took action.

He ordered the War ended. A message was sent to the U.S., asking if the Japanese could keep their Emperor if they surrendered. The U.S. agreed to this one condition. The War in the Pacific was over.

Unlike World War I, World War II had been a just cause. Both Nazi Germany and Japan had been ruled by evil governments, unleashing aggression against other nations, taking innocent lives and spreading suffering and destruction. The U.S. was justified in entering the War, and its men fought courageously and honorably.

But in the 20th century, wars were fought by nations which no longer honored Christian principles. Hence even nations fighting for a just cause could commit evils. Because it no longer accepted moral restrictions on how war should be waged, the U.S. could firebomb Dresden and incinerate Hiroshima and Nagasaki. Because the Allies were eager to appease Stalin, so that he would keep the Soviet Union in the War, they could send Russians back to the Soviet Union to face certain death and could agree to the establishment of Communist tyranny over the helpless people of Eastern Europe.

Nazi and Japanese tyranny were utterly destroyed. But no new moral, constructive order was established in the countries they once ruled. Eastern Europe was under Communist domination, and Western Europe and Japan became imitators of American materialism and secularism. Because the world had rejected Christ, it was doomed to continue searching for the genuine peace which only He can give.

REVIEW QUESTIONS

1. How did the U.S. respond to World War II during 1940 and 1941?
2. Summarize the circumstances of the attack on Pearl Harbor.
3. What was the first great U.S. victory against Japan and why did we win?
4. Summarize the battle for Guadalcanal.
5. What contribution did the U.S. make in North Africa and Italy?
6. What were the policies of unconditional surrender and strategic bombing?
7. Summarize the Normandy invasion.
8. Why did Germany not have V-1 and V-2 Rockets operational in time to help them win the War?

9. What was the Stauffenberg Conspiracy? What was the reaction in the U.S.?
10. Summarize the battles of the Philippine Sea and of Leyte Gulf.
11. What mistakes did the U.S. make at Yalta?
12. What was the firebombing of Dresden?
13. What was Operation Keelhaul?
14. Why did the U.S. decide to use the atomic bomb? What were the consequences?
15. Why was World War II a moral cause?

PROJECTS

1. Hold a series of debates on the issues raised in this chapter such as the firebombing of Dresden, Operation Keelhaul, and the atomic bombing of Hiroshima and Nagasaki.
2. Do research and prepare a report on the American homefront during World War II.
3. Write an imaginary interview of an important figure from World War II including at least ten questions and answers.

Chapter 24

The Birth and Death of Anti-Communism

As THE ASHES OF Europe's and Japan's ruined cities settled into the earth, the United States clung to an optimistic belief that co-operation with the Soviet Union would ensure world peace. After all, the U.S. and England had made many concessions to Stalin. Besides, there was the United Nations, for which Poland and much else had been sacrificed. But the Soviet Union turned the West's dreams of peaceful harmony into a nightmare.

The Truman Administration

At the Potsdam Conference (July-August 1945) the three wartime Allies seemed to be in agreement on all major points. In the Declaration on Liberated Europe, they agreed to work together to direct the former German satellites and other liberated countries. But the declaration contained the proviso that all three powers had to agree on all polices, effectively giving the Soviet Union a veto. The Soviets immediately brought three former German satellites under their control: Romania, Bulgaria and Hungary. When the U.S. brought up the subject of democracy, the Soviets said they were establishing "totalitarian democracy," which they defined as the union of all elements of society against Fascism. What they meant was the establishment of Communist dictatorship. Each country was nominally under a Control Commission, but the Soviet member of each commission was the commander of the Communist army in that country. He would act first and inform the other members later. President Truman was angry with the concessions being made to the Soviets and wrote a letter to Secretary of State Byrnes in which he said, "I'm tired of babying the Soviets."

But the letter was never sent, and the three countries slipped under Communist rule.

The original attitude toward post-war Germany was that the Germans had to be kept weak, left to get along as best they could with what they had or could produce. But by the winter of 1945 it was obvious that such a policy would result in starvation and epidemics, so the U.S. and Great Britain began to ship food to Germany. The country was divided into four zones, each one occupied by Great Britain, France, the United States and the Soviet Union, with the capital, Berlin, similarly divided, though it was in the Soviet zone. Each of the four occupying powers was to prepare its zone for a new government for all of Germany at an early date. The French were the first to refuse to cooperate. Since they wanted the Saar and the Rhineland, they would not permit centralization of railroads and postal service or trade with other zones. This intransigence gave the Soviet Union an excuse to behave similarly. The Soviets put only pro-Communists into office, including some former Nazis who were willing to take Communist orders. They confiscated all large farms and estates, closed all private banks, and nationalized industries. They dismantled German factories and shipped the parts to Russia.

By December 1946 the U.S. and British zones were mostly fused as the two governments realized the necessity for rebuilding Germany. The French, in an attitude reminiscent of World War I and Versailles, still wanted to punish Germany. The Soviet Union, of course, was not cooperating.

The winter of 1946-1947 brought heavy snowfalls and extreme cold. Throughout war-ravaged Europe, the suffering was intense. Many U.S. government officials realized that Europe needed massive aid and that the only country economically healthy enough to provide it was the United States. On June 5, 1947, Secretary of State George Marshall announced the Marshall Plan (named after him, though he did not originate it) to provide comprehensive aid to all European nations which would reveal their economic condition and announce what raw materials they could contribute. The Soviet Union was invited to participate, but they had no intention of revealing their economic condition, nor would they allow their Eastern European satellites to be part of the program. At a July 12 conference, 16 countries signed up for the Marshall Plan (Austria, Belgium, Denmark, France, Greece, Iceland, Ireland, Italy, Luxembourg, Netherlands, Norway, Portugal, Sweden, Switzerland,

Turkey, and Great Britain). The plan began in July 1948 and was immensely successful, even though Communists in France and Italy tried to disrupt it.

The U.S. and Great Britain realized that Germany must be brought into the program as well and began making plans to set up a bi-zonal government. On March 20, 1948, the Soviets walked out of the Four-Power Control Council, never to return. England, France, the U.S., Netherlands, Belgium and Luxembourg held a six-power conference to set up a government for the non-Soviet parts of Germany. In retaliation, the Russians began harassing travel to Berlin, stopping trains, cars and trucks for tedious inspections. On June 11 they halted all rail traffic for a day and closed a main highway on the excuse of bridge repair. By June 25, the Soviet Union had imposed a full-scale blockade on Berlin. By troops and road blocks, they prevented all movement by rail, road or water between Berlin and the Western zones. They also cut off the flow of electric power from the Soviet sector of Berlin to the Western sectors.

The U.S. and Great Britain had three options: to allow the Communists to get away with their power play, thereby giving them control of all of Berlin; to resupply the city by land; to resupply the city by air. The first alternative was not seriously considered. The second was rejected because it might provoke a violent confrontation. The third alternative was chosen, and a massive airlift began.

By July 22, U.S. planes were making 250 deliveries a day, with 2500 tons of cargo; by December, 4,500 tons a day; and by spring, 8,000 tons a day, with a plane landing in West Berlin every two minutes. Finally, on May 12, 1949, the Soviets gave in and lifted the blockade. The Communists had no way of stopping the airlift, short of all-out war, and U.S. firmness had forced the Soviet Union to back down.

Also in May 1949, the West German constitution was completed, and the German Federal Republic was formed with its capital at Bonn. Its chancellor was Konrad Adenauer, a strong Catholic and a committed anti-Communist who believed in natural law and emphasized the preservation of the family. He presided over an economic and cultural resurgence in West Germany. The Soviet Union countered by setting up the German Democratic Republic, a Soviet satellite state.

Meanwhile, the Communist guerrillas were stepping up action in Greece and Turkey. The Communists had been active in the fight against Nazi occupation of Greece, but as soon as the war was over, they turned all their attention to overthrowing the government. In Turkey, the Communists were demanding control of the Dardanelles and were facing a Turkish army of 1910 quality. Neither country would be able to resist a Communist take-over without assistance.

The U.S. was faced with a decision: stand up to the Communists or allow them to carry on aggression. President Truman decided to defy the Communists. He announced the **Truman Doctrine** of supplying economic and military aid to nations threatened by Communist takeovers (a policy later known as "containment"). He stressed the importance of giving nations a free choice as to their type of government and said that the Communists must be confronted and checked. Thanks to this help, the revolutionaries in both Greece and Turkey were defeated and the independence of those nations was safeguarded.

To protect West Europe against Communist aggression, the U.S. helped bring into being the **North Atlantic Treaty Organization (NATO)**, to provide for containment and mutual defense. An integrated **NATO** military force was set up under command of General Eisenhower. As part of the treaty agreement, West Germany was rearmed as a safeguard against a Communist attack.

The U.S. had committed itself to the **Cold War**, a confrontation between Communism and the West. The U.S. and the U.S.S.R. never actually went to war against each other, but each was committed to opposing the other. In a document issued by the National Security Council in March 1949, the U.S. acknowledged that as the greatest free power, it had a moral, political and ideological obligation to preserve freedom throughout the world, and a corresponding obligation to be militarily prepared to do so.

Unfortunately, throughout the Cold War the Communists were nearly always on the offensive, attacking here, probing there, to spread Communist power and influence; whereas the U.S. restricted itself to *reacting* against Communism, rather than trying to liberate countries already under Communist rule or to spread Western values. The underlying problem was perhaps that the West did not know what values to spread. The Communists were quite sure what they believed and what kind of world they wanted to establish. The West, no longer united by Christianity, was unsure of itself. It was not committed to any system of beliefs and values which it could oppose to Communism and offer to the world as a strong and meaningful alternative.

The Loss of China

The most spectacular U.S. failure in the early days of the Cold War came in Asia. Since 1927, civil war had raged intermittently in China between the Communists, led by Mao Tse-tung, a fanatically dedicated Communist, and the Nationalists, led by Chiang Kai-shek, a Christian and a strong anti-Communist. During World War II, both sides fought the Japanese, but Mao also took advantage of the situation to strengthen his strategic position. The Soviet Union declared war on Japan just before the War ended. The Soviet troops made no contribution to the ending of the War against Japan, but they were allowed to seize territory and supplies, which they then handed over to the Chinese Communists. After the War, the Soviet Union poured aid into China for Mao. Worn down by twenty years of fighting the Communists and the Japanese, Chiang needed U.S. help to carry on his fight for China's freedom.

But in the U.S., the climate of opinion was being turned against Chiang. Assistant Secretary of the Treasury Harry Dexter White, probably himself a Communist, stymied economic aid to Chiang. State Department officials John Stewart Service, John Carter Vincent and Owen Lattimore undermined support for Chiang and encouraged support for Mao as a "simple agrarian reformer." They agitated for an end to aid to Chiang and called for a "strong, united, democratic" China. The main source of information in the U.S. on China was the Institute for Pacific Relations and its publication *Pacific Affairs*. The Executive Secretary of the IPR was Frederick Vanderbilt Field, a Communist; Alger Hiss, another Communist, was on the board of IPR. Chiang was described as "cruel, corrupt, reactionary, inept, undemocratic and unpopular," and Mao was praised as the main hope for a democratic China.

On November 27, 1945, General George Marshall became special representative to China. Marshall came with instructions from Truman to bring about a coalition government including Nationalists and Communists. He did not come to help Chiang achieve victory. When Chiang refused to participate in a coalition government, Marshall ordered an arms embargo and the U.S. ceased giving aid to Chiang. When the Truman Doctrine was announced, Chiang expected that the embargo would be lifted and he would receive the same kind of aid that Greece was receiving. But the Truman Doctrine was not applied to China.

In June 1947, the Chinese Communists launched a new offensive. The Nationalists were almost helpless. In some battles their soldiers had only three or four cartridges each. The *New York Times* reported that the guns of the Nationalists were so worn that bullets fell through them to the ground. At times, a division of soldiers coming to the front to relieve another division had to take the retiring division's rifles because they had none of their own.

The U.S. Congress was dominated by anti-Communists and in April 1948 approved a shipment of arms to Chiang. But the State Department, which was responsible for carrying out the legislation, sent guns without bolts, machine guns without ammunition clips, planes without fuel.

On January 21, 1949, Peking fell. On October 1, the **People's Republic of China** was proclaimed, with Mao Tse-tung as Chairman. In December, Chiang and his supporters fled to Taiwan (then called Formosa), where he set up a free Chinese government.

In spite of pressure from the pro-Mao forces in the U.S., the U.S. did not grant diplomatic recognition to Mao's government. The Communists ruined their chances for recognition by mistreating Americans in China and by vicious anti-American propaganda. When the American consular property in China was seized in January 1950, that was the last straw. The Truman government officially recognized Chiang as the legitimate ruler of China and supplied economic support to prevent a Communist takeover of Taiwan.

But the damage had been done. The Communist government slaughtered millions of innocent people, outlawed the practice of religion, persecuted both native Christians and foreign missionaries, and set up a brutal dictatorship. Mao held the country in an iron grip, and the Chinese were consigned to slavery.

Witness

On August 2, 1948, an editor of *Time Magazine*, Whittaker Chambers, was subpoenaed to appear before the **House Un-American Activities Committee**, then investigating the influence of Communists in the U.S. government. Chambers would have given anything not to appear before the committee. He had joined the Communist Party in 1925, working zealously for Communism, until a gift of God's grace opened his eyes to the evil of Communism and the truth of Christianity. He repudiated the Party in 1938, and after a year of hiding in terror of retaliation, he built a peaceful life for himself and his family. Chambers knew that, if he testified, he would reopen all the wounds of his past and cause many others besides himself to suffer. But he also knew that he had no choice:

> I believed that I was not meant to be spared from testifying. I sensed with a force greater than any fear or revulsion, that it was for this that my whole life had been lived. . . . Everything that made me peculiarly myself and different from all others qualified me to testify. My failure to do so, any attempt to evade that necessity, would be a betrayal that would measure nothing less than the destruction of my own soul.

Chambers saw himself as a witness (the title he later gave to his autobiography), a Christian witness against the evils of Communism, which had insinuated itself into the highest councils of the American government and was dedicated to the destruction of everything moral and decent and healthy in America. On August 3, Chambers appeared before the committee, testifying that he had been "a member of the Communist Party and a paid functionary of the Party." Chambers gave a detailed description of his activities, naming those who had been in his Party group, the Ware Group, in Washington. At one of the names, everyone in the room gasped: Alger Hiss, one of Roosevelt's closest advisers at Yalta, an architect of the United Nations, a pillar of the liberal establishment in Washington, now President of the Carnegie Endowment of World Peace. All of the other men Chambers named had been previously identified or suspected to be Communists. No one had suspected Hiss. He was too famous, too important, too respected.

Hiss demanded to be heard by the Committee, testifying on August 5 that he had never set eyes on Whittaker Chambers. Faced with two contradictory statements, the Committee—primarily under the urging of California Congressman Richard Nixon—determined to solve the mystery. Both men were questioned separately and in detail in executive (non-public) session to determine who was lying. The two men presented quite a contrast. Chambers was quiet, nervous, obviously deeply moved by emotion. Hiss was cool, calm, confident, self-possessed. But Chambers gave countless details of the way Hiss and his wife had lived, the furnishings in their apartment, the cars they drove, their habits and hobbies. Hiss was an ornithologist, and one of his greatest moments, Chambers said, was the sighting of a rare prothonotary warbler near the Potomac. When Hiss was questioned the next day, having no idea of anything Chambers had said, he confirmed detail after detail of Chambers' testimony. He mentioned his bird-watching hobby. A Committee member casually asked if he had seen any especially rare specimens.

Yes, he said excitedly, a prothonotary warbler. The committee room was absolutely silent for a few seconds; then one of the members quickly asked a question to hide the shock and surprise.

Hiss realized that the committee was inclined to believe Chambers, so he changed his strategy. Instead of denying that he had ever known this man, he pretended to have known him once under the name of George Crosley, to have sublet his apartment to him and loaned him a car, thus explaining Chambers' knowledge of his home and his habits. But that ploy did not work either. In a public hearing on August 25, Hiss contradicted himself, especially on the issue of his 1929 Ford roadster, which he claimed to have given to Chambers but which had actually been sold to the Communist Party.

Then Hiss prepared still another strategy. To deflect attention from himself, he attacked Chambers. He received permission from the Committee to read a letter, in which he asked ten questions of Chambers. Each question referred to a crime or immoral behavior, one of them inquiring if Chambers had ever been in a mental hospital or treated for mental illness. Hiss was clever enough not to say outright that Chambers was insane, but by asking the question, he implied doubts about Chambers' mental health. The public therefore assumed that Chambers must have been insane, though he had never in his life so much as consulted a psychiatrist or psychologist. Thus did Chambers' real agony begin. Few among the ordinary people could quite believe that the popular, influential Hiss could be guilty. Few in political life could dare admit it even if they did believe, because to do so would have cast doubts on all their causes and on their own judgment in trusting such a man. To give just one example: If Hiss really were a Communist, then the American public would begin to doubt the value of the United Nations, since Hiss had done so much to set it up. But the Liberals could not bear to have the U.N. criticized. So they *had* to believe Hiss innocent. And if they had to present Hiss as a noble man unjustly accused, they had to attack Chambers. From this point on, Chambers was subject to vicious attacks against his character, his morals and his sanity, attacks which continued long after his death.

As the committee continued its investigations, Hiss stayed on the attack, filing a $75,000 libel suit against Chambers. In the pre-trial examinations, Hiss's lawyers made every effort to degrade Chambers and his wife with insults and accusations. But the lawyers outsmarted themselves. Casually, with no idea of what he was getting into, Hiss's lawyer asked Chambers to turn over any written material Hiss had ever given him, sure that there was none to be turned over. Chambers reluctantly agreed. One of his duties in the Ware Group was to collect secret government documents, which Hiss then copied for the Soviet Union. When he fled the Party, Chambers—not knowing why he did it—saved the last of these documents, a sheaf of papers and rolls of microfilm, hiding them in his wife's nephew's apartment. Now he retrieved them from New York, turning the papers over to the court. The microfilm he decided to keep temporarily. Afraid that his home might be searched, Chambers hollowed out a pumpkin and hid the film in it. Hence the documents came to be known as the ***"Pumpkin Papers."***

With the documents now in public possession, it would seem that Hiss would at last tell the truth. But he did not. Called before a New York Grand Jury investigating Communism, he cooly denied under oath ever having passed secret documents and ever having been in a Communist group with Whittaker Chambers. The Grand Jury had already heard lengthy and agonized testimony from Chambers. They believed Chambers. In December 1948, the Grand Jury indicted Hiss on two counts of perjury. (They could not indict him for treason because the statute of limitations on those actions had expired.)

But Chambers' witness had still not ended. At the perjury trial, Hiss's lawyer, Lloyd Paul Stryker, pulled out all the stops. In his opening argument he listed all of Hiss's achievements and all of the leading figures who trusted him. He violently attacked Chambers, concluding with a vicious tirade: "In the warm southern countries, you know, where they have leprosy, sometimes you will hear on the streets among the lepers a man crying down the street 'Unclean, unclean,' at the approach of a leper. I say the same to you at the approach of this moral leper."

The government prosecutor, Thomas Murphy (a Catholic and an able lawyer), concentrated on the hard evidence: that the documents had been typed on Hiss's typewriter, that the factual details Chambers knew of Hiss's life could not have come from the slight acquaintance Hiss had admitted to with "George Crosley." The judge, Samuel Kaufman, allowed Hiss's lawyers practically everything they asked for, while continually overruling Murphy's objections. The jury could not agree among themselves. They came back a hung jury, eight for convicting Hiss, four for acquitting him.

At the second perjury trial, Chambers was once again subjected to personal attack. This time Hiss's lawyers brought in a psychiatrist named

Dr. Carl Binger, who testified that Chambers was a psychopath, though Binger had never in his life so much as spoken to Chambers. But Murphy calmly dismantled Binger's testimony by showing that everything he pointed to as evidence of Chambers' insanity could also be part of a perfectly sane behavior pattern. The new judge, Henry W. Goddard, was much more objective; the government had made its case against Hiss even tighter. This time the jury had little difficulty. They found Hiss guilty on both counts.

Hiss was sentenced to five years in prison. After his release he was eventually readmitted to the bar and became a practicing lawyer, steadfastly protesting his innocence all the while. In 1978 a liberal historian named Allen Weinstein published *Perjury: The Hiss-Chambers Case*. Weinstein had undertaken his investigations in order to exonerate Hiss; instead his researches showed him that Hiss was indeed guilty. Weinstein was attacked by other Liberals, who still defended Hiss, but no one could refute the evidence of his book.

After the fall of the Soviet Union and the opening of Communist archives, there was a reconsideration of the Hiss-Chambers case. Confirmation was found of an active Soviet espionage ring, just as Chambers had described it. In a March 30, 1945 cable from the Soviet intelligence representative in Washington to Moscow, mention was made of a Soviet agent, code named "Ales." The National Security Agency identified "Ales" as "probably Alger Hiss."

In the last years of his life, Chambers became very pessimistic about the chances of the West's ever defeating Marxism if no one would face up to the reality of Communism. But whether he realized it or not, Chambers' witness had a vital impact on America. His testimony and his book influenced thousands of Americans to appreciate more fully the menace of Communism. American anti-Communism was shaped largely by Chambers; like all martyrdoms, his witness was not in vain.

The Atomic Bomb and the Soviet Union

In August 1949, the Soviet Union exploded its first atomic bomb. This news shocked Americans, who had assumed that it would be years before the Communists obtained this weapon. The American government, in fact, had been agonizing over what and how much to tell the Soviet Union about the bomb, thinking that perhaps sharing information with them would make it less likely that they would ever use the bomb against the U.S. Now, suddenly, that question had become obsolete. A new question had arisen, however. How did the Russians manage to produce a bomb so quickly? The answer to that question gradually emerged: espionage.

On February 2, 1950, U.S. newspapers carried headlines that Klaus Fuchs, a German refugee scientist working on the British atomic bomb project, had been giving information on the project to the Soviet Union. Fuchs said that his contact, to whom he gave the information for transmittal to Moscow, was code-named Raymond. The F.B.I. eventually identified Raymond as American chemist Harry Gold, who confessed to having been Fuchs' courier. Besides Fuchs, Gold said, he had also received information from a U.S. soldier working at Los Alamos. He did not remember the soldier's name, but he did remember where he lived in New Mexico. The F.B.I. identified the soldier as David Greenglass, who immediately admitted having passed information to Gold and who also implicated his wife Ruth and his brother-in-law, Julius Rosenberg. Thus began the highly controversial **Rosenberg Spy Case**.

Greenglass and his wife gave the F.B.I. extensive information implicating Rosenberg and Greenglass' sister, Rosenberg's wife Ethel. Liberals accused Greenglass of fabricating most of the information as part of a deal with the U.S. government to give him a lighter sentence. As with the Hiss case, however, a book by Liberals originally begun as an attempt to exonerate the Rosenbergs instead corroborated the government's case on all essential points. This was *The Rosenberg File*, by Ronald Radosh and Joyce Milton.

Before the War, Julius and Ethel, who were married in 1939, were both committed Communists. But during 1943, they suddenly dropped their party membership, a standard procedure whenever a party member was recruited into espionage work. In January 1945, Greenglass returned to New York from Los Alamos and had dinner with the Rosenbergs. The Greenglasses testified that at this dinner Julius persuaded David to obtain information on the atomic bomb and to give it to a courier. Ruth was to meet this courier outside a Safeway store in Albuquerque, New Mexico. The recognition signal was provided by Julius. He cut a Jello box in half, gave one half to Ruth and told her that the courier would have the other half. On June 3, 1945, Harry Gold showed up at the Greenglass apartment with the other half of the box. Greenglass wrote out for him all the information he had on an implosion lens which would be used for detonating the bomb, illustrating the explanation with drawings. Gold then passed the information to his Russian contacts. In September 1945, on a trip to New York, Greenglass gave Rosenberg further information on the bomb.

After the War, Rosenberg and Greenglass went into business together, but the business failed, largely, according to Greenglass, because Rosenberg spent too much time on Communist activities. Greenglass also stated that Rosenberg boasted of other espionage successes. Then in 1950, when Fuchs was arrested, Rosenberg began urging David and Ruth to leave the country before they could be tracked down as part of the same spy ring. The Greenglasses found it difficult to take the warnings seriously, until David was arrested on June 15. David signed a confession that same day, but he did not decide to make a full disclosure of everything he and the Rosenbergs had done until June 26. He did so at that time because he believed that was the only way to salvage something from the situation for his wife and children. The Korean War had just broken out, and Americans were not in a mood to be merciful to Communist spies. Greenglass, who had become increasingly disenchanted with Communism after the War, felt that his only loyalty now was to his family.

In July, Julius was arrested, and on August 11, Ethel. There was very little evidence against Ethel at this time, but the government hoped that her arrest might shake Julius into confessing, or that she herself might break down and give damaging admissions. But neither Julius nor Ethel would budge from their protestations of complete innocence. (Ruth Greenglass was never arrested; she was named an unindicted co-conspirator.)

The Rosenbergs were charged with conspiracy to commit espionage, and their trial began March 6, 1951. Prosecutor Irving Saypol's main witnesses were David and Ruth Greenglass, who testified that Julius had brought them into his espionage ring and arranged for David to give atomic secrets to Harry Gold. Defense lawyer Emmanuel Bloch cross examined ineptly and was unable to shake the testimony of either Greenglass. The next witness was Harry Gold, who confirmed the Greenglass' story. Bloch did not cross-examine him at all, most probably because Rosenberg knew Gold could implicate him further and did not want to make things worse than they already were.

Julius was the first witness for the defense. He provided other explanations for everything in the Greenglass testimony which could not be denied outright, but frequently took the Fifth Amendment. The Fifth Amendment to the Constitution states that a person cannot be required to incriminate himself. It was used by Julius whenever he was asked a question about any connection with Communism in his past, even regarding facts that were common knowledge. His frequent use of the Fifth Amendment perhaps convinced the jury that he had something to hide. His stony, unsympathetic demeanor also helped to create an unfavorable impression.

Ethel testified next. The defense had hoped that the jury would see her solely in her role as wife and mother of two young children and therefore sympathize with her. But she too presented a cold, unsympathetic demeanor. Her testimony confirmed Julius on all points, but some of the questions she answered were those on which she had taken the Fifth Amendment when appearing before the Grand Jury. This contradiction was an opening for Saypol to sow doubts in the jury's mind as to what the truth really was.

Bloch's summation was emotional, referring to Greenglass's willingness to testify against his own sister as "repulsive." Saypol stressed the evil of Communism, which should erase any sympathy for the Rosenbergs. During their deliberations, the jury of eleven men and one woman was unanimous from the beginning in their belief that Julius should be convicted. All of them also agreed that Ethel was guilty as well, but one juror, James Gibbons, did not want to convict her because he did not want to see a young mother executed. Finally, under pressure from the other jurors, Gibbons voted for conviction for both Rosenbergs.

Judge Irving Kaufman announced the sentence on April 5, 1951, condemning both Rosenbergs to the electric chair. Many were surprised that he gave Ethel the death sentence, but Kaufman said that their crime was worse than murder and that their selling atomic secrets to the Communists had helped lead to the Korean War. Greenglass was sentenced to fifteen years in prison, more than he expected.

The defense lawyers filed two separate appeals with the U.S. Court of Appeals. But in spite of the fact that the three judges on the court were known to be Liberals, the convictions were upheld on both appeals. In October 1952, the U.S. Supreme Court refused to review the case. President Eisenhower denied a clemency appeal in February 1953. The National Committee to Secure Justice in the Rosenberg Case mounted a world-wide campaign, first to get a new trial for the Rosenbergs, and then for clemency, but a last-ditch effort to get the Supreme Court to stay the executions and review the case failed when the Court voted

5-4 to uphold the convictions and executions. The Rosenbergs were executed on June 19, 1953.

Though Liberals still maintain that the Rosenbergs were innocent, evidence in files opened after the fall of Communism in the Soviet Union indicates that they were guilty and in fact were part of a wider espionage ring. The question of the justice of their sentence remains open, however. They were convicted of conspiracy to commit espionage, not treason, and no one else in U.S. history has ever been executed for such a crime. The argument given by Eisenhower and others was that the Communists must be sent a clear message of American firmness in opposition to Communism. The mood of the country, as American soldiers were dying in the Korean War, supported Eisenhower on this issue. But the main effect of the executions was to make the Rosenbergs into martyrs, a situation from which the Communists extracted maximum propaganda advantage.

But the crime was real, and it was one more example of Soviet determination to get the best of the U.S. even when, as during World War II, the U.S. thought the Soviet Union was its friend.

Korea

Americans who had doubts that the Communists really did desire world domination were shaken out of their complacency on June 25, 1950, as thousands of North Koreans poured across the 38th parallel into the **Republic of Korea** (South Korea). Korea had been divided after World War II when the Communists had refused to allow the territory they had occupied in the closing days of the War to be reunited with the rest of the country. Now they were launching a drive to conquer the South. The aggression was also a test to see whether America would have the will and the ability to resist a limited Communist aggression not directed against the U.S. or Western Europe.

The initial invasion was instantly successful. The Communists had infiltrated the South Korean army so that the **NKPA** (North Korean People's Army) knew the location of every **ROK** (Republic of Korea) defense unit. The ROK and its American advisers were taken by surprise. ROK soldiers fled in terror at the sight of Russian T-34 tanks. The ROK Seventh Division was cut to pieces; the High Command panicked and ordered the evacuation of Seoul, though the capital could have been defended. The bridges over the Han River south of Seoul were blown up while covered with refugees and while 44,000 ROK

Russia
Mongolia
North Korea
South Korea
Japan
China
Southeastern Asia
Burma
Laos
North Vietnam
Thailand
South Vietnam
Philippines
Cambodia
Pacific Ocean
Malaysia
Borneo
New Guinea
Sumatra
Java

troops, with their equipment and artillery, were still on the other side. On June 28, the ROK could account for only 22,000 out of the 98,000 troops they had had on June 25.

The U.S. was aghast. Though Truman had pursued a policy of containment (not allowing Communism to spread), he and his advisers had never expected the Communists to start a limited war in an out-of-the way area. After Hiroshima and Nagasaki, American military leaders had assumed that the next war would be total and atomic. They were unprepared to fight a limited, conventional war. Further, after World War II, there had been a revulsion against having a strong and highly trained military. Liberal leaders pushed through legislation and policy directives to reduce the effectiveness of military training. Instead of a battle-ready army, Americans had a group of civilians who knew little more than how to fire a rifle. The Communists had no doubt counted on this unpreparedness in their planning for the invasion.

But the aggression having taken place, the U.S. acted. The Joint Chiefs of Staff authorized General MacArthur in Japan to send ammunition, equipment and a survey party to Korea. The United Nations convened its Security Council, which passed a resolution calling for a cessation of hostilities and the withdrawal of the invading forces, and authorizing UN members to take all necessary steps to implement the resolution. Normally such a resolution would have been vetoed by the Soviet Union. But the Soviet delegate was boycotting the Council in protest of the UN's refusal to recognize Red China. Hence the U.S. could send troops into Korea under the sponsorship of the UN, thereby blunting what would otherwise have been strong Liberal opposition to helping South Korea.

But having the desire to help South Korea and actually being able to were two different things. U.S. combat teams were at 70 per cent strength. There were not enough weapons and equipment, such weapons as were available were mostly old and worn; and the soldiers of the 21st Division, who had been trained as occupation troops for police duty, were unprepared for combat. They had not been given the type of training required for this situation.

MacArthur sent over the 500 men of Task Force Smith, expecting them to hold the line until he could get a larger force together. The Task Force was assigned to protect the airport of Suwon against T-34 tanks and NKPA infantry. But the American weapons had so little effect that the tank drivers did not even know they were being attacked. And the Americans were no match for the North Korean infantry. When the Americans realized that they were losing the battle, many of them ran, dropping their weapons, disappearing into the hills, leaving their wounded behind. The American combat team delayed the Communists exactly seven hours.

The 24th Infantry Division arrived. They were unprepared for the 120 degree heat and searing drought of Korea's summers. Not having enough water, they drank from rice paddies and came down with dysentery. They sweated until their shirts and belts rotted. In seventeen days of combat they suffered 30 per cent casualties and left behind enough equipment to supply a full infantry division. Making a valiant personal attempt to hold the line, the commanding officer, General William F. Dean, was captured and spent the rest of the war in a Communist prison camp. The 21st and 24th Divisions received Unit citations for heroism and General Dean received the Congressional Medal of Honor.

The NKPA had overrun all of the Korean peninsula except for a perimeter around the Port of Pusan. Here the Americans and South Koreans made a last desperate stand behind the Naktong River. They blew the bridges over the river and dug in, knowing that they had to keep the port open come what may, because that was their only way to bring in more men and supplies. At last the U.S. was able to set up a defensive line, secure its flanks and station reserves in the rear. And the Communists could not shake American control of air and sea. Our ships brought in men and supplies; our planes bombed the enemy supply lines. Without this vital help, there would have been virtually no chance at all to hold the Pusan Perimeter.

But the North Koreans did not give up. They crossed the river and pushed a huge bulge into the American lines. But the Marines had arrived. The Marine Corps had maintained its standards and its toughness. All the way over to Korea on the troop ships, they had made bets as to whether they could get to Korea before the War was over. They did, and were immediately thrown into the battle to hold the Perimeter. Two hundred forty Marines made the first assault. Twenty three were killed and 119 wounded. But the next day they forced the NKPA back across the river.

On August 31 the NKPA launched a concentrated night attack across the Naktong, and for the next two weeks the Americans endured heavy fighting and war casualties. The Communists put pressure at five points and made a dramatic breakthrough at the Naktong Bulge. But this time the Americans did not run. They regrouped their forces and held the line.

Now the Americans were ready to go on the offensive, and MacArthur had a plan. He would land the Marines on the west coast, in the rear of the Communist lines, at the port of Inchon, only eighteen miles from Seoul. No one else was enthusiastic about the plan. The tides around Inchon were extreme, among the highest in the world, and a landing would be possible during only a few hours each day. The landing force risked being trapped on the mud flats. But MacArthur knew what the Marines had done in World War II. He was confident, and the attack was ordered.

On September 15 at 6:30 a.m., the Third Battalion, 5th Marine Division landed on Wolmi Island, which was connected to the mainland at Inchon by a causeway. In less than two hours, they had secured the island with only seventeen American casualties. Then the tide went out, and the Marines were left to hold the island. They did, with the help of naval and air bombardments. When the tide came in around 5:30 p.m., the Marines went on to the mainland. By 1:30 a.m. September 16, the city had been taken with only twenty Marines killed.

The successful Inchon landing gave tremendous momentum to the U.S. By September 25, Marines were inside Seoul. On September 29, MacArthur and ROK President Syngman Rhee rode in triumph through the city and re-established the government. It was a proud moment, but it was sobered by the discovery that, before evacuating, the North Koreans had executed thousands of men, women and children from the families of South Korean policemen, government employees and soldiers.

With the U.S. on their rear, interdicting the supply lines, the North Koreans could not hold the Americans within the Pusan Perimeter. By the end of September, the 8th Army was in Seoul, and on October 7, they crossed the 38th parallel at Kaesong on their way north.

The U.S. and ROK goal was not simply to drive the Communists out of South Korea. It was to drive them out of the peninsula altogether and reunite the country. At a high-level conference on October 15 at Wake Island, Truman gave MacArthur the go-ahead to push on to the Yalu River, the border between Korea and China, after MacArthur assured him that there was no danger whatsoever that the Chinese Communists would enter the War.

But as MacArthur gave Truman those assurances, 120,000 Chinese Communist troops, hardened in the war against Chiang, crouched by day under camouflage and marched by night through Korea. Every night between 9:00 p.m. and 3:00 a.m. they covered eighteen miles. The U.S. had not the slightest idea that they were there.

The NKPA had virtually collapsed, and the U.S. drove forward. Down the center of North Korea was a chain of virtually impassable mountains. On one side marched the First Marine Division, on the other side the 8th Army, with no real communication possible between them. Even for units on the same side of the mountains, communication and coordination were difficult because of the up and down terrain; the forces were strung out and vulnerable.

During November sub-zero winds whistled down into Korea from Siberia, dropping the temperature to 24 degrees below zero, freezing food and water and medical supplies. On the night after Thanksgiving, the Chinese attacked the 8th Army. Many Americans had thrown away their equipment during the march because it was too heavy to carry. They no longer had their bayonets or helmets or grenades. The 8th Army units were cut into pieces, as each individual unit was singled out and enveloped by overwhelming numbers. The Chinese swarmed through to the rear, destroying unit after unit. Without realizing where the Chinese were, the commanders ordered a retreat south. The Second Division started through Kunu-ri Pass. It was an ambush. Chinese opened fire on all sides. The U.S. force was decimated.

On the other side of the mountains, the Chinese commanders told their men: "Kill these Marines as you would snakes in your homes." The strategy was the same as against the Army: cut the line into pieces, break through to the rear, and wipe out the Marines. The attack came on November 27. The fighting was ferocious, but the individual units held, in spite of terrific losses. D Company was driven from its hill three times, and three times came back, though at the end it had only fourteen men left out of 150. Walt Phillips of E Company stuck his bayonet in the ground and said, "Easy Company holds here." He died there, along with 156 other Marines. But they held. The individual Marine units fought back together and consolidated a line. One Marine battalion marched and fought for two days over the frozen hills around the Chosin Reservoir, without rest; they were exhausted, cold, suffering from dysentery. Then they attacked. They took the Chinese in the flank by surprise and drove them off the hills so that their fellow Marines could get out. By December 3 the Marines had fought out of the trap, bringing out every single one of their wounded men, leaving none behind to be tied with wire and shot or bayonetted in the back. They marched into Hagaru erect and in cadence. They had inflicted 37,400 casualties on the Communists. Four Red Chinese armies were completely eliminated as effective fighting forces by one Marine division.

Now the War settled into still another phase. The U.S. consolidated a line just south of the 38th parallel, holding it in spite of repeated Chinese assaults. MacArthur wanted to bomb the supply lines on mainland China and allow Chiang's army to invade. But Truman did not wish to widen the War or risk a nuclear war. When MacArthur publicly attacked the President, Truman fired him and appointed Matthew Ridgeway as commander-in-chief. Ridgeway led the Americans back to the 38th parallel.

And there the War remained, throughout 1951, 1952 and early 1953. Many men fought and died, but the lines scarcely moved. Aware that they were getting nowhere militarily, the Communists agreed to truce talks, which opened at Panumjon on October 25, 1951. It soon became obvious that both sides were willing to let the boundary between North and South Korea be where it had been when the War began, though the Communists wanted to gain every possible propaganda advantage and therefore forced the talks to drag on.

Meanwhile, it was not only on Pork Chop Hill and Heartbreak Ridge and other battlefields along the parallel that Americans were suffering. In a bauxite mining camp nicknamed by the Americans "Death Valley," U.S. prisoners of war suffered from poor diet, lack of medical care and constant Communist indoctrination. They lived in filthy huts with no room to sleep comfortably. The medical corpsmen were given only enough sulfa each day for four men, and no other medicines. So many men died by March 17, 1951, that they were consolidated with other prisoners in a camp on the Yalu River. They started with 3200 men. Between March and October, that number fell by 50 per cent. Those with no religion generally gave in and died first; those with weak faith generally died next. But those with a strong religious faith usually held on, despite the worst the Communists could do to them. There was one exception: the chaplains, who were the Communists' particular target. For the slightest offense, a chaplain could be put in solitary confinement and deprived of food and medicine. Not a single chaplain survived the Communist prison camps.

By the spring of 1952, the Communists had extracted almost every drop of propaganda advantage, so the truce talks were moving toward a conclusion. Then arose the issue of the return of POW's. Perhaps remembering the anguish of Operation Keelhaul, the U.S. adamantly refused to force anyone to return to North Korea or Red China who did not want to go. When the Communists found that 80 percent of the Chinese prisoners and 50 percent of all the Communists in American hands refused to return, they balked. They could not let the world know the strong aversion these men felt against returning to Communism. They declared that all prisoners had to be returned or there would be no peace treaty.

But the Communists could not hold out forever. World opinion began to turn against them. Stalin died, and the new Communist leaders were less hard line. The Communists suffered a bad harvest and could no longer afford to devote so much of their resources to the War. The armistice was at last signed on July 27, 1953.

The Korean War was a high point of the Cold War. The U.S. steadfastly opposed Communist aggression and served notice to the Communist leaders that they could not attack other nations with impunity. The Communists learned their lesson well. Their next aggression would be guerrilla warfare and terrorism, disguised as a civil war. They would no longer try to challenge the Americans in stand-up battles in a conventional war. The U.S. was less ready to learn. In spite of this clear evidence of Communism's continuing drive toward world domination and its unyielding hostility to all Christian and moral values, the U.S. continued to believe that some accommodation could be reached with the Communists, if only the magic formula could be found.

Joseph McCarthy

Whittaker Chambers had won his battle with Alger Hiss in the fight against Communism within America, though he suffered greatly during and after it. Shortly after the Hiss-Chambers case, another major battle would be fought.

Joseph McCarthy was an Irish-German Catholic from Wisconsin. After World War II, in which he had served as a Marine, he had gone into politics, being elected to the Senate in 1946. With both an Irish and a German Catholic heritage, he was deeply sensitive to the implacable enmity of Communism toward the Catholic Faith and all decent values. He did not put his feelings clearly into words because he was not an intellectual, but he knew in his heart that Communism was an enemy which must be *fought*. He knew also, as had become clear in the Hiss case, that the problem was much bigger than a few traitors in the government. The whole Liberal Establishment had lined up against Chambers; men in the government, in the press and in the universities had attacked the Christian and defended the Communist. The members of the leadership elite of America, although relatively few were actual Communists, saw no strong reason for opposing Communism because they had abandoned Christian truth. These were the men McCarthy fought; these were the men who fought him.

McCarthy began his war against Communism on February 9, 1950 in a speech to the Ohio County Women's Republican Club of Wheeling, West Virginia, in which he said that he knew the names of a number of Communists working in the State Department. The claim was exaggerated. What he knew was that a number of State Department employees were security risks because of their sympathy to Communism. As would often be the case, McCarthy would make exaggerated statements which unfortunately would obscure the genuinely serious problems which he was trying to bring out into the open.

In a speech on the Senate floor on February 20, McCarthy repeated the essence of the Wheeling charges. As a result, the Senate established a committee under Senator Millard Tydings of Maryland to investigate McCarthy's charges. The committee was mandated to conduct a "full and complete study . . . as to whether persons who are disloyal to the U.S. are or have been, employed by the Department of State." But the bias of Senator Tydings was made clear in a statement before the investigation began: "Let me have McCarthy for three days in public hearings and he will never show his face in the Senate again."

Though the Tydings Committee condemned McCarthy and not the security risks, and though McCarthy often over-stated his case, the fact is that most of the people whose names he brought up before the committee were in fact security risks. The most significant was Owen Lattimore, one of the chief architects of U.S. policy toward China. The Tydings Committee exonerated Lattimore. But on June 27, 1952, the Senate Subcommittee on Internal Security announced that Owen Lattimore was "a conscious articulate instrument of the Soviet conspiracy" and that he had testified falsely before the Tydings Committee on at least five separate items.

The Liberals launched a counterattack against McCarthy, accusing McCarthy of creating a "climate of fear" in the United States, of trying to suppress free speech and of "character assassination." Walter Lippmann, a widely-read political columnist wrote, "This is the totalitarianism of the man: his cold, calculated, sustained and ruthless effort to make himself feared . . . he respects nobody, no office, and no institution in the land." His enemies coined a word, "McCarthyism," to mean any kind of attack on the character and decency of others. Yet the very men who complained that McCarthy had suppressed free speech were freely writing and publishing and speaking against him; the men who accused him of destroying the reputation of others were calling McCarthy a monster, insane and a threat to the United States.

McCarthy reacted with his emotions instead of his intellect. He always said exactly what he thought, even if not especially polite. He was fond, for example, of referring to Arkansas Senator William Fulbright as "Halfbright," and Liberal newspaper columnist Joseph Alsop as "All-slop." He would lose his temper and make charges which he could not prove. These mistakes were seized upon by the press and the Liberals, while they ignored all the charges he had made which were true.

As chairman of the Permanent Investigations Subcommittee of the Senate Committee on Government Operations, McCarthy had been conducting his own investigations into Communist infiltration in the government. During late 1953, his investigations had centered on the Signal Corps installations center in Fort Monmouth, New Jersey (where Julius Rosenberg had once worked). Eventually McCarthy began to investigate the case of an officer in the Army, Irving Peress, who had been promoted and then honorably discharged, though he was known to be a Communist. The Army fought back, supported by almost every influential person in the country. Army officials accused McCarthy's chief staff member, Roy Cohn, of using his position to get special favors for his friend David Schine, who had been drafted into the Army. These charges and counter-charges led to a special investigation known as the Army-McCarthy hearings, nationally televised in the summer of 1954.

The Army had a clever lawyer, Joseph Welch, who knew how to make McCarthy and Cohn look bad. McCarthy lost his temper. Cohn projected an image of a conceited, young know-it-all. As Hiss's lawyers had distracted attention from Hiss by attacking Chambers, Welch distracted attention from Communist infiltration in the Army by attacking McCarthy on three main points: the cropped photo, the purloined document and Fred Fisher. The cropped photo was a picture of Secretary of the Army Robert Stephens, David Schine and Colonel Bradley which McCarthy used to show that Stephens was friendly to Schine though the opposition was trying to show that Stephens was furious with him.

In the version of the photo McCarthy submitted to the committee, Colonel Bradley had been cropped from the picture so that only Schine and Stephens were visible. Though Bradley's presence or absence had no relevance to the point McCarthy was making, Welch described the photo as "doctored," an "altered, shamefully cut-down picture," and refused to accept it as evidence of anything.

The purloined document was a letter which McCarthy possessed which listed persons at Fort Monmouth who were security risks. The letter was similar to an FBI document on the same subject, and Welch accused McCarthy of having stolen the letter and of having unethically publicized its contents. But McCarthy had received the letter from an Army intelligence officer and had publicized it because the Army was doing nothing about the security risks. Nevertheless, the public received the impression that McCarthy was using stolen evidence.

Fred Fisher was a law associate of Welch and a former member of the National Lawyers Guild, a Communist front organization. Welch had decided not to use Fisher in the Army-McCarthy hearings because of his associations, and had publicly announced his decision three months before the hearings. But when McCarthy mentioned that Fisher belonged to a Communist-front organization, Welch became outraged and with tears in his eyes accused McCarthy of destroying the man's career: "Until this moment, Senator, I think I never really grasped your cruelty or your recklessness. . . . Let us not assassinate this lad further, Senator. You have done enough. Have you no sense of decency, Sir, at long last? Have you left no sense of decency?"

McCarthy's support in the country plummeted. Before the hearings, polls showed that 50 percent of the people supported his efforts to expose Communists in the government. Now the figure dropped to 35 percent. His fellow Senators turned against him, voting to censure (condemn) him. The vote was strictly political. The Democrats and Liberal Republicans (under the leadership of President Eisenhower) voted against McCarthy; only the conservative Republican Senators voted for him.

McCarthy needed public approval to carry on his work. But what was worse, the attacks against him took a personal toll. He went into a depression and began drinking too much. His body could bear the stresses no longer, and he died on May 2, 1957, the victim of an irrational hatred which has not entirely disappeared even forty years later.

Eisenhower's Foreign Policy

The destruction of McCarthy was the beginning of the end of consistent and widespread anti-Communism in the U.S. President Eisenhower (elected in 1952 and re-elected in 1956) had supported the censure vote, and the foreign policy of his Administration was a mixture of firmness and failure.

Eisenhower and his Secretary of State John Foster Dulles presided over the end of the Korean War and held out for the rights of POW's to refuse to return to their home countries. At the end of 1953, the Chinese Communists seized Yikiang, an island north of Taiwan, and talked of invading Quemoy and Matsu, two small islands near Taiwan and even of invading Taiwan itself. Eisenhower and Dulles proclaimed that they would defend the islands and received Congressional authorization to move American forces into the area. Though the Communist threats continued, the islands were never invaded, thanks to America's firm policy.

In 1955, Dulles' strong support of Austria helped bring about the Austrian Peace Treaty of 1955, which was the only instance since World War II when Soviet troops ever retreated until the evacuation from Afghanistan in 1989.

In 1956, however, when the **Hungarian Freedom Fighters** attempted to free their country from Soviet domination and begged the U.S. for help, Eisenhower refused. Said Eisenhower: "Hungary couldn't be reached by any of the U.N. or U.S. units without traversing neutral territory. Unless the major nations of Europe would, without delay, ally themselves spontaneously with us (an unimaginable prospect) we could do nothing. Sending troops into Hungary through hostile or neutral territory would have involved us in a general war." Though there would indeed have been risks in aiding the Freedom Fighters (although providing them with weapons and supplies would have been less risky than sending troops), the U.S. refusal to offer any aid at all caused the Eastern Europeans to conclude that they would have to learn to live with Communism, since they could not count on the U.S. to help them liberate themselves from Soviet tyranny.

Communism made a major gain in 1959, the year that Dulles died, with Castro's take-over of Cuba (discussed in the next chapter).

Summary

The moral decline in America found its expression in foreign policy. The Cold War had proud moments—the planes over Berlin, Chambers' witness, the Marines fighting out of the North Korean mountains. But it could not last. The Liberals in the media and the universities, the shapers of public opinion, presented a favorable view of Communism which increasingly would find fulfillment in American foreign policy.

REVIEW QUESTIONS

1. Why was the U.S. optimistic about world peace after World War II? What events showed this optimism unfounded?
2. How did the U.S. oppose the earliest Communist attempts to extend their power?
3. How did the U.S. contribute to the loss of China to the Communists?
4. Why did Whittaker Chambers call himself a witness? Who opposed him? How did they oppose him?
5. How was Hiss convicted? Why did Chambers feel that he had failed? What actually had he accomplished?
6. What events led to the arrest of Julius and Ethel Rosenberg?
7. Summarize the events of their trial and the appeals following it.
8. What happened in the early days of the Korean War? Why was the U.S. unprepared?
9. What was the significance of the Pusan Perimeter? What was the significance of the Inchon Landings?
10. What mistakes did MacArthur make in Korea?
11. What happened when the Red Chinese attacked?
12. Describe conditions in Communist prison camps.
13. What delayed the signing of a truce? What were the results of the war?
14. How did McCarthy try to fight Communism? What mistakes did he make?
15. What happened at the Army-McCarthy hearings and what were the results?
16. Why did the U.S. decided not to help the Hungarian Freedom Fighters?

PROJECTS

1. Prepare a mural showing the major events of the Cold War during the administrations of Eisenhower and Truman.

2. Do research and then prepare a report on the Hungarian Freedom Fighters.
3. Do research and prepare a report on the Berlin Airlift.

Chapter 25

Communists vs. Christians in Latin America

THE HISTORY OF THE 20th century in Latin America is the story of the war between the Catholic Church and its enemies for the souls of men. The battle was fought in Mexico in the 1920's, with the Cristeros proudly bearing the banner of Christ the King against the Liberals and Freemasons, who sought to destroy His Church. In other countries the same war was waged in the second half of the century.

Cuba

After the Spanish-American War, Cuba's business and commerce were heavily influenced by the U.S., which bought the bulk of Cuba's main crop, sugar, at prices favorable to the buyer. The U.S. also had dominant political influence. If the U.S. did not like the way the Cuban government was handling an issue, it would intervene and tell the Cubans what to do or even send in the Marines if that proved necessary. Cubans came to rely on the U.S. for political leadership and did not develop good leaders of their own. Cuba adopted U.S. materialism and secularism so that the Church was not as strong as in other Latin American nations.

In 1952, a former army sergeant named Fulgencio Batista marched on Havana and took over the government with the backing of the Army. Batista quickly restored order and settled down for what he hoped would be a long rule.

But on the campus of the University of Havana, a bearded part-time law student and full-time revolutionary had stored arms and ammunition and trained men for war. The University had traditionally been a hotbed of liberalism and Marxism, and many rebellions had been born on the campus. Using the campus as his base, Fidel Castro planned an attack on the Moncada military barracks, as a first step toward overthrowing Batista. The attack on July 26, 1953 was a disaster. Only a few of Castro's men forced their way inside the barracks. Castro himself was captured and imprisoned.

But the failure of one violent act did not end opposition to Batista's rule. Students attacked the police; the police fought back with brutality; the brutality spawned more riots. Even ordinary citizens were unhappy with Batista for refusing to allow elections or to allow anyone who opposed him (except the Socialists and Communists) to have a voice in public affairs. Upon his release from prison, Castro intended to capitalize on the continuing unrest. He went to the United States, collecting funds for his revolution and organizing his followers into the 26th of July Movement. Meeting with student leaders in Mexico in 1956, Castro outlined plans for an invasion of Cuba to be supported by student riots in Havana.

On December 1, 1956, Castro and a group of 80 revolutionaries, including his brother Raul and Argentinian Che Guevara (a terrorist and dedicated Communist), landed in Oriente Province, touching off a wave of sabotage, terrorism and bombing. But neither the general public nor the Army showed much interest in Castro's revolt, and Batista's forces quickly crushed the movement. But Castro and a dozen survivors found refuge in the Sierra Maestra mountains and began waging guerrilla warfare.

Thinking to eliminate the source of revolutionary activity, Batista closed the University of Havana, throwing 18,000 students into the general confusion and hardening them in their resolve to overthrow the regime. Because he held out in the mountains while other anti-Batista groups were defeated in the streets, Castro grew in prestige, strength and adherents. In April, 1958, he was finally ready to launch full-scale warfare: raids, sabotage, attacks on military bases. The U.S., partly in response to Liberal agitation and partly in response to general disenchantment with Batista, stopped supplying him with weapons in March, 1958, making his army even weaker.

Finally, at the end of 1958, the Army refused to continue fighting. Batista's regime crumbled, the president and his followers fleeing to the Dominican Republic in the early hours of January 1, 1959. Castro stepped into the vacuum. Able to speak extemporaneously for hours, he mesmerized many Cubans into believing that he was the solution to all their ills. He eliminated opposition by the simple expedient of firing squads.

Many Liberals in the U.S. admired Castro, but those who followed his policies carefully could see that he was nothing less than a Communist dictator. He nationalized natural resources, utilities, banks, the media, and most large and medium industries. The upper classes and most of the middle classes were wiped out, many of them fleeing to the United States to set up Cuban exile communities, largely in Florida. He organized neighborhood committees to spy on Cuban citizens, forcing everyone to live in fear. Those who represented a threat to his regime were thrown into inhuman prisons; many of the prisoners were Catholics, who would write on the walls of their cells the Cristero battle cry, *Viva Cristo Rey!* Castro deliberately set out, as most Communist leaders have done, to destroy the family. Women were forced to work; children were taken from their parents and placed in boarding schools to be indoctrinated in Communism. Not content to turn Cuba into a Communist slave state, Castro sent **Che Guevara** to other countries to stir up revolution. Of these attempts, Castro boasted that he would convert "the Cordillera of the Andes into the Sierra Maestra of Latin America."

Though many innocent people died in the terrorism fomented by Guevara, Castro's attempts to export the revolution were largely unsuccessful, and Guevara himself was killed trying to start a revolution in Bolivia. In Cuba, Castro held an iron grip on the people, despite the obvious failure of Communism to help them. Imposing a communistic economy led to inflation, bureaucratic chaos and inefficiency. Agricultural production declined sharply, and in 1961 food rationing was introduced for the first time in Cuba's history. Cuba had once had one of the highest standards of medical care in Latin America; under Castro it disintegrated. Many more Cubans fled the island, risking their lives to escape Castro's tyranny.

U.S. relations with Castro began to deteriorate early in his regime, and in 1960 the U.S. withdrew diplomatic recognition. At the same time, groups of Cuban exiles were being trained under the supervision of U.S. officials in Central America, with the goal of invading the Island and overthrowing the government. The Cubans willing to fight and die for the freedom of their country possessed enormous courage, but every sort of problem beset their heroic enterprise. Although the Castro government did not know the exact date or place of the planned invasion, Castro was well aware that an invasion was planned. To be successful, the invading force needed the support of the anti-Communist underground within Cuba, but communications between the underground and the exiles broke down so that those in Cuba did not know the date of the invasion until it actually took place. The site for the invasion, the Bay of Pigs, was swampy, with little access to the mountains where future guerrilla activities could have been launched.

But the worst problem the invading force had to face was caused by the U.S. The invasion had been planned under the administration of President Eisenhower. But it was scheduled for early 1961. By that time, a new President had been inaugurated, John F. Kennedy. Kennedy allowed the plans to proceed, but he did not give the invasion full backing. When some of his Liberal advisers learned of it, they reacted with shock and horror. Finally, on April 17, the day of the invasion itself, Kennedy withdrew the order to U.S. planes to give air cover to the landing force. The Cuban exiles were pinned down on the beach by Communist troops who should have been eliminated by U.S. planes. Almost all of the brave Cubans were killed or taken prisoner.

Castro brutally repressed all remaining opposition to his regime, smashing the anti-Communist underground and arresting thousands. The invasion's failure and the repression which followed broke the back of anti-Communist resistance in Cuba.

Then, in 1962, the USSR secretly put bombers and missiles into Cuba, hoping to force the U.S. into concessions over Berlin. When U.S. spy planes photographed the missiles, Kennedy ordered the Navy on October 22 to blockade Cuba until the missiles were withdrawn. The whole world was frightened that the U.S. and the Soviet Union were going to war. But a frantic exchange between Kennedy and Soviet Dictator Nikita Khruschev led to a compromise. Khruschev agreed to remove the bombers and missiles, and Kennedy agreed never again to support in any way a Cuban exile attempt to liberate the Island.

Castro at first was furious that Khruschev had given in, but soon the Soviet Union was using Cuba as a base for its missile-bearing submarines, at least as great a threat as the original missiles. And even more to Castro's gain, the Cuban exiles were deprived of help they needed to free their homeland.

Gradually, the U.S. tended toward more friendly relations with Castro, accepting a Communist nation only 90 miles away from its shores. In the meantime, the Cubans themselves suffered a miserable oppression, grinding poverty and little hope for the future.

Argentina

Argentina had been slightly less chaotic than most Latin American countries after independence, largely because the British dominated its economy. Nevertheless, the government tolerated the usual corruption and the lower classes suffered the usual poverty. Then, in June 1943, a military coup overthrew the corrupt dictator Ramón Castillo. From the *junta*, **Juan Perón** emerged as the strongest man, with the support of the badly paid industrial workers in the cities and the friendless farm workers in the country. On February 24, 1946, in remarkably honest elections, Perón, with 52.4 per cent of the vote, became president.

He set up an authoritarian rule which controlled the press, abolished the autonomy of the universities, had veto power over strikes and eliminated the opposition Labor Party. At the same time, the ***Peronata***, as his regime was known, embodied Catholic social doctrine from the papal encyclicals, encouraged private industry, protected private property and met the needs of the poor.

The main source of hope for the poor was actually **Evita**—Perón's wife Eva Duarte—who rose out of poverty and the lower classes to rally the workers in Perón's support. She married Perón in 1944 when she was 24 and became virtual minister of labor in his government. Perón created the Eva Perón Foundation and gave her authority over all charities. She used her power to gain more support for Perón, but she also used it to the benefit of the poor, personally dispensing money to those in need, establishing hospitals, clinics and nursing homes, conducting the first effective campaign against tuberculosis and malaria, setting up a nursing school, and organizing a country-wide soccer league for children, which provided the opportunity to give the children health checkups and ensure that they were going to school. She worked 18-hour days, supervising the distribution of aid so that it was far more effectively spent than if it had been administered by a bureaucracy.

The most important result of Perón's policies and Evita's charities was that the lower classes had no interest in Communism, unlike the lower classes elsewhere in Latin America. This channeling of lower class discontent away from Marxism was Perón's greatest service to his country.

But in 1950, problems began to develop. Perón's attempt to industrialize the country quickly led to inflation. Perón lost support from the Church when he sent official greetings to a spiritualist conference and neglected to appear at a Eucharistic Congress until the last day. Then in January, Evita fainted at a public ceremony. She was operated on for appendicitis, but it was probably at this time that she was diagnosed as having cancer, though the seriousness of her illness was kept secret even from her.

A presidential election was scheduled for November, 1951. Evita wanted to run for vice-president with her husband. The ordinary people fanatically supported this idea, though the army and Perón himself were opposed. On August 22, 1951, the CGT (Argentinian labor organization) held a mass rally at which Evita and Perón appeared. They demanded that she declare her candidacy for vice-president. After refusing several times to make a commitment, she finally said, "I will do what the people say." Nine days later, she made a radio broadcast saying that she would not "exchange one battle position for another." The people idolized her all the more, referring to August 22 as her "Day of Renunciation." In reality, Perón had forbidden her to run for vice-president.

Shortly after the radio broadcast, she collapsed from pain and was confined to bed. She was slowly dying, and nothing could be done because the cancer was too far advanced. On November 11, in another honest election, Perón was re-elected with 66 per cent of the vote. Most of his increase in support came from the recently enfranchised women voters.

The whole country watched Evita's dying. After her death on July 26, 1952, hundreds of thousands crowded around her casket as she lay in state, the Argentinians petitioned the Pope to canonize her, every province had at least one school named after her, and her autobiography was made required reading in the public schools.

But with Evita dead, the people became aware of the problems afflicting their country. They became restless. Then Perón made his biggest mistake. He turned against the Church, which had represented a check on his power. He legalized divorce, proposed to end the Church's participation in public education, and threatened to tax Church property. In June 1955, 100,000 Catholics demonstrated in the Plaza de Mayo in front of his residence and then marched to the capitol, over which someone raised the papal flag.

Perón retaliated. Gangs of ***Peronistas*** attacked churches in Buenos Aires, setting fires and smashing statues. When two priests protested, they were put on a plane for Rome, whereupon the Vatican excommunicated Perón for "trampling on the rights of the Church." In July and

August, more demonstrations took place, countered by police violence. On September 16, the Army revolted. Perón was forced to resign, eventually going into exile in Spain. He left behind an economy in ruins.

Post Perón Argentina was confused and chaotic. Then in 1966, General Juan Carlos Onganía seized the Casa Rosada (presidential residence) and threw out the Liberal government then in power. His greatest act was to dedicate the country to the Immaculate Heart of Mary. The national shrine of Argentina is that of the Basilica of the *Virgen de Lucan*. In the Basilica, is a statue which had been imported from Italy for a church in Buenos Aires in the 1920's. But when the car carrying the statue reached a small town outside Buenos Aires, it broke down. When the escort tried to take the statue out of the car to shift it to another, it became so heavy that no one could lift it. They concluded that the Virgin wanted the statue to stay where it was. A basilica was built there in her honor, becoming the National Shrine of the country. Onganía led a pilgrimage to the Shrine, attended by thousands of Argentinians, who enthusiastically pledged their loyalty to the Immaculate Heart of Mary.

Unfortunately Onganía did not know what else to do with his government. He had only a vague social program, and the government began to drift. In 1970, he was overthrown. In 1973, Perón was called out of exile and took over the government at the age of 77. Again the working class supported him, along with the conservative and firmly Catholic middle class. But Perón was a sick man; he had lost his master touch. He infuriated the people by appointing his third wife, Isabelita, as vice-president. When he died, on July 1, 1974, Isabelita succeeded him. Though a Catholic, she was in over her head. The country fell into disorder until she was overthrown by a military coup in 1976.

But Peronism did not die with Perón. As late as 1983, the Peronist Party garnered 40 per cent of the votes. And Argentina remains anti-Communist.

Chile

In Chile, pro-Communists came to power through elections. Therefore, many Americans thought that this government should be allowed to remain in power, no matter how evil. Fortunately, the Chileans did not have the same illusions about democracy.

In the 1960's, President Eduardo Frei and his Christian Democratic Party had made Chile more liberal and had exploited the poor. Disenchanted with the Christian Democrats, many people, during the 1970 elections, supported Salvador Allende and his platform of social reform. Allende received 36 percent of the vote, more than any other candidate, but short of the majority needed for election. Allende promised concessions to some of the minority parties, which lined up behind him, giving him the 50 percent needed. He never kept his promises, saying later: "I accepted [them] as a tactical necessity to assume power. The important thing at that moment was to get hold of the government." Thus, Allende came to power through a lie. He would do many worse things before he was finished.

Allende wasted little time moving toward the communization of Chile's economy, nationalizing over 500 industries. He claimed that they would be run for the benefit of the people. Instead they were run for the benefit of Allende and his cronies. The nationalized industries had a deficit of 150 billion escudos per year, yet the Allende-appointed managers accumulated personal fortunes. The stores were empty, and Chileans waited hours in long lines to buy what few goods were available. Yet Allende and his friends did a brisk business of their own, selling goods on the black market for huge prices and pocketing the profit. Allende's secretary had at least 22 and perhaps as many as 45 new cars delivered to her to sell. Allende sent $6 million to Canada to be deposited to his personal account.

As a campaign slogan, Allende had once said that "violence is living in opulence while thousands of Chileans live in shacks." As president, he bought a huge mansion with swimming pool and tennis courts and a vacation home with four swimming pools and a movie theater. As Chilean women marched in the streets beating empty pots to symbolize their children's hunger, Allende's home had five refrigerators bulging with food.

Opposition to Allende's destruction of Chile met with harsh repression. The trucking industry was in the hands of many individuals, each owning one or two trucks. After Allende nationalized the spare parts industry, making it virtually impossible to obtain parts or tires, the truckers went on strike. In mid-August 1973, thousands had hidden their vehicles in the hills. Then the government invited the strikers to a meeting to settle their grievances. When the truckers left to attend the meeting, the Minister of the Interior led an armed assault on the hidden vehicles. Three hundred were driven away by the attackers in a shoot-out.

There was worse. Edmundo Searle, a young leader of the *Patria y Libertad*—"Fatherland and Liberty"—organization described his experiences: "I was tortured by Allende's police. I was blinded. . . . I was given no water, no food, no sleep. I was told I would be killed without anybody knowing it. . . . When I got out . . . I was really damaged physically and mentally."

Scarcely any institution in Chile was left untouched. Allende put Communists into the hospitals and medical centers, though they knew nothing about medicine. The infant mortality rate almost doubled; no one could get a vaccination unless he was loyal to Allende. The government took over the food distribution industry, driving out of business the widows and wives of pensioners who ran the small neighborhood groceries.

Allende arranged to sell Chile's entire gold reserve on the black market, to enrich himself while bankrupting his country. He secretly armed guerrillas and lied about it. His thugs terrorized people in the streets. He fortified his home by a high concrete wall, stocking automatic weapons including a 50 mm. cannon and even erecting anti-aircraft defenses.

By 1973, the country was in such chaos that Allende's party, the *Unidad Popular*—"Popular Unity"—was in serious danger of losing the election, which would lead to Allende's impeachment. But Allende took care of that. Voter identification cards were forged in the names of people who were dead or who had left Chile. On election day, trucks took people from polling place to polling place to vote with the forged cards. The *Unidad Popular* won 43.4 per cent of the vote by stealing more than 100,000 votes.

But Allende knew that opposition to his tyranny would soon erupt. With his henchmen, he developed Plan Z, a violent purge which would sweep through the armed forces, destroy the opposition and kill 50,000 Chilean traditionalists. The coup would be carried out by a force of armed foreign leftists, mostly Cubans and Mexicans.

The Chilean generals found out about this murderous plan. On September 10, the Chilean fleet abruptly turned from Pacific maneuvers and headed for Valaparaiso. Allende called out his Communist troops. They did not even show up. The next day the Army and the Air Force attacked *La Moneda*, the presidential palace. The troops defending Allende soon fled. He was left with his personal bodyguard of 60. He gave them a choice: stay and fight with him or escape. To a man, they escaped. Allende committed suicide.

The new government was a military junta of five generals, four of whom were Catholics, led by Augusto Pinochet. Chile slowly began rebuilding the wrecked economy, and the generals arrested the Communists and purged all Allende's fellow criminals from the government. The new government was supported by the Chilean bishops in a major statement on Christmas Day, 1973.

The government knew what steps it should take first, organizing a national pilgrimage to the shrine of the Blessed Mother. No fewer than two and a half million Chileans took part. Folk dancers from every province, even from every town, performed. Banks of flowers were piled high. It was a great outpouring of Catholic faith and of gratitude to God for saving the country from the misery and terror of Communist tyranny.

Except in Cuba, Latin American Catholics held the line against Communism during the 20th century. Our Lady of Guadalupe was watching over the people she had helped bring to the Faith 400 years before.

REVIEW QUESTIONS

1. Outline the steps by which Fidel Castro came to power.
2. Describe Castro's regime.
3. Why did the Bay of Pigs invasion fail?
4. What were the results of the Cuban Missile Crisis?
5. How did Juan Peron come to power? What role did his wife Eva play?
6. What were the good and harmful elements of Peron's regime? Why was he overthrown?
7. What happened in Argentina after Peron?
8. How did Allende come to power in Chile?
9. Describe his regime.
10. How was he overthrown?

PROJECTS

1. Do research and write a report on Cuba, Argentina or Chile today.
2. Find out who are the leading cardinals and bishops in Latin America today.
3. Interview someone in your area who is from Latin America to find out conditions in his country today.

Chapter 26

The Moral Decline of America

IN 1952, THE REPUBLICANS were optimistic that for the first time in 20 years they could elect a President. The two main candidates seeking the nomination were Ohio Senator Robert Taft, who opposed the growth of power in the national government and tended to favor the principle of subsidiarity, and Dwight D. Eisenhower, the World War II hero, whose political views were not well known. Eisenhower had the lead as the convention neared, but needed the support of California to be sure of victory. He received that support by promising California Governor Earl Warren an appointment to the Supreme Court at the earliest opportunity. Eisenhower won the nomination on the first ballot; his vice presidential choice was California Senator Richard Nixon, who had gained fame as Whittaker Chambers' supporter. The election was a Republican landslide over Adlai Stephenson of Illinois, the Democratic candidate, as scandals in the Truman administration, the continuation of the Korean War, Eisenhower's popularity and a general desire for a change brought Eisenhower to victory.

We have already seen the major foreign policy events of Eisenhower's administration—the ending of the Korean War and the sometimes firmness (Quemoy and Matsu) and sometimes weakness (Hungary) in the face of Communism. Eisenhower also refused to support Senator Joseph McCarthy and encouraged Republican Senators to vote to censure him. In domestic policy, Eisenhower's most significant act was to fulfill his promise to Earl Warren by appointing him Chief Justice of the Supreme Court in 1953.

The Warren Revolution

At times, a strong President such as Wilson or the two Roosevelts had dominated the government. Occasionally, Congress had been especially powerful, as during Post Civil War Reconstruction. Now it was the Court's turn. Before Warren, the Court had more often than not regarded its function as the exposition of the law. If the law was unclear, the justices would try to determine what the law's authors had meant. This is not to say that the Court had never given its own opinions more weight than the views of the legislators. For example, the Court had first rejected, then accepted governmental regulation of business as the law of the land. But even in these instances, the justices had tried to find support for their decisions in previous cases and in the words of the Constitution or of the law under review. It remained for the Warren Court to declare the supremacy of the justices' own opinions. In addition, previous courts had rarely declared any law unconstitutional. The Warren Court would frequently declare laws unconstitutional, becoming in effect legislators with no check on their legislative powers.

The Warren Court's first major case was **Brown v. Topeka Board of Education**, in May 1954. The plaintiffs argued that state laws requiring Blacks to attend segregated schools were a violation of the 14th Amendment's guarantee of "equal protection of the laws." The defendants argued that the authors of the 14th Amendment did not intend it to apply to schools, that only the states could end segregation in the schools. The defendants had the better legal case. The 14th Amendment itself said nothing whatever about schools, and debates in Congress at the time of the Amendment's passage indicated that the Amendment was specifically not meant to apply to schools, that the states and local governments had full authority over the operation of public schools. The Warren Court ignored the evidence, declaring, "In approaching this problem, we cannot turn the clock back to 1868 when the Amendment was adopted . . . We must consider public education in the light of its full development and its present place in American life throughout the Nation." Chief Justice Warren then concluded that "separate education facilities are inherently unequal" and therefore unconstitutional.

Certainly it is right for public schools to be open to members of all races. But other means existed for desegregating schools. For example, Congress could have cut off all federal funds from states which had segregated schools. Furthermore the constitutionally designated task of the Supreme Court is to explain the Constitution. Instead the Warren

Court declared that their own opinions were the law of the land. In so doing, they left in a shambles two cherished American ideas. The first was that the Constitution represented an ideal form of government. But if the Supreme Court can put its own opinions into the Constitution, the Constitution is meaningless. The second is that the checks and balances in our government are foolproof. But the Supreme Court gave itself precedence over all other branches of government and over the states. The *Brown* case was the beginning of **judicial activism**, actions by the courts which write laws and make major social changes.

The Warren Court went on to strike down state laws against Communist subversion, to tell the states how to set up their legislative districts and to put serious restrictions on the ability of the police to solve crimes and convict criminals. In each of these cases, the Court simply wrote new laws instead of interpreting existing laws and the Constitution.

Among the cases which caused the most outcry were the **Schempp-Murray** cases, concerning school prayer. In 1963, the Court upheld Pennsylvania Unitarian Schempp and Maryland atheist Murray, who were opposed to prayer in the schools on the ground that it violated the First Amendment. The First Amendment states only that Congress may not establish a national religion. But the Warren Court declared that, instead, the government must possess toward religion "strict neutrality." "The test . . . may be stated as follows: to withstand the strictures of the establishment clause there must be a secular legislative purpose and a primary effect that neither advances nor inhibits religion." In other words, religion was to have no part in the public life.

The Kennedy Era

Religion became a major public issue in the 1960 elections when the first major Catholic candidate since Al Smith in 1928 ran for President.

The Republican nominee was certain to be Eisenhower's Vice President, Richard Nixon. The Democratic race was wide open, however, with the leading prospects being Senate Majority Leader Lyndon Johnson from Texas, Senator Hubert Humphrey from Minnesota and Senator John F. Kennedy from Massachusetts, a Catholic. All the candidates were Liberals, so there was little to choose among them in ideology. Johnson and Humphrey had been active in politics much longer than Kennedy, but Kennedy had other assets. He was young, handsome, energetic and had an equally young, handsome, energetic family of brothers and sisters who campaigned for him with a highly organized, highly professional campaign. He also had a millionaire father who provided all the campaign funds needed. On the other hand, he was a Catholic. Could a Catholic win the election or even the nomination?

Johnson stayed out of the primary elections, but Kennedy realized that he had to prove that he could win by running well in the primaries against Humphrey. The first primary contest, in Wisconsin, was inconclusive. Kennedy won by a narrow margin, carrying the Catholic industrial districts, while Humphrey carried the Protestant farming areas. The next primary was West Virginia, where there were almost no Catholics but strong anti-Catholic prejudice. Though his advisers told him to ignore the religion issue, Kennedy chose to meet it head on in a state-wide television appearance in which he said that he would be faithful to his presidential oath to uphold the constitutional separation of church and state. He cast the issue in terms of tolerance vs. intolerance: a vote for Kennedy, he implied, is a vote for tolerance. Though Humphrey himself was not at all intolerant, somehow voting for him was made to seem an act of bigotry. That, plus the Kennedy money lavishly spent, gave Kennedy a landslide victory. Humphrey withdrew from the race. Kennedy went on to win other primaries and received the nomination on the first ballot of the Democratic convention. Knowing that he would need Southern votes to win the election and that the South was the most anti-Catholic area of the country, he chose Lyndon Johnson, a Texas Senator, as his running mate.

Early in the campaign, the old 1928 rumors were circulating about direct phone lines to the Vatican, should a Catholic be elected President. Kennedy again decided to meet the Catholicism issue head on. On September 12, he appeared before the Greater Houston Ministerial Alliance, telling the Protestant ministers, "Whatever issue may come before me as President, if I should be elected—on birth control, divorce, censorship, gambling, or any other subject—I will make my decision . . . in accord with what my conscience tells me to be in the national interest, and without regard to outside religious pressure or dictation, and no power or threat of punishment could cause me to decide otherwise." Kennedy thus declared that his religion took second place in his life, that it had no relationship to his political career, thereby endorsing the view found also in the Supreme Court school prayer decisions: God must be kept separate from the public life.

Nixon ran on a platform of experience, peace and prosperity. Kennedy's slogan was "Get America moving again," calling for more of the liberal social policies and a stronger commitment to anti-Communism. But perhaps the key issue turned out to be Nixon's image on television. For the first time, the two candidates held a series of nationally televised debates. In the four debates, Nixon was unattractive, exhausted, defensive. Kennedy, after some early nervousness, presented an attractive image of vigor, wit and intelligence. The visual media, from that point in time, assumed a dominant role in presidential campaigns which it has not yet relinquished.

On election day, Nixon carried the farm, mountain and border states, the industrial Midwest, and the Pacific coast. Kennedy carried the big cities, the Northeast, and the Old South. He took 70 per cent of the Catholic vote. But the election was extremely close, and into the early hours of November 9 the decision remained in doubt. Illinois votes were the longest coming in and were crucial. If Nixon carried Illinois, several Southern electors were prepared to switch their votes from Kennedy to Nixon, throwing the election into the House of Representatives where the Southern states—fearful of the new tide pushing for equal rights for Blacks—could demand concessions as the price of support. But if Kennedy carried Illinois' then 27 electoral votes, the southern electors would not be able to make a difference. By early morning it appeared that Illinois had given its electoral votes to Kennedy, by a 6000 to 7000 vote majority, attained by a heavy Democratic vote in Chicago. It was later discovered, however, that massive vote fraud had been engineered in Chicago by the Democratic machine of Mayor Richard Daley; the state's electoral votes probably should have gone to Nixon.

Nevertheless, Nixon did not protest or call for a recount, and John F. Kennedy was the nation's first Catholic President. He proclaimed a "New Frontier" and gave a stirring inaugural speech, with the well-remembered line, "Ask not what your country can do for you. Ask what you can do for your country." But the fine rhetoric was not followed by action. Congress blocked Kennedy's legislative program. Conservatives—those who called for less power in the central government and a strongly anti-Communist foreign policy—grew in popularity.

In foreign policy, Kennedy faced many problems: Cuba (which we have already discussed); Berlin, where the Communists built a wall separating the Communist side of the city from the free side to prevent escapes; and the nightmare of the Vietnamese War.

The Vietnam Nightmare

The French had conquered Indochina—the area including Vietnam, Cambodia and Laos in Southeast Asia—late in the 19th century, and missionaries brought Catholicism to many Vietnamese. During the aftermath of World War II, the Communists had pressed forward in Southeast Asia, as throughout the world, starting a revolution in 1946 under the leadership of Ho Chi Minh. The war dragged on, and by 1954 the French were exhausted. After the fall of the fortress of Dienbienphu and the capture of a French army of 10,000, negotiations opened at Geneva, Switzerland. Laos and Cambodia were given independence, and Vietnam was divided into North Vietnam with Ho Chi Minh leading a Communist government and South Vietnam under Ngo Dinh Diem.

Many expected South Vietnam to fall to the Communists within months. The Chief of Staff of the Vietnamese Army boasted openly of planning an anti-Diem coup; Vietminh (Communist) agents were everywhere; the economy was in chaos. But Diem was a man of integrity, insight, courage and deeply Catholic faith. In 1946 he had survived several months of torturous imprisonment by the Vietminh and had refused an offer of a high position in Ho Chi Minh's government. He knew that Vietnam needed a strong national government to unite the country and to give it the will to carry on the fight against the Communists. Diem was firm against all who represented a threat to the unity of Vietnam, thereby making enemies. But by 1959, a million refugees escaping from the Communists had been resettled, the army had been brought under control, and South Vietnam had the highest per capita income in Southeast Asia.

Ho Chi Minh realized that South Vietnam would not fall by itself. He formed the National Liberation Front, which pretended to be a group of South Vietnamese who wanted to be free of Diem's rule, but which was in fact thoroughly Communist. During 1959 and 1960, the Communists concentrated on a war of terror, kidnapping and killing village leaders. In 1961, the Viet Cong (Communist Viet) launched guerrilla warfare and hit and run raids. In February 1962, at Diem's request, an American mission began to train and equip the South Vietnamese army. In 1963, Ho Chi Minh added conventional ground warfare to the terrorism of the preceding years. The Viet Cong were well armed with Russian and Red Chinese weapons.

Nevertheless, the South Vietnamese, who were receiving military aid from the U.S., were holding their own, thanks to the firm and uncompromising stand of Diem, who had once said: "The Communists say that individuals exist for the good of the state. In contrast, we hold that the state exists for the good of the individual, whose welfare and liberty must be protected." Faced with this spirit, the Communists knew that they must destroy Diem.

Communist agents infiltrated Buddhist pagodas throughout South Vietnam to stir up hostility toward the Catholic Diem. Though Diem's regime had never oppressed other religions, Communist agents convinced Buddhists that the Catholics meant to persecute them. These Buddhists, led by the pro-Communist Thich Tri Quang, made up a list of supposed grievances against the government. When Diem offered to work with an international commission to investigate the grievances, Tri Quang quickly rejected the offer. He did not want an investigation because the grievances were false.

The command post for Buddhist subversion was the Xa Loi Pagoda in South Vietnam's capital city Saigon. In the summer of 1963 the pagoda looked less like a place for prayer and meditation than a political campaign headquarters, with mimeograph machines, ringing telephones and daily press conferences. Tri Quang would stop at nothing. Beginning the spring of 1963, a number of Buddhists burned themselves to death in public places. Before dying they would proclaim that they were protesting Diem's religious persecution. Immediately afterwards, Xa Loi would have press releases ready. Within 24 hours Americans would see pictures of the tragic suicides and read stories blaming Diem for the deaths. Yet the suicides were instigated by Tri Quang, who had a special Suicide Promotion Group. Buddhists would be persuaded that persecution existed and that the only way to stop it was to die. They would be told that they would receive a heavenly reward for their deaths and be provided with cans of gasoline and pills to reduce the pain (in fact the pills were fakes, since Tri Quang did not want any traces of drugs to be found in their bodies). None of these details appeared in the newspapers; Americans were convinced that Diem's regime was tyrannical, since people were willing to die in protest of it.

Liberals in America took up the anti-Diem outcry. Their main theme was that Diem's regime was not democratically elected. Americans, conditioned to believe that democracy is the only correct, legitimate form of government, turned against Diem. But the last thing Vietnam needed was elections. A war raged in the countryside, and the Vietnamese had always had a society built on discipline and respect for authority, not elections.

On August 21, Diem's government raided Xa Loi and other pagodas which had been used for Communist subversion. The raids had the support of the people and of Buddhists who simply wanted to practice their religion. But on August 24 the anti-Diem faction in the U.S. government met in Washington. They drafted a cable to the new ambassador in Vietnam, Henry Cabot Lodge, telling him that if Diem did not release the Buddhist rebels and end press censorship (neither of which he dared to do for the safety of his country), the U.S. should encourage South Vietnamese generals to overthrow Diem.

At first the generals were reluctant, fearing the consequences of a revolt, but U.S. threats to cut off all aid finally persuaded them. On November 1, 1963, the generals began shelling the presidential palace in Saigon. Diem telephoned Lodge and asked what was the U.S. policy toward this attempted overthrow of Vietnam's rightful government. Lodge said only, "I'd like to get you safely out of the country," indicating that he supported Diem's ouster. Then Lodge asked, "What will you do?" Diem replied: "I shall do what duty and good sense dictate. I shall attempt to restore order." The Third Corps of the Vietnamese Army, which should have come to Diem's aid, went over to the plotters. At 8:00 p.m. Diem and his brother Nhu took refuge at the home of a friend. After a night of fruitless telephone calls, the brothers decided to go to 8:00 a.m. Mass at a next-door church, then call military headquarters to surrender, having previously been offered safe conduct to a place of exile of their own choosing.

The next morning, All Souls Day, they were standing on the church steps when a convoy rolled up. They were put into the back of an armored personnel carrier, and the convoy returned to the headquarters of General Minh, leader of the coup. When the convoy arrived and the carrier was opened, the bodies of Diem and Nhu were found. Diem had been shot in the back of the head, Nhu stabbed in the chest and shot many times in the back of the head and the back. Both men had their hands tied behind their backs.

Diem had once said, "If they overthrow me, whoever comes after will have to be far more of a dictator than I." He was right. Martial law was invoked more often in the two years after Diem's death than in the entire nine years of his rule. The Viet Cong mounted new raids. The plotters fought among themselves and jailed the most talented men in the Vietnamese government simply because they had once supported Diem. The Buddhist radicals continued their anti-government agitation, becoming openly pro-Communist and anti-American. Viet Cong successes increased. The country Diem loved and died to save slipped slowly into the grip of the Communists.

Lyndon Johnson in the White House

John Kennedy did not have to face these consequences of his role in Diem's overthrow. Less than a month after Diem's murder, on November 22, 1963, President Kennedy was assassinated in Dallas, Texas. A pro-Communist named Lee Harvey Oswald was arrested but never brought to trial because he himself was murdered by Dallas night club owner Jack Ruby. Overwhelming evidence pointed toward Oswald's guilt, but rumors persisted that others had been involved in the plot. Oswald's murder and Ruby's death January 3, 1967 made it unlikely that the full story would ever be uncovered.

In the aftermath of the assassination, Americans indulged in an orgy of grief, glorifying Kennedy, his family and everything he had done. For a while, they even transferred their affection to his successor, Lyndon Johnson, who had never been particularly popular outside Texas.

Since Kennedy was a Liberal, and since Dallas was a conservative city, conservatives were seen as somehow to blame for the President's death, even though Oswald was a Communist sympathizer. Conservative Arizona Senator Barry Goldwater was able to capture the Republican nomination in 1964, but he and the rising conservative movement in America were buried in the landslide Johnson victory in the presidential election of that year. Nationwide support for Johnson continued through 1966, as a liberal Congress enacted his **"Great Society"** program, the greatest wave of social welfare legislation since the New Deal.

Part of the Great Society was aid for medical expenses. Medicare (which went into effect July 1, 1966) and Medicaid provided federal money to help the elderly and the poor pay medical bills. But the result was not always better and less expensive medical care. Previously, doctors had often reduced their rates for poor patients, and church-operated or charity hospitals had been available. Now, many doctors and hospitals simply increased their bills, collecting from both the government and the patient. Rates rose steadily because doctors and hospitals were sure the government would pay, with the citizen who was neither poor nor rich being hit hardest.

Johnson's aid-to-education program put the federal government into the business of financing local schools, previously the sole responsibility of local communities and states. Many educators became more interested in obtaining money than in providing a service. As more money poured into the schools, the quality of education declined because of too much concern with externals—buildings, equipment, audio-visual aids—and not enough with the transmitting of truth and the formation of character.

Johnson also declared a **"War on Poverty,"** and called for massive federal education, job training, and employment programs which would supposedly wipe out poverty. Some of the programs were useful, but most were not and in general encouraged the poor to expect instant solutions to all their problems.

The final major element of the Great Society was civil rights legislation, designed to end the discrimination against Blacks which had existed since Reconstruction, even in the North. **The Civil Rights Movement** began during the Kennedy administration under the leadership of Martin Luther King, Jr., a Baptist minister. King stressed non-violence, peaceful sit-ins at segregated establishments, passive resistance and moral pressure. Others in the movement, however, encouraged violence and rioting, though King never approved of violent tactics. Civil rights laws passed included the prohibiting of discrimination in public accommodations such as restaurants and hotels, in the selling of one's house, in hiring and in voting rights.

Though the Civil Rights Movement contained many immoral aspects, as we shall see, on balance the movement resulted in an end to much discrimination against Blacks in our society. Though personal prejudice is a matter of the individual will and cannot be affected by legislation, at least Blacks were allowed a better chance to achieve a full role in society and to escape the stigma of being second-class citizens.

In foreign policy the U.S. became more deeply involved in Vietnam. Having removed from power the one man who could have helped South Vietnam to save itself, the U.S. was faced with a choice of committing ground troops to the war or of watching South Vietnam be overrun. In 1965, Johnson, supported by Congress with the **Tonkin Gulf Resolution**, made the choice of trying to save South Vietnam and on March 2 began large scale bombing of North Vietnam. On March 8, two battalions of Marines were sent to guard Da Nang, though they were not supposed to engage in combat with Communist forces, and finally on June 27 the first American combat troops arrived in Vietnam.

American soldiers found themselves fighting against an enemy they could never really pin down, and in a war with no front lines. The bombing was unsuccessful, especially since it was not accompanied by a blockade of Haiphong harbor, through which North Vietnam imported most of its war material. In addition, U.S. trade with Soviet Russia increased at the same time as the Russian Communists were supplying North Vietnam with 80 per cent of its armaments and military supplies. The U.S., frustrated in its attempt to win the War, gradually stepped up its troop commitments, until eventually there were over half a million Americans fighting in Vietnam.

America and the Second Vatican Council

The Second Vatican Council, called by Pope John XXIII, was in session from October 1962 until December 1965. Though the Council documents were orthodox, many passages could be seen as ambiguous, and Liberals in the Church misinterpreted or ignored the documents in the name of "**The Spirit of Vatican II**," which they took as a license to spread their Liberal ideas. This subversion of Vatican II was most apparent in Western Europe and in the United States.

Sadly, the Church in America did not use the opportunity presented by Vatican II to strengthen itself to meet the challenge of secularism, relativism and materialism in America. Instead, far too many Catholics and Catholic leaders succumbed to these temptations themselves.

The results have been tragic. There has been a serious decline in religious and priestly vocations. Almost all the Catholic colleges and universities, founded in the days when the Church was under siege, have become dominated by Liberals, who deny doctrinal and moral absolutes and the authority of the Pope. The feminist movement in the Church demands ordination of women, in spite of Pope John Paul II's definitive statement that the "Church has no power whatsoever to confer priestly ordination on women." Liberation theologians encourage cooperation with Marxists, ostensibly to aid the poor, but in fact to advance the cause of socialism and revolution. Catholics get divorced and remarried at almost the same rate as non-Catholics, often with the approval of Liberal diocesan tribunals (Church courts) which grant marriage annulments for almost any reason. The Americanist heresy has resurfaced with American Church leaders claiming that the Church must adapt its doctrinal and moral teachings to meet America's needs.

The disunity in the Catholic Church in America was most clearly illustrated in the reaction to the encyclical *Humanae Vitae*, issued by

Pope Paul VI on July 29, 1968. The encyclical declared that artificial contraception was intrinsically immoral and that the Church was not going to—and was not able to—change this teaching. Many Americans had convinced themselves that the Church would change its teaching after Pope John XXIII appointed a commission to study the matter, and they had begun using contraceptives. But though the majority of the commission's members approved of artificial contraception, commissions are not infallible. Only the Pope is infallible, and Pope Paul VI knew that he must speak out in order to make the moral issues clear. In a beautiful teaching on the true nature of marriage and conjugal love, he declared that "each and every marital act must remain open to the transmission of life."

Liberal Church leaders in America, led by Father Charles Curran of Catholic University, had seen advance copies of the encyclical. As soon as the document was made public, they issued a statement rejecting the teaching and declaring that each person must make up his own mind on contraception. The encyclical was rejected and even ridiculed by many Liberal intellectuals, as well as by many rank-and-file Catholics. American Catholics used contraceptives in about the same percentages as non-Catholics, and far too often their priests told them that no sin was involved. While few bishops spoke out openly against *Humanae Vitae*, they often allowed their subordinates to do so and did not take the decisive disciplinary action needed to restore doctrinal and moral orthodoxy to the Catholic Church in America.

1968: Year of Revolution

In 1968 the United States came close to revolution. A combination of forces led large numbers of people to hate their government and their country and to take steps that could have led to its destruction.

The first factor was that the long years of moral relativism in higher education finally bore their unwholesome fruit. For years, many professors had been teaching that absolutes did not exist, that all was relative. From there it was a short step to telling the students that anything they really wanted to do was all right for them to do. And from there it was an exceedingly short step for the students to take their teachers at their word. In addition, America's growing affluence and admiration for higher education had led to there being more young people on college and university campuses than ever before. Many of them were not really qualified for a college education and many others did not really want one. These students were ripe for agitation.

A second factor was the Vietnam War. The United States had no clear purpose in fighting the War and therefore could not convince many American people that the War was worth fighting. Since the military draft was still in effect, many young men hated the War simply because they might get drafted to fight in it and be killed or crippled. As the War stretched on and on with no end in sight, many Americans felt that they must do whatever was necessary to bring the War to an end. Though not numerous, Communist agitators helped stir up hostility to the War, finding a ready and willing audience.

A third factor was that the Civil Rights Movement and civil rights legislation had led many Blacks to expect an immediate end to discrimination. Their frustration with segregation, whether imposed by law or simply by desire, was encouraged by revolutionaries who wanted to destroy the American system of government. They were also encouraged, in many cases, by their own greed. These factors combined to bring about Black riots.

A fourth factor was the expectations that were stirred up by Great Society promises of a War on Poverty. Poverty can never disappear entirely, and even amelioration takes time. Again, revolutionaries were fed on frustrations and unrealistic expectations in order to encourage violence.

A final factor was the mass media. The media in the United States was dominated by Liberals. They fostered each of the preceding factors by espousing moral relativism, hostility to the Vietnam War, and hatred for the American system of government, which was unforgiveably guilty, they claimed, of racial prejudice and oppression of the poor.

Revolutionary violence did not begin in 1968. In 1966 there were serious Black riots in the Watts area of Los Angeles and in 1967 equally serious ones in Detroit, along with other city riots during those two summers. Anti-war demonstrations had been mounting, including a march of 35,000 people on the Pentagon on October 21-22, 1967. Campus violence had been on the increase, especially on the sprawling campuses of the University of California. But 1968 saw the violence reach its peak, as the President of the United States virtually abdicated his authority to restore and insure order, and there was no one else to exercise it for him.

On January 31, 1968 the Communists launched a major offensive during the Vietnamese holiday known as Tet. Every major South Vietnamese city and town came under attack. The only city where the Communists made major gains was Hue, but even there the offensive was stopped and the Communists driven out, though not before they had murdered hundreds of people.

At the same time as the Tet offensive, the siege of Khe Sanh was underway. U.S. Marines held a base at Khe Sanh. The Communists launched a major attack on the base on January 21 and kept it up for 77 days. On March 31, the Communists lifted the siege, and the U.S. then abandoned the base.

In both the Tet Offensive and the battle for Khe Sanh, U.S. forces had been victorious, but the average American would never have known it from the press and television reports. The Liberal media presented only the dark side of the War, especially emphasizing American casualties. Nightly television reports from Khe Sanh brought the War right into American living rooms and made it appear as if America was losing. For the first time the Gallup public opinion poll showed that the majority of the American people disapproved of the War. Another poll revealed that 65 per cent of the American people regarded Tet as a defeat for U.S. objectives. Demonstrators burned draft cards and U.S. flags and chanted, "Hey, hey, L.B.J., How many boys did you kill today?"

1968 was an election year, and everyone expected Johnson to seek re-election. But Minnesota Senator Eugene McCarthy announced his candidacy as a peace candidate in opposition to Johnson. On March 12, Senator McCarthy came within 300 votes of Johnson in the New Hampshire primary; on March 16 Senator Robert Kennedy, brother of President John F. Kennedy, announced his candidacy against Johnson; on March 19, 139 members of the House of Representatives passed a resolution calling for an immediate review of U.S. war policy.

Faced with the mounting opposition to his war policy, Johnson consulted a number of foreign policy advisers. Almost all of them urged him to get out of the War. So Johnson scheduled a nationwide address for March 31. He announced that he would freeze troop levels, limit the air war and seek negotiations. Then came the bombshell conclusion: "I shall not seek, and I will not accept the nomination of my party for another term as your President." The War was lost, though Vietnam would be a longer time dying.

On April 4, civil rights leader Martin Luther King was killed by a sniper in Memphis, Tennessee. The assassination served as the excuse for a wave of violence throughout the U.S. As buildings burned and rioting spread in Washington, D.C., President Johnson could do nothing more than ring the White House with troops and let the rioters have their way with the rest of the city. At least 46 persons were killed, 2,600 were injured, and 21,000 arrested, with property damage estimated at more than $45,000,000.

That same month, the biggest campus riot of all occurred, at Columbia University in New York, beginning on April 23 with a demonstration to protest construction of a gym in neighboring Morningside Park (opposed by Negroes in nearby Harlem), as well as the school's association with the government's Institute of Defense Analysis. After the demonstration, led by Mark Rudd, president of Columbia's Students for a Democratic Society (S.D.S.), probably the most revolutionary of all campus groups, the students occupied the administration building and held three officials hostage for 24 hours. Later they ransacked the office of the university's president and demanded complete amnesty. By April 26, they had taken over five buildings, classes were canceled, and the university was under the control of the rioters. On April 26, the administration suspended work on the gym. Finally, on April 30, city police forcibly removed the protesters, arresting 707 persons.

On May 3, students seized the business offices of Northwestern University in Evanston, Illinois and forced the administration to capitulate to their demands. Major student riots also occurred during May at Stanford, Cornell, Duke, Princeton, the University of Chicago, Ohio State, Southern Illinois, the University of Oregon and elsewhere.

Also in May, a so-called "March of the Poor" was held in Washington, led by Ralph Abernathy, Martin Luther King's successor as head of the Southern Christian Leadership Conference. After the march, some 3000 people camped in West Potomac Park to continue their protest.

On June 5, at a party celebrating his victory in the California primary, Senator Robert Kennedy was killed by a Jordanian Arab, Sirhan Sirhan. This left the two major Democratic candidates to be McCarthy, who was running on a strong anti-war platform, and Johnson's Vice President, Hubert Humphrey. The Democratic Party split between the old line Liberals led by Humphrey and the radicals, supported by the students and the press and led by McCarthy.

On July 23 and 24, major riots took place in Cleveland, including a four-hour gun battle between Black extremists and police, followed by massive rioting that left 23 wounded and $1.5 million in property damage.

In August, the Republicans nominated Richard Nixon at a heavily guarded convention in Miami Beach. Nixon had lost the election for Governor of California in 1962. After this humiliation, he had built a strong and skilled campaign organization and raised hundreds of thousands of dollars. Then the Democrats held their nominating convention in August. The convention soon degenerated into chaos, with violence in the streets sparked by 10,000 young, wild anti-war protesters and pandemonium on the floor. Hubert Humphrey was finally nominated, but his party was deeply divided. The election was close, but the split in the Democratic Party gave Nixon the win.

Former Alabama Governor George Wallace ran as a candidate for a third party, the American Party. Wallace had supported segregation in Alabama and some of his supporters were doubtless racist. But he was also supported by those who wanted less government interference in their lives and who opposed the Liberal policies of the Johnson administration. Wallace won 13.5 percent of the popular vote, carrying five southern states with 46 electoral votes.

Richard Nixon in the White House

Nixon knew that the continuation of the Vietnam War would destroy him politically, as it had destroyed Johnson. He sought to stabilize the military situation and began peace talks. Nixon's other main foreign policy goal was to achieve friendly relations with the Soviet Union and Red China—a policy known as **detente**. Nixon had once been anti-Communist; but now anti-Communism was ceasing to be a popular position.

And Nixon was determined to be popular. In the 1972 elections, he made it clear to his supporters that he wanted the biggest landslide possible. The Committee to Re-elect the President (CREEP) raised $52 million to finance the campaign. Nixon told his supporters to do anything necessary to ensure a landslide re-election, and several of them took him at his word. G. Gordon Liddy and E. Howard Hunt decided to wiretap the Democratic National Committee Headquarters in the Watergate Hotel in Washington. Besides being illegal, the action was unnecessary, since Nixon's re-election was assured anyway, his Democratic opponent, George McGovern, being far too radical to attract much support. The men hired to break into the headquarters were caught on June 17, but no involvement of anyone close to Nixon was known at that time.

George Wallace campaigned for the Democratic nomination. He ran well in the primaries, with a victory in Florida and strong showings in Wisconsin, Pennsylvania and Indiana. His vote totals showed that many Democrats did not support the liberal candidates. But in May, while campaigning in Maryland, he was shot by Arthur Bremer. He was paralyzed from the waist down and had to withdraw from the campaign. (Even after the shooting, he won the Maryland primary handily.)

Nixon went on to win the election with 67 per cent of the vote, the largest majority in the history of the nation. The 1972 election had a third party candidate, American Party nominee John G. Schmitz, a California Congressman, a Catholic and a former Marine, who offered the American people a thoroughly moral platform stressing the principle of subsidiarity in government and firm, dedicated anti-Communism. One million Americans voted for him. The total would have been higher, except that the newspapers and television ignored his candidacy, and the Nixon forces persuaded many pro-Schmitz people that if they voted for Schmitz, McGovern might win (though he had no chance whatever). Nevertheless, at least some of the American people had a chance to hear that the only solutions to America's problems were Christian solutions.

Nixon had won by the greatest majority in history. His popularity increased when a peace agreement was concluded for Vietnam in January, 1973, even though the agreement allowed the Communist forces to remain in South Vietnam. Then the roof fell in. By mid-1973 it was known that Attorney General Mitchell and Legal Counsel to the President John Dean had known in advance and approved of the Watergate break-in. The U.S. Senate set up the Select Committee on Presidential Campaign Activities to investigate the crime. In March 1974, Mitchell and top Nixon aides Robert Haldeman and John Ehrlichman were indicted by grand juries for conspiring to cover up the Watergate burglary.

During the investigations, it became known that Nixon had taped conversations in his office. On April 16, the committee subpoenaed the tapes relating to the Watergate break-in. Nixon refused to release the tapes, but on April 30 released edited transcripts. On May 9 the House of Representatives opened impeachment hearings. On May 24, Special Prosecutor Leon Jaworski appealed to the Supreme Court for access to 64 key tapes, and on July 24 the Court unanimously ordered Nixon to release the tapes. Finally, on August 5 Nixon released the full transcripts, which showed that he had given orders to the FBI to halt any inquiry into the Watergate break-in, thereby making the President an accessory to the crime. On August 9, Nixon became the first President to resign. He was succeeded by his Vice President, Gerald Ford, who had been appointed after the elected Vice President, Spiro Agnew, had been forced to resign because of having accepted bribes when still governor of Maryland.

The Liberal newspapers said that democracy had triumphed in America because the lawbreaker Nixon was out of office. But it was clear to any thinking person that it was precisely American democracy which had failed, as America was governed by a man who had not been elected to the presidency or vice presidency, after the man who had been elected by the greatest majority in history was found to be a criminal.

Roe v. Wade

On January 22, 1973 occurred the most important domestic event of the Nixon administration, more important by far than Watergate or anything else relating to Nixon, except the ending of our resistance to Communism in Vietnam. On that day the United States Supreme Court issued the most far-reaching decision in its history, condemning millions of unborn babies to death, as it declared all laws prohibiting abortion to be unconstitutional.

The push for legal abortion was the result of the sexual revolution and accompanying moral decline of the late 1960's and of the feminist or Women's Liberation Movement. The anti-life movement made its first drive to legalize abortion in state legislatures. Colorado, in 1966, was the first state to legalize abortion. California, the nation's most populous state was next. There, the bill was approved in the Senate Judiciary Committee by only one vote, the vote of a Catholic state senator from San Francisco, who was the only Catholic in either house of the legislature to vote for the bill. The bill still would not have passed without the support of Governor Ronald Reagan. Reagan insisted that the bill's sponsors remove the provision allowing abortion in the case of a deformed child, but did not object to the provision which allowed abortion for the sake of the mother's "mental health." Reagan was warned that this opened the door to abortion on demand, since almost anything could be said to be damaging to a woman's "mental health," but Reagan did not listen. He signed the bill. Later, after it became obvious that the bill did permit abortion on demand, he had the courage to admit his mistake and to apologize. He became a pro-life advocate, and continued to support the pro-life position even after he became President.

In spite of the anti-life success in California, pro-lifers were winning more legislative battles than they were losing. The anti-lifers therefore turned to the courts, realizing that they had a far better chance to succeed with Liberal, activist courts than with state legislatures which were responsive to the will of the people, the majority of whom at this time still opposed unrestricted abortion.

Anti-life groups sponsored a suit by a pregnant single woman in Texas, known in the case as "Roe," challenging the constitutionality of Texas' criminal abortion statute, which prohibited abortion unless necessary to save the life of the mother, as did most state abortion laws at this time. A three-judge federal district court declared the statute void and the state of Texas appealed to the U.S. Supreme Court. The nine judges who heard the case were Chief Justice Warren Burger, Harry Blackmun, Lewis Powell, and William Rehnquist, all Nixon appointees; Thurgood Marshall, the first black Supreme Court Justice, appointed by Johnson; Byron White, appointed by Kennedy; Eisenhower appointees Potter Stewart and William Brennan (the Court's only Catholic); and William O. Douglas, who had been appointed by President Roosevelt in 1939. Douglas was the most liberal member, and it was assumed beforehand that he would want the most sweeping pro-abortion decision possible; Marshall and Brennan were also known Liberals. But the other justices were regarded as moderate to conservative and unlikely to give the anti-lifers everything they wanted. Some pro-life groups were even predicting a pro-life decision, or at worst a "states-rights" decision, which would continue to allow each state to pass its own laws, restrictive or non-restrictive as the legislators chose.

But none of the predictions came true. The Court voted 7-2 to legalize abortion on demand, right up to the moment of birth.

All of the justices, except Rehnquist and White, endorsed the decision written by Justice Blackmun. The decision made three main points. First, anti-abortion laws violate the due process clause of the Fourteenth Amendment, which states that no one may be deprived of life, liberty or property without due process of law. Though that would seem to protect the right to life of the unborn child, the Court declared that "freedom of personal choice in matters of marriage and family life is one of the liberties protected by the due process clause of the Fourteenth Amendment."

Next, the Court proclaimed a right to privacy which was violated by anti-abortion laws. Though Blackmun admitted that the "Constitution does not explicitly mention any right of privacy," he stated that it was implied in the First Amendment (freedom of religion), Fourth and Fifth Amendments (freedom from illegal searches and seizures), Ninth Amendment (the enumeration of specific rights in the Constitution does not preclude the existence of other rights), in "the concept of liberty guaranteed by the first section of the Fourteenth Amendment" and in the "penumbras" of the Bill of Rights. This right, he said, "is broad enough to encompass a woman's decision whether or not to terminate her pregnancy."

Finally, the Court denied that the unborn child was a person who had rights that the Constitution protected. Blackmun stated that the text of the Constitution does not define the unborn as persons; and since American anti-abortion laws were once less restrictive than later, and since the courts have not before clearly upheld Fourteenth Amendment rights for the unborn, he concluded, therefore, that the unborn did not have any such rights. He added that there is too much disagreement on when life begins to say that it begins at conception. While he presented feminist arguments for why a woman would want to terminate a pregnancy, he presented no arguments at all that the unborn child is a living human person.

He concluded by stating that during the first trimester (three months) of pregnancy, there can be no legal restrictions whatsoever on abortion. During the second trimester, the state may pass laws to safeguard maternal health (such as requiring abortions to be performed by a licensed physician), but not to limit the right to an abortion. In the last trimester, in view of the existence of "potential" life, the state "may go so far as to proscribe abortion during that period except when it is necessary to preserve the life or health of the mother." Though this last might sound like a restriction, it is not. The word health can be and has been interpreted to mean mental as well as physical health. Therefore, all a woman needs to do is say that her pregnancy is mentally distressing and she can get an abortion. In effect, the decision legalizes abortion on demand right up to the moment of birth.

Various states and cities attempted to provide some regulation of abortion, as for example by requiring parental notification before a minor can have an abortion, or requiring the father's permission, or requiring the woman to receive information on the harmful effects of abortion. A few restrictions were let stand in the *Webster* (1990) and *Casey* (1992) cases, but the Court still upheld a woman's "Constitutional right" to abortion.

Attempts by pro-lifers to have Congress pass a Constitutional amendment protecting the right to life also failed. There nevertheless remains an active Pro-Life Movement in the United States, engaged in education, lobbying, and sidewalk counseling and other activities to persuade women planning abortion to consider other alternatives.

In the meantime, the death toll from abortion reached a million and a half babies a year in the United States by the mid-1980's.

The Fall of Vietnam

The truce agreement signed by the United States and North Vietnam in January 1973 had allowed 150,000 North Vietnamese troops to remain in the South. But the Communists waited until January 1975 to launch their final offensive. They began with a test thrust from Cambodia into South Vietnam. When the U.S. did nothing more than issue a protest at the treaty violation, the Communists launched their major offensive on March 10. The South Vietnamese fought well but were hopelessly outnumbered. On April 10, with Saigon itself under attack, President Ford asked Congress to appropriate a billion dollars of aid to the South Vietnamese. Congress responded by authorizing $200 million for the purpose of evacuating U.S. personnel from the doomed country. The only question that remained was whether the U.S. would also help evacuate those South Vietnamese who had worked for and with them over the past 20 years, or would they be abandoned to a tragic fate in a Communist-ruled country.

On April 17, the U.S. Ambassador in Saigon received a cablegram from Secretary of State Henry Kissinger telling him not to assist the evacuation of any South Vietnamese, but instead to evacuate Americans as quickly as could be done without creating "panic." When Admiral Noel Gayler, commander-in-chief of U.S. naval forces in the Pacific, suggested to Ambassador Grew that his ships be used to help evacuate Americans and South Vietnamese, Grew refused on the grounds that the use of ships would create panic.

By April 28, 18 Communist divisions ringed Saigon, and the Communist high command was preparing its final assault for the next day. On the same day, Ambassador Grew ordered four cargo ships at the

Saigon docks to sail empty for the open sea. Also that same day, the embassy staff debated whether to cut down the tamarind tree in the parking lot of the embassy to make landing space for evacuation helicopters. The ambassador vetoed cutting down the tree, because it might create panic. The Communists launched an air strike on Tan Son Nhut, the only remaining airfield. General Homer Smith sent out a party of Marines to cut down the tamarind tree so that helicopters could land. Ambassador Grew made them stop.

At 4:00 a.m. on April 29, the Communists launched a rocket attack on Tan Son Nhut. The airfield was put out of commission for anything but helicopters. At 10:51 a.m., Ambassador Grew finally allowed a helicopter evacuation of the embassy. At noon, the tamarind tree was cut down. At 3:00 p.m. Ambassador Grew took a car and some Marine guards to his house to pick up his poodle, Nit Noy, who was safely rescued. Meanwhile, thousands of South Vietnamese crowded around the embassy, begging for escape. The Marine guards were ordered to charge the crowd and fire if necessary to keep them out, because they would have overrun the embassy.

Even so, some South Vietnamese were saved before the evacuation was ended by direct personal order from President Ford at 5:24 a.m. on April 30. At most, 60,000 were rescued, less than one-third of those who needed to escape and had a claim on America's help. Last out of the embassy was the commander of the Marine guard and 10 of his men. Below their helicopter as it rose, desperate Vietnamese leaped in vain, trying to catch its departing wheels.

The Communists occupied Saigon and renamed it Ho Chi Minh City. They murdered or sent to prison camps all those who had been associated with America during its involvement in Vietnam.

President Carter and the Hostage Crisis

The Republicans nominated President Ford for re-election in 1976, and the Democrats nominated a man who had been virtually unknown before the campaign began, former Georgia governor Jimmy Carter. Carter won because he seemed to offer an image of integrity and incorruptibility after the scandals of the Watergate era. Though Ford himself had nothing whatever to do with Watergate, he had identified himself with it when he had granted Nixon a full pardon of any crimes he might have committed.

In April 1978, the U.S. Senate ratified a treaty which would turn over the Panama Canal Zone to Panama at the end of 1999. During the heated debate, opponents of the treaty argued that this strategic waterway should not be turned over to a country whose government had often been unstable and even anti-American.

On January 1, 1979, the United States granted full diplomatic recognition to the People's Republic of China and terminated its recognition of the Nationalist Chinese government on Taiwan as the official government of China. The groundwork for this action had been laid by Richard Nixon, and his work reached fruition with the official acceptance of the Chinese Communists as the legal government of the billion people they had subjugated.

In June of 1979, the Communist Sandinista government gained control of Nicaragua, and that same month Carter and Soviet leader Leonid Brezhnev signed the Strategic Arms Limitation Treaty (SALT I). Carter agreed to the treaty because he was erroneously convinced that the Soviet Union would take action to end various human rights violations. At the end of 1979 the Soviet Union invaded Afghanistan to keep a Communist government in power. Carter took several actions in response: a cutoff of sales of high technology equipment to the Soviet Union, a limitation of their fishing privileges in U.S. waters, an embargo on grain sales to the Soviet Union, a deferral of cultural and educational exchanges and a boycott of the 1980 summer Olympic Games to be held in Moscow. These actions made no difference whatsoever. Only the courageous resistance by the Afghan freedom fighters prevented the Soviets from solidifying their control of the country.

But the most embarrassing episode of the Carter administration was the Iranian hostage crisis. On November 3, 1979, 90 people including 63 Americans were taken hostage at the American embassy in Teheran by militant students who demanded the return for trial of the overthrown Shah of Iran, who was at that time undergoing medical treatment for cancer in New York City. Carter's first response was to suspend all Iranian oil imports to the U.S. and to freeze all Iranian assets in this country. The terrorists freed all women, Blacks, and non-Americans, but 53 American men remained in captivity. Carter sent a personal note to the Ayatollah Kohmeni, who held dictatorial power in Iran, but the Ayatollah refused to read it. On November 10, Carter warned that he might take military action, but nothing came of the threat. On December 15 the Shah went to Panama, but the militants still demanded his return to Iran. The U.S. appealed to the United Nations, which sent an investigatory commission in February 1980. The commission accomplished nothing, and on April 7 Carter severed diplomatic relations with Iran.

Then on April 24, the U.S. made a dramatic attempt to rescue the hostages. At a secret landing strip in Iran, code-named Desert One, three of the eight helicopters involved in the rescue, for various reasons, were unable to complete the mission. The commander on the scene made the decision to cancel. As the evacuation got under way, a helicopter sliced into a plane. Both craft burst into flames and eight men died. In view of the enormous amounts of money, men and resources available to the U.S., it was hard to understand why the mission ended so ignominiously.

The Shah died on July 27, but there was little movement on the hostage crisis until after the November election, in which Republican candidate Ronald Reagan overwhelmed Carter, carrying 43 states. In November, the Iranian government began serious negotiations to gain concessions in return for releasing the hostages. The main issue was the return of Iranian assets to the country. The Iranians demanded $30 billion at the beginning of the negotiations, but agreed finally on $8 billion. The hostages came home on January 20, after 444 days in captivity.

Reagan, Bush, Clinton

Carter also went home on January 20, and Ronald Reagan was President. Reagan had run on a conservative platform. He was an excellent speaker and helped give Americans confidence in themselves and their country, in contrast to the negativism and defeatism that had plagued the United States since the late sixties.

In foreign policy, the main thrust of his administration was to weaken the Soviet Union. Assisted by Central Intelligence Agency Director William Casey, this policy first involved support of the anti-Communist freedom fighters throughout the world. Though this policy often faced opposition from Congress and from the State Department, which was still dominated by Liberals, the "Reagan Doctrine," as it was called, provided valuable assistance to the freedom fighters. Aid to Afghanistan helped the freedom fighters there hold their own against the mighty Soviet army; aid to Angola was resumed in 1985, so that freedom fighters there were able to stop every Communist offensive; and assistance was given to Nicaragua, though a scandal involving illegal sales of weapons to Iran for the purpose of raising money for the **Contras** (patriotic Nicaraguan resistance fighters) weakened the effort to help them.

The second aspect of the Reagan-Casey policy was to undermine the Soviet Union economically. The Soviet economy depended on its exports of oil and gas. Reagan administration pressure encouraged Western European countries to reject trade with the Soviets, making it impossible for the U.S.S.R. to obtain the necessary equipment to build a new natural gas pipeline to Western Europe. The Reagan administration also persuaded Saudi Arabia to quadruple its oil production and drop the price of oil, so that the Soviet Union could not compete. It is estimated that this policy cost the Kremlin $10 billion.

These policies played a role in helping to economically weaken the Communist system, which finally fell in the Soviet Union in 1991, at least in its external structures. But Communists still retain positions of power in the former Soviet Union.

Little progress was made on the pro-life front, in spite of the anti-abortion stand of Reagan and his successor George Bush. Pro-lifers turned to more militant tactics such as abortion mill sit-ins, as well as emphasizing sidewalk counseling in front of abortuaries to persuade girls not to have abortions. The general moral decline of America continued.

Bush was defeated in 1992 by radical liberal Democrat William Clinton, former governor of Arkansas. Clinton's first official actions as President were to sign executive orders assisting the abortion industry. On January 22, 1993, he authorized the following anti-life policies: abortions in military hospitals, fetal experimentation, investigations leading to the approval of RU-486 (a chemical abortifacient), the use of tax dollars to fund abortions and provision of contraceptives overseas (overturning the "Mexico City Policy" of the Reagan administration), and permission for federally funded clinics to provide counseling on abortion. The day chosen for these actions—January 22—was the anniversary of the *Roe v. Wade* decision legalizing abortion, when thousands of pro-lifers were in Washington to participate in the annual March for Life. In 1996 Clinton vetoed a bill to ban partial-birth abortions (whereby a child is delivered except for his head, killed, and then completely delivered). This bill had bi-partisan support in Congress. The Pope's personal spokesman, Joaquin Navarro, said that the veto "amounts to an incredibly brutal act of aggression against innocent human life and the inalienable rights of the unborn." Never before had America been governed by a man so openly opposed to Catholic moral principles and even to the principles of natural law.

America and the Future

The widespread acceptance of contraception and abortion is leading inevitably to an acceptance of assisted suicide and euthanasia. These last two evils will become more widely accepted as the population ages. For example, fewer wage earners will be paying into the social security system which will then have fewer resources with which to support the elderly. Without sound moral principles to guide them, the younger generation will see euthanasia as the logical solution to the nation's problems.

America desperately needs spiritual renewal. Her future will depend on whether and to what extent this renewal takes place. And that will depend largely on America's Catholics, members of the Church Christ founded, partakers of His Body and Blood, who thus alone possess the spiritual resources to lead a Christian rebirth in America.

An exhortation to spiritual renewal was the message delivered to Americans by Pope John Paul II in his visits to the United States in 1979, 1987, 1993 and 1995. During the first visit, he defended the infinite value of every human person in an address to the United Nations. On all four visits he told the U.S. bishops to teach absolute moral values and to reject any compromise with the modern world. He told priests that their vocation was a permanent commitment to Christ, that having once received the grace from God to say "Yes," they must not then say "No." He told religious women to imitate the obedience and humility of Mary in service to the people of God. In the final Mass of his 1979 visit, held on the Mall in Washington, D.C., the Holy Father issued a ringing defense of the right to life of every human person from the moment of conception, proclaiming that each person is unique and irreplaceable; of the indissolubility of marriage, where two truly become one flesh; and of the inviolate union of life and love in marriage, pointing out to parents that instead of giving their children material goods, they should give them brothers and sisters. Everywhere the Pope went, he was met by cheering crowds who were captivated by the love that radiated from his every word and action.

Relying on the prayers of America's saints and the example of its Catholic heroes, then, American Catholics have the responsibility to show forth Christ, so that Christ the King may reign over our land.

REVIEW QUESTIONS

1. How did Earl Warren lead the U.S. Supreme Court to a position of unchecked power?
2. What was the significance of the 1960 election?
3. Summarize the events surrounding the assassination of Diem. What role did the U.S. play in his overthrow?
4. Why was Johnson elected by a landslide in 1964?
5. What were the consequences of Johnson's election in terms of domestic legislation?
6. What was Johnson's policy in Vietnam?
7. Summarize the causes and main events of the near-revolution of 1968.
8. What were the two main elements of Nixon's foreign policy and what were the results of them?
9. Summarize the election of 1972, the Watergate scandal, and Nixon's resignation.
10. Summarize the main points in the decision on *Roe v. Wade*.
11. What have been the consequences of this decision in the United States?
12. Discuss the final fall of Vietnam and explain why most of the pro-American South Vietnamese were not rescued.
13. What were the main events in the administration of Jimmy Carter?
14. What were the main events in the administration of Ronald Reagan?
15. What were the main events in the administrations of George Bush and William Clinton?

PROJECTS

1. Prepare a written or oral report on the Pro-Life Movement in America today.
2. Hold a class discussion on which events occurring in the past year are likely to be historically significant for the future.
3. Choose the "Man of the Century" in American history—that individual who has made the greatest impact on history, for good or ill, in this century. Write a paper defending your choice.

Afterword

This Afterword is being written in the summer of 1996. From many standpoints this time is not one of optimism for American Catholics. The President recently vetoed legislation that would have banned the horrific procedure known as partial-birth abortion. Television and the movies are displaying increasingly immoral behaviors for all to see. Various so-called Catholic organizations are in outright rebellion against the Holy Father, most specifically in their demand for women priests, though the Pope has definitively stated that the Church will never confer priestly ordination on women. Polls indicate that almost as many Catholics as non-Catholics use contraceptives, and other polls indicate that over half of Church-going Catholics no longer believe in the Real Presence of Our Lord in the Blessed Eucharist.

Realistically, we see many grave problems in our society. But realism should not be pessimism. Pessimism might say that there is no way to turn our society around and therefore there is no reason to fight its evils any longer. Or pessimism might say that the only hope is to retreat far from society and have as little to do with it as possible.

But both of these attitudes are opposed to Christian hope. The man and woman of Christian hope does not sit around waiting for the perfect candidate to be elected President or for the leaders of the media to undergo a mass conversion. The person of Christian hope heeds the words of the first native-born saint of the United States, St. Elizabeth Ann Seton: "Let His will of the present moment be the first rule of our daily life and work." Each of us, no matter who we are, can look for and accomplish God's will of the present moment.

Our country is still free in many ways. We are still free to live a virtuous life, to obey the teachings of the Church, to get involved in parish or other Catholic organizations, to support good religious orders and faithful bishops, to home school our children or find good schools for them, to follow the plan God has in mind for each of us.

The Second Vatican Council speaks in *Lumen Gentium* of the universal call to holiness. Holiness is not just for those living long ago in a culture hospitable to Christianity. It is not just for priests and nuns and monks. It is for each of us. Each of us is called to develop an intimate personal relationship with Jesus Christ primarily through the Holy Eucharist, but also through mental prayer and penance. And by becoming holy, we will help our country. As the Gospel tells us, there are devils which can be cast out only by prayer and fasting. If we pray and fast, we can cast the devils out of our country.

If the task seems overwhelming, think of what life must have looked like to a faithful Catholic in Eastern Europe or the former Soviet Union as recently as 1989. Yet in those areas, Communism was finally overthrown, at least in its external structures. A greater transformation can happen here.

The beginning of a transformation of Eastern Europe surely began with the quiet prayers and sacrifices of countless Christians. The transformation of the United States can begin the same way. Let the conversion of America begin with you.

Praised be Jesus Christ, now and forever.

Manassas, Virginia
Solemnity of the Assumption
1996

Bibliography

Ambrose, Stephen E. *Nixon: The Triumph of a Politician, 1962-1972.* New York, 1989.

———. *Nixon: The Education of a Politician, 1913-1962.* New York, 1987.

———. *Nixon: Ruin and Recovery, 1973-1990.* New York, 1991.

———. *Eisenhower, The President.* New York, 1984.

Bailey, David. *Viva Cristo Rey.*

Beals, Carleton. *Eagles of the Andes: South American Struggles for Independence.* Philadelphia, 1963.

Blair, Clay. *The Forgotten War: America in Korea, 1950-1953.* New York, 1987.

Brandt, Irving. *James Madison, 1787-1802.*

Buckley, William F. and L. Brent Bozell. *McCarthy and His Enemies.* New Rochelle, NY, 1954.

Cameron, Roderick. *Viceroyalties of the West.*

Caro, Robert A. *The Path to Power: The Years of Lyndon Johnson.* New York, 1981.

———. *Means of Ascent: The Years of Lyndon Johnson.* New York, 1990.

Carroll, Warren H. *Our Lady of Guadalupe and the Conquest of Darkness.* Front Royal, Virginia, 1983.

———. *The Rise and Fall of the Communist Revolution.* Front Royal, Virginia, 1995.

———. *Isabel of Spain: The Catholic Queen.* Front Royal, Virginia, 1991.

Chambers, Whittaker. *Witness.* New York, 1952.

Collier, Richard. *Bridge Across the Sky: The Berlin Blockade and Airlift, 1948-1949.* New York, 1978.

Commager, Henry Steele and Richard B. Morris, eds. *The Spirit of Seventy-Six: The Story of the American Revolution As Told By Participants.* New York, 1958.

Costain, Thomas. *The White and the Gold: The French Regime in Canada.*

Costello, John. *The Pacific War.* New York, 1981.

Cunningham, R. B. Graham. *Vanished Arcadia: Jesuits in Paraguay, 1607-1767.*

DeVoto, Bernard. *Year of Decision 1846.*

Dirvin, Rev. Joseph. *Mrs. Seton.* New York, 1975.

Edmonds, Walter. *The Musket and the Cross: The Struggle of France and England for North America.* Boston, 1968.

Elkins, Stanley and Eric McKitrick. *The Age of Federalism: The Early American Republic, 1788-1800.* Oxford, 1993.

Fehrenbach, T. R. *Fire and Blood: A History of Mexico.* New York, 1973.

Follett, Ken. *On Wings of Eagles.* New York, 1984.

Foner, Eric. *Reconstruction: America's Unfinished Revolution, 1863-1877.* New York, 1988.

Freeman, Douglas Southall. *George Washington.*

———. *Robert E. Lee.*

Gurn, Joseph. *Charles Carroll of Carrollton, 1737-1832.* New York, 1932.

Hammer, Ellen J. *A Death In November.* New York, 1987.

Haslip, Joan. *The Crown of Mexico: Maximilian and His Empress Carlota.* New York, 1971.

Higgins, Marguerite. *Our Vietnam Nightmare.* New York, 1965.

Horgan, Paul. *The Great River.*

———. *Lamy of Santa Fe.*

James, Marquis. *The Life of Andrew Jackson.* New York, 1938.

Jensen, Merrill. *The New Nation.*

Johnson, Paul. *Modern Times: The World from the Twenties to the Eighties.* New York, 1983.

Keyes, Frances Parkinson. *The Rose and the Lily.*

Korngold, Ralph. *Citizen Touissaint.*

Kubek, Anthony. *How the Far East Was Lost: American Policy and the Creation of Communist China, 1941-1949.* Chicago, 1963.

Lazo, Mario. *Dagger in the Heart: American Policy Failures in Cuba.* New York, 1968.

Leckie, Robert. *The March to Glory.* New York, 1960.

Maclear, Michael. *The Ten Thousand Day War: Vietnam, 1945-1975.* New York, 1981.

Madariaga, Salvador de. *Hernan Cortes, Conqueror of Mexico.* Chicago, 1955.

———. *The Rise of the Spanish-American Empire.* New York, 1947.

Malone, Dumas. *Jefferson The Virginian.*

Manchester, William. *The Glory and the Dream: A Narrative History of America, 1932-1972.* Boston, 1973.

Marks, Frederick W. *Velvet On Iron: The Diplomacy of Theodore Roosevelt.* Lincoln, Nebraska, 1979.

Marshner, William H. *Chile First Hand: A Report from Santiago.* St. Paul, Minnesota, 1974.

Maxwell-Scott, M. *Gabriel Garcia Moreno: Regenerator of Ecuador.*

Maynard, Theodore. *History of American Catholicism.*

McCullough, David. *Truman.* New York, 1992.

Melville, Annabelle M. *John Carroll of Baltimore: Founder of the American Catholic Hierarchy.* New York, 1955.

Morgan, Edmund. *Puritan Dilemma.*

Morgan, Ted. *F.D.R.: A Biography.* New York, 1985.

Morison, Samuel Eliot. *The European Discovery of America: The Southern Voyages.* New York, 1974.

———. *Admiral of the Ocean Sea: A Life of Christopher Columbus.* Boston, 1942.

———. *History of United States Naval Operations in World War II.* Boston, 1959-1960.

Morris, Richard B. *Encyclopedia of American History.* New York, 1953.

———. *The Forging of the Union 1781-1789.* New York, 1987.

Page, Joseph A. *Peron: A Biography.* New York, 1983.

Parkman, Francis. *The Battle for North America.* New York, 1948.

Parmet, Herbert S. *Eisenhower and the American Crusades.* New York, 1972.

Parsons, Wilfrid. *Mexican Martyrdom:* Rockford, Illinois, (1936) 1987.

Peterson, Merrill D. *The Great Triumvirate: Webster, Clay, and Calhoun.* Oxford, 1987.

Posner. *Case Closed: Lee Harvey Oswald and the Assassination of JFK.* New York, 1993.

Potter, George. *To the Golden Door.*

Powell, Philip. *Tree of Hate.*

Prange, Gordon W. *At Dawn We Slept: The Untold Story of Pearl Harbor.* New York, 1981.

Prange, Gordon W. *Miracle at Midway.* New York, 1982.

Pratt, Fletcher. *A Short History of the Civil War.* New York, 1935.

———. *Battles That Changed History.*

———. *The Heroic Years: Fourteen Years of the Republic, 1801-1815.* New York, 1934.

———. *The Navy—A History: The Story of a Service in Action.* Garden City, N.Y., 1938.

Radosh, Ronald and Joyce Milton. *The Rosenberg File: A Search for the Truth.* New York, 1983.

Reeves, Richard. *President Kennedy: Profile of Power.* New York, 1993.

———. *The Life and Times of Joe McCarthy.* New York, 1982.

Repplier, Agnes. *Father Serra.*

Rhodes, Richard. *The Making of The Atomic Bomb.* 1986.

Robertson, William Spence. *Rise of the Spanish-American Republics.* New York, 1946.

Royer, Fanchon. *Padre Pro.*

Rozek, Edward J. *Allied Wartime Diplomacy: A Pattern in Poland.* New York, 1958.

Ryan, Cornelius. *The Longest Day: June 6, 1944.* New York, 1959.

———. *A Bridge Too Far.* New York, 1974.

Safire, William. *Freedom.* New York, 1987.

Simpson, Colin. *The Lusitania.* Boston, 1972.

Smith, Page. *John Adams.* New York, 1962.

Smith, Gene. *When the Cheering Stopped: The Last Years of Woodrow Wilson.* New York, 1964.

Snepp, Frank. *Decent Interval.* New York, 1977.

Talbot, Francis. *Saint Among Hurons.*

———. *Saint Among Savages.*

Terrill, J. *Black Robe.*

Tolstoy, Nikolai. *The Secret Betrayal.* New York, 1977.

Valladares, Armando. *Against All Hope.* New York, 1986.

Weinstein, Allan. *Perjury: The Hiss-Chambers Case.* New York, 1978.

White, Theodore H. *The Making of the President 1964.* New York, 1965.

Willison, George. *Saints and Strangers.*

Index

About The Author

Anne W. Carroll is the founder and director of Seton School in Manassas, Virginia, where she has been developing and teaching an authentically Catholic curriculum at the junior and senior high school levels since 1975.

Holding an M.A. in English, Mrs. Carroll has taught many subjects over the years and has a special love for history. She uses *Christ and the Americas* for a History of the Americas course at Seton School. She is also the author of *Christ the King—Lord of History*.

Mrs. Carroll resides in Manassas, Virginia with her husband, Dr. Warren H. Carroll, noted Catholic historian and founder of Christendom College.